THE HOLY WARRIOR
OSAMA BIN LADEN AND HIS JIHADI JOURNEY IN THE SOVIET-AFGHAN WAR

2nd Edition

Reagan Fancher, M.A., Ph.D.
Texas Woman's University

Series in World History

Copyright © 2024 Vernon Press, an imprint of Vernon Art and Science Inc, on behalf of the author.

All rights reserved. No part of this publication may be reproduced, stored in a retrieval system, or transmitted in any form or by any means, electronic, mechanical, photocopying, recording, or otherwise, without the prior permission of Vernon Art and Science Inc.

www.vernonpress.com

In the Americas:
Vernon Press
1000 N West Street, Suite 1200
Wilmington, Delaware, 19801
United States

In the rest of the world:
Vernon Press
C/Sancti Espiritu 17,
Malaga, 29006
Spain

Series in World History

Library of Congress Control Number: 2023943477

ISBN: 978-1-64889-946-1

Also available: 978-1-64889-764-1 [Hardback]; 978-1-64889-780-1 [PDF, E-Book]

Product and company names mentioned in this work are the trademarks of their respective owners. While every care has been taken in preparing this work, neither the authors nor Vernon Art and Science Inc. may be held responsible for any loss or damage caused or alleged to be caused directly or indirectly by the information contained in it.

Cover design by Vernon Press. Cover image by OpenClipart-Vectors from Pixabay.

Every effort has been made to trace all copyright holders, but if any have been inadvertently overlooked the publisher will be pleased to include any necessary credits in any subsequent reprint or edition.

TABLE OF CONTENTS

Note: Readers unfamiliar with the major terms relating to this topic are encouraged to consult the Glossary that I have included in this book before reading the main body of text.

	PREFACE: Osama bin Laden in the Soviet-Afghan War – an introduction	vii
	PROLOGUE: The war that made the modern world	xv
CHAPTER 1	**The historical origins of Salafi jihadism, 1744-1979**	1
CHAPTER 2	**Brezhnev's boast, Osama's early actions, and U.S.-U.K. perceptions of the Islamic guerrillas, 1979-1985**	13
CHAPTER 3	**Gorbachev's gamble, Reagan's response, and increased Arab involvement, 1985-1987**	37
CHAPTER 4	**Osama in the spring and the birth of a vanguard, 1987-1989**	57
CHAPTER 5	**South Arabia's model insurgency and its global ramifications, 1989-1994**	73
	EPILOGUE: The inspirer	85
	AUTHOR'S AFTERWORD TO THE SECOND EDITION: U.S.-U.K. Perceptions of Osama's 1994 South Arabian guerrilla war – a conclusion	89
	ACKNOWLEDGEMENTS	141
	GLOSSARY	143
	NOTES	153

BIBLIOGRAPHY 239

INDEX 259

For my beautiful bride, endless love, and forever queen, Graziele

For my awesome number one Mom, Rebecca, and my wonderful in-laws and Brazilian father and mother, Vanderlei and Suzel

For Eissa Nasraldeen, M.B.A., truly a brother, now, always, and forever

For the courageous men and women warriors of the U.S. Army, Marine Corps, and CIA, the republic's best, brightest, and most uncredited defenders

PREFACE:
Osama bin Laden in the Soviet-Afghan War – an introduction

"Knowledge comes only from God, the Mighty One, the Wise One."- Ibn Khaldun, *The Muqaddimah – An Introduction to History: The Classic Islamic History of the World*[1]

In late 1979, Soviet forces invaded Afghanistan to bolster an unpopular communist regime and crush a growing resistance movement of Islamic guerrillas calling themselves *mujahedin*. As a result, the leaders of Pakistan, Saudi Arabia, North Yemen, the United States, and Britain launched a program of limited financial and material support for the Afghan insurgency. As the fighting spread, thousands of devout young men from Arab nations began gathering in Pakistan to offer their support to their Afghan coreligionists. Prominent among these volunteers, a wealthy Saudi named Osama bin Laden persuaded Afghan insurgent leaders to allow his small Arab band to face the Soviets. Bin Laden's subsequent actions as a guerrilla fighter and leader helped to launch al-Qaeda as a deadly and well-trained insurgent organization.

In the decades since the 9/11 terror attacks successfully drew U.S. and UK troops into Afghanistan, scholars have produced a multitude of works analyzing bin Laden's life, including his exploits in the Soviet-Afghan War. After learning that bin Laden and other Arab volunteers had fought the Soviets in Afghanistan, I became fascinated with this topic and authored a short high school paper on it in late 2001. A lifelong fascination was born, and my passion continued to grow as I devoured numerous books and articles about bin Laden and al-Qaeda that emerged in the decades after 9/11, researching various aspects of the topic until earning my M.A. in History in 2017.

This book is the culmination of my lifelong interest in bin Laden and my desire to produce a readily available and original monograph to help explain the significance of his wartime experiences fighting the Soviet occupation forces in Afghanistan in his rise to prominence as a historical figure. Born in 1985, I grew up as part of what is sometimes known as "Generation 9/11," defined as those who were between the ages of 10 and 20 years old at the time of the 9/11 attacks and began saving my money and buying books about the al-Qaeda leader after starting work at my first job as a teenager. My interest only grew with time as I learned more, leading to my decision to write the dream book on this topic that I envisioned rather than pursue publication in a journal.

Bursting with ideas and refusing to put off my dream of pursuing the topic of my true historical passion any longer, I finally sat down and began writing the first chapter of this book during my second semester as a Ph.D. student at the University of North Texas (UNT) in April 2020.

From the moment of his 1996 declaration of war on the United States and its European allies until his much-deserved 2011 death, bin Laden consistently and ruthlessly demonstrated al-Qaeda's position as the deadliest threat to Westerners and their security. It therefore remains unfortunate but necessary for me to point out that by focusing this book on his wartime anti-Soviet exploits, I am not in any way, shape, or form seeking to praise him, but to help improve scholars' understanding of his true motivation and still lethal legacy. As the native of a small, sleepy southern town in the United States, my fascination with bin Laden as a historical figure, irrespective of positive or negative connotations, has always been and remains strictly historical in nature. The qualities that he possessed according to most of the primary sources consulted for this work, including those authored by critics that turned against the al-Qaeda chief for various reasons, appear to have led others to follow him and transformed him into an uncompromising and vicious foe of those he deemed the enemies of Muslims.

Bin Laden's own statements, those of his closest former associates, and the excellent books written by those whose expertise has contributed many remarkable findings on the al-Qaeda leader's life have proved to be invaluable sources. Housing many of bin Laden's additional statements, as well as those by Afghan, Soviet, and Western leaders, the digital and online archival collections of *The Wilson Center, The National Security Archive, The Bukovsky Archives*, the *Congressional Record*, the *Parliamentary Record*, and the *Combating Terrorism Center at West Point* have also proved to be equally invaluable. In writing and researching this book, I have also located many detailed and informative newspaper reports, journal articles, and other primary and secondary sources that were readily available. All these sources proved to be indispensable to this book's development as I consulted them while completing my required classwork and began studying for my doctoral dissertation on a separate and unrelated topic between spring 2020 and fall 2021. The work that I have hopefully produced here, aided only by the many sources that I have cited and the moral support of the very few loved ones who were aware of my project, has resulted in the completion of this book and the realization of a lifelong dream.

From my perspective, the biographies of bin Laden authored by Peter Bergen, Steve Coll, and Michael Scheuer served as the most informative of the numerous secondary sources cited in this book. Peter Bergen's 2001 book *Holy War, Inc.: Inside the Secret World of Osama bin Laden*, a *New York Times*

Bestseller, is the first book that I read on bin Laden's life after I became interested in this subject in my late teenage years. Throughout the work, Bergen emphasizes the ways in which al-Qaeda is organized along the lines of a multinational corporation and pays close attention to bin Laden's actions, including two chapters discussing his role in the Soviet-Afghan War.[2]

Bergen rebuts some claims by another early bin Laden biographer, Yossef Bodansky, arguing that the earlier author erred in his 1999 book *Bin Laden: The Man Who Declared War on America* by describing the al-Qaeda leader as a violent, womanizing drunkard in Beirut during his teenage years and later ally of Iran that settled in London, a, "fantastic assertion" that Bergen points out is contradicted by the accounts of those closest to bin Laden at the time and later.[3] Bergen also briefly visits bin Laden's motivation to attack the United States, arguing that the bulk of primary source evidence indicates that the al-Qaeda leader sought to fight those he regarded as oppressing Muslims through specific policies rather than attacking Americans for their secular, democratic freedoms.[4] In his outstanding 2006 book *The Osama bin Laden I Know: An Oral History of al-Qaeda's Leader*, essentially a primary source collection including many of bin Laden's own statements, Bergen provides scholars with a detailed look at the words of those that knew the al-Qaeda chief, including the accounts of several of his former anti-Soviet comrades.[5]

Steve Coll's 2004 book and Pulitzer Prize winner *Ghost Wars: The Secret History of the CIA, Afghanistan, and bin Laden, from the Soviet Invasion to September 10, 2001*, also discusses bin Laden's anti-Soviet activities much like Bergen's *Holy War, Inc*. Like Bergen however, Coll largely focuses on the al-Qaeda leader's later war with the United States, while providing invaluable information on his interactions with Afghan and Arab militants during the war against the Soviets.[6] In another Pulitzer Prize-winning 2008 book *The Bin Ladens: An Arabian Family in the American Century*, Coll appears to part with Bergen by inferring bin Laden to have been a cowardly participant seeking to avoid combat in the Soviet-Afghan War, an assertion also popularized by other authors including Lawrence Wright, Abdullah Anas, and Rob Schultheis.[7] Coll then contradicts this statement by arguing that during his first taste of battle in 1987, bin Laden fought, "honorably" and earned his place among the Islamist zealots fighting the Soviet occupation forces.[8]

Out of all these fantastic biographical accounts that have emerged, I have found Michael Scheuer's 2011 biography *Osama bin Laden* to be particularly well-researched and authoritative, especially regarding bin Laden's actions in the Soviet-Afghan War. Scheuer's bin Laden biography appears to be the most thoroughly researched of these excellent works, relying heavily on the words of bin Laden and his closest associates, including some previously untranslated documents and unavailable material.[9] Characterizing bin Laden's time fighting the Soviets as a holy warrior, "apprenticeship" alongside the Palestinian-born Islamist scholar *Shaykh* Abdullah Azzam, Scheuer emphasizes the militant educational value of the al-Qaeda chief's early years as a jihadi.[10]

Focusing much of the book on bin Laden and al-Qaeda's war on the United States and the West in the manner of previous scholars, Scheuer nevertheless provides an informative portrait of his subject's years as a guerrilla volunteer in the Soviet-Afghan War. He revisits and emphasizes Bergen's earlier argument regarding bin Laden as a deadly threat but rational operator focused on striking those perceived as attacking Muslims while caring very little about the perceived debauchery of Western culture.[11] Scheuer also rebuts the allegations of bin Laden behaving in a cowardly fashion during the Soviet-Afghan War suggested not only by Steve Coll but by Lawrence Wright in the latter's 2006 book *The Looming Tower: Al-Qaeda and the Road to 9/11*.[12] Scheuer points out that while the primary source for Wright's claim, the former Algerian jihadi Boudejema Bounoua, known as Abdullah Anas, knew bin Laden during the Soviet-Afghan War, he also quickly became his enemy and sought to discredit him after the al-Qaeda chief won control of Azzam's fundraising and militant recruitment networks.[13] Citing the accounts of men that fought alongside the al-Qaeda leader including some that became his harsh critics after tactical disagreements or alleged pressure and lucrative offers from the Saudi and other Arab regimes, Scheuer points out that all eyewitnesses appear to agree that bin Laden acquitted himself bravely in battle.[14]

Indeed, Anas admits in his 2019 memoir *To the Mountains: My Life in Jihad, from Algeria to Afghanistan* that while he met bin Laden at the time, he never participated in the engagements in which the al-Qaeda leader reportedly fought, opting to fight alongside the Afghan commander Ahmed Shah Massoud in northern Afghanistan instead.[15] While providing a valuable eyewitness account of the Soviet-Afghan War including a brief, passing encounter with bin Laden in his 2008 book *Hunting bin Laden: How al-Qaeda is Winning the War on Terror*, the journalist Rob Schultheis also appears to imply the al-Qaeda chief as a coward in battle.[16] Like Anas, Schultheis does not appear to have been present at the battles in which bin Laden is said to have participated.[17] This stands in contrast to the primary accounts by men such as Abdullah Azzam, Saudi cleric Musa al-Qarni, former Yemeni jihadi Tariq al-Fadhli, and former Egyptian journalist and military intelligence officer Isam Darraz, all battle participants attesting to the al-Qaeda leader's combat actions.

The statements of bin Laden and the memoirs and interviews of his closest associates have also collectively produced a goldmine of information on the impact of the Soviet-Afghan War on al-Qaeda's martial origins. Foremost among these firsthand accounts and second only to bin Laden's words, the written and oral statements of Musa al-Qarni, Tariq al-Fadhli, bin Laden's first wife and fourth-eldest son, Najwa and Omar, his former bodyguard Nasser al-Bahri, and his childhood friend Khaled al-Batarfi serve as the absolute best primary sources to date. Of all these invaluable primary accounts, I have found Nasser al-Bahri's 2010 memoir *Guarding bin Laden: My Life in al-Qaeda* and Najwa and Omar bin Laden's 2009 memoir *Growing Up bin Laden: Osama's Wife and Son Take us Inside Their Secret World* to be especially courageous and remarkable in their honesty.

The outstanding quality of these memoirs, along with the interviews of al-Batarfi, al-Fadhli, and al-Qarni, is further enhanced by the fact that their authors have reportedly lived and worked under daily pressure from regimes staunchly opposed to bin Laden and yet still openly acknowledge his wartime record and effective leadership skills. While each of these authors has contributed invaluable information, none have yet produced a book focusing exclusively on bin Laden's wartime role as a *mujahid* or "holy warrior" fighting the Soviets. This book's original contribution lies in its focus on his life and actions in the Soviet-Afghan War and the practical training in combat and insurgency support that he and his lieutenants received courtesy of their unwitting Soviet foes.

This is a book about bin Laden's participation in guerrilla warfare and rise to prominence, about his transformative and arduous journey from a resistance financier, engineer, and fighter to a tactical combat commander. His battlefield exploits transformed him into a respected insurgent leader in the multinational Arab contingent fighting in Afghanistan, propelling him to hero status in his native Saudi Arabia and triggering the birth of al-Qaeda. Bin Laden's successful efforts to assist the beleaguered Afghans and acquire combat experience for his Arab guerrilla unit were enabled by the ongoing fighting resulting from the prolonged Soviet military occupation of Afghanistan.

Fearing the potential rise of a fundamentalist Sunni version of neighboring Iran's Shia Islamic Revolution or U.S. and Pakistani military involvement, Soviet leaders from Leonid Brezhnev to Mikhail Gorbachev desperately sought to stabilize Afghanistan's communist central government to crush the resistance fighters.[18] Frustrated by the Soviet Army's failure to achieve a decisive victory and sufficiently bolster the regime's security, they waged a limited campaign often executed through brutal means in hopes of ending an increasingly costly and destructive war.[19] As a result of the insurgency's resilience, Soviet leaders were repeatedly forced to delay their army's withdrawal, and their generals served as the unwitting instructors for the leaders and foot soldiers of al-Qaeda by providing a key window of opportunity for the Arab fighters to obtain battlefield experience.

This intense practical training, acquired by their eager participation in guerrilla warfare against the Soviet troops, enabled bin Laden and his lieutenants to launch al-Qaeda as a battle-hardened insurgent organization, steeled in combat and capable of training others. In addition, the perseverance of bin Laden's guerrilla unit in the battles fought between 1987 and 1989 appears to have inspired militant Islamists worldwide and triggered an immense boost in jihadi recruitment efforts. As Gorbachev and the Soviet Politburo began withdrawing their troops, bin Laden and al-Qaeda prepared to channel their rich combat experience in a guerrilla campaign to aid local Islamists in eventually expelling all remaining infidel forces from Muslim countries.[20]

It may seem odd to the reader that despite the dozens of books written about bin Laden and al-Qaeda since the 9/11 terror attacks, no author until now has focused a single monograph on the group's origins and activities in the Soviet-Afghan War. I have found this puzzling for years, given the considerable amount of material available on this subject and the war's impact on training the al-Qaeda top brass militarily. While several authors have alleged that the Arab fighters received CIA training and have blamed the agency for "creating" al-Qaeda, the historical record reveals a far larger factor in the group's rise resulting from practical combat experience.

The Soviet invasion itself created the opportunity for the Arab fighters to obtain this crucial training, providing militant Islamists worldwide with the traditional Koranic justification for a *Faridat al-Jihad* or "holy war of resistance" against the infidel occupiers.[21] For many Westerners, memories of the 1980s conjure up images of Nelson Mandela and the end of *apartheid* in South Africa, nuclear war scares, or summits between Ronald Reagan and Gorbachev. While these events were remarkable, Afghanistan is often treated as a Cold War sideshow by scholars overlooking the Islamist awakening in the Sunni Muslim world triggered by the Soviet invasion.

Perhaps this is the reason why Western historians, until now, have yet to produce a work focusing primarily on bin Laden's role in this conflict that gave birth to al-Qaeda and the global jihadi movement. In writing this book, I have sought to produce an original work by exploring the topic of the war's impact on training al-Qaeda, dispelling many of the false assumptions about the group's origins along the way. In addressing several misconceptions about the role of bin Laden and his Arab guerrilla unit in battle, I hope to help ignite a discussion and open the way for future research into this fascinating topic in the history of the world.

For many people, history is little more than a hobby. For me, it is a passion, a profession, and an art. As I sit down to indulge this passion by opening a book or beginning to write, my mind calmly wanders into another world. Current global affairs, controversies, and concerns disappear, and the lives of people and cultures far away illuminate my mind. Studying history professionally is not for everyone. It takes a great deal of patience, dedication, and an acknowledgement that one's research and findings may not be understood or appreciated either by colleagues or much of the broader public. This is especially true for historians specializing in what may someday receive recognition in our field as "Bin Laden Studies." As one such person, I have also found that the study of history comes with great rewards in the form of the personal satisfaction of researching topics, cultures, and historical figures that continue to fascinate me.

Focusing on the role of prominent individuals in history remains somewhat of a controversial subject among scholars. In some ways, this controversy results from a popular misinterpretation of the "Great Man" theory of history, a nineteenth-century concept stating that individuals with natural talents or social influence determine the course of world civilization. Part of the reason for this controversy is the assumption of many people, scholars and students alike, towards a profession often stereotyped as the study of kings, queens, "old dead white guys," and events that transpired centuries ago.

Since graduating with my M.A. in History from the University of Louisiana at Monroe (ULM) in 2017, I have had the pleasure of pursuing my lifelong dream of teaching history and doing my part to break this and other negative perceptions about the field. As I have often taught my students, history is something far larger than most people assume, and I hope that they take this lesson with them as they continue their academic careers as college students and members of the U.S. military. History is a journey, an unfurling ribbon that continues to paint and shape the present, just as the present will someday be classified as history and inevitably impact the future.

Yet none of this is possible without the human element, the key role of individual men and women in determining the course of events. While there is certainly much more to history than the mere study of great individuals, the actions of such people complete the puzzle of our world's past as scholars seek to connect every piece. While economics and impersonal social forces certainly matter, it is people that make the crucial difference. Contrary to popular assumptions, great figures arise in all social classes, religions, and cultures, and do not necessarily hail from the ranks of royalty or even hold economic or political power. Nor are all such world-changing individuals great in a positive sense, a somewhat subjective perception in and of itself.

This book is intended first and foremost to serve as a teaching tool and to enhance the previous findings of the experts by refocusing the historiographical conversation surrounding the origins of bin Laden and his al-Qaeda unit on their actions in the Soviet-Afghan War. In particular, the book theorizes that Moscow's invasion and the opportunity to fight the world's greatest military machine at that time provided bin Laden and his lieutenants with the training that they needed to launch al-Qaeda and prepare it for later struggles. By focusing on this psychological and physical battle baptism of the Arab fighters, the book also serves as a cautionary tale regarding the strengthening of local jihadi groups as an unintended result of counterproductive military interventions in traditional Muslim societies.[22]

Other theories regarding the origins of al-Qaeda are also addressed in the book, particularly the claim that the Arab fighters enjoyed the support of the West as their Afghan hosts did. Although this book's subject is highly specialized in many ways, I have sought to make it accessible to all interested readers with the intention of producing a readily available book answering the "how and why" of bin Laden and al-Qaeda's martial origins. I trust that the book's findings have produced a focused but approachable work on bin Laden's beginnings and the birth of al-Qaeda that may prove valuable to students of history and casual readers alike.

PROLOGUE:
The war that made the modern world

At 7:00 a.m. on the morning of 25 May 1987, 30-year-old Osama bin Laden watched in awe as a Soviet MiG-27 "Flogger" ground attack plane suddenly broke apart while falling helplessly from the sky above his mountaintop base overlooking the valley of Jaji.[1] Afghan insurgents had landed a parting shot as they withdrew from the area, inspiring bin Laden and his lightly trained Arab unit to hold their ground and fight the advancing Soviet onslaught themselves. In the ensuing battle, the 70-man guerrilla band faced merciless attacks by 200 Soviet troops, including elite *Spetsnaz* commandos.

As the Soviet assault began, the zealous, inexperienced young men braced for martyrdom at the hands of their foes, a chance to die fighting in God's path. Instead, during the months that followed, they received intense practical training in conducting a determined resistance against the forces of a superpower. For bin Laden and his lieutenants, the Battle of Jaji served as the ultimate test of leadership, management, and insurgency combat skills as holy warriors defending besieged Muslims from infidel invaders.

The conflict that propelled bin Laden to prominence and trained al-Qaeda in guerrilla warfare began almost a decade before the defiant stand of the Arab fighters at Jaji in the spring and summer of 1987. The Soviet-Afghan War began as a civil war within Afghanistan and escalated into an international conflict involving the Soviet Union, Pakistan, Saudi Arabia, North Yemen, the United States, Britain, and thousands of jihadi volunteers from dozens of Islamic countries. Initially planning to withdraw quickly after Soviet forces equipped and trained a new and more reliable Afghan Army and regime, Brezhnev reportedly expected all resistance to crumble quickly in the face of the Soviet Army's overwhelming preponderance of mechanized forces and airpower.[2] Lasting more than a decade, the ensuing conflict destabilized much of South Asia, accelerated the Soviet Union's collapse, and motivated the birth of the modern Salafi jihadi movement and its multinational guerrilla vanguard, al-Qaeda. In short, it may reasonably be concluded that the Soviet invasion and subsequent war in Afghanistan helped to usher in the modern world.

More than a decade after his long overdue death, courtesy of the U.S. Navy SEALs acting on CIA intelligence, bin Laden remains an example of one such historical figure whose legacy continues to damage U.S. and Western security interests. Born into a wealthy and pious Saudi family of Yemeni origin, bin Laden decided on a life-changing course of action following the Soviet invasion of Afghanistan in December 1979, eventually changing the world. Rather than limiting his support of the besieged Afghan Muslims to charitable work as many wealthy Saudis initially did, he embraced the Spartan lifestyle of a mujahid, rejecting a billionaire's life of luxury as advised by the medieval Arab scholar Ibn Khaldun.[3]

Bin Laden won the respect of his Saudi and Yemeni compatriots and the Afghan and Pakistani border tribes due to his willingness to sacrifice worldly riches and match his beliefs with actions. While this basic fact has been documented in several books, most notably in former CIA officer and historian Michael Scheuer's indispensable biography *Osama bin Laden*, this book reexamines the impact of the specific interactions and events that propelled the al-Qaeda chief to prominence. The accounts of bin Laden's associates, especially those of his son Omar, anti-Soviet colleagues Tariq al-Fadhli and Shaykh Musa al-Qarni, and former bodyguard Nasser al-Bahri provide useful windows into the Soviet-Afghan War's impact on al-Qaeda's martial growth.

Among other aspects of bin Laden's actions in the Soviet-Afghan War, this book emphasizes the significance of practical combat on his Arab unit that served as the forerunner to al-Qaeda between his establishment of a guerrilla base for Arab fighters in October 1986 and the group's participation in the rebel assault on Jalalabad in 1989. The book also emphasizes the importance of the connections that bin Laden forged with the Afghan warriors and the impact of Washington's Afghan policy in unintentionally provoking Islamist resentment. While researching this topic, I have found that several of the dates often associated with the intense Jaji battles of 1987 have been inaccurately documented in previous secondary accounts. In the interest of historical accuracy, I have sought to provide the correct dates of these key engagements that propelled bin Laden to leadership by a careful check of the Muslim *Hijri* calendar dates for 1987 (or 1407 *Hijri*) listed in the primary sources.

I have also included a chapter on the historical origins of the Salafi jihadi movement embraced by bin Laden and his closest associates during their youth in Saudi Arabia. By doing so, I hope to clarify the key role of religious fervor in inspiring the founding fathers of al-Qaeda to bear arms against a superpower once perceived as invincible by many people worldwide. This deep religious conviction spurred bin Laden and his comrades to action and distinguished them as warriors in a society whose clerics called for holy war but displayed a noticeable reluctance to join the guerrillas on the battlefield.

I also hope to encourage current and future scholars to explore these engagements in further detail to provide students of history with a greater understanding of al-Qaeda's formation. The book also addresses many of the popular assertions of CIA support for the Arab fighters and assesses the documented impact of U.S. and Saudi material aid to the Afghan resistance.

Following a detailed assessment of the Arab guerrillas in combat between 1987 and 1989, I have included a chapter on the subsequent civil war fought between various factions in Yemen in 1994. This conflict provided bin Laden with a second opportunity to test al-Qaeda's combat capabilities acquired while fighting the Soviets. It also allowed him to strengthen al-Qaeda's connections in a largely rural and tribalized society dear to his heart as he and his lieutenants prepared to launch their war against the West.

Bin Laden based his strategy to engage the United States and its allies that he regarded as Islam's foes on his Arab guerrilla unit's practical experience fighting the Soviets in Afghanistan.[4] As the war that he twice declared on the United States, Britain, and Israel in 1996 and 1998 remains far from over even a decade after his death, Americans and their allies must continue to arm themselves with detailed knowledge of their most determined enemies.[5] Only by understanding the origins of their martial skills can we hope to decisively defeat them in the present and thereby safeguard our future.

From a mud hut in Afghanistan in a 28 May 1998 interview with former *ABC News* journalist John Miller, bin Laden predicted a day of societal and political division and disunity in the United States not unlike the collapse of the Soviet Union after its defeat in Afghanistan. Bin Laden warned Miller that, "We predict a black day for America and the end of the United States as the United States, and it will become separate states and will retreat from our land and collect the bodies of its sons back to America, God willing."[6] Bin Laden ruthlessly labored to draw U.S. forces and their allies into Afghanistan to make this day a reality, successfully inflicting more damage on U.S. security interests than any individual since Robert E. Lee. Bin Laden and his lieutenants mastered their fighting skills during fierce battles with the Soviet troops, just as the Mexican-American War (1846-1848) trained Lee and his officers for their later rebellion against the American Union.[7] Al-Qaeda's leaders successfully emerged as battle-seasoned insurgent commanders courtesy of the unwitting Soviets, just as the Army of Northern Virginia's officers received their battle baptism, more effective than any West Point education, on the Mexican battlefields.[8] Bin Laden concluded that Allah had provided a blueprint for defeating far superior forces through uncompromising patience, faith, and determination, as well as the practical training in conducting a ruthless guerrilla war to eventually emerge victoriously.[9]

I also hope that the book will call readers' attention to the key role of individuals in history and clarify the importance of understanding bin Laden's vicious and lethal anti-Western legacy while emphasizing the ability, even of those holding no official title or government post, to make an impact on world affairs, whether positive or negative. While I focus on the impact of the Soviet invasion and subsequent war in Afghanistan in tactically training the militants in the art of guerrilla warfare, I also want to emphasize the role of bin Laden's personal characteristics, skills, and leadership example. His decision to act on his militant convictions and lead his comrades on the frontlines served as the key factor in propelling him to leadership in the international jihadi movement triggered by the Soviet invasion.

In many ways, readers may find my thesis in this book to be comparable to the scholarly school of thought emphasized by Karl Marx in his 1852 masterpiece *The Eighteenth Brumaire of Louis Bonaparte*, a work focusing on Napoleon III and the events that propelled his rise to power. Arguing that existing social conditions in mid-nineteenth-century France "created circumstances and relationships that made it possible for a grotesque mediocrity to play a hero's part," Marx concludes that great individuals arise and shape history by cleverly channeling events outside of their control to their advantage, essentially taking control of the situation.[10] Influenced by Marx's findings, Russian revolutionary leader Vladimir Lenin later spoke of a "vanguard of the revolutionary forces in our time," subsequently demonstrating that even a small, determined group led by committed zealots can impact history as he and his comrades seized power in the world's largest country.[11]

While I have not sought to portray bin Laden as playing "a hero's part," or in any way praise his actions, readers will notice that I also view him as having been far from a "grotesque mediocrity," as Marx describes his subject.[12] Whether positive or negative, such opinionated portrayals of the late al-Qaeda leader do not move scholars any closer to an accurate understanding of his true motivation and his still lethal legacy as reflected in the primary sources. Had bin Laden either proven to be a mediocre leader or overinflated his wartime role by crediting the small number of Arab guerrillas that fought the Soviets with victory rather than their Afghan hosts, it seems unlikely that he could have won the respect and comradeship of both Afghan and Arab militants. This book seeks to provide readers with an informed understanding of how and why bin Laden succeeded in taking control of the situation presented to him and applying the martial skills that he and his senior lieutenants acquired fighting the Soviets in establishing al-Qaeda's deadly legacy of inciting Islamist insurgencies through training and guerrilla support operations.

Through al-Qaeda's vicious terror attacks on U.S. interests in the 1990s, the 9/11 attacks, the 3/11 attacks in Madrid, Spain in March 2004, and subsequent terror attacks in London, Paris, and elsewhere, bin Laden demonstrated an ability to impact Western governmental policies and public perceptions of those policies despite being one man commanding a small organization. Like Lenin, bin Laden worked to establish a militant vanguard, not for leading an immediate revolution in the Western sense, but for inspiring a protracted, multigenerational struggle to motivate aspiring jihadis to acquire the training and fighting experience necessary to overthrow Muslim regimes perceived as corrupt or tyrannical. By skillfully acting within the existing framework of events far outside of his control, bin Laden succeeded in forging global connections and acquiring combat experience in command of a small Arab guerrilla band while fighting the Soviet troops. His successful mission enabled the vanguard organization that he and his comrades subsequently founded to export their improved combat skills to jihadis elsewhere, while eventually drawing U.S. and NATO forces into Afghanistan and winning another 20 years of practical battle experience for new generations of Islamist militants.

While his family's wealth and status initially enhanced bin Laden's reputation and enabled him to secure financing for the Afghan cause from other wealthy Saudis, his decision to join his guerrilla comrades in the trenches against the Soviet troops seems to have propelled him to leadership in their ranks and helped him to command their respect and build a following. Saudi society remains dominated by thousands of royals, all of whom are far wealthier than the bin Ladens, and reportedly even look down on them as ethnic Yemenis from modest origins.[13] Yet few of these royals or their regime clerics appear to have been prepared or willing to risk their earthly pleasures and comforts for the arduous Afghan mountains and face the Soviets' cold steel and hot lead.

Bin Laden's initiative to act on his beliefs and to match them with deeds earned him the respect of Afghan and non-Afghan Islamists alike, and highlights the importance of individuals, even those holding no official power or public office, in making a historical impact. Along with the reluctance of many of the Saudi regime's clerics to act on their own professions of faith, bin Laden's leadership example demonstrates that finances and impersonal social factors contributed very little to the respect that he commanded and the militancy that he inspired. Rather, as Marx states of Napoleon III, bin Laden's willingness to display initiative by cleverly working within existing conditions that he could not control propelled his rise to prominence, enabling him to manage the situation and forge a history-shaping guerrilla vanguard in battle, transforming him into a deadly adversary.[14] If readers of this book can walk away with some understanding of these conclusions, I will feel that I have succeeded in my efforts to teach about one of the most significant events and individuals in the contemporary history of the world.

CHAPTER 1

The historical origins of Salafi jihadism, 1744-1979

The 9/11 terror attacks did not come out of nowhere, nor did the entire history of events in the two decades preceding them. Bin Laden did not suddenly and randomly spawn in the middle of South Asia's steep mountains as the chief of the Muslim world's first multiethnic and multilingual global insurgent organization. His story, and that of al-Qaeda, begins not in the snow-capped mountains of Afghanistan, but in the desert oases of the Arabian Peninsula in the form of a religious reformation beginning two centuries before the war that trained them in the deadly art of insurgency. To fully understand the role of bin Laden and his Arab unit in the Soviet-Afghan War, it is necessary to first examine the religious ideology that prompted him to act on receiving the news of the Soviet invasion.

In his book, *The Landscape of History: How Historians Map the Past*, Cold War scholar John Lewis Gaddis points out that the crucial factor differentiating the historian from the social scientist is the latter's insistence on locating the "independent variable" in his or her findings.[1] By contrast, the historian rejects the notion of an independent variable altogether, adhering to the belief that events cannot simply and randomly occur without causes, in most cases, human interaction.[2] The proper role of the historian, then, is to emphasize the dependence of one variable on a preceding one, as every reaction depends on a prior action.

Of all the key interdependent variables leading to and motivating bin Laden's involvement in the Soviet-Afghan War, religious fervor is perhaps the most important. To understand the significance of this factor, it is necessary to briefly explore the history of the fundamentalist reform movement within Sunni Islam known as Salafism.[3] Established as a doctrine in the thirteenth century by a Syrian Islamic scholar that bin Laden frequently quoted, *Shaykh al-Islam* Taqi al-Din Ahmad Ibn Taymiyyah (1263-1328), Salafism's roots date back centuries.[4] Yet only in the late twentieth century did these roots spread and bear fruit on a truly global scale.

The label of Salafi comes from the Arabic term *salaf*, meaning "pious ancestors," and refers to the Prophet Muhammad, his companions, and the first three generations of Muslims under the first four *caliphs* or successors to Muhammad.[5] Modern Salafists believe that following the death of the last of these "rightly-guided" *caliphs* in 661 CE, Islam became corrupted by tyrannical and decadent rulers. Often governing as monarchs, these rulers ceased abiding by strict adherence to the words of the Koran and the example of the Prophet and his companions, exposing the faithful to infidel influences.[6]

One of the key Koranic concepts that militant Salafists seek to revive among their fellow Sunni Muslims is the practice of a defensive *jihad*, often simplified in translation as "holy war" but perhaps more accurately rendered as defining an act of resistance. The term jihad itself derives from the root word *jahada* meaning a "striving" or "effort" and traditionally refers to almost any action ranging from personal self-improvement to warfare.[7] In the case of modern Islamists, the term refers to an armed military struggle, essentially a holy war, to defend the faith and brethren from perceived aggressors and reclaim the lands taken from Muslims by military force in the manner of medieval Muslim war heroes such a Nur al-Din and Saladin.[8] The eventual reconquests of such lands, ranging from Spain to the Filipino island of Mindanao, remains the ultimate objective of Salafi jihadi groups today and are considered to be defensive wars as these lands were perceived as being seized from Muslims by infidel invaders.[9]

Many Westerners and others mistakenly believe that all Islamist groups throughout the world advocate and plot a war of aggression or *Kifayat al-Jihad* to force the entire non-Muslim world to convert or submit to the rule of Islam.[10] While there are certainly groups that seek to do this through endless proselytizing and hope to impose Islam on regions of the world in which it has never been dominant, this is not the case with those strictly adhering to Salafi teachings.[11] Ignoring bin Laden's consistently professed motives, many Western officials assumed the al-Qaeda leader to be driven by a radical urge to force all Americans to convert to Islam or be killed. This assumption succeeded in keeping U.S. troops in Afghanistan for nearly two decades after 7 October 2001, bleeding the West economically and galvanizing the global Salafi jihadi movement while training its new recruits in combat just as bin Laden hoped and prayed.[12]

During the 1980s, Iran's revolutionary Shia Islamist regime under the Ayatollah Ruhollah Khomeini called for the destruction of the United States based on the perceived debauchery and decadence of American culture. Bin Laden and his Sunni Salafist colleagues watched quietly from the trenches of Afghanistan as their Shia adversaries in Tehran failed miserably to ignite such an offensive jihad against the West. Indeed, few Muslims, even within Khomeini's minority Shia sect, proved willing to martyr themselves waging such a cultural offensive against U.S. and Western freedoms and democratic values.[13]

Ruthless in battle though they were, bin Laden and his compatriots from the Arabian Peninsula did not seize the initiative and rush to fight the Soviets based on Moscow's dictatorial rule at home, the consumption of *vodka* by many ordinary Russians, or Soviet sexuality. Rather, an act of outright aggression in the form of Soviet bullets and bombs killing Muslims in their own country motivated the militant Salafists to act. Within Afghanistan, many rural village *mullahs*, later collectively known as Taleban or "students," initially remained passively content in their traditional Islamic seminaries or *madrassas* until pressure from the communists mounted, inciting them to lend their support to the various guerrilla factions.[14]

Militant Salafism emerged on the Arabian Peninsula during the first half of the eighteenth century and became a potent force following the 1744 alliance of Muhammad bin Saud with a strict desert preacher following Ibn Taymiyyah's teachings, Muhammad ibn Abd al-Wahhab.[15] While bin Saud desired temporal control and aspired to earthly greatness, al-Wahhab sought to revive the teachings of Ibn Taymiyyah and implement them on the Arabian Peninsula, restoring Islam to its original form as practiced by the early Muslims.[16] Following bin Saud's agreement to promote Salafism in exchange for al-Wahhab's religious backing, the two men embarked on a campaign to purify Islam in Arabia under the rule of the al-Saud clan.[17]

Before continuing this chapter's examination of al-Qaeda's fundamentalist ideological roots, a brief discussion is necessary to clarify the key difference between Wahhabism and Salafism. While the two movements are essentially one regarding the duty of Muslim rulers to govern in accordance with Islamic law, known as *Shariah*, Wahhabis display an attitude of superiority towards Muslims outside of their sect.[18] They also display outright hostility towards diversity of belief and thought among other Sunni Muslims, a trait rejected by their Salafi brethren.

While agreeing entirely with the Wahhabi view of cultural isolationism as necessary and proper, traditional Salafists display a far greater tolerance of the diversity of belief within the Sunni Muslim world.[19] Salafi jihadis such as bin Laden also disregard the calls of prominent Wahhabis, such as the Egyptian scholar Said Qutb, for an offensive war against all unbelievers, monotheistic or otherwise, and do not agree that non-Muslims are automatically enemies of the faith.[20] A traditional Salafi does not automatically view a Bulgarian, for example, as a legitimate target or a foe of Islam unless he or she has participated in or supported an action against Muslims.

Throughout his career as the al-Qaeda leader, bin Laden consistently voiced his staunch opposition to sectarian violence and advised his compatriots to avoid unnecessary attacks against nominal Sunni Muslims, Shia Muslims, Christians, and Jews.[21] By contrast, his second-in-command, the former Egyptian surgeon Ayman al-Zawahiri, displayed a marked intolerance of non-Muslims and other Islamic sects. Al-Zawahiri often advocated violence against such groups, receiving regular rebuffs from bin Laden as a result.[22] Documented by former al-Qaeda members and contemporaries, the stark contrast between al-Zawahiri's rush to violence and bin Laden's patient, persuasive approach illustrates the key difference in attitude between Wahhabis and Salafists.

According to several scholars, including Professors Khaled Abou El Fadl and Quintan Wiktorwicz, Wahhabis also display an aura of superiority towards non-Arab Muslims, a trait not shared by bin Laden and his closest associates.[23] For this reason, Wahhabism's appeal is largely limited to al-Wahhab's descendants in the Saudi regime's official religious establishment and some Egyptian organizations such as al-Zawahiri's former group, Egyptian Islamic Jihad (EIJ). Bin Laden's traditional Salafism, while militant, remains focused on the teachings of the Koran and the *sunnah* or *hadith*, the practices of Muhammad and the first three generations of the faithful, seeking to persuade nominal Muslims and infidels rather than forcibly convert them. For this reason, Salafism continues to appeal to countless men and women in the Arabian Peninsula, South Asia, sub-Saharan Africa, Europe, and the Americas.[24]

Throughout the eighteenth century, the Saudi-Salafi alliance gathered many followers in central Arabia and struck far and wide, driving the decadent Ottoman Empire and its local clients from much of the region.[25] Following the death of bin Saud and al-Wahhab, their heirs maintained the traditional alliance and formula for success, unifying much of the Arabian Peninsula under Saudi rule by the end of the eighteenth century. The al-Sauds and Al Ash Shaykh, as al-Wahhab's descendants became known, intermarried as they consolidated their joint religious dynasty.[26]

Seeking to follow the path taken by Muhammad's immediate successors and purify Islam among all Arab peoples, Saudi raiders struck deep into modern-day Iraq, then an Ottoman province, in 1802.[27] They sacked and destroyed the Shia shrine of *Imam* Hussein in Karbala on 21 April, killing more than 2,000 Shia worshippers. The shrine's destruction propelled the First Saudi State, also called the Emirate of Diriyah, to notoriety outside of Arabia and ignited centuries of tension and hostility between Sunni and Shia Islamists across the region.[28]

In 1811, Ottoman Sultan Mahmud II launched a campaign against the Saudi Emirate and drove deep into Arabia.[29] Despite the tenacity of the Saudi warriors, Ottoman forces advanced quickly under superior firepower and numbers. In September 1818, Ottoman troops under Ibrahim Pasha captured Diriyah and razed it to the ground. They seized the Saudi ruler, Abdullah bin Saud, and sent him to Istanbul for public humiliation and execution.[30]

Salafism returned to central and eastern Arabia in 1824 with the rise of Abdullah's heir, Turki bin Abdullah al-Saud.[31] Rallying local allies of the Sudairi tribe, Turki seized the town of Riyadh, modern Saudi Arabia's capital, and swathes of land along the Persian Gulf coast. Throughout the nineteenth century, al-Saud's descendants continued raiding and restoring the lands ruled by their ancestors until their overthrow in 1891 at the hands of the rival al-Rashidi clan of Hail in northern Arabia, allied to the Ottomans. Ottoman and al-Rashidi forces defeated the Saudis at the Battle of Mulayda in 1891, driving them into exile once again.[32]

Militant Salafism re-emerged in Arabia as the nineteenth century led to the twentieth. Following the collapse of the Emirate of Riyadh in 1891, the young Saudi heir Abdul Aziz Ibn Saud escaped into exile with the staunchly Salafi Bedouin warriors of the al-Murrah tribe. The al-Murrah provided protection throughout their extensive tribal domain, while Ibn Saud steadily re-organized his relatives and their allies to reclaim their seat of dynastic power.[33]

In 1903, Ibn Saud led a daring raid with about 40 of his cousins to seize the al-Rashidi-occupied fortress of Riyadh, surprising the occupiers and establishing a third and new Saudi State that he simply called Najd and Its Dependencies.[34] Following this initial success, Ibn Saud experienced a series of blistering defeats at the hands of his al-Rashidi rivals and their Ottoman backers throughout 1904 and 1905. The young Saudi chieftain realized that to reclaim the lands of his forebearers, he needed the assistance of committed warriors.[35]

At the time of Ibn Saud's campaign of reconquest, a Salafi reform movement called the *Ikhwan*, the plural form of the word *akh* or brother, began emerging among the Bedouin tribes of central Arabia.[36] Initially small, the movement slowly began converting adherents across the Arabian Peninsula, eventually providing Ibn Saud with a reliable military force for expanding his domain. The Ikhwan sought to restore traditional Islamic law as practiced by Salafists throughout Arabia and organized themselves into communal, intertribal agricultural communities that they called *hujar* or *hijra* in the singular.[37]

The term *hijra* contains deep religious significance to Muslims of all religious schools and sects, referring to the Prophet Muhammad's journey from his unbelieving Quraish tribe in Mecca to the shelter offered by the faithful Muslims of Yathrib, now known as Medina, in 622.[38] By exchanging their Bedouin lifestyle for a communal life in the *hujar*, the Ikhwan believed themselves to be emulating Muhammad's example of abandoning a place of unbelief for a place of belief. To emphasize their strict Salafi adherence to Muhammad's example, they wound white turbans or *imamah* around their traditional *qutra* headdresses to emulate the dress of the Prophet and his companions and built mud huts as living quarters in place of Bedouin tents.[39]

Sensing a window of opportunity, Ibn Saud tapped into the Ikhwan movement and quickly gained the support of its leaders due to his family's historical promotion of Salafism in the eighteenth and nineteenth centuries. With the support of his father, the last ruler of the Second Saudi State, he became the chief religious leader or *imam* of the Ikhwan, ensuring the family's religious legitimacy in the eyes of the movement's faithful.[40] Fighting for Ibn Saud provided the Ikhwan with an opportunity to face infidel forces in battle as holy warriors waging a defensive war to reclaim former al-Saud territory and restore Salafism as the state religion. According to Saudi scholar Dr. Madawi al-Rasheed, they were often referred to as *jund al-tawhid* or "soldiers enforcing the doctrine of the oneness of God."[41]

Bedouin men from the Mutair tribe established the first major Ikhwan colony at al-Artawiyah, while warriors from the Utaybah and Qahtan tribes settled the colony of al-Ghat Ghat shortly afterwards in 1912.[42] By the mid-1910s, tens of thousands of volunteers from almost all the Arabian Peninsula's tribes had answered the call to holy war fighting under *al-Raya*, the black flag of jihad, alongside Ibn Saud's loyal regular army that he raised from the population of Riyadh.[43] Under Ibn Saud's oversight, Salafi jihadism had entered the twentieth century.

Throughout the First World War (1914-1918), Ibn Saud received limited Allied material support, particularly from Britain, in the form of arms, ammunition, and government financing.[44] This support provided a critical boost to his regular Saudi forces fighting the al-Rashidis and the Ottoman Turkish forces in northern Arabia. Simultaneously, the Ikhwan conducted daring raids against al-Rashidi and Ottoman strongholds throughout Arabia, recruiting further volunteers to their cause and fighting ferociously.[45]

The Ikhwan quickly earned a reputation for ruthlessness and reckless bravado in battle, hurling themselves at terrified Turkish soldiers manning their artillery positions. Although lightly armed and facing a modernized and professional army, the Ikhwan compensated for their lack of conventional firepower with uncompromising tenacity in combat.[46] With a reputation for being fearless of death and willing to die in battle as martyrs or slay their "apostate" enemies, the warriors liberated large swathes of Arabia from Ottoman rule.[47]

While on a campaign, the Ikhwan raiders often utilized their war camels or *zalul* as mobile infantry transport in the same manner as the early Muslim armies.⁴⁸ This allowed the warriors to conserve their energy for combat and to strike quickly, using the few horses at their disposal for cavalry support. Before battle, they presented their enemies with the same options that the Rashidun general Khalid bin Walid gave his Byzantine and Persian opponents during the Islamic expansion of the 630s, "Islam, the *jizya* [a special tax on non-Muslims], or the sword."⁴⁹ If the Ottomans or their Arab clients refused the first two options, they faced the full fury of Ibn Saud's holy warriors.

The Ikhwan played a key role in contributing to the destruction of Ottoman power in Arabia and strengthening Ibn Saud's position. As war-ravaged European countries returned to an uneasy peace at the end of the decade, fighting continued to rage across Arabia as the Ikhwan achieved further victories, extending Saudi rule and their Salafi creed. Between 1924 and 1926, the Ikhwan scored a series of successes against the rival Hashemite dynasty backed by Britain in the Hejaz region, driving its ruler King Hussein into exile in Transjordan.⁵⁰

The Ikhwan's victories in the Hejaz region placed Ibn Saud in control of the holiest cities of Islam, Mecca and Medina, and alarmed the British authorities in control of Iraq and Transjordan. Following the fall of the Hejazi Hashemites, British troops began building a series of forts along their borders with Najd and Hejaz. The Ikhwan subsequently attacked the British forts and raided into Iraq and Transjordan, reaching as far as the modern Jordanian capital of Amman.⁵¹ British forces in the region retaliated with an aerial bombing campaign into Saudi territory.⁵²

Realizing that his holy warriors must be restrained if he hoped to retain control of the regions that they had reconquered for him, Ibn Saud ordered the Ikhwan to refrain from further raiding into territories controlled by Britain.⁵³ He ordered his Islamist *ulema* or clergy to issue religious rulings in his favor to control the Ikhwan's actions and began introducing modern technology into his regular tribal army as a balance against his religious militia. Denouncing these measures as a betrayal of Islam, many Ikhwan began to perceive Ibn Saud as a tyrant and a puppet of the British infidels.⁵⁴

In their arguments, Ikhwan chiefs sought to persuade Ibn Saud that the British had committed an act of aggression by occupying Muslim territory and threatening Najd with their forts and bomber aircraft.⁵⁵ This is a key point, because it reveals the Ikhwan's perception of their military struggle as a defensive war against infidels occupying Muslim lands, a perspective shared by al-Qaeda and its international wings. On 29 March 1929, Ibn Saud defeated the rebellious Ikhwan at the Battle of S'bala with the support of 200 armored cars supplied by Britain and the intervention of British fighter pilots.⁵⁶

Consolidating his power in the following years, Ibn Saud announced the birth of the Kingdom of Saudi Arabia in 1932 and permitted the remaining loyal Ikhwan to stay on their agricultural colonies practicing an ideal, communal Salafism unhindered by the state. These Salafi loyalists among the Ikhwan subsequently participated in a border war with *Imam* Yahya of Yemen in 1934 but saw little action after this brief and bloody affair.[57]

The following decades after modern Saudi Arabia's birth saw a period of increasingly firm control by the al-Saud dynasty over its lands covering much of the Arabian Peninsula. During the reign of Ibn Saud's son King Faisal (r. 1964-1975), a grassroots Salafi reform movement developed among the Saudi clergy unaffiliated with the regime. The followers of this movement, known as the *Sahwa* or "Islamic Awakening" sought to support peaceful reforms and the full implementation of all the *Shariah* laws to end official corruption.[58]

King Faisal tolerated and promoted the movement as a counterweight to the spread of Soviet-backed Arab nationalism supported by the Egyptian ruler Gamal Abd-al-Nasser, despite its origins among Salafi clergy not belonging to the regime establishment.[59] In the early 1970s, Faisal also began allowing Awakening scholars and their non-governmental organizations (NGOs) to use the wealth generated by the country's booming oil industry to export Salafism. Faisal staunchly opposed the spread of Nasserism and communism and allowed Salafi scholars to debate communist teachings in the Kingdom's universities. He supported these activities with increased vigor after a Marxist regime seized power in South Yemen in 1970, an event that also alarmed Western leaders, as emphasized by UK MP Lord Reginald Prentice in a 26 March 1979 House of Commons debate.[60]

In a March 2006 interview, Saudi cleric Shaykh Musa al-Qarni, a former *mufti* or religious mentor of bin Laden, recalls the Saudi regime's promotion of the Islamic Awakening as a counterweight to the appeal of Nasser's Soviet-backed Arab national socialism. Under regime encouragement, Salafi scholars engaged in intense debates with supporters of Nasserism in Saudi universities throughout the late 1960s and early 1970s. The challenge presented by the Arab national socialist movement grew into a more lethal threat during and after the North Yemen Civil War fought between 1962 and 1970.[61]

During the fighting in Yemen, Nasser intervened on the side of the Arab national socialists backed by Moscow and its Warsaw Pact client states, sending Egyptian troops and tanks to support the secularists while Faisal and his predecessor, King Saud, supported the Shia Muslim royalists opposing them.[62] On 7 November 1962, Egyptian bombers struck several Saudi cities and towns in the neighboring provinces of Najran and Jazan, reportedly killing and injuring Saudi and Yemeni civilians and escalating tensions to the state of an international crisis.[63] Fiercely independent and uncompromising in their struggle against foreign intervention, the Yemeni warrior tribesmen, or *qabili*, doggedly resisted the invaders.[64] While simultaneously fighting the British during the struggle for independence in Aden, they inflicted a humiliating defeat on Nasser's Soviet-backed troops, forcing the invaders to retreat in 1969.[65]

While UK leaders opposed Nasser's military intervention in North Yemen's civil war and reportedly joined with the Saudi, Israeli, and Jordanian governments in backing the royalists, Whitehall faced a growing tribal insurgency against its collapsing rule in the strategic port of Aden.[66] Beginning in October 1963, Yemen's devout *qabili* warrior tribes began inciting revolts against Britain's rule in Aden and challenging the colonial forces that had controlled the key Arabian Sea port city since 1839. Throughout the 1960s, local resentment towards the perceived British and Egyptian occupiers galvanized the resistance of the defiant Yemeni tribes to all foreign forces stationed in the country's northern and southern regions.[67]

Concerned that a British withdrawal could leave Aden and the neighboring Yemeni region then called the Federation of South Arabia open to Nasser's expansionism, UK MP Sir Neil Marten recommended that London continue its military presence despite the rising opposition encountered by UK troops in a 27 February 1967 House of Commons debate.[68] Urging Whitehall to either deploy enough troops to crush the insurgency or withdraw immediately, MP Sir Peter Tapsell seconded Marten's criticism of London's February 1966 decision to withdraw while maintaining a limited presence for several more years as, "sheer nonsense and folly."[69] Advising Whitehall to either, "stay in the Arabian Peninsula in sufficient force or get out altogether," Sir Tapsell concluded by expressing his view that, "There is no middle way in the Middle East."[70]

On 30 November 1967, British forces completed their withdrawal from Aden, and Nasser's Egyptian forces began retreating from the North that same year after suffering a series of stinging defeats by the rural, devout Yemeni tribes.[71] Despite the Egyptian defeat, North Yemen's secularists won enough tribal support to depose the minority Shia royalists, and Faisal immediately switched Saudi Arabia's support to the military regime that they subsequently established in the northern capital of Sanaa. Following Britain's defeat in the south, Aden became the capital of the newly established state of South Yemen following unification with the former Federation of South Arabia and the three neighboring sultanates of the eastern desert region of Hadramut.[72]

In 1970, a Marxist clique seized control in Aden, South Yemen's capital, and declared the nation the Arab world's first and only communist state.[73] Backed by Faisal's Saudi regime, the military republic remained in power in North Yemen, and the nation remained divided for several decades, with a largely tribal and devout Sunni majority ruled by minority military or Marxist elites in each respective case. This forced division of fiercely independent tribes and families ruled by tyrannical minority central governments in both cases lit the fuse of resentment in Yemeni society, later creating fertile ground for al-Qaeda.[74] Both ruling factions represented minority ideologies, and the fighting and subsequent rule of Marxists in southern Yemen displaced numerous families and forced large numbers of devout Sunni Muslims into exile in North Yemen and Saudi Arabia. Several of these Yemeni refugee immigrant families later produced prominent al-Qaeda fighters and leaders, including Tariq al-Fadhli, Jamal al-Hadhi, Obadah al-Wadihi, and Nasser al-Bahri.[75] Their traditional family connections to Yemen's devout and defiant tribes later proved to be decisive in securing a thoroughly entrenched base on the Arabian Peninsula for bin Laden and al-Qaeda.

Despite Nasser's defeat, the Marxist presence in South Yemen enhanced the secular and national socialist threat to the Saudi Kingdom on its very borders while continuing to concern Western governments by allowing Soviet commanders to dock naval vessels and station troops in Aden.[76] King Faisal continued to provide strong official support to the Islamic Awakening, hoping to bolster the Kingdom's defenses against the secular threats of communism and nationalism, and earn the trust of its devout tribal population. Faisal also continued encouraging the Salafi NGOs to channel the profits from Saudi Arabia's growing oil revenues towards the promotion of Salafism abroad.[77]

Traveling on regime approval and both official and private funding, Saudi Salafi clerics began performing missionary work throughout the Muslim world, establishing Islamic religious seminaries or *madrassas*, and spreading their message of restoring Islam to its purest form as practiced by the Prophet and his companions. This process eventually created strong local cadres of militant Salafists, particularly in Yemen and South Asia, and enhanced the message of local Sunni Islamist movements such as the Deobandis in Afghanistan and Pakistan and their religious students, some of whom later reportedly organized the Taleban movement at the White Mosque in Afghanistan's Kandahar Province on 10 October 1994.[78] This regional ideological struggle between the Sunni Islamists backed by Riyadh and the Arab national socialists backed by Moscow earned Faisal the respect of Salafists inside the Kingdom, and he remains the only Saudi monarch that bin Laden never denounced.[79]

Bin Laden's former religious mentor Shaykh Musa Al-Qarni recalls the growing threat of communism emanating from the South Yemeni regime, despite the regime's inability to enforce its control outside of its capital city of Aden. In a March 2006 interview, al-Qarni emphasizes the determination of the Saudi royals to prevent a communist invasion by fostering Salafism's growth.[80] Born in Jeddah, Saudi Arabia in 1972, Nasser al-Bahri, the first son of a Yemeni *qabili* couple fleeing Yemen's southern Shabwah province, recalls that even his father could not help but admire Egypt's Nasser to the point of styling his hair in a similar manner.[81] Yet al-Bahri's father, Ahmed, an employee of the Bin Laden Company, nevertheless resented those calling themselves Muslims yet forgetting to pray. While admiring Nasser's efforts to unify the Arab world, and critical of the Islamic Awakening for its perceived excesses, al-Bahri's father remained traditional in his religious outlook and at one with the Salafis in their promotion of Islamic values.[82]

In 1973, a devout 16-year-old boy from a wealthy and hardworking Yemeni immigrant family named Osama bin Laden joined the Salafist *Sahwa* movement sweeping Saudi society.[83] Bin Laden never forgot Faisal's promotion of the movement and its support for Salafi missionary work abroad. His childhood friend, Khaled al-Batarfi, states that bin Laden earned a solid reputation working and eating alongside his family's employees at construction sites as a manual laborer for the Bin Laden Company, Saudi Arabia's largest construction firm.[84]

Bin Laden's father, a devout Yemeni laborer named Muhammad born in 1908, had set an example for his sons to follow, bringing his work ethic and construction skills from Yemen's impoverished Hadramut region to help build Saudi Arabia's infrastructure in 1931.[85] In the 1960s, Muhammad bin Awad bin Laden had physically connected his homeland with Mecca, completing a road running from the holy city through the mountains of southwestern Asir province to the Yemeni border, a task reportedly rejected by European engineers as impossible.[86]

Citing the accounts of bin Laden's childhood friends, several biographers have pointed out that he likely met his father on barely a handful of occasions in his life, as the elder bin Laden died in a plane crash near the city of Oom in the Asir mountains on 3 September 1967.[87] Nevertheless, as bin Laden biographer Michael Scheuer points out, Muhammad bin Laden's example provided his heirs with a blueprint for success, and Osama applied it in working alongside Muslims of diverse ethnic and national origins.[88] Osama's approachability, a product of a devout childhood influenced by his family's modest origins and work ethic, won him the respect of his coworkers, a trait that subsequently benefitted him during the Soviet-Afghan War.[89]

Following Faisal's assassination in 1975, his brothers and successors Kings Khalid and Fahd largely continued to follow his policies but acted with far less piety. This double standard provoked fear and resentment among militant Salafists in the Kingdom and the birth of an underground movement led by Juhayman al-Utaybi, the son of an Ikhwan warrior.[90] As the Islamic New Year 1400 dawned on 20 November 1979, al-Utaybi led hundreds of his followers, recruited via the illegal distribution of pamphlets and cassette tapes, into Mecca's Grand Mosque, Islam's holiest house of worship.[91]

The rebels denounced the al-Saud royal family as corrupt and insufficiently pious and held countless pilgrims as hostages for 10 days.[92] With the help of French Special Forces, Saudi National Guardsmen eventually engaged the insurgents in battle, arresting the survivors and beheading al-Utaybi on 9 January 1980.[93] During its 10-day duration, al-Utaybi's seizure of the Grand Mosque ignited a series of turbulent events throughout the Muslim world. Angry Pakistanis besieged the U.S. consulate in the capital city of Islamabad, killing a U.S. Marine while denouncing the mosque seizure as a CIA conspiracy. In the southern Indian cities of Calcutta and Hyderabad, a series of violent clashes erupted as Islamist protesters reportedly targeted Westerners and Hindu businesses.[94]

In Saudi Arabia itself, Islamic Awakening members such as bin Laden sympathized with many of the insurgents' complaints about the growing corruption in Saudi society but disagreed with both sides committing violence inside of Islam's holiest mosque.[95] Bin Laden's brothers had aided the Saudi National Guard by providing blueprints of the Grand Mosque, which they had continued to renovate since the time of their father's work on the site. Some bin Laden brothers also faced scrutiny from the security forces after allegations emerged that they had sought mediation between the regime and the rebels to avoid violence at Islam's holiest shrine.[96]

Bin Laden later expressed disappointment with King Fahd's handling of the event by answering violence with violence inside of the holy Grand Mosque and for flying in infidel French troops to participate in the operation.[97] As documented by biographers such as Michael Scheuer and Steve Coll, the young militant remained intensely loyal to his king and country despite his growing reservations about the royal family's perceived hypocrisy.[98] One month after the upheaval in Mecca, Saudis were shocked by a far greater assault on Islam in South Asia that triggered the Awakening's transformation from a peaceful reform movement into a vanguard of Sunni Islamist resistance.

CHAPTER 2

Brezhnev's boast, Osama's early actions, and U.S.-U.K. perceptions of the Islamic guerrillas, 1979-1985

One month after the new Ikhwan uprising in Mecca rocked Saudi society and the wider Muslim world, a reluctant decision by the Soviet Politburo sent Moscow's forces surging into Afghanistan, creating shockwaves still reverberating into the third decade of the twenty-first century.[1] This reluctant act of aggression, executed for the limited purpose of ensuring a friendly regime on the Soviet Union's southern borders, drew swift condemnation from the West but the war that it triggered has largely been minimized in importance as a local theater of the global Cold War. For many devout Muslims, the invasion represented an unprovoked assault on their brethren in one of the world's poorest countries, leading many Salafists in Saudi Arabia and elsewhere to join the resistance fighters seeking to oust the Soviet occupiers. Although they represented a diverse range of ethnicities and nationalities from North Africa to the South Pacific, these zealous volunteers became known collectively as the "Afghan Arabs."[2] The bulk of these young men were indeed ethnic Yemenis, known as *Qahtanis* or "South Arabians," hailing from devout tribes native to southern Saudi Arabia or Yemen.[3]

The roots of the Soviet military intervention in Afghanistan date to 1973, a year that marked the end of Afghan King Zahir Shah's 40-year reign.[4] During the latter years of his rule, Zahir Shah had reportedly become increasingly corrupt, allegedly spending much of his time traveling to Italy and engaging in numerous affairs while the small Afghan Communist Party infiltrated his government. On 17 July 1973, the king's cousin and prime minister Muhammad Daud Khan overthrew him in a successful coup staged in conjunction with an elite clique of leftist army officers.[5]

After exiling his royal cousin to Italy, Daud gradually strengthened his support from military elites by forging a power-sharing alliance with communist politician Nur Muhammad Taraki.[6] Between 1973 and 1978, Taraki consolidated his position and that of the People's Democratic Party of Afghanistan (PDPA) in the new regime hierarchy by promoting communist military officers to positions of authority. He also attempted to persuade Daud to adopt Marxist reforms and forge a closer relationship with Brezhnev's Soviet Union.[7]

While allowing promotions to placate his communist allies in the elite military class, Daud moved slowly in implementing reforms out of fear of provoking the resentment of the tribal religious leaders in Afghanistan's vast rural regions.[8] While Islamist leaders such as Gulbuddin Hekmatyar and Abdul Rasul Sayyaf certainly welcomed Zahir Shah's ouster, they also feared the anti-religious policies of the communists and a potential Soviet invasion. Following Daud's July coup, Hekmatyar and Sayyaf denounced the regime with calls for a defensive jihad against the regime and launched a small-scale insurgency from their bases in neighboring Pakistan.[9]

Frustrated by Daud's reluctance to implement communist policies, Taraki and his deputies staged a coup against him on 27 April 1978, and quickly reached out to the Soviet Union for economic and diplomatic aid.[10] Actively backing communist regimes and insurgencies as part of the global Cold War but surprised by the Afghan Marxists' successful coup, Brezhnev began providing Soviet financial and military aid despite the Kremlin's prevailing perception of the PDPA as an unimpressive and ineffective party.[11] Emboldened by Moscow's backing, Taraki moved quickly in ushering in reforms steeped in communist ideology. As Islamist resistance to the central government mounted, Taraki dispatched police and military personnel, sometimes advised by their Soviet counterparts, into the Afghan countryside to root out the opposition.[12]

To co-opt religious support and counter the message of the Islamists, some PDPA leaders reportedly sought to enlist the help of traditional tribal mullahs and adherents of the traditional Deobandi sect of Sunni Islam in Afghanistan's ethnic Pashtun regions.[13] According to former Taleban ambassador to Pakistan, Mullah Abdul Salam Zaeef, the regime's agents briefly succeeded in recruiting several prominent religious scholars led by *Mawlawis* Mir Hatem and Niaz Muhammad, to support the government's efforts at land redistribution.[14] Zaeef claims that many other scholars such as *Mawlawi* Abdul Qadir and Mullah Muhammad Sadiq viewed such policies as theft and therefore an affront to Islam, and joined local guerrilla units as government pressure mounted, directing the assassinations of many of the pro-regime clerics.[15] As tensions mounted, Afghan Army units began to mutiny and desert to the resistance, prompting Brezhnev and KGB Chairman Yuri Andropov to dispatch Soviet military and KGB advisers in larger numbers to Afghanistan to gather information and to advise Taraki accordingly.[16]

Between the communist coup in April 1978 and the Soviet invasion of December 1979, an estimated 27,000 people were reportedly killed in Pul-i-

Charki prison in the Afghan capital, Kabul.[17] Many of these victims were reportedly devout Muslim clerics and others deemed to be threats to the new regime and potential supporters of the growing insurgency. Inspired by Khomeini's recent Islamic Revolution in neighboring Iran, Afghan Army Captain Ismail Khan staged a mutiny in the city of Herat on 15 March 1979.[18] During Khan's revolt, his Shia Islamist followers reportedly seized and slaughtered more than a dozen Soviet military advisers and their families residing in the city, prompting the Afghan Air Force to strike Herat in retaliation.[19]

Violating an agreement between the Afghan central government and the rebels not to engage in violence on Fridays, the Muslim day of congregational prayer, regime forces reportedly surrounded the village of Kerala with their Soviet-supplied tanks and armored cars before executing more than 1,100 male villagers suspected of supporting the guerrillas in the early morning hours of 20 April 1979.[20] According to eyewitnesses interviewed by the Swiss-American journalist Edward Girardet, the Afghan troops allegedly executed the massacre in the presence of a "Slavic-looking" senior officer whom the witnesses referred to as the "commandant."[21] The government soldiers reportedly herded their captives into the village square before unleashing a hailstorm of machine gun bullets as the men recited the *shahada* or Muslim profession of faith from the Koran, while shoving back the female villagers praying for their husbands, fathers, and sons, and begging to say goodbye.[22]

Many Afghan civilians are said to have lost their lives to other massacres allegedly executed by regime forces between April 1978 and December 1979.[23] During this time, Soviet KGB advisers also reportedly instructed their Afghan colleagues on ways to wire their victims' rectal areas and administer electric shocks.[24] As atrocities mounted and the resistance continued to spread, large numbers of Afghan civilians began fleeing to Pakistan and Iran, bringing stories of the regime's brutality and its perceived assaults on Islamic traditions with them.[25] The resentment that these accounts gradually generated against the regime and its foreign backers appears to have motivated many young zealots from Saudi Arabia and elsewhere to leave home and join the Islamic guerrillas in a war of resistance against the occupiers that Salafists worldwide regarded as the irrefutable Koranic justification for a defensive jihad.[26]

As the fighting between the government forces and the rebels continued to spread, KGB Chairman Andropov reportedly began joining Taraki's desperate lobbying for Brezhnev and the Soviet Politburo to launch a Soviet military intervention to strengthen the regime enough to crush the Islamic resistance.[27] Acknowledging that such intervention constituted aggression despite Taraki's demands for Soviet military action, Andropov is said to have insisted in a Politburo session on 17 March 1979 that Moscow could not afford to stand by idly while the Afghan communists fought for survival.[28] While expressing reservations about the deployment of a large military force to Afghanistan, Andropov concluded that a direct, limited intervention by the Soviet Army could be necessary save the hated central government from collapse and preserve Moscow's image as socialism's champion in the Third World.[29]

Yet while some major decision-makers within the Kremlin hierarchy appear to have felt a military intervention to be the only logical solution, other Soviet officials reportedly cautioned against acting with such haste. Although the Soviet leadership feared the potential spread of U.S. or Pakistani influence in Afghanistan, a situation that meant hostile forces approaching Soviet borders, the hostility of the rural Afghan Islamist leaders toward perceived infidel influences posed a problem for any temporary occupation force.[30] In his splendid book *Afghanistan: The Soviet Union's Last War*, historian Mark Galeotti points out that several key Soviet leaders sought to prevent the debacle that occurred after Soviet forces invaded Afghanistan, emphasizing the need for a cautious approach while taking into consideration the complexities of traditional Afghan society.[31]

On 29 June 1979, a key group of leading Politburo Central Committee members of the Communist Party of the Soviet Union (CPSU) including Brezhnev, Andropov, Defense Minister Dmitry Ustinov, Foreign Minister and later Chairman of the Presidium of the Supreme Soviet between 1985 and 1988 Andrei Gromyko, and International Department Head Boris Ponomarev met to discuss the situation in Afghanistan.[32] Citing the example of the recent Islamic Revolution in neighboring Iran, Andropov, Gromyko, and others expressed alarm at the growing threat to the Kabul regime posed by the rural, "reactionary clergy."[33] Dreading the potential takeover of Kabul by a hostile, fundamentalist regime, the Committee members concluded with a decision to send a small detachment of experienced Soviet officers and a parachute battalion to ensure the protection of Soviet planes at Bagram Air Base near Kabul.[34]

The Committee also decided to dispatch more KGB and military intelligence (GRU) advisers in Afghan uniform to quench Taraki's constant pleas for more aid and to, "pass the Indian leadership disinformation" about alleged Islamist plans to create a, "world Islamic republic" in Afghanistan and Kashmir.[35] Concerned with growing Pakistani support for the Afghan Islamist groups, the Committee members declared the objective of their disinformation campaign to influence Indian officials into increasing pressure on Pakistan's leaders to cease supporting the growing resistance movement.[36] Seeking to avoid a full intervention and potential quagmire that could result from religious and nationalistic resentment of a large Soviet military presence in Afghanistan, the CPSU delegates expressed hope that their decision may prove sufficient to safeguard the PDPA government from a rebel takeover.[37] In an August 1979 meeting, Lieutenant General Leonid Gorelov reportedly urged further restraint on the Afghan issue despite the growing demands of PDPA officials for a larger Soviet assistance force, advising against a direct military intervention that could potentially boomerang to the Kremlin's detriment.[38]

Demands for an invasion intensified in September 1979 with Taraki's overthrow in a coup by Communist Party rival Hafizullah Amin, a fellow member of the party's *Khalq* faction that the Soviet leadership viewed dimly due to its unrealistic approach of forcing communist reforms onto the religious Afghan rural population quickly.[39] After imprisoning Taraki and his family, Amin continued to implement Marxist policies while attacking the country's traditional Islamic values, further angering Moscow by purging alleged party rivals.[40] As pointed out by Mark Galeotti and Robert Kaplan, the rural population's perception of Amin as an even greater tyrant than his predecessor drove increasing numbers of young men into the arms of the growing insurgency.[41] Amin's factionalism and the political infighting that he exacerbated within the PDPA further threatened the regime's stability, rendering him a less reliable client ruler for Moscow and reportedly triggering frustration and calls for his removal within the KGB.[42]

Noting that the situation continued to spiral out of control, Andropov's KGB Residency in Kabul printed false stories alleging that Amin had become an agent of the United States.[43] Brezhnev and Andropov became suspicious that Amin secretly sought both a compromise with Islamist leaders and U.S. support to save himself and retain some degree of political power.[44] In a 31 October 1979 Central Committee discussion, Andropov, Gromyko, Ustinov, and Ponomarev cited Amin's growing excesses as a growing threat to the regime's stability.[45] The CPSU officials proceeded to denounce Amin's alleged desire to seek compromise with the "right-wing Muslim opposition" as well as his excessive mass arrest campaign and the possibility that U.S. officials could successfully manipulate the situation to Washington's advantage.[46]

Expressing growing reservations about Amin's unreliability, the Committee members appear to have concluded that Amin's reign threatened "the gains of the April Revolution," inevitably leading either to the establishment of an Islamist or pro-U.S. and Pakistani regime in Kabul.[47] In a Politburo session on 26 November 1979, Brezhnev declared an invasion of Afghanistan to be necessary to replace Amin with a more trustworthy Kremlin puppet, destroy his loyal units within the Afghan Army, and withdraw within a short period after training a new Afghan military and police force to crush the insurgency and ensure the PDPA's survival.[48] Reportedly boasting that the world could expect Soviet troops to achieve a rapid victory over Amin's Soviet-trained and equipped Afghan Army in, "three to four weeks," Brezhnev appears to have expected Soviet forces to withdraw quickly after consolidating a new regime and military while avoiding prolonged combat with the insurgents.[49]

On the evening of 24 December 1979, the Soviet invasion of Afghanistan, code-named Operation *Storm-333*, commenced as Soviet airborne troops landed in Kabul and killed Amin while storming his palace.[50] Babrak Karmal, the former Afghan ambassador to Czechoslovakia and a member of the PDPA's rival *Parcham* faction favored by the Kremlin for its proposed policies of a slower, more careful progression to communism in rural, religious Afghanistan, assumed power as his country's new ruler. At 11:30 p.m. on the following night, 52,000 troops of the Soviet 40th Army surged across the Amu Darya River in a two-pronged assault into northern Afghanistan and quickly fanned out across the country.[51] They immediately occupied the major Afghan cities and roads, attempting to consolidate their holds to secure Karmal's position in power while the Afghan Army engaged the insurgents in battle.[52] Soviet forces reportedly crushed the last of the pro-Amin resistance within the Afghan Army on 5 January 1980, smashing the conventional military opposition within the timeframe expected by Brezhnev while remaining unprepared for the protracted struggle ahead.[53]

Initially planning for a struggle with the pro-Amin factions within the Soviet-trained and equipped Afghan Army, the generals of the 40th Army invaded Afghanistan with enormous material advantages over the resistance fighters that they subsequently encountered. Enjoying total air supremacy, the Soviet Air Force completely dominated the skies, while tanks and armored columns enjoyed the close support of motorized rifle formations, and unlike Amin's Soviet-equipped regime forces, the Islamic guerrillas that the occupiers were gradually drawn into combat against boasted neither aircraft nor armored units.[54] The guerrillas could initially resist Moscow's mechanized forces mainly with the Lee Enfield rifles that their grandfathers and great grandfathers had used to fight the British during the Third Anglo-Afghan War in 1919.[55]

In addition to overwhelming conventional firepower, armor, air supremacy, and the relentless airstrikes of the Sukhoi Su-25 *Grach* or "Raven" close air support jet, Soviet troops could rely on the aid of the world's best attack helicopter, the Mil Mi-24 gunship.[56] Known to Soviet pilots as the "flying tank" and *krokodil*, each of these war machines reportedly boasted at least 128 rockets and four missiles.[57] Their constant presence in the skies above the advancing armored columns caused many international observers to concur with Brezhnev's expectations of a rapid and inevitable Soviet victory.[58]

Initially, Soviet forces also appeared poised for victory in terms of morale. Under the "Brezhnev Doctrine," Soviet KGB and GRU operatives had overseen the successful rise of communist regimes throughout the world during the 1970s, culminating in the invasion of Afghanistan.[59] Communist regimes or insurgencies had spread aggressively across Asia, Africa, and Latin America with Soviet support, and *Storm-333* marked the first instance since 1968 that Soviet troops had been deployed to crush a rebellion.[60] Believing the Soviet Army to be irresistible, many Western observers also expected the Afghan resistance to collapse quickly. This factor reportedly led to congressional authorization for the CIA to initially supply only a limited amount of material aid to the rebels through Pakistan's Inter-Services-Intelligence (ISI) for fear that arming the fighters amounted to throwing U.S. arms into Soviet hands.[61]

Throughout the 40th Army's Afghan campaign however, Soviet forces also suffered from several crucial disadvantages that hampered the Kremlin's mission to stabilize the Kabul regime to enable a quick and victorious withdrawal. Initially planning for a short operation, the Soviet leadership does not appear to have been prepared for the prolonged campaign that resulted as Soviet forces became increasingly drawn into battle against a lightly armed but determined enemy fired by faith.[62] Afghanistan's complex topography that combines some of the world's highest mountains with thickly wooded hills and vast, arid deserts also presented a challenging environment.[63] Prepared for a conventional conflict in Western Europe, the nature of the war that Soviet commanders faced forced them to rely heavily on airpower and Special Forces operations in bloody and destructive but ultimately unsuccessful attempts to dislodge the guerrillas and their supporters from their rural strongholds.[64]

The limited nature of the Soviet campaign also appears to have impaired the 40th Army's operations. Whether under Brezhnev, Gorbachev, or the general secretaries that ruled briefly between their respective tenures, Kremlin leaders reportedly shared the goal of bolstering the pro-Soviet regime in Kabul and withdrawing their forces quickly after accomplishing this objective.[65] As the primary motive for the temporary but often brutal occupation of a country that they otherwise appear to have had little interest in, the objective of stabilizing the hated regime in Kabul prevented Soviet leaders from withdrawing their forces as quickly as they intended.[66] This, in turn, led to an unexpected and prolonged war of attrition that strongly favored the resistance and later provided vital combat training for the founding generation of al-Qaeda.

According to an after-action report on the war by the Russian General Staff, the campaign's primary decision-makers also underestimated the power of religion to incite the rural population against the perceived occupiers, disregarding prewar concerns by some Politburo members.[67] The Soviet High Command also reportedly leaned heavily on the belief that the Soviet Air Force's sustained bombing campaigns supported by helicopter gunship raids could eliminate the insurgents' logistical capabilities and willpower to resist by interdicting the fighters and the horses, camels, and pack mules used for transporting their supplies through the mountains.[68] Along with this overreliance on airpower, an aversion to casualties also reportedly afflicted the 40th Army.[69] By contrast, the more militant Afghan Islamist groups and the small number of Arab guerrillas fighting alongside them appear to have suffered less psychologically from this factor, propelled by religious fervor to fight with an, "indifference to death."[70]

While crediting Soviet soldiers with admirable martial qualities and a willingness to pursue the resistance fighters in battle, bin Laden later cited the Soviet High Command's perceived underestimation of religious fervor in motivating their adversaries to fight back as a weakness that also afflicted U.S. leaders.[71] Expressing his perception that the Soviet-Afghan War's outcome "cleared from Muslim minds the myth of superpowers," the al-Qaeda chief taunted Washington in several interviews in the late 1990s while executing deadly terror attacks to draw U.S. forces into Afghanistan.[72] Reflecting on the battle experience obtained by the Afghan and Arab fighters resisting the Soviets, bin Laden reportedly calculated that the Taleban insurgency with the support of al-Qaeda guerrilla cadres, could overcome the U.S.-NATO Afghan campaign, describing U.S. troops as "paper tigers" in comparison to the more merciless Soviet troops.[73]

Despite the fears that the insurgents could not resist the Soviet Army for long, U.S. and other Western leaders launched a bold effort to arm them during the decade of war following the Soviet invasion, greatly expanding their efforts as the lightly armed rebels continued persevering against the odds.[74] Relations between Washington and rebel leaders soured later in the war however, after some U.S. officials reportedly supported an initiative that offended several key mujahedin commanders by promoting the creation of an "interim government" including members of the hated PDPA regime.[75] Perceived as an attempt to exclude the major resistance factions, the four that reportedly fielded the most uncompromising fundamentalist fighters, from attaining power after achieving victory, this suggestion provoked harsh rebukes from several Afghan commanders and U.S. congressmen. Along with a subsequent proposal by the U.S. Department of State to permit President Mohammad Najibullah a role in an Afghan transitional government, the congressional arguments favoring a power-sharing interim regime exacerbated tensions and mistrust between some U.S. officials and mujahedin commanders.[76]

The tensions that sometimes resulted from the Afghan insurgent leaders' growing mistrust of their Western backers later provided rhetorical ammunition for bin Laden to utilize in emphasizing the alleged hostility of U.S. and U.K. politicians to the establishment of a religious-oriented regime in Kabul.[77] Bin Laden's actions and the rapport that he gradually established with the Afghan and Pakistani Pashtun tribes and insurgent commanders while fighting the Soviets likewise later guaranteed a strong local constituency for al-

Qaeda as the group launched its war with the West. These key factors appear to have coalesced in heightening the mistrust of many Afghan commanders and their supporters towards the United States and Britain and strengthened the relationship of the Arab jihadis with the Afghan Islamists from the later years of the anti-Soviet jihad until the U.S.-NATO Afghan campaign.[78]

Moscow's invasion drew sharp criticism from U.S., U.K., and Pakistani leaders and triggered calls for an anti-Soviet defensive jihad throughout Saudi Arabia, North Yemen, and much of the Muslim world.[79] Pakistani military dictator General Muhammad Zia ul-Haq concluded a Tripartite agreement with U.S. President Jimmy Carter and Saudi King Fahd to supply the rebels with a limited amount of funding and arms.[80] Learning of the Soviet Army's aggression while at prayer, bin Laden flew to Pakistan two weeks after the Soviet invasion and offered his services to the insurgents.[81]

As Muslim sources began reporting on the carnage, Salafists in Saudi Arabia became increasingly occupied with the war between Moscow's puppet regime and the Islamic guerrillas. Even while beginning his studies at King Abdul Aziz University, working for the Bin Laden Company, and celebrating the 1979 birth of his third consecutive son, Saad, bin Laden grew increasingly concerned with the ongoing strife in Afghanistan.[82] His first wife and cousin, Najwa, recalls that her husband perceived an unforgivable and "great evil" being inflicted on Muslim women and children prior to the Soviet invasion. Stating that these accounts burned bin Laden's heart "to a crisp," Najwa suggests that her husband had fully developed a desire to support the Afghan cause before Soviet forces fully invaded Afghanistan.[83]

Bin Laden's jihadi journey and his desire to act stemmed from his commitment to the militant Salafism dominant in Saudi Arabia's grassroots Islamic Awakening movement in addition to the teachings of the medieval Muslim historiographer Ibn Khaldun (1332-1406). In his detailed biography of bin Laden, historian and former CIA officer Michael Scheuer emphasizes Ibn Khaldun's influence on the al-Qaeda chief's choice of a "Spartan" lifestyle.[84] Scheuer points out that bin Laden's rejection of modern comforts and his genuine love of nature and the outdoors reflects Ibn Khaldun's theory that rural tribal societies remain physically strong, unified, and true to their faith while avoiding weakness and corruption.[85]

In his 1377 masterpiece called the *Muqaddimah* or "Introduction," Ibn Khaldun promotes the concept of *asabiyah* a term meaning "group feeling", but perhaps more accurately understood as referring to solidarity, a central theme of his work.[86] This concept emphasizes the key role of social and tribal solidarity in restoring civilization after its inevitable collapse due to the divisions caused by corruption and tyrannical urban governments. Ibn Khaldun argues that rural and united societies, through their rejection of luxuries and arduous daily living, are the best prepared to spearhead a restoration of civilization. By avoiding the corruption, injustice, and division brought about by luxurious urban living while promoting a Spartan rural life, such societies strengthen warriors to physically and mentally surmount the inevitable obstacles that serve as God's test for Muslims to overcome.[87] Bin Laden's staunch adherence to this concept is reflected in the way that he militantly avoided luxuries and reportedly regarded all Muslims as equals no matter their wealth or status.[88]

Scheuer's theory regarding Ibn Khaldun's influence is backed by the accounts of bin Laden's closest associates. Khaled al-Batarfi recalls that during their teenage years, bin Laden lived modestly, maintaining close friendships with poor peers and driving Bin Laden Company tractors from dawn to dusk in the stifling summer heat in the Saudi Red Sea port of Jeddah.[89] From at least the time of his teenage years in Jeddah, bin Laden based his life and actions on Ibn Khaldun's teachings, rejecting air-conditioning, indoor plumbing, household electronics, and ice cubes not as sinful inventions but as luxuries leading to physical weakness.[90] Najwa recalls that her husband began regularly voicing his concern that Jeddah had become overpopulated in the early 1980s, a key condition identified by Ibn Khaldun as promoting luxuries and leading to urban corruption and tyranny.[91]

As Scheuer points out, bin Laden's actions reflected Ibn Khaldun's teachings throughout his life.[92] Bin Laden's former bodyguard Nasser al-Bahri recalls in his memoir *Guarding bin Laden: My Life in al-Qaeda* that the al-Qaeda chief selected the "Spartan" conditions of Tarnak Farm, an agricultural center and former Soviet Army barracks near Kandahar Airport, as living quarters for his family and fighters in the summer of 1997. "We want to live a primitive life," al-Bahri quotes bin Laden repeating as he politely rejected Taleban chief Mullah Omar's offer of a more spacious living facility equipped with modern comforts.[93] Al-Bahri's recollections further reinforce Scheuer's theory that bin Laden embraced Ibn Khaldun's teachings during his youth and applied them consistently throughout his life.[94]

The scholar Malise Ruthven points out that bin Laden's organization of al-Qaeda reflects Ibn Khaldun's promotion of rural warrior societies needed to conduct the inevitable "cyclical revolt and dynastic renewal" in civilizations corrupted by material indulgence and tyranny.[95] Bin Laden's stated desire to base al-Qaeda in either Afghanistan or Yemen further reinforces this view.[96] Stating that both countries remained ideal locations for basing al-Qaeda, bin Laden referred to Yemen, his ancestral land, as, "one of the best Arab and Muslim countries in terms of adherence to traditions and the faith."[97]

In addition to his rejection of physical comforts and adoption of arduous living, Ibn Khaldun influenced bin Laden in his belief that while all blessings come from God alone, individuals must do their part and act to produce the desired results in any situation. The medieval scholar used this example while referring to profits acquired from the hard work, trade, and defensive warfare mandated by *Shariah* law.[98] Scheuer points out that bin Laden applied this logic beginning with his response to the Soviet invasion of Afghanistan, just as he had done working in his father's company during his youth.[99]

Bin Laden's unshakeable commitment to this article of faith propelled him to rush to support his Afghan brethren following Moscow's assault, and only deepened as he faced Soviet troops in battle alongside his Arab unit at the height of the war. Bin Laden openly emphasized his perspective in later interviews, calling on devout Muslims to abandon the comforts of home and join the guerrilla ranks.[100] Bin Laden's statement reveals that from the very beginning of his jihadi journey, he adhered firmly to Ibn Khaldun's theory that the blame for Muslim suffering lay not on Allah, but on the failure of the faithful to conduct armed resistance against their oppressors.[101]

As the war raged in Afghanistan throughout the 1980s, the Afghan Islamists began securing greater amounts of financial support from wealthy Arab individuals and NGOs, primarily from Saudi Arabia.[102] Initially, Arab volunteers began gathering in Peshawar to perform charitable work along the Afghan frontier, working as medical doctors and aid workers in the clinics established by Saudi NGOs to treat wounded guerrillas and refugees fleeing the fighting.[103] Bin Laden initially supported the resistance by rising to a leading role in the field of humanitarian work, building field clinics and hospitals for the wounded fighters and their families in Pakistan's crowded refugee camps. From 1985 forward, he also began building homes, villages, and roads for the local Pashtun tribes in Pakistan's border region, spending his private money as with his other construction activities, and earning the staunch support of the tribal chiefs.[104] The excellent personal rapport that he gradually established with the Afghan insurgents and local tribal leaders eventually enabled him to obtain frontline combat experience in command of his own band of Arab holy warriors.[105]

Bin Laden's charitable activities earned him a solid reputation for great persnoal generosity and selfless giving toward the Afghan cause.[106] Often visiting injured fighters in the clinics and hospitals that he built for them, he became known as "the Good Samaritan or the Saudi Prince," writing generous checks and distributing cashews and chocolates for their families. Bin Laden's humanitarian contributions during this period are well-documented and backed by the accounts of those closest to him.[107] According to Shaykh Abdullah Azzam, bin Laden's close anti-Soviet jihadi colleague, the Saudi zealot once persuaded his sister to write a check for 8,000,000 riyals, Saudi currency, for the Afghan Islamists. Azzam states that after she returned to bin Laden asking for him to return the money for her to build a new house in Jeddah, he refused, pointing out that the Afghan people lacked even shoes and tents for shelter.[108]

Aspiring to play a supporting military role even as he continued with his humanitarian aid work, bin Laden also purchased 4x4 Toyota pickup trucks, equipping each vehicle with antitank missiles and mine detectors, to help the beleaguered guerrillas improve their logistical support operations.[109] He also built mountainside caves for ammunition storage as well as roads and tunnels through the mountains along the Afghan-Pakistani border to ensure the more effective transportation of the arms and fighters packed inside the trucks to reach the battlefield quickly. While the insurgents largely relied on horses, pack mules, and camels to carry ordnance and fighters to the frontlines, bin Laden's trucks later proved to be a valuable supplementary addition to local logistical operations.[110] In 1987, Robert Kaplan witnessed insurgents in the Kandahar region speeding through enormous minefields in the surrounding desert even under fire from Soviet Mi-24 gunships, returning fire with their truck-mounted 23mm antiaircraft guns.[111]

Children named after prominent historical figures are often said to grow up to emulate their namesakes. This appears to apply to bin Laden's first name, Osama, meaning "lion," and honors a beloved companion of the Prophet Muhammad, Osama bin Zaid.[112] Bin Laden reportedly displayed lion-like courage under fire as he performed his construction work in support of the Afghan resistance.[113] His subsequent actions earned him other honorific titles from Afghan and Arab fighters, and he used these as pseudonyms or *kunyas* during the war against the Soviets and later against the United States and NATO. One title, "the Director," refers to his effective management skills and the "cost-benefit-calculating businessman" demeanor that he displayed during the Soviet-Afghan War and later as the leader of al-Qaeda.[114] On some occasions, Saudi and Yemeni jihadis addressed bin Laden affectionately as *khal* or, "uncle," in a display of deep respect for his personal modesty and willingness to apologize to his subordinates and admit mistakes.[115]

Najwa bin Laden recalls that while many wealthy Saudis contributed financial donations, none did so as zealously as her husband and his family.[116] Bin Laden's generosity toward the besieged Afghans reflects his firm belief in the equality and solidarity of all Muslims, regardless of race, customs, or socioeconomic status, and that those physically or financially strong must aid their brethren in times of war and suffering. These charitable actions constitute a form of *zakat* or almsgiving, a pillar of Islam, and serve as further supporting evidence of Michael Scheuer's theory that bin Laden embraced the teachings of Ibn Khaldun from his youth forward, despite never directly quoting the scholar.[117] Advocating an egalitarian approach to Islamic solidarity, Ibn Khaldun shamed wealthy Muslims for committing acts of perceived hypocrisy by giving to their orphaned and poor coreligionists while also treating them as lesser in importance and expressing disgust at their existence.[118] Ibn Khaldun argued that while some may appear generous, God knows the contents of the heart, and only those with sincere intentions backed by selfless gestures earn His appreciation and eternal paradise. Bin Laden often displayed strong agreement with this thesis by his modesty and approachability in his dealings with the Afghans, earning their appreciation and gradually establishing an excellent personal rapport with them.[119]

Spearheading the funding efforts of wealthy Saudi NGOs and individual donors, bin Laden traveled frequently between Saudi Arabia and Pakistan between 1980 and 1984.[120] His first visit to Pakistan following the Soviet invasion involved a meeting in the city of Lahore with Qazi Hussain Ahmed, the leader of Pakistan's largest religious party Jamaat-e-Islami. Knowing of the bin Laden family's immense wealth and influence in Saudi Arabia, Ahmed assigned to Osama the task of collecting donations for the insurgents.[121]

While authors such as Lawrence Wright, Steve Coll, Rob Schultheis, and Abdullah Anas have implied bin Laden to be a reluctant fighter uninterested in frontline combat, mounting evidence suggests that he simply respected the wishes of his Afghan hosts until earning their permission to fight.[122] Afghan commanders greatly appreciated the generosity of their Arab supporters, a factor that played a key role in the ultimate success of their holy war, but disliked the Salafists' criticism of local customs and their urge to charge into battle without first preparing to attack.[123] This factor proved to be an obstacle for many of the Arab fighters seeking a combat role until bin Laden successfully persuaded the Afghan commanders to permit the establishment of an Arab guerrilla unit under his command.

Far from shying away from battle, bin Laden appears to have aspired to serve in a combat role as a resistance fighter to prepare himself for leadership from the very beginning, yet respected the wishes of the insurgent leaders that he limit his participation to a financial jihad in the war's early stages.[124] Citing, "the brutality of the Russians bombing" that he reportedly observed as his motivation to move beyond financing and play a greater role in supporting the beleaguered guerrillas, bin Laden began volunteering for frontline tasks, performing tunnel construction and digging trenches with equipment from his family's construction firm.[125] Recalling his 28 May 1998 interview with bin Laden, John Miller states that Afghan guerrilla veterans recalled their admiration of the young Saudi bravely riding the bulldozers and digging trenches even under intense Soviet bombing and strafing from Mi-24 gunships.[126]

Bin Laden reportedly suffered injuries during one vicious and heavy strafing assault by the Mi-24s, the first of four occasions on which he is said to have received combat wounds. Undeterred, he stubbornly resumed his work, laboring under lethal Soviet fire and inspiring other militants with his example, refusing to allow his key supporting role in the Afghans' holy war to be interrupted.[127] Bin Laden's documented courage under fire and refusal to stop the work as it progressed even as Soviet bombs and shells came crashing down appears to contradict the claims that he shied away from danger before his first taste of combat in 1987.[128]

Bin Laden's deference to the wishes of the Afghan commanders and prolific fundraising efforts eventually earned him their trust and gratitude, ultimately helping him to establish an Arab guerrilla base and join the fighting.[129] Peter Bergen and Michael Scheuer point out that since his youth, bin Laden had participated in his family's hosting of evening *halaqat* meetings for visiting Islamist scholars performing the *umra* or lesser pilgrimage to Mecca. These gatherings acquainted him with insurgent leaders such as Abdul Rasul Sayyaf and Burhanuddin Rabbani and instilled in him a tolerance for the diversity of thought and customs in the Muslim world.[130]

While embracing his financial support role with zealous enthusiasm, bin Laden wasted no time in preparing to join the holy war on the frontlines at the earliest possible opportunity. During his lengthy fundraising drives in Saudi Arabia, he began taking his older sons on desert hikes, teaching them to go for days without water.[131] Following his first trip to Pakistan in early 1980, he also used his family's connections to secure permission to train in hand-to-hand combat with Saudi Arabia's national judo team.[132]

Judo instructor Jimmy Wu served as the teacher of the Saudi national team and recalls bin Laden's participation in his classes between 1980 and 1984. In several interviews following the al-Qaeda chief's death in 2011, Wu recalls being introduced to a distinctively quiet, thin, and tall young man known to him only as "Osama" at the time.[133] Concerned that bin Laden's unusual height at about six feet five inches tall may have rendered him unfit for judo, Wu attempted to persuade the shy student to pursue another sport more suited for tall people. Undeterred and true to the determination documented by his associates, bin Laden persisted, persuading Wu that he could master the art.[134]

Described by Wu as a "serious student," bin Laden succeeded in his quest, regularly attending classes in Riyadh, and eventually earning a blackbelt.[135] Wu recalls that he no longer saw bin Laden after 1984, a claim that squares with Najwa and Omar bin Laden's recollection that he moved his family to Peshawar that year to pursue a more direct role in the holy war.[136] Bin Laden's intense dedication to training and preparation while performing his role as a financier and fundraiser reflects his determination to prepare for the mission ahead while patiently waiting. This preparation for battle while supporting the Afghan warriors through financing seems to fully justify Michael Scheuer's conclusion that bin Laden consistently sought to prepare himself for leadership roles in any actions in which he participated.[137]

During this time, bin Laden worked closely with Prince Turki al-Faisal, the director of Saudi Arabia's General Intelligence Directorate (GID) and his assistant Ahmed Badeeb. While not a GID agent himself, bin Laden nevertheless enjoyed the cordial appreciation and support of his country's intelligence service.[138] Badeeb expressed deep respect and appreciation for bin Laden's efforts to support the Afghan insurgency. As Turki and Badeeb arranged construction projects, bin Laden responsibly performed the work, deferring to Abdullah Saadi, an expert Bin Laden Company engineer that he had recruited for planning and directing each project, and earning profits that he used to further his support for the Afghan Islamists.[139]

While bin Laden began preparing for his jihadi journey through combat training, financial support, and frontline construction work, the nations of the West were also taking a keen interest in Moscow's Afghan debacle. On 27 December 1979, the day after Soviet troops entered Afghanistan from the north, U.K. Foreign Secretary Lord Carrington denounced Moscow's brazen aggression and urged Whitehall to begin supporting the guerrillas as a way of making the Soviets, "uncomfortable."[140] Three weeks later, U.K. Cabinet Secretary Sir Robert Armstrong began holding talks discussing ways of arming the resistance fighters against the Soviet invaders.[141]

Emphasizing the determination of the guerrillas to carry on their struggle in the face of seemingly insurmountable odds, Armstrong stated that Britain could not afford to stand by idly and allow such an opportunity to go to waste.[142] U.K. Prime Minister Margaret Thatcher, a staunch anti-communist, quickly agreed, immediately authorizing Britain's MI-6 intelligence agency to begin working with President Carter's CIA to support the rebels.[143] Characterizing the Soviet invasion of Afghanistan as, "brutal" in a 28 April House of Commons debate, U.K. MP Lord Geoffrey Rippon voiced strong support for the prime minister's bold approach and her efforts to strengthen Britain's military defense capabilities against potential Soviet aggression.[144]

Following prewar combat support doctrine, the Soviet occupation forces initially remained in their garrisons protecting their gains and advising and overseeing Afghan Army operations against the insurgents.[145] As Afghan Army defections mounted throughout early 1980, Soviet troops found themselves increasingly drawn into combat.[146] In March 1980, Brezhnev reinforced the 40th Army, deploying the 201st Motorized Rifle Division and two additional motorized rifle regiments, boosting the Soviet military presence in Afghanistan to more than 80,000 troops.[147] More than 600 tanks, 4,400 armored combat vehicles and personnel carriers, and 1,000 aircraft and artillery pieces spearheaded Soviet assaults on the guerrilla strongholds.[148]

In addition, small numbers of Bulgarian, Vietnamese, East German, Cuban, and Czechoslovak troops arrived to support the 40th Army's "Limited Contingent" in Afghanistan.[149] According to Lieutenant-Colonel Scott R. McMichael (U.S. Army, Ret.), the Bulgarian troops were the largest contingent of foreign forces invited to participate in the occupation by the Soviets, performing guard duties at the airports in Jalalabad and Mazar-e-Sharif. Cuban troops largely served in an advisory role for the elite Soviet Special Forces or *Spetsnaz* units conducting counterinsurgency operations in the Afghan countryside beginning in 1985.[150]

Seeking to prevent the insurgents from executing raids from across international boundaries and interdict their supply routes through the Hindu Kush mountains, Soviet troops mined Afghanistan's borders with Pakistan and Iran, as well as numerous mountain roads.[151] Many of these mines, as well as countless unexploded "bomblets" released from Soviet cluster bombs, remain in the country today, maiming and killing civilians well into the twenty-first century. Between March 1980 and April 1985, Soviet commanders focused on encirclement operations against the insurgents.[152] Motorized rifle formations conducted raids from the main roads into villages and valleys suspected of hosting guerrilla bases.[153] Often resulting in temporary gains and the destruction of civilian infrastructure, these offensives failed to achieve a decisive victory over the mujahedin as the insurgents persistently infiltrated the villages from their bases in the mountains.[154]

As resistance against the occupiers intensified, the traditional, loosely organized networks of village mullahs and religious students of southern Afghanistan continued joining the mujahedin, and a brief description of the Taleban movement that these rural veterans later founded in 1994 is in order before continuing. Strict adherents of the Deobandi sect of Sunni Islam, the founders of the Taleban differ from the traditional Arab Salafists in several ways. Bin Laden's son Omar explains that while Salafists from the Arab world reject and tear down grave markers as a form of idolatry, Taleban members traditionally mark the graves of their martyred comrades. Omar adds that while both Arab jihadis and the majority Pashtun Taleban interpret dreams, Taleban leaders often base their decisions on them, while the Salafists reject such notions.[155]

Arab jihadis in al-Qaeda traditionally did not oppose the education of women, while the Taleban staunchly opposed women's education. Nasser al-Bahri further explains that the Taleban shared the fear of many Afghans regarding death by fire, and sometimes tended to retreat from enemy flamethrowers, while Arabs jihadis suffered from no such fears.[156] Afghans also traditionally rejected the use of suicide bombers embraced by some Arab jihadi groups, yet this has changed in recent years as the Taleban have begun to embrace the tactic.[157] Soviet atrocities in Afghanistan swelled the insurgent ranks by galvanizing the resistance, while also creating countless war orphans, particularly around Kandahar, and instilling a practical resentment of foreign infidels among the mullahs and orphans that later organized the Taleban and a gradual appreciation of their Arab allies.[158]

Joining the mujahedin at the age of 15 in 1983, former Taleban ambassador to Pakistan Mullah Abdul Salam Zaeef states in his autobiography *My Life with the Taliban* that he and his colleagues initially knew nothing of combat other than the duty to defend beleaguered Muslims until the Soviet invasion. Stating, "But the Russian front lines were a tough proving ground," Zaeef recalls that he and other Afghan guerrilla fighters learned quickly as a necessity under constant pressure from Soviet bombardment.[159] By the late 1980s, Zaeef and his comrades had honed their martial skills considerably, commanding their own guerrilla units while striking back and regularly besieging their unwitting Soviet teachers in their garrisons.

As the fighting intensified throughout this period, so did outside efforts to assist the Afghan rebels.[160] In January 1983, U.S. President Ronald Reagan, Carter's presidential successor in the White House, greatly increased his country's efforts to support the insurgents with National Security Decision Directive Number 75 (NSDD-75).[161] A type of presidential directive used during Reagan's presidency in which he issued instructions to his advisers on matters of U.S. national security, the NSDDs enabled U.S. officials to support the Afghan resistance. NSDD-75 authorized the CIA under its devout Catholic and staunch anti-communist Director William J. "Bill" Casey to increase the pressure on the Soviet occupation forces.[162] While the president stopped short of directly calling for the defeat of the Soviet Army, NSDD-75 allowed Casey to increase weapons purchases for the insurgents and maintain maximum pressure on the occupiers.[163]

The day after Reagan issued NSDD-75, Soviet General Secretary Andropov, Brezhnev's Kremlin successor, chaired an 18 January 1983 Politburo session addressing a possible withdrawal from Afghanistan.[164] After a brief discussion with Foreign Minister and later Supreme Soviet Chairman Gromyko, Andropov concluded that Soviet forces could not be immediately withdrawn due to the threat of "American imperialism" in the country, dismissing Pakistani complaints about the Soviet military presence.[165] Describing Afghanistan as a "feudal country" in which tribes had historically resisted central governments and reminding the Politburo members of their hesitance to endorse an invasion during Brezhnev's reign, Andropov concluded by ordering Gromyko to revise the "demanding" recommendations for Soviet and Afghan regime operations in the Politburo's report.[166]

Between 1981 and 1985, President Reagan and CIA Director Casey gradually persuaded Saudi King Fahd to match U.S. spending on the united effort.[167] After a meeting with Congressman Charles "Charlie" Wilson (D-TX), a staunch supporter of the mujahedin, Senator Gordon J. Humphrey (R-NH) organized the Congressional Task Force on Afghanistan.[168] While Wilson reportedly worked closely with the CIA to generate congressional support for Operation *Cyclone*, the agency's covert action aid program, Humphrey enthusiastically embraced a more public role. Publicly shaming some of his U.S. Senate colleagues for their perceived disinterest in supplying the Afghan resistance and reportedly spending the night outside their office doors to persuade them to vote for increasing aid, Humphrey appears to have displayed a zealous determination to ensure congressional support for the CIA's program.[169]

According to Mohammad Yousaf, the former chief of the "Afghan Bureau" for Pakistani military intelligence (ISI), half of the U.S. and Saudi government funds were channeled through the CIA to ISI headquarters in Islamabad. The remaining half reportedly went to the purchasing of weapons from individual arms dealers in the United States, Britain, and Israel, and corrupt government officials in Egypt and China that were then delivered to ISI's offices in Rawalpindi and Quetta.[170] The bulk of weaponry and ordnance reportedly arrived in the Pakistani port city of Karachi, delivered by the CIA in cargo ships throughout much of the war. From Karachi harbor, ISI officers then transported the material to storage facilities in Peshawar and Quetta under the direction of Director Major General Akhtar Abdul Rahman Khan. Yousaf claims that U.S., Saudi, and Chinese planes occasionally delivered weapons and ordnance to the Pakistani Air Force base in Islamabad, yet the alleged failure of many Saudi pilots to commit to their delivery schedules greatly frustrated many guerrilla commanders, eventually forcing ISI officers to rely on the U.S. Air Force instead.[171]

In an 8 May 1987 article for *The Washington Post*, authors Jack Anderson and Dale van Atta criticized the CIA for allegedly equipping the Afghan fighters with faulty arms and ordnance, thereby betraying the trust of U.S. taxpayers and their elected congressional representatives.[172] While agreeing with Anderson and van Atta that the CIA often allegedly supplied, "outdated weapons systems" until 1986 because of U.S. and Pakistani fears of provoking a Soviet retaliation, Yousaf contradicts the notion that the agency bore responsibility for the inherent problems in the arms pipeline to the guerrillas.[173] Rather, limited logistical capabilities on the part of Pakistan's ISI with a crew of only 200 men operating seven days a week and delayed arms deliveries by the Saudi Air Force reportedly created delays that sometimes reduced the insurgents' stock of weaponry, increasing their mistrust of the Pakistani authorities.[174]

Due to staunch congressional opposition to supplying U.S. arms and the fears of a potential Soviet invasion of Pakistan or nuclear retaliation against the West by Pakistani and U.S. diplomats, Reagan and Casey initially authorized the CIA to purchase only Soviet-designed weaponry for the insurgents.[175] Despite Washington's burning desire to repay Moscow for its support of the Vietcong guerrillas during the Vietnam War, many individual congressmen viewed the lightly armed insurgents as little more than a temporary bump in the road. Many congressional leaders feared that the resistance could not resist the mechanized Soviet onslaught for long, and initially opposed Reagan's proposals to supply them with U.S. arms fearing such weapons falling into Soviet hands.[176]

This is not to say that the U.S. Congress did not generally provide bipartisan support for the CIA's efforts, but that few representatives shared Congressman Wilson's view that a steady flow of arms could help the beleaguered resistance fighters to achieve victory. In an 8 March 1982 Congressional Session, Senator Charles H. "Chuck" Percy (R-IL) chaired a hearing of the second session of the 97th U.S. Congress addressing the situation in Afghanistan.[177] Heading the Senate Committee on Foreign Relations, Percy and several colleagues delivered a stinging rebuke of Soviet actions in Afghanistan. U.S. Deputy Secretary of State Walter J. Stoessel echoed their sentiments, voicing approval of President Reagan's designation of 21 March as "Afghanistan Day" and assessing the Soviet Air Force's ongoing bombing of Kandahar as barbaric.[178]

In a 27 March 1984 Congressional Staff Report, U.S. Senate Staff Advisor John B. Ritch III presented a report to the Senate Committee on Foreign Relations. Headed by Senator Percy, the committee members listened to Ritch's detailed account of his travels to the embattled Afghan frontier, followed by a visit to Moscow.[179] Urging his colleagues to abandon their comparisons of the Soviet campaign to the Vietnam War, Ritch stated that in stark contrast to Washington's openness, Moscow blatantly denied the devastation being caused by its war.[180]

While emphasizing the perseverance of the insurgents against the odds, Ritch called attention to Soviet domination of the skies and the Soviet troops' frequent planting of millions of PFM-1 "butterfly mines" in Afghan fields, sometimes fired in large numbers by Soviet Mi-24s.[181] Concluding that the dependence on Soviet weaponry captured in the field or supplied by Afghan Army defectors and the Egyptian and Chinese regimes handicapped the fighters, Ritch stated that French humanitarian organizations had provided more than the U.S. government thus far. Later that year, Congress voted to approve Senate Congressional Resolution 74, a bill renewing congressional support for Operation *Cyclone* and the Reagan administration's efforts to arm the Afghan Islamist insurgents.[182]

According to former CIA Director and U.S. Defense Secretary Robert Gates, many lower-level CIA bureaucrats shared congressional pessimism despite the determination and zeal of Casey and numerous operations officers and analysts such as Frank Anderson, a CIA officer reportedly working closely with the guerrillas to ensure the delivery of material.[183] Opposition to sending U.S. ordnance to the rebels within the CIA and the Congress largely stemmed from fears that Soviet troops could capture the weapons, steal U.S. technology, and retaliate against Washington. With the key support of Congressman Wilson and Senator Humphrey, Reagan and Casey eventually prevailed, successfully sending more than 1,000 FIM-92 "Stinger" missiles to the rebels beginning in late 1986.[184]

In 1987 however, some U.S. officials reportedly began suggesting that the Afghan Islamist groups accept a transitional government that included former communists that many resistance fighters perceived as having ordered the torture and killing of captured guerrillas and their civilian supporters.[185] Many U.S. senators and congressmen such as Humphrey and Wilson voiced staunch opposition to supporting any transitional government that the mujahedin rejected, as well as a subsequent proposal by the U.S. State Department to include former Afghan communists in such a government. Others such as Senator Anthony Beilenson (D-CA), appear to have incurred the resentment of Afghan commanders such as Gulbuddin Hekmatyar and Abdul Haq, with the latter man later criticizing the U.S. senator and the State Department's proposal in a 9 June 1989 opinion piece for *The New York Times*.[186] While U.S. officials favoring the State Department's proposition reportedly viewed it as a positive step in calming Soviet concerns that a hostile regime may emerge in Kabul, commanders such as Haq perceived this practical diplomatic approach as an attempt to undermine their holy war efforts.[187]

Throughout the 1980s, Reagan consistently hailed the Afghan warriors as "freedom fighters" in his presidential addresses as he and Casey ordered the CIA to wage an undeclared war as part of the administration's "Reagan Doctrine."[188] Through this policy, Reagan and Casey sought to counter communist aggression on a global scale in a way that saved American and European lives and avoided nuclear war by supporting those already actively resisting Soviet invasion and occupation.[189] The U.S. president regularly declared "Afghanistan Days" every year to mark the struggle of the rebels against the Soviet occupiers and invited guerrilla commanders to the White House.

While attending one such ceremony with Reagan on 20 March 1987, Senator Humphrey, a staunch supporter of the mujahedin, replied, "Don't you guys know that a million people have died in Afghanistan? Why don't you ask some important questions?" in response to reporters inquiring about the president's thoughts on other matters.[190] Humphrey subsequently traveled to Afghanistan on 13 April 1987 and pointedly refused to meet with Afghan regime officials in Kabul in a show of solidarity with the resistance. Describing his visit to Moscow on the previous day, Humphrey reported that the "overconfident and cocky" Soviet officials that he met with on his "fact-finding tour" boasted that three Afghan insurgent commanders with some 37,000 men had recently defected to the regime as a result of its national outreach program.[191]

While some Islamist commanders such as Hekmatyar refused to meet with Reagan, others such as Burhanuddin Rabbani, Ishaq Gailani, and Abdul Haq traveled to Washington, D.C. and received warm receptions at the White House on a handful of occasions between 1983 and 1986. Hekmatyar's reluctance to meet the U.S. president is somewhat understandable considering the desperate attempts of Soviet leaders to paint the resistance groups merely as paid tools of U.S. imperialism rather than fighting for their own various motives, including nationalistic, religious, and local interests. For this reason, Pakistani ISI officers pointedly refused to allow CIA agents or U.S. officials to meet with guerrilla commanders during their visits to the Afghan-Pakistani border regions.[192] Fearing morale damage due to relentless Soviet propaganda, many Afghan insurgent commanders displayed considerable reluctance to meet U.S. officials, triggering frustration in Washington, D.C. and exacerbating mutual feelings of mistrust.

Undeterred by these relentless Soviet efforts to defang their holy war, Rabbani, Gailani, and other commanders met the U.S. president in hopes of making a positive impression and securing more effective aid from the West.[193] On 12 November 1987, Reagan also met with Islamist commander *Mawlawi* Muhammad Yunis Khalis during a White House visit in which the red-bearded rebel gave a speech in the presence of top U.S. officials including Congressman Wilson of Texas.[194] Khalis also met with and provided guerrilla escorts for Robert Kaplan during several of the journalist's courageous forays into wartime Afghanistan. He also became a close ally of bin Laden, admiring the Saudi zealot's solid support of the Afghan warriors, and later facilitating his return to Afghanistan from Sudan on 18 May 1996.[195]

Fearing a repeat of Khomeini's Islamic Revolution in Iran, CIA officials frequently complained that ISI favored the most hardline Islamist insurgent organizations.[196] Despite American concerns, Pakistani leaders continued to justify this policy by pointing out that these groups also fielded the most uncompromising fighters dedicated to defeating the communists. Ahmed Shah Massoud, a French-speaking ethnic Tajik responsible for defeating several Soviet offensives, is described by some authors as a moderate insurgent leader.[197] He also concluded a temporary truce with the Soviets in 1983, while fundamentalist guerrillas doggedly resisted a merciless Soviet offensive.[198]

One of the few Western journalists to cover the Soviet-Afghan War, Peter Bergen has criticized the CIA for not insisting that American funds and arms be channeled to Massoud.[199] According to Yousaf, ISI officers did not give the CIA a choice. Massoud's truce and his Tajik ethnicity made him an unreliable asset for the Pakistanis and an unacceptable leader for Afghanistan's ethnic Pashtun majority.[200] Islamist insurgent leaders such as Hekmatyar, Sayyaf, and Khalis, drew significant support from the Pashtun tribes, rendering them more desirable and reliable recipients of ISI support.[201]

In addition to the funds provided by the U.S. and Saudi governments, financing from individual Arab donors began to play an immense role in supplying the Afghan Islamists in their anti-Soviet struggle.[202] After collecting donations, Arab non-governmental organizations (NGOs) delivered them directly to the Afghan Islamists based in the Pakistani border city of Peshawar. These extra funds helped the fighters to account for the losses of ordnance due to delayed arms deliveries by the U.S. and Saudi governments.[203] Insurgent organizations based in Pakistan also confiscated weapons from the ISI pipeline for later use or personal gain, elevating the importance of the direct delivery of funds and supplies by Arab individuals and Saudi NGOs.[204]

While Western political leaders and commentators welcomed the rise to power of Mikhail Gorbachev in the Soviet Union in March 1985, the people of Afghanistan could only expect further bloodshed. Addressing the Afghan debacle that he inherited the following month, Gorbachev initially expanded the 40th Army's military campaign with the goal of crippling the resistance enough to ensure the regime's survival and begin withdrawing Soviet forces, slightly increasing the Soviet military presence to more than 115,000 troops.[205] He also deployed one-third of the Soviet Union's elite Special Forces or GRU *Spetsnaz* commandos to Afghanistan along with fresh T-62 tanks, BMP-2 armored combat vehicles, and KGB *Kaskaz* operatives.[206]

One of the few Western journalists to enter Afghanistan during the Soviet-Afghan War, Robert Kaplan reportedly witnessed the destructive nature of Gorbachev's temporarily reinvigorated military campaign firsthand. Embedded with a group of Afghan insurgents, Kaplan describes the Soviet Air Force's intense carpet bombing of the city of Kandahar in southern Afghanistan throughout 1987.[207] While Gorbachev appears to have mesmerized Western audiences with promises of *glasnost* and *perestroika*, Soviet *Red Star* and *Izvestia* correspondents allegedly denounced the mujahedin as, "bandits" in desperate need of communist reform.[208]

According to Kaplan, the Soviet Air Force bombed Kandahar and the surrounding region for months in 1987, while planes, Mi-24 gunships, and mortar teams flooded the desert with land mines in a destructive campaign targeting the insurgents.[209] Soviet tanks and armored cars reportedly smashed through shops, mosques, and homes, while engineers built a road to enable the easier advance of armored forces. Yet the local guerrillas reportedly thwarted many of these operations while fighting their way back into Kandahar even as the Soviet assault commenced. The Islamist and royalist rebel factions of the Kandahar region refused to surrender the city, conducting a determined resistance motivated by their deep faith and the Pashtun tribal tradition of *badal* or "revenge."[210]

As the fighting intensified and the Kremlin remained committed to stabilizing its puppet regime before ordering a full withdrawal of Soviet forces from Afghanistan, an atmosphere enabling the growth in strength of Sunni Islamist militancy gradually emerged.[211] By prolonging the Afghan campaign, Gorbachev and his generals unwittingly provided a chance for bin Laden and al-Qaeda's founding generation to acquire intense combat training, strengthening the international movement that they eventually led and inspired. Persisting in their efforts to secure Afghanistan's communist central government from collapse, the Soviet leaders inadvertently enabled the largely untrained but zealous Arab guerrilla volunteers to obtain crucial combat experience by facing Soviet troops in battle.

On 14 April 1988, Soviet, U.S., Pakistani, and Afghan officials concluded the Geneva Accords, agreeing on the full withdrawal of Soviet combat troops from Afghanistan by 15 February 1989 and a symmetrical approach to further aid the warring factions within the country.[212] U.K. Prime Minister Thatcher had already voiced her approval of Gorbachev's recent announcement to exit the South Asian country in a 4 March 1988 address to the House of Commons, commending the Soviet leader on "the very welcome decision to withdraw from Afghanistan."[213] Alleging betrayal by the U.S. and Pakistani governments, insurgent commanders such as Gulbuddin Hekmatyar, Abdul Rasul Sayyaf, and Abdul Haq later expressed their resentment that the meeting in Geneva had excluded representatives of the resistance.[214] In compliance with the Geneva Accords, Soviet General Boris Gromov subsequently began withdrawing the 40th Army's troops on 15 May 1988, while U.S. officials reportedly refocused their efforts on promoting a transitional government in Kabul to contain the rise of Islamic fundamentalists.[215]

In a 14 May 1988 Congressional Staff Report introduced by the U.S. Senate Committee on the Judiciary, U.S. officials recommended that the various insurgent groups consider finding common ground with all factions within Afghanistan, "including Najibullah's PDPA."[216] Chaired by Senator Edward "Ted" Kennedy (D-MA), the Committee concluded that a "political resolution" to produce an interim government including royalist resistance factions and PDPA members remained an essential objective of U.S. policy.[217] After acknowledging Islamist commander Hekmatyar's list of specific complaints regarding aspects of the Geneva Accords, Kennedy suggested that an all-inclusive transitional government remained crucial to ending the bloodshed in Afghanistan.[218]

Sensing betrayal, insurgent commanders opposed to negotiating a settlement with both the Kabul regime and the Afghan royalists that they viewed as corrupt reportedly incorporated anti-monarchical slogans into their anti-communist religious propaganda.[219] In 1988, Robert Kaplan witnessed the open resentment of Islamist fighters perceiving a slight from the West. During a demonstration in Peshawar, one young guerrilla reportedly grabbed a microphone declaring that only God deserved to rule Afghanistan due to the mujahedin's enormous sacrifices during the war.[220] Perhaps the insurgent commander Abdul Haq delivers the best explanation of his compatriots' perceived betrayal by the West following their hard-won victory over the Soviet Union. "American won't give a visa to Kurt Waldheim because he was alleged to have a role in war crimes more than 45 years ago. But you want us to compromise with the Hitler of our country."[221]

CHAPTER 3

Gorbachev's gamble, Reagan's response, and increased Arab involvement, 1985-1987

As bin Laden gradually established a reputation for generosity and fearlessness along the borders of Afghanistan and Pakistan, some Western officials and observers debated their governments over the need to continue supplying the Afghan resistance. Several of these men and women are also said to have voiced approval of the Soviet occupation, reportedly portraying it as a progressive crusade against religious ignorance and medieval mindsets. In a 1980 debate, U.K. scholar David Selbourne reportedly compared Afghan society to medieval feudalism, while commending the Soviet Army and PDPA regime for achieving "social progress" regarding women's education and the elimination of the Afghan heroin trade.[1]

In an 18 June 1986 parliamentary debate on the floor of the House of Commons, MP Harry Cohen accused U.K. Foreign Secretary Sir Geoffrey Howe of "a succession of slurs of undiluted hostility" against the Afghan central government and its Soviet backers.[2] Cohen reportedly proceeded to portray the struggle of the insurgents and their civilian supporters as an obstacle to progress while urging Whitehall to reassess Britain's policies toward the hated Kabul regime of the Soviet puppet ruler Mohammad Najibullah.[3] Describing Sir Howe's denunciation of the PDPA regime as "no way to create the conditions that will lead to the Russian troops leaving that country and enable Dr. Majeeb [sic] to emerge with his country from feudalism," Cohen spoke of his recent visit to Kabul and called for, "an informed debate in the House on Afghanistan."[4]

In *The Mail on Sunday* Julie Burchill reportedly implied the Soviet 40th Army and its Afghan regime clients to be civilized forces serving as a progressive red shield defending Western values from the fanatical green cloud of Islamic fundamentalism inevitably bent on heading West to enforce its medieval views.[5] Burchill is said to have proceeded to denounce the U.S. war in Vietnam as the case of a backwards power imposing its will on a civilized and progressive one, while arguing that the Soviet war in Afghanistan constituted a "completely reversed" situation.[6]

In a May 1988 article, journalist Mary Kenny reportedly characterized the Afghan rebels as fanatical and the Soviet troops as defenders of Western civilization in their ongoing efforts to crush the insurgency.[7] Reportedly referring to the officially atheist Soviet regime as "the Christian Russians" and the mujahedin as "Moslem fanatics," Kenny predicted an alliance between the Western and Eastern Blocs to contain the alleged threat of Islamist expansion from Afghanistan.[8] Such sentiments appear to have reinforced Islamist resentment of the West and the sense of betrayal felt by the guerrillas over Western attempts to persuade them to work with some former communists, including Moscow's final puppet ruler Najibullah, following the Soviet retreat.[9]

In a discussion with Robert Kaplan, Afghan guerrilla Ismail Gailani described a conversation he had had with some of his wife's friends in London. Gailani reportedly told Kaplan that the women had tried to persuade him of the hopelessness of the insurgents' struggle and had asked him why the mujahedin did not simply reconcile themselves to communist rule.[10] The baffled fighter reportedly asked Kaplan how an Afghan patriot could possibly reason with such mindsets.[11] Kaplan points out that although Gailani hailed from a royalist party, his presence on the battlefield near Kandahar reflected a religious devotion no less sincere than the fundamentalist guerrillas. Even as he arranged for his wife's safety in London, an opportunity neither affordable nor desired by Islamist fighters, Gailani's consternation at the Westerners' lack of understanding reportedly reflected that of many frontline fighters.[12]

Bin Laden and other Arab jihadis also experienced and expressed frustration and confusion over a similar perceived lack of support and expectation of Soviet victory among members of the Islamic clergy in their native countries.[13] The al-Qaeda leader later described the reluctance of members of the Saudi *ulema* to match their words with deeds by joining the young men they incited to holy war on the frontlines.[14] Reportedly, many of these scholars privately confessed their fears that the Soviets could not be defeated, and that the Arab volunteers and their Afghan hosts could only hope for martyrdom and Allah's blessings of eternal paradise.[15]

Bin Laden found this attitude strange, and although he continued to express a deep respect and deference toward official Islamic scholars throughout the war, he likely began to question the motives of the Saudi clergy during this period.[16] Hoping to prevent future uprisings such as the Grand Mosque siege of 1979, the Saudi royals and their regime clerics promoted the idea of holy war in Afghanistan. This ultimately unsuccessful policy served the dual purpose of portraying the Saudi regime in a positive image for Islamists and sending the militants to their deaths at the hands of the Soviets.[17]

Bin Laden later cited this reluctance among the religious scholars of the Arab world to join the faithful on the frontlines as an early indication of the al-Saud's betrayal of Islam.[18] While remaining a loyal subject of his king and country during the Soviet-Afghan War, he began quietly noting the contradictions between the statements of the regime's scholars and their lack of action. Combined with the al-Saud's later support of the Marxist regime in South Yemen, followed by their invitation of U.S. and Western troops into the Arabian Peninsula, the actions of the Saudi establishment proved to be the tipping point for bin Laden and his lieutenants.[19]

Bin Laden also witnessed the considerable ideological inroads made by the Soviet KGB deep inside Pakistani territory during this period. He later described seeing "pictures of Ka[r]mal, Lenin and Stalin" as well as red flags adorning the villages and tribal meeting places while passing through the Baluchistan region of southwestern Pakistan, "from Quetta to the Gulf of Oman."[20] Local Communist Party officials became even more daring in their celebrations every year on 27 December to mark the anniversary of the Soviet invasion of Afghanistan.[21] The sight of a fiercely independent Sunni Muslim region allowing itself to be "intellectually invaded by the Soviet Union," at the expense of its Afghan Muslim neighbors, steeled bin Laden's resolve to seek a combat role for Arab fighters in the holy war.[22]

Throughout the war, Soviet KGB and GRU agents and the Afghan regime's KhAD intelligence agency successfully exploited disunity between the various rebel factions and impaired guerrilla operations by bribing some tribes to turn against the insurgents. Accepting many of these bribes, Nadar Khan, the chief of the Afridi tribe along the Afghan-Pakistani border, turned against his fellow Pashtuns and received Soviet money and arms in exchange for their attacks on the resistance.[23] Combined with attempts by Najibullah's regime to promote civilian support by invoking Islam and seeking to co-opt religious support, these Moscow-backed efforts occasionally succeeded in provoking violent clashes between rival guerrilla factions.[24]

The tensions between the insurgent groups sown by the Soviets and their Afghan clients further motivated bin Laden and his holy war comrade Abdullah Azzam to focus on promoting Islamist solidarity by refusing to become involved in disputes between rebel commanders. Setting an example for other Arab guerrilla recruits to follow, bin Laden addressed these Soviet attempts at dividing the resistance by refusing to permit criticism of the Afghan insurgent leaders or their backers in the Saudi royal family in the camps that he financed and built for the fighters.[25] Bin Laden reportedly rebuffed attempts by his compatriots to criticize Saudi King Fahd after the monarch accepted a British medal perceived as resembling a Christian cross in 1986, and later advised al-

Qaeda members to "be careful of your enemies, particularly the hypocrites who penetrate into your ranks to spark strife."[26]

Several authors and politicians, including at least one former head of state, have alleged that bin Laden and other Arab volunteers enjoyed a relationship with the CIA during the war against the Soviets. These claims have contributed to a popular perception of bin Laden and al-Qaeda being creations of Operation *Cyclone*, the U.S.-led effort to support the Afghan rebels against the Soviets. Author Chalmers Johnson served as a CIA consultant from 1967 until 1973 and once described bin Laden as a "former protégé" of the CIA.[27] Johnson argues that the United States virtually created al-Qaeda, resulting in a classic example of "blowback," in which CIA efforts intended to further U.S. security interests boomerang in harmful ways.[28]

U.K. MP Robin Cook contributed his thoughts to the issue in a 2005 article stating that the United States and Saudi Arabia had knowingly funded bin Laden's anti-Soviet operations.[29] In his 2017 book *A Military History of Afghanistan: From the Great Game to the Global War on Terror* Afghan guerrilla veteran Ali Ahmad Jalali makes a similar claim. Jalali briefly states that U.S. leaders spearheaded an effort to gather jihadi fighters from around the world and organize them into an "international network" to fight the Soviets.[30]

Following the 9/11 terror attacks, American filmmaker Michael Moore claimed that the CIA bore responsibility for the "creation" of bin Laden and al-Qaeda during the Soviet-Afghan War.[31] Indian novelist Arundhati Roy echoed this claim shortly afterwards in an opinion piece for *The Guardian*.[32] In 2010, former Cuban President Fidel Castro also repeated the assertion during an interview yet declined to elaborate further after being asked to provide supporting evidence.[33] In support of this theory, Cook, Johnson, and Jalali point to the Reagan administration's well-known support of the Afghan insurgency, arguing that this aid enabled al-Qaeda to flourish, and contributing to the notion that the CIA deliberately recruited Arab guerrillas.

Several primary sources cited throughout Jalali's book include the memoirs written by Robert Kaplan and Mohammad Yousaf. Each author strongly refutes the notion that the CIA ever supported the Arab fighters.[34] The argument that the CIA "created" bin Laden and al-Qaeda to fight the Soviets is so often repeated that it has largely been accepted as fact by many in the West and throughout the world. Several of bin Laden's former contemporaries have alluded to the possibility that the al-Qaeda chief maintained cordial relations with the CIA during the war against the Soviets. A brief examination of some of the more intriguing of these accounts coming from several close associates and former comrades of the al-Qaeda chief is therefore in order before continuing.

Bin Laden's fourth-eldest son Omar states in his memoir *Growing Up bin Laden: Osama's Wife and Son Take Us Inside Their Secret World* that the West considered his father a "hero" and appreciated his anti-Soviet efforts in the 1980s.[35] Coming from the words of one of bin Laden's sons, Omar's statement appears to provide strong supporting evidence of cordial relations between his father and the CIA. Omar implies that his father received the West's approval, yet does not discuss details and never specifically states that his father served as an agent of the CIA or other Western intelligence agencies.[36]

In a February 2010 interview, bin Laden's former anti-communist colleague, Tariq al-Fadhli, states that he and bin Laden were "allies" of the United States against the Soviets.[37] Al-Fadhli did not provide further details but maintained that his current struggle against the Yemeni regime constituted a continuation of the alliance and urged the West to support the cause of South Yemeni independence.[38] Following bin Laden's death in May 2011, al-Fadhli mourned his fallen former comrade, and expressed deep admiration for the al-Qaeda chief's success in taking on a second superpower and its international allies.[39]

In his insightful memoir *Guarding bin Laden: My Life in al-Qaeda*, the al-Qaeda chief's former bodyguard Nasser al-Bahri recalls his desire to join the Saudi guerrilla contingent at the age of 16 in 1988 while his father criticized the fighters as U.S. agents.[40] Al-Bahri strongly disagreed, but curiously states that after joining al-Qaeda he understood that he had been, "naïve" in his belief that the West had not been, "using" the Arab fighters to fight the Soviets.[41] Al-Bahri later served as bin Laden's personal and most trusted bodyguard between 1997 and 2000 and the al-Qaeda chief expressed his most intimate thoughts to the man with whom he entrusted his life.

Each of these primary accounts seems to provide circumstantial evidence of Western awareness and appreciation of al-Qaeda's anti-Soviet operations but fails to produce conclusive evidence of CIA support for bin Laden's organization. However, Omar bin Laden's mention of the West's perception of his father as a hero is included in his overall description of the Reagan administration's characterization of the guerrillas as "freedom fighters."[42] Omar does not specifically refer to bin Laden as an agent or ally of the CIA and describes his father denouncing the West as the next target for his holy war since the early 1980s.[43]

Referring to bin Laden's resentment of the U.S. government, Omar recalls that his father began preparing his sons for combat in a future war with the West from an early age. Stating that "this idea formed in my father's head when I was a toddler [born in 1981] and grew with each passing year," Omar recalls his father leading his oldest sons in arduous treks deep into the Saudi desert and teaching them to go for days without water.[44] Omar further states that during these extensive desert excursions, bin Laden stated that all Muslims needed to train for desert warfare in preparation for an inevitable invasion by the United States.⁴⁵

Al-Fadhli's use of the word "allies" to describe an alleged relationship between the CIA and al-Qaeda conveys deeper meaning. At the time of the interview however, al-Fadhli also desperately sought U.S. support for Yemen's Southern Independence movement to which he had just switched his allegiance. He made his statements as an internet video circulated showing him standing beside an American flag with the "Star-Spangled Banner" playing loudly as he spoke. Al-Fadhli also mourned bin Laden's death and expressed deep admiration for the al-Qaeda chief and his war with the West, along with gratitude for his comrade's solid support of the mujahedin in their resistance to the communist regimes in Afghanistan and Yemen.⁴⁶

While omitting further details regarding the alleged alliance between the CIA and al-Qaeda, al-Fadhli insisted that he did not approve of terror attacks targeting civilians and that he and bin Laden never considered such attacks during their war against the Soviets.⁴⁷ He also did not hesitate to join forces with al-Qaeda on the Arabian Peninsula (AQAP) in 2013 and offered to use his jihadi connections to forge a dialogue between the organization and the United States. Until further evidence emerges, al-Fadhli's brief mention of an alliance appears to be an attempt to persuade Western audiences that he never opposed the United States and that the country's best interests lay in supporting his current political aspirations.⁴⁸

Al-Bahri's claim that the West "used" bin Laden and al-Qaeda to fight the Soviets is initially intriguing considering his former close relationship with the world's most wanted man.⁴⁹ His statement strongly indicates that the West took advantage of the fact that the Arabs fought against Soviet troops, and he does not state that al-Qaeda and the CIA forged an alliance. Indeed, al-Bahri's statement strongly implies that the Arab fighters and their supporters perceived Western fears of the Soviet Army and hopes that the guerrillas may indirectly further U.S. interests by driving Soviet occupation forces from Afghanistan. Echoing bin Laden's words on the subject, al-Bahri's account suggests that the Arab fighters felt "used" by the West in the sense of fighting in the trenches while the U.S. government and the Arab regimes could write checks and claim credit for victory while relaxing at home.⁵⁰

The claim that bin Laden and al-Qaeda served as agents of the CIA is an easy one to accept for many in the West. Rooted in Soviet attempts to discredit the Islamist mujahedin, it conveniently allows Americans, Europeans, and others to assume that nothing happens in the world without the express approval of Washington or Moscow. This is a very strange notion, because it assumes that Muslims, whether nominal or fundamentalist, are incapable of fighting their own wars without a superpower's support. Such an assumption represents the height of both Western and Soviet arrogance and is belied not only by al-Qaeda's ongoing war with the West since 1996 but the organization's resilience nearly a decade after bin Laden's death.[51]

Conversely, such thinking ignores the fact that prolonged military campaigns or occupations of traditional Muslim countries promote Islamist unity by transforming local insurgencies into international movements and providing battlefield experience. This crucial combat training allows new recruits, such as the non-Afghan Salafi fighters in the Soviet-Afghan War, to emerge as seasoned warriors capable of inspiring new generations and helping them to hone their fighting skills in their home countries and abroad.[52] Juhayman al-Utaybi's rebel group, not unlike bin Laden's al-Qaeda, had the sympathy of many militant Salafists in Saudi Arabia.[53] Yet without the support of a trained guerrilla vanguard such as al-Qaeda, the insurgents stood little chance of ousting the Saudi regime's National Guard troops from the holy city of Mecca, let alone inspiring and training enough recruits to overthrow the regime across the entire country.

Moscow's invasion of Afghanistan, less than a month after al-Utaybi's failed Mecca uprising, provided the ideal solution for the Islamists' dilemma by creating an opportunity for the militants to forge global connections, obtain battle experience, and inspire and train new generations in guerrilla war tactics. Throughout the war, Brezhnev, Gorbachev, and the intervening Soviet general secretaries desperately sought to defang the Afghan jihad and deflect Islamist resentment towards their temporary occupation by claiming that the insurgents were not true Muslims at all but agents of the West.[54] By making these claims, they appear to have taken many Muslims for fools, apparently hoping that the Islamic faith's more devout members might somehow ignore Moscow's limited but often brutal occupation of Afghanistan and its continued support for the perceived Islamophobic and dictatorial communist regime in South Yemen.[55]

To be sure, the U.S. and Saudi governments together undeniably contributed a significant amount of financial and material aid to the Afghan resistance throughout the 1980s, reportedly totaling some $6,000,000,000 in support.[56] This aid, surpassed by the financing from wealthy Saudi NGOs and individual efforts led and spearheaded by bin Laden's prolific fundraising successes, certainly contributed to the Afghans' eventual triumph. This fact of history often causes many in the West to assume that without CIA support, the Afghans were doomed to defeat.[57]

By enabling the guerrillas to resist the Soviet Army with AK-47 assault rifles instead of only the Lee Enfield rifles wielded by their ancestors against the British troops, the CIA, MI-6, GID, and ISI certainly helped to render Moscow's temporary occupation and the Afghan regime's operations far costlier in blood and treasure. The Afghan Islamists also launched their resistance movement to communist rule and continued fighting the Soviets well before Western aid began making a difference. Initial CIA support provided by the Carter administration amounted to "peanuts", in the words of Pakistani President Zia, a factor that changed significantly as the arms flow greatly increased during Reagan's presidency.[58]

Even after the Reagan administration began successfully introducing the Stinger missile in limited numbers in 1986, the insurgents faced an uphill battle with no air force of their own as Soviet pilots began flying their planes at higher altitudes. They continued their bombing and airstrikes from this range, even if less accurately, and continued to pose a constant threat to the rebels and Afghan civilians.[59] According to historians Mark Galeotti and Rodric Braithwaite, the Stinger also appears to have had little effect on the final decision by Gorbachev to withdraw, a decision reportedly reached in late 1985 due to the resilience of the guerrillas rather than the introduction of new U.S. technology.[60] Had the Afghan fighters been unwilling to persevere even as their homes and families were ravaged by warfare, it appears unlikely that outside assistance could have made a difference.

Ultimately, as bin Laden himself consistently admitted, the glory of victory in the anti-Soviet jihad properly belongs to the Afghan guerrillas and their civilian supporters, not to outside financing, manpower, or material support.[61] While Western and Arab financing certainly played an important role, none of this mattered without manpower and the willingness of the Afghans to suffer enormous losses and continue fighting.[62] Crediting outside support also denies the importance of the religious factor with providing the true motivation of the Islamists to resist the merciless, mechanized, and far superior Soviet forces.

Arguing that Western aid created the Afghan resistance as well as al-Qaeda and the Taleban fails to credit the tenacity of both the Afghan and Arab fighters and underestimates the power of religion to keep committed warriors in the field, even against a superpower. Such arguments assume the Islamists to be incapable of fighting independently, despite outlasting an invader reputedly capable of ravaging most of the Northern Hemisphere.[63]

During the brutal years of fighting in the mid and late 1980s, Robert Kaplan traveled alongside the Afghan insurgents, sometimes during vicious combat, and experienced the anti-Western hostility of the Arab volunteers. In his firsthand account of the war, *Soldiers of God: With Islamic Warriors in Afghanistan and Pakistan*, Kaplan recalls a visit with a colleague to insurgent commander Jalaluddin Haqqani, a close ally of bin Laden during the anti-Soviet jihad.[64] Shortly after their arrival, the journalists encountered Haqqani's other guests, a group of Saudi jihadis. The Saudis eyed Kaplan and his friend coldly and the two Westerners decided to leave.[65]

Mohammad Yousaf's memoir *Afghanistan – The Bear Trap: The Defeat of a Superpower* offers a clear description of the role of Arab jihadis during the war. The funds supplied by the mostly Saudi NGOs and wealthy Arab individuals helped the insurgents compensate for unusable weaponry or delayed arms deliveries flown to Pakistan by the Saudi government with fresh purchases directly from the arms bazaars in the Pashtun tribal regions. Yousaf states that this, in turn, increased the effectiveness of the most militant Islamist factions within the Afghan resistance as the Arab NGOs enjoyed the advantage of bypassing Pakistan's military bureaucracy and providing cash and arms to the fundamentalist rebel factions.[66] Independently wealthy and capable of delivering their funds and supplies directly to the Afghan factions of their choice, the Salafi NGOs had no use for the West and remained hostile to the Americans over U.S. support for secular Muslim regimes and Israel.[67] Yousaf also states that his ISI superiors refused to permit CIA agents any contact with the Afghan insurgents or the anti-Western Arab volunteers.[68]

Despite the adamant protests of several insurgent leaders, CIA and ISI officials continued to rely on Egyptian and Chinese suppliers for Soviet-made weaponry.[69] While the CIA managed to provide effective material support in the majority of cases, the dilemmas caused by occasional delays in the U.S.-Saudi arms air delivery routes to Pakistan led some insurgent leaders to forge closer relations with the militant Salafists that they perceived as more reliable sources of arms.[70] Traveling alongside his Afghan hosts, Robert Kaplan found that while U.S. aid may have appeared impressive to officials in Washington, D.C., the daily struggles that the insurgents faced on the battlefield proved otherwise from the perspective of those waging their war of resistance.[71]

While President Reagan and Bill Casey reportedly remained unwavering in their support of the guerrillas, many others in the administration and the U.S. Congress were motivated only by a desire to repay the Soviet Army for its support of Vietcong guerrillas and their North Vietnamese allies.[72] With the notable exceptions of Congressman Wilson of Texas, Senator Humphrey of New Hampshire, Congressman Gerald Solomon (R-NY), and briefly, Senator Chuck Percy of Illinois and Congressman Clarence "Doc" Long (D-MD), few members of the U.S. Congress appear to have remained firm supporters of Operation *Cyclone*.[73] Like their communist opponents, many U.S. officials considered Soviet victory over the rebels to be inevitable, and simply hoped for Moscow to receive a bloody nose at best.[74]

Despite Casey's determination to help the insurgents drive the Soviets back, few other CIA officials appear to have firmly believed in such a positive outcome for the resistance. In late 1986, Deputy CIA Director Robert Gates placed a bet with Michael H. Armacost, the U.S. Under Secretary of State for Political Affairs, that Soviet forces could be expected to remain in Afghanistan.[75]

Gates recalls that he discounted the possibility of Gorbachev withdrawing the 40th Army at any point during the final years of the Reagan presidency.[76] During this period, Casey reportedly met regularly with Pakistani ISI officers to discuss Operation *Cyclone* and to coordinate CIA efforts with them, while Wilson and Humphrey continued ensuring congressional support for the CIA Director's Afghan program through their efforts.[77]

In a 21 May 1987 session of the House of Representatives at the 100th U.S. Congress, Congressman Wilson called attention to the allegedly ongoing Soviet atrocities in Afghanistan and cross-border bombings of Pakistani villages, seeking to generate a sympathetic response and further galvanize congressional support for the resistance fighters. Referring to the limited but often brutal Soviet campaign as "genocide," Wilson emphasized the reports of murders of pregnant women, drownings of men, and the more than 250 Soviet bombing raids across the Pakistani border for the first half of 1987 alone.[78] Echoing his House colleague Congressman Gerald Solomon of New York's assessment of the Soviet campaign as "a holocaust," Wilson concluded with a positive appraisal of the noble efforts of independent humanitarian aid organizations and the Pakistani government.[79]

At a 26 February 1988 session of the U.S. Senate, Senator Humphrey called attention to the ongoing negotiations between U.S. and Soviet officials and stated that President Reagan should refuse General Secretary Gorbachev's recent demand that the CIA immediately terminate Operation *Cyclone*.[80] Humphrey then cited an article from *The New York Times* alleging that, without the president's knowledge and in contradiction of his recent pledge before a White House summit, "senior State Department officials" had promised to "end military aid to the Afghan guerrillas at the beginning of a Soviet troop withdrawal."[81] Humphrey and Senator Robert Byrd (D-WV), another staunch congressional advocate of Operation *Cyclone*, proceeded to voice support for a resolution authorizing Reagan to declare another "Afghanistan Day" ceremony on 21 March and remain firm in his commitment to the CIA's program.[82]

As the war raged throughout the late 1980s, U.S., U.K., Saudi, and Pakistani leaders generally succeeded in providing a largely steady flow of arms and significant humanitarian aid to the Afghan rebels and refugee families in Pakistan. Reagan, Casey, Turki, and Badeeb launched a bold united effort and worked zealously to supply ordnance to the fighters and humanitarian aid to the Afghan refugees in the Pakistani border regions. Yet while the CIA and GID cooperated in the overall effort, many low-level decisions regarding the distribution of weapons reportedly created difficulties while tensions and mistrust between insurgent commanders and individual CIA and ISI bureaucrats exacerbated the problem.[83]

Robert Kaplan recalls one U.S. official mocking Afghan commander Yunis Khalis and sarcastically asking whether the insurgent leader accomplished anything other than prayer alongside his men at their guerrilla base in Afghanistan.[84] In late September 1986, U.S. officials, at the urging of Reagan, Casey, Wilson, and Humphrey, began supplying the new heat-seeking Stinger missiles to equip the Afghan fighters with striking capability against Soviet helicopters. These missiles, and to a lesser extent their British counterparts, the Blowpipes, had a tremendous morale-boosting effect on the resistance.[85] Yet the insurgents had also persevered for more than eight years by this point and had previously been denied the Stingers due to the fears of U.S. and Pakistani officials of handing the Soviets a propaganda victory.[86]

Kaplan recalls that guerrilla commanders such as Abdul Haq regarded President Reagan and Prime Minister Thatcher as genuine supporters of the resistance while voicing their frustration with lower-level officials in their governments responsible for the aid distribution.[87] Haq traveled to Washington, D.C., and London in 1985 and 1986, meeting with both leaders and expressing appreciation for their efforts. These meetings and the strong impression that Haq made on both leaders steeled Reagan and Thatcher's determination to increase their support for the resistance, resulting in the late 1986 introduction of the Stinger.[88]

Haq's visit demonstrated the sheer determination and resolve of the Afghan resistance groups to carry on their holy war even during a time of increased pressure and conventional Soviet successes due to Gorbachev's limited and temporary but brutal escalation. Arguing that Britain had paid more attention to Afghanistan during the colonial period, Haq provided Reagan and Thatcher with rhetorical ammunition to shame their congressional and parliamentary opponents into approving stronger support of the resistance.[89] Beyond the determination of Reagan, Thatcher, and Zia to drive the Soviet forces from Afghanistan, few officials responsible for the aid distribution appear to have worked as feverishly to support the rebels. Director Casey and ISI's General Akhtar Abdul Rahman Khan remained utterly uncompromising in their support of the resistance, and their efforts generally ensured a steady flow of arms overall.[90]

Successful deliveries of arms were reportedly sometimes hampered by individual officers in Pakistan's army seeking to procure additional weaponry in the event of war with India or an invasion by the Soviet Union.[91] Peter Bergen points out that Pakistani military and civilian leaders, like their Israeli counterparts, have historically perceived their nation as being surrounded by hostile regimes and believe in the necessity of ensuring their nation's survival in a tough neighborhood.[92] These fears heightened during the years of Soviet occupation in Afghanistan and likely again during the more recent U.S. and NATO military campaign against the Taleban and al-Qaeda.

Abdul Haq voiced his frustration in numerous conversations with Robert Kaplan, complaining that his group received little aid at all. Kaplan himself states that the scant attention of Western media outlets served as a form of betrayal of the Afghan fighters and U.S. taxpayers, recalling little evidence of effective aid deliveries until the war's final years.[93] Bin Laden recalled seeing very few signs of Western aid to the guerrillas in a December 1993 interview with British journalist Robert Fisk. The al-Qaeda chief credited the perseverance of the guerrillas first to God, and second to the utter determination and tenacity of the Afghans.[94]

Yousaf points out that the limitations on CIA and ISI aid at the local level, despite the overall massive contribution of the U.S., U.K., Pakistani, and Saudi governments, propelled the aid of Arab NGOs to even greater importance.[95] He further asserts that without the role of bin Laden and his colleagues spearheading the financing efforts of Saudi NGOs and individual donors, the flow of arms to the insurgents, "would have been cut to a trickle."[96]

Swiss-American journalist Edward Girardet states that beginning in the middle of the 1980s, he observed Arab volunteers arriving in Peshawar in growing numbers, bringing cash for humanitarian aid and weapons purchases.[97] He recalls that open hostility to Western aid workers and diplomats in the region also increased with the arrival of the Arab jihadis. On several occasions, Arab fighters voicing anti-U.S. and anti-Israeli sentiments reportedly spat and shook their fists at Girardet and his colleagues as they crossed the border into Afghanistan.[98]

Despite the complaints of Girardet and other Western journalists and aid workers, Pakistani authorities warned Westerners to beware and took no direct action against the militant Salafists.[99] Wealthy Saudi NGOs and individuals such as bin Laden helped the insurgents to compensate for unusable weaponry or delayed ordnance deliveries with purchases from arms dealers working in the bazaars of the Pashtun tribal regions.[100] Pointing out that Arab financing, "saved the system," Yousaf states that this in turn increased the effectiveness of the most militant Islamist factions within the Afghan resistance.[101]

Peter Bergen also describes the importance of Arab funding for the Afghan insurgents.[102] Bergen discounts the notion that the CIA had any relationship with the Arab fighters, pointing out that the Arabs displayed intense hostility during encounters with Westerners at the time. He acknowledges that by allowing Pakistan's ISI to arm the most militant Afghan Islamist factions, the CIA may have indirectly assisted the Arab fighters, but states that rumors of a direct relationship remain only rumors.[103] While highlighting two cases of a known jihadi recruiter receiving a U.S. visa as well as a CIA informant later found to be working for al-Qaeda, Bergen concludes that all allegations of U.S. aid to al-Qaeda are erroneous.[104]

Steve Coll also points to an indirect connection between bin Laden and the U.S. leadership, citing one of President Reagan's speeches in February 1985. Coll states that shortly before this speech, the U.S. president hosted a White House visit from the Saudi ambassador, a close friend of bin Laden's older brother Salem.[105] At the time, Salem had recently visited the ambassador with a video documentary of bin Laden's humanitarian work on the war-torn Afghan frontier. Coll argues that Reagan's mention of Saudi charitable contributions to the Afghan cause and his emphasis that "we all worship the same God" constitutes circumstantial evidence that the president at least knew of bin Laden's role in the anti-Soviet jihad.[106]

Journalist Rob Schultheis also encountered hostility from a bus of Arab fighters entering Afghanistan. Schultheis states that the Arabs began voicing threats and expressing anti-Western taunts while "dry sniping" at him with small arms and RPG-7 grenade launchers. The jihadi fighters reportedly withdrew without attacking only after Schultheis's Afghan hosts intervened and ordered them to do so.[107]

British journalist John Simpson reportedly encountered bin Laden himself in July 1989. According to Simpson, he and his camera crew were filming a band of guerrillas executing a mortar barrage until bin Laden appeared and urged the Afghans to kill the Westerners.[108] Otherwise engaged, the fighters refused, prompting the Saudi mujahid to turn to, "a nearby lorry driver" with a $500 offer to run over the Westerners. Again refused, bin Laden appeared to grow in frustration at the Westerners' presence, and Simpson's team decided to leave before the fighters reconsidered the al-Qaeda chief's offer.[109]

Bin Laden later acknowledged a "confluence of interests" between the Arab jihadis and the West during the anti-Soviet jihad, stating that such a situation did not make them allies while pointing to the early Muslim Caliphate's simultaneous battles against the Byzantines and Persians during the early history of Islam as an example.[110] Pointing out that such shared interests did not amount to an alliance, he also referred to rumors that he had worked with the CIA as distortions, issuing a challenge for those alleging otherwise to present evidence of their claims. Bin Laden also recalled feeling intense resentment for the U.S. government since the early 1980s and claimed to have seen no evidence of American help during the war.[111]

Perhaps a question may arise asking that if bin Laden and his fellow Arab fighters also opposed the United States and the Western powers during their guerrilla war against the Soviets, why did they not target Western security interests at the time? Bin Laden and his closest associates always believed that Islam's foes had to be confronted one at a time, not all at once. Indeed, the fact that the Arab fighters, including bin Laden himself, came very close to attacking Western journalists and threatened them on numerous occasions indicates an irresistible urge to kill Americans and others wandering in the war zone of a "holy war" that the jihadis regarded as rightfully belonging to Muslims.[112]

Yet while threatening and targeting individual Americans and Westerners indicates strong resentment, it does not indicate outright warfare with the Western countries. Bin Laden later expressed this to his son Omar and former bodyguard Nasser al-Bahri on several occasions, stating that Islam's enemies had to be confronted one at a time based on the greater threat to the faith.[113] During the late 1990s, militants from the Levant and other regions expressed confusion over al-Qaeda's reluctance to target Israeli interests or attack Shia Islamist groups like Hizballah and Amal. Bin Laden repeatedly replied that by wounding the United States, al-Qaeda created future problems that "would impact on the Hebrew state" and advised his fellow Salafi jihadis to resist the urge to strike the Shia "heretics" as this could distract from their war with the West.[114]

Bin Laden's main goal while fighting the Soviets, as it was later with the United Stated and NATO, centered on repulsing the perceived greater threat to Islam at that time, while acquiring crucial combat experience in the process. Michael Scheuer states that bin Laden sought to "lure" U.S. and U.K. forces into Afghanistan to engage them in guerrilla warfare and drain their governments economically, just as the Afghan and Arab fighters had done to the Soviets.[115] Bin Laden consistently advised al-Qaeda members on the need to focus on striking the Americans and other interventionist powers before the group could shift its attention to its main goal of wearing down tyrannical Muslim regimes.[116]

His emphasis on striking one infidel superpower at a time reflects the Arab fighters' Soviet-Afghan War experience. Since Soviet forces had already invaded Afghanistan and triggered a global Islamist response, no luring had been necessary, and the Arab fighters could focus on acquiring combat experience and honing their martial skills.[117] While bin Laden's associates, including his son Omar, recall the Saudi zealot expressing resentment of the U.S. government at the time, he did not shift al-Qaeda's focus from fighting the greater Soviet threat.[118] Even after the Soviet Army's defeat, bin Laden remained determined to finish the struggle that Moscow had started by fighting South Yemen's communist regime before shifting al-Qaeda's focus to the United States.[119]

Even in his August 1996 declaration of war on the United States, Britain, and Israel, bin Laden emphasized his resentment, and that of Salafi jihadis everywhere, of the Arab regimes and powers that he perceived as Islamophobic, particularly those in Russia, China, and India.[120] Bin Laden expressed this resentment in other statements over the years and allowed seasoned al-Qaeda veterans to train militants and join them in guerrilla operations in the Balkans, Chechnya, and Kashmir. This demonstrates that even while focusing his main efforts against the Americans and their allies, bin Laden and his lieutenants did not refrain from supporting jihadi groups engaged in other struggles. By the same token, they threatened and came close to attacking U.S., U.K., and French journalists and aid workers in the Afghan war zone of the 1980s yet remained undeterred from their main mission of driving the Soviets from Afghanistan.[121]

Bin Laden's documented anti-U.S. and anti-Western statements and actions from the 1980s, even while fighting communist aggression in Muslim countries, reflects his later focus on the United States and NATO even while supporting operations against other large powers.[122] He and his lieutenants certainly believed war with the West to be inevitable but did not actively pursue such a confrontation until the 1990 arrival of U.S. forces and their allies in Saudi Arabia. Focusing their postwar efforts instead on driving the tyrannical communist clique from power in South Yemen, al-Qaeda's leaders sought to fully conclude their anti-Soviet struggle before focusing on their operations against the United States.[123]

Bin Laden's reluctance to confront the West militarily until defeating the Soviets and their puppet regimes in Afghanistan and Yemen seems to justify Michael Scheuer's conclusion that "Al-Qaeda was not looking for a war of its own in 1988-1989."[124] Adhering strictly to the militant Salafi teachings that he had embraced in his youth, bin Laden persuaded numerous jihadis in the organization to focus on the communist enemy. While doing so, he consistently lectured them and his sons on the hostility of the U.S. government towards Muslims and prepared them for a clash with the West that he increasingly viewed as inevitable.[125]

While little evidence has emerged in support of claims that bin Laden and the Arab contingent in Afghanistan acted as agents of the CIA, the jihadis benefitted immensely from combat experience as the resistance persevered and Soviet leaders prolonged their temporary occupation. Mikhail Gorbachev assumed power as General Secretary of the Soviet Union on 10 March 1985, bin Laden's 28th birthday.[126] Although unclear at that time, Gorbachev's rise proved to be an unintended gift for the militant young Saudi.[127] The new Soviet leader immediately began escalating his army's war in Afghanistan, before gradually de-escalating the campaign after 1986, in the hopes of stabilizing the situation sufficiently to withdraw the 40th Army. According to historian Artemy Kalinovsky in *A Long Goodbye: The Soviet Withdrawal from Afghanistan*, Gorbachev appears to have been convinced by Marshal Sergei Sokolov that while the 40th Army could not "deal with the counterrevolution," it could seal off the Afghan-Pakistani border and interdict the insurgents' arms supply caravans based in Pakistan.[128]

While desiring an exit from the Afghan quagmire as soon as possible like his Kremlin predecessors, Gorbachev is said to have vainly sought to ensure the survival of the PDPA before committing to a full troop withdrawal, thereby prolonging the Soviet military presence before beginning the withdrawal process in May 1988.[129] Hoping to seal off the Afghan-Pakistani border to sufficiently aid the Kabul regime, Gorbachev reportedly rejected the idea of an imminent withdrawal and ordered one-third of the elite Soviet GRU *Spetsnaz* commandos into Afghanistan along with fresh deployments of tanks, combat vehicles, and KGB assassins. He also promoted Generals Valentin Varennikov and Mikhail Zaitsev to positions of overall command of the 40th Army in Afghanistan. These highly decorated officers had climbed to the highest echelons of power and influence in the Soviet Army.[130]

Gorbachev appears to have intended his intensified campaign and promotion of these generals to both intimidate and cripple the resistance sufficiently to stabilize the regime and allow Soviet troops to return home.[131] Varennikov had previously overseen successful Soviet efforts to bolster communist regimes and insurgencies in Angola, Nicaragua, El Salvador, and Mozambique, while Zaitsev had mercilessly crushed the Czechoslovak "Prague Spring" in 1968. Desiring a decisive victory to finally ensure the survival of Kabul's pro-Soviet regime, Gorbachev reportedly sought to finish the war quickly in the hopes of withdrawing the 40th Army and saving the Soviet economy from collapsing in part because of the increasingly expensive and bloody campaign.[132]

Under Varennikov and Zaitsev, Soviet occupation forces increasingly focused on striking the insurgent strongholds in eastern and southern Afghanistan, particularly in the provinces of Nangarhar, Paktia, and Kandahar.[133] Following intensified bombing by the Soviet Air Force, Mi-24 gunships inserted commandos into mujahedin rear areas in attempts to drive the rebels into the open and annihilate them with tanks and armored cars. As in the case of earlier Soviet operations, these tactics failed to achieve decisive victory despite causing incalculable damage, and the guerrillas persistently infiltrated the rural villages and engaged the occupiers in urban combat.[134]

In response, Soviet forces increasingly focused on cluster bombing and mining villages in addition to targeting crops, irrigation, and livestock for destruction in hopes of flushing out the guerrillas or killing, injuring, and starving their civilian supporters into surrendering.[135] Often painting their small bomblets and "butterfly mines" brightly to attract and injure, but not kill, children, Soviet troops hoped to demoralize and undermine guerrilla morale and momentum, as caring for wounded civilians and fighters drained more manpower than burying the dead.¹³⁶ In stark contrast to Czechoslovakia, Hungary, and Poland however, Afghanistan proved to be impossible for the invaders to pacify as these scorched earth tactics only served to further galvanize the resistance and boost its effective recruitment efforts.¹³⁷ Gorbachev's brief escalation appears to have ultimately achieved little more than causing more destruction in parts of Afghanistan and creating a critical opportunity for the Arab jihadis to obtain practical combat experience in battle with the Soviet Union's most elite troops.

In September 1986, Gorbachev also replaced Babrak Karmal with another member of the PDPA's *Parcham* faction, the former head of the regime's KhAD intelligence agency Mohammad Najibullah.¹³⁸ Seeking to undermine the resistance and save his regime, Najibullah announced the creation of a, "national reconciliation" policy in December, a program offering amnesty to insurgent leaders that surrendered and promising an inclusive government consisting of multiple political parties.¹³⁹ The PDPA's program appears to have achieved some temporary successes, reportedly convincing three guerrilla commanders and most of their men to lay down their arms according to Soviet officials in a conversation with U.S. Senator Gordon Humphrey in April 1987.¹⁴⁰ Najibullah's program may also have served as motivation for the proposal reportedly made by some U.S. State Department officials and congressmen that the insurgent parties accept a transitional government including PDPA members, straining relations between Washington and many insurgent leaders.¹⁴¹

As Gorbachev briefly escalated and prolonged the Soviet military presence in Afghanistan, U.S. and Saudi leaders redoubled their efforts to arm the resistance.¹⁴² In addition to daily news coverage in Saudi media outlets, Saudia Airlines even offered a 75% discount to jihadi volunteers traveling to Afghanistan, with the remaining cost being paid for by private grants.¹⁴³ North Yemeni President General Ali Abdullah Saleh mirrored Riyadh's actions, taking them several steps further by strengthening his alliances with Yemen's powerful tribal leaders and Salafi clerics to recruit jihadi fighters. Spearheaded by the efforts of Shaykhs Abd al-Wahhab al-Daylami and Abd al-Majid al-Zindani, Salafist clerics throughout the country's large cities and small, rural villages began recruiting thousands of Yemeni warriors for the Afghan holy war. Saleh regularly welcomed the pious and determined young men to his presidential palace in the capital of Sanaa while continuing his encouragement and support for the recruitment efforts of the Yemeni clerics and tribal chiefs.¹⁴⁴

In a 1985 visit to the Saudi capital Riyadh, CIA Director Casey persuaded Saudi King Fahd to match U.S. spending efforts on the two countries' united effort to arm the Afghan Islamists.¹⁴⁵ Beginning in August 1985, Fahd also slowly began lowering Saudi oil prices to strike an economic blow against the

Soviet Union in a daring move that historian Paul Kengor refers to as "economic warfare."[146] In addition, Reagan and Casey sought a way to deliver the much-needed arms more effectively to the mujahedin in the field.

Overruling his presidential advisers' demands that all CIA-supplied weaponry must be Soviet-designed, Reagan signed NSDD-166 in early 1985, declaring the objective of helping the guerrillas to triumph over the Soviet occupiers.[147] While little initially changed in terms of the inherent difficulties in the CIA-ISI arms pipeline, Reagan and Casey's determination played a key role in the eventual delivery of the heat-seeking Stinger anti-aircraft missiles to the insurgents.[148] Even after the limited introduction of the formidable Stinger in late 1986 however, Soviet fighter-bombers and attack helicopters remained a constant threat to the guerrillas and a daily nightmare for Afghan civilians throughout the war.[149]

On 1 May 1987, Reagan authored NSDD-270 focusing exclusively on Afghanistan and the CIA's support for the rebels as Soviet forces continued launching vigorous offensives in the south and east of the country.[150] While continuing to engage in firm diplomacy with General Secretary Gorbachev, the U.S. president reportedly remained determined and active in his efforts to help the mujahedin force a Soviet retreat.[151] Yet alleged statements by some administration officials reportedly supporting the creation of an Afghan "interim government" to temporarily allow the PDPA regime to share power and entice Gorbachev to commit to a firm withdrawal date led to expressions of mistrust by some guerrilla commanders.[152]

Following a meeting with U.S. Under Secretary of State for Political Affairs Michael Armacost on 12 November 1987, insurgent commander Yunis Khalis, later a staunch ally of bin Laden, met with Reagan in a White House visit attended by Charlie Wilson and other congressional supporters of the guerrillas.[153] Promising that his administration sought to have Operation *Cyclone* "strengthened, rather than diminished," the U.S. president attempted to allay the rebel leader's fears of a potential "sell out" of the resistance by Washington, D.C.[154] Expressing gratitude for Reagan's support, Khalis pointedly warned the gathering of U.S. officials that, "We do not accept the preferences of others" regarding the creation of a post-Soviet Afghan government before departing for a meeting with U.S. Secretary of State George P. Shultz on the following day.[155]

As Gorbachev escalated Moscow's Afghan campaign to bolster the regime sufficiently to enable a Soviet withdrawal, bin Laden also redoubled his efforts to assist the Afghan Islamists. He had already begun working closely with a Palestinian-born Islamist scholar Shaykh Abdullah Azzam in 1984.[156] Together, the two men established a guest house and a hostel in the Pakistani city of Peshawar bordering Afghanistan. Traveling throughout the Sunni Muslim world, bin Laden and Azzam worked to expand the participation of guerrilla volunteers from Arab nations in the fighting.[157]

Known as the *Makhtab al-Khadamat* (MK) or "Services Bureau," the guest house served as a gathering area for pious young men from throughout the Islamic world.[158] Bin Laden and Azzam covered the costs for the fighters to travel to Pakistan, connected them with one of the Afghan insurgent groups, and arranged for their paramilitary training.[159] The volunteers collectively became known as the "Afghan Arabs," although they hailed from diverse nationalities and ethnic groups. In his biography of bin Laden, Michael Scheuer states that the al-Qaeda chief acted as Azzam's holy war "apprentice" as a way of preparing for leadership, further contributing to this effort by personally covering the expenses of MK's operations. This commitment ultimately cost him about $1,200,000 by the end of 1988.[160]

Bin Laden also financed the publication of Azzam's monthly magazine *Al-Jihad*. The magazine extolled the virtues of jihad and the Afghan holy warriors waging it against the barbarity of the Soviet Army.[161] Through these articles, the holy war colleagues sought to motivate able-bodied young men to go to Afghanistan, and bin Laden later acknowledged their limited successes, pointing out that relatively small numbers of Arab fighters answered the call in comparison to their Afghan brethren.[162] Scheuer points out that bin Laden's involvement in the monthly publication of *Al-Jihad* strongly influenced the way that he later promoted al-Qaeda's agenda first through published and later through digital media.[163]

Bin Laden also admired the effectiveness of Saudi Arabia's official news outlets in covering the Afghans' heroic struggle to defeat their oppressors. During the five daily prayer times, the Saudi media reported on the guerrillas' ongoing fight to liberate Afghanistan and encouraged young men throughout the kingdom to come to the aid of their faith and brethren.[164] Bin Laden subsequently devoted a considerable amount of effort into al-Qaeda's media operations, bearing in mind the effectiveness of Saudi recruitment work during the anti-Soviet jihad.[165]

Bin Laden and Azzam also sought to expand the participation of these young men in the anti-Soviet struggle. Before 1984, most of the Arab volunteers gathering in Pakistan came to Peshawar to serve the insurgents in humanitarian and charitable roles as relief agency workers or medical doctors, while only a handful managed to join the holy warrior ranks on the frontlines.[166] With the formation of MK in 1984, volunteers from the Arab world began arriving in even larger numbers in hopes of serving in combat roles on the frontlines.[167]

Bin Laden also established a nearby hostel called Abu Othman or "Father of Othman," referring to the 1983 birth of his fifth-eldest son, Othman, and in honor of a Kuwaiti volunteer and former Ph.D. student killed in battle with Soviet forces near Herat.[168] The hostel served as a resting area for the Arab relief workers and the small numbers of jihadi volunteers successful in their quest to fight alongside their Afghan brethren. As mentioned in an earlier chapter, after establishing the hostel in 1984, bin Laden moved his growing family from Jeddah to Peshawar to take a more direct role in MK's operations and to expand his support for the Afghan holy war.[169]

CHAPTER 4

Osama in the spring and the birth of a vanguard, 1987-1989

Despite his financial, construction, and recruitment contributions to the holy war effort, bin Laden remained dissatisfied. Inspired by the accounts of Muslim war heroes such as Saladin and Khalid bin Walid, as well as the Prophet Muhammad's triumph over overwhelming odds during the early days of Islam, bin Laden sought to join the fighting as a mujahid himself.[1] He also expressed disappointment that many of the young recruits were barred from combat by Afghan insurgent leaders.[2] Afghan commanders appreciated the Arabs' generosity and zeal for battle but viewed them as reckless and overly anxious for martyrdom, placing guerrilla operations in unnecessary danger.[3]

Bin Laden's desire to form a separate guerrilla unit to help Arab volunteers obtain fighting experience independently of the Afghan groups was initially met with opposition from Azzam.[4] While Azzam agreed with bin Laden's position that the Arabs were not receiving the combat experience that they required for later struggles to oust corrupt regimes and restore conquered Muslim lands to Islamic rule, he feared that the non-Afghan fighters could not succeed independently. Despite their differences, relations between the two holy war comrades remained cordial, and bin Laden continued financing MK's operations and expenses into 1988.[5]

In late 1984, bin Laden secured the permission of Afghan insurgent commander Sayyaf to establish a base for non-Afghan fighters in the Jaji region of Afghanistan's eastern Paktia province bordering Pakistan.[6] Located along an important arms-smuggling route for the insurgents, Jaji had been the target of major Soviet offensives throughout the war. Hoping that the Arab fighters could finally gain practical experience fighting the Soviet troops, bin Laden began building the new base in late 1985 and settled the camp with 11 Saudi compatriots from Medina and Taif on 24 October 1986.[7] Michael Scheuer points out that the delay in establishing the camp, initially called Camp al-Madinah, likely resulted from bin Laden's construction commitments for GID and his ongoing efforts to aid Azzam and MK.[8]

In May 1986, a group of impatient and inexperienced Arab volunteers formed a unit known as the al-Khurasa Battalion and launched a daring attack on

Soviet troops in the Khowst region near the Pakistani border.[9] The untrained men fought fiercely but suffered severe losses and were defeated with little effort by the Soviets. Such a waste of life reinforced Azzam's belief that the Arab fighters should not confront the Soviet troops on their own and needed to limit their involvement to small numbers fighting in Afghan units. Conversely, the episode strengthened bin Laden's position that because the Arabs were often barred from combat by their hosts, they were not obtaining proper combat training and experience to potentially prevent such disasters.[10]

Despite his opposition to bin Laden's decision to form an Arab guerrilla unit, Azzam continued referring fresh recruits to his jihadi colleague throughout the winter months of 1986 and 1987.[11] Hailing primarily from Saudi Arabia and Yemen, the main group of these fighters shared bin Laden's ethnic *Qahtani* origins as well as a fearless determination to attack the enemy, while others came from diverse North African or Kurdish backgrounds.[12] Two Egyptian volunteers with prior military experience, Abu Ubaydah and Abu Hafs, helped bin Laden to organize and train the young zealots. Both men previously fought alongside Massoud's forces early in the war and channeled their fighting experience in preparing the volunteers for the battles that they all prayed lay ahead.[13]

Despite the challenges presented by heavy snowstorms and ice in the steep mountains surrounding Jaji, bin Laden and his men labored intensely to complete their base, which they renamed *Al-Masadah al-Ansar* or "Lion's Den of the Companions."[14] In addition to the Afghan winter, bin Laden and his lieutenants had to persuade the young fighters to be patient and complete their training before attacking the enemy. Bin Laden sought to lead the overzealous militants in a raid on a nearby Soviet garrison, but he refused to grant permission for an attack until Abu Ubaydah and Abu Hafs determined the men to be ready for battle.[15] Bin Laden's thinking appears to reflect the teachings of Mao Zedong in his masterpiece about guerrilla warfare regarding the need for guerrilla fighters to prepare a reliable base before beginning operations. According to Mao's theory, bases for training and careful preparation must be completed to support lightning-fast tactical attacks in a strategically defensive war, enabling guerrillas to remain on the offensive in small local engagements that steadily wear down the enemy.[16]

Many of the fighters had never committed themselves to construction work in arduous winter conditions before and had rarely encountered Muslims from outside their native countries, despite some being well-educated.[17] Bin Laden's persistence in completing the mountaintop base along with military training not only helped prepare the men for the battles ahead but forced them to put aside their ethnic and national differences and work together as an organized unit. Azzam continued referring fresh recruits from the Services Bureau in

Peshawar and the population of the Lion's Den continued to grow, eventually housing 120 fighters by the middle of April 1987.[18]

Many of the young recruits displayed the characteristic battle drive and desire for martyrdom at the first possible opportunity that had irritated the Afghan commanders and had cost the Arab fighters numerous opportunities to participate in combat. Utilizing the management skills that he had mastered while working on his father's construction sites during his youth, bin Laden patiently and consistently reminded the young men of the necessity to complete the base.[19] Persuading them that future combat operations depended on the Lion's Den's completion, he sought to channel their zeal for battle into the creation of a fortified redoubt capable of withstanding Soviet assaults in which the men could train and hone their martial skills. Only after completing their preparations, bin Laden said, could the fighters truly assist their Afghan brethren in the field.[20]

In addition to channeling the men's battle drive toward completing the base, bin Laden and his lieutenants had to persuade Afghan commander Sayyaf that his decision to allow the Arab presence in Jaji had been a wise one.[21] Despite their closeness to the Saudi regime, Sayyaf and his comrades maintained the largely negative view of Arab fighters in combat and were initially reluctant in permitting the men to operate in the region. Bin Laden persisted in his assurances to Sayyaf that the men could become a disciplined fighting force once properly trained and seasoned in battlefield experience. He also persuaded the Afghan commander to remain in the Jaji region for the winter to allow the Arabs to continue their training while fortifying the surrounding mountains.[22]

Bin Laden also had to contend with Azzam's doubts and those of his assistants, such as his son-in-law, the former Algerian jihadi Abdullah Anas. A son-in-law of Azzam, Anas describes passing through the Jaji region with a group of Arab fighters on their way to join Massoud's forces in the north.[23] In his memoir, Anas recounts a brief visit to the Lion's Den base in the mountains. Reportedly witnessing bin Laden hard at work alongside his men, Anas states that he tried unsuccessfully to persuade the zealous Saudi of the difficulty in defending Jaji in the event of an unexpected Soviet attack.[24] According to Anas's claims, bin Laden remained undeterred and persisted in his work, allegedly inspiring Anas himself with the example of a wealthy Saudi construction heir entirely committed to the anti-Soviet jihad risking his life and health on the arduous Afghan frontlines.[25]

Bin Laden's brother-in-law Muhammad Jamal Khalifa recalls visiting the Lion's Den in early 1987, seeking to convince him of the hopeless position of the young volunteers in the event of a sudden Soviet offensive. The camp's mountaintop location inevitably rendered it an enticing target for Soviet aircraft and artillery despite serving as a tactical vantage point allowing the Arab fighters to observe enemy troop movements in the valley below.[26] As in his dealings with Azzam, Anas, and Sayyaf, bin Laden listened patiently to Khalifa's arguments, but remained undeterred, explaining his belief that abandonment of their Afghan brethren constituted sinful behavior. Bin Laden's interactions with his Arab band, Azzam, Anas, Khalifa, and Sayyaf attest to his effective management skills, determination, persuasiveness, and steadfastness under pressure from multiple directions.[27]

Passing through Jaji in early 1987, Edward Girardet observed bin Laden's men at work digging trenches with his bulldozers. Resenting the American's presence, several of the men emphatically stated that they were engaged in humanitarian work and that Girardet needed to clear out immediately. While complying with their order, Girardet observed that "It was more substantial than that", and noted the zealous commitment of the young men as they persisted in their work.[28]

Rob Schultheis also encountered bin Laden during this period while passing through Jaji on a return journey from the nearby city of Azrow. Schultheis recalls seeing bin Laden working into the evening hours, driving a bulldozer, and fortifying a hill. As Schultheis passed by dressed in traditional Pashtun attire, he briefly exchanged greetings with the Saudi zealot and the two men continued in their separate ways.[29]

In January 1987, bin Laden's unit participated in a brief confrontation with Soviet forces that has not been addressed in previous secondary works. As new recruits continued arriving, the young militants continued pressing bin Laden to allow them to participate in combat, yet he repeatedly refused until they had acquired more training. In late January however, bin Laden sensed a key training opportunity and a chance to participate in an attack on the enemy.[30]

Gorbachev's generals had stationed about 1,000 troops in a large garrison called Chowni and several smaller outposts near Jaji. In late January 1987, as the garrison commanders were engaged in drunken revelry celebrating the 75th anniversary of the CPSU, bin Laden coordinated an attack with Afghan commanders on the Soviet forces. Working together, the Afghan and Arab mujahedin executed a brief and intense mortar barrage, surprising the Soviets, disrupting their festivities, and boosting guerrilla morale.[31]

While the far larger Jaji battles of spring 1987 have been described by some authors as bin Laden's first taste of combat, the brief January engagement has been largely overlooked, despite its mention by several mujahid veterans of the Jaji fighting. This is important, because the surprise attack represents the first true engagement fought by bin Laden's unit, and enabled the men to obtain their first taste of combat. It also created a small, experienced cadre of lightly trained artillerists to support further operations. The attack also temporarily satisfied the battle drive of the inexperienced Arabs and demonstrated to Afghan commanders that they could potentially become disciplined and coordinate their attacks as a cohesive unit.[32]

At 6:00 p.m. on the evening of 16 April 1987, bin Laden's Arab band executed its first independent operation called Operation *17 Shaban* in an attack on the two Soviet outposts in the valley below the Lion's Den as Afghan units attacked six Soviet targets elsewhere in the region.[33] The 120 Arabs approached the base perimeters but, in their haste, they had failed to conduct enough reconnaissance and were surprised by lethal enemy fire. Bin Laden's seasoned artillerists maintained a steady mortar barrage from their vantage point in the mountains as intense fighting ensued throughout the night with Soviet forces attempting to dislodge the guerrillas, inflicting heavy losses. Bin Laden ordered a withdrawal to the Lion's Den as the unit's ammunition supply began to run low and Soviet aircraft and artillery struck the mountains around Jaji.[34]

On 15 May 1987, two days after Soviet MiG-27s and Su-25s had swept over the mountains around Jaji to identify the guerrilla positions for bombing by attracting antiaircraft fire, Abu Ubaydah led a second raid on the Soviet outpost called Operation *17 Ramadan*.[35] Returning that day from Peshawar with two other Saudi recruits, bin Laden quickly joined the attack which again resulted in failure to capture any of the Soviet bases. Despite several weeks of thorough preparation, the fighters suffered heavy losses and were again forced to withdraw under heavy fire from Soviet planes, helicopter gunships, and artillery.[36] Between the two failed raids in mid-April and mid-May respectively, bin Laden's unit suffered a loss of 50 men, leaving 70 fighters to man the Lion's Den as Soviet troops prepared to launch an assault on the mujahedin bases in the mountains on 20 May 1987. The day after the Soviet attack on the Afghan rebel strongholds began, two Mi-24s surprised several of the Arab fighters as they swept low over the Lion's Den in preparation to storm bin Laden's base.[37]

On 22 May 1987, bin Laden seized the initiative, preempting the Soviet attack and leading his men in another raid on the Soviet outpost located directly below the Lion's Den with the objective of "totally destroying" the enemy base.[38] After taking the enemy by surprise and executing a tenacious attack, the Arabs were eventually forced to withdraw under heavy fire from BM-21 *Grad* or "Hail" multiple rocket launchers. Bin Laden and his lieutenants braced for a major confrontation as Soviet bombs and shells began crashing into the mountains around the Lion's Den, precipitating three weeks of vicious engagements. Bin Laden rose to a prominent leadership role in the ensuing fighting that raged for 22 days as Sayyaf's insurgents initially withdrew to a rear location, leaving the Arabs to confront the Soviet juggernaut with no help from their Afghan brethren.[39]

Soviet forces launched a massive artillery barrage of 120mm shells against the guerrilla positions in the mountains in preparation for the assault. A sudden hailstorm, interpreted by the Arab fighters as a sign of God's divine favor, broke out over the Lion's Den, inspiring the jihadis to hold their ground and endure the bombardment.[40] On 26 May 1987, a mixed squadron of 24 Soviet MiG-27 and Su-25 aircraft repeatedly struck the mountains around The Lion's Den with cluster bombs, incinerating large swathes of trees to deny ambush positions to the guerrillas, while Soviet mortar teams delivered further damage.[41]

In the late afternoon, a mechanized force of eight Soviet tanks and 12 armored cars advanced quickly towards the mujahedin positions.[42] The armored column approached the 70-man Arab band armed with two 4x4 Toyota pickup trucks equipped with mine detectors and antitank missiles, three 82mm mortars, and a captured BM-21 rocket launcher with an ordinance lorry. The advancing Soviets maintained a steady mortar barrage as they approached the Arab positions, but bin Laden forbade his comrades from returning fire until the enemy drew closer. As the Soviet tanks entered within range, the Arabs retaliated with bin Laden leading shouts of, *"Allahu Akbar! (God is Greatest!),"* destroying several enemy vehicles and throwing them back in disarray.[43]

At sunlight the following morning, 200 Soviet troops, including elite *Spetsnaz* commandos, attempted to breach the Arab defenses three times and were repulsed during each assault, surprised by the dogged resistance of the Arab fighters, including bin Laden himself.[44] Observing as Mi-24 gunships swept in to insert the commandos, bin Laden deferred to Abu Ubaydah and Abu Hafs, men with far greater military experience, to prepare for battle. Dividing the 70-man unit into two groups, bin Laden remained with 35 men to defend the base, while Abu Ubaydah led his group around the other side of the mountain to ambush and engage the Soviets from the rear.[45]

Bin Laden then led a group of nine fighters out of the Lion's Den cave complex and occupied a small cave that they referred to as the "Forward Base", to observe the advancing Soviets at a closer range and engage them in a diversionary operation. Seeking to prevent an enemy encirclement, bin Laden divided his small group further, leading two Saudis, Khidr al-Haili and Muhammad al-Azman, to occupy the peak of a hill located between the "Forward Base" and the Soviet force.[46] Armed with hand grenades and RPG-7 rockets, bin Laden and his small group observed Soviet troops gathering on another hill in preparation to resume their advance.[47]

Answering to the pseudonym Abu al-Kaka to confuse enemy radio interceptors, bin Laden radioed the rest of his men from the "Frontal Base" to join his smaller group on the hill. As the Soviets began leaving the hill that they had occupied, the Arabs prepared to launch their grenades. Suddenly and unexpectedly, the Soviet troops attacked, launching a mortar barrage that preempted bin Laden's planned ambush, and forcing the jihadi group into a defensive position.[48]

Believing that the Arabs had been killed or severely wounded during the intense bombardment, the Soviets began ascending the hill. As they reached its peak, they were surprised by tenacious resistance as bin Laden and his surviving fighters ambushed them with their grenades in close quarters fighting. The Arabs killed several Soviet commandos in this confrontation, forcing the remainder to retreat in confusion.[49]

Bin Laden's successful diversionary operation had caused the Soviets to assume that the guerrilla ranks contained a far greater number of men than the 70 Arabs present at the beginning of the battle. It also demonstrated the Arabs' tenacity in combat to Afghan commanders.[50] Inspired by the Arabs' determined resistance, Sayyaf dispatched 20 of his fighters to reinforce the Lion's Den and replenish its losses. That night, the Afghans launched a brief mortar barrage against the enemy garrison as Soviet shells continued to crash in the mountains.[51]

On 28 May 1987, 100 Soviet troops and *Spetsnaz* commandos resumed the attack on the Lion's Den. As the Soviets advanced, nine fighters, including Abu Ubaydah, advanced around the opposite side of the mountain into a remaining wooded area to outflank the advancing enemy force and attack it from the rear.[52] Bin Laden managed to execute another diversionary operation despite suffering from a particularly severe episode of low blood pressure, forcing him to lie down at times. As Abu Ubaydah's men began assembling in the woods to the rear of the large Soviet force, bin Laden led a group of four guerrillas to engage the enemy.[53]

Advancing under the cover of a heavy artillery barrage, the Soviets quickly approached the entrance of the Lion's Den. Bin Laden's small group engaged the attackers from the peak of a small hill close to the base, and a rocket-propelled grenade exploded close to him. Distracting the Soviets with carefully planned cover fire, bin Laden's small group successfully executed their diversion, allowing Abu Ubaydah's men to strike the Soviet rear.[54]

Led by Muhammad al-Azman, the Arabs surprised the Soviets with sniper fire from the trees, sowing confusion and causing them to fire on each other. Sweeping over the mountains, Soviet Mi-24 gunships quickly incinerated the trees with napalm, rockets, and missiles, but the Arabs successfully executed their ambush. At the end of the fighting, the jihadis counted 35 *Spetsnaz* commandos killed and 45 taken prisoner, at a cost of 17 Arab fighters dead.[55]

Following the ambush, Soviet artillery and aircraft pulverized the mountains relentlessly and bin Laden wisely led a tactical withdrawal to a rear location across the Pakistani border at Sada, a guerrilla base that he had built for Sayyaf's men, hoping to minimize casualties. After turning over their captives to Hekmatyar and Sayyaf, bin Laden and his men performed their morning prayer or *fajr* alongside their Afghan brethren on the *Eid al-Fitr* holiday the following morning, 29 May 1987. Bin Laden then returned with about 30 fighters from his Arab unit and ambushed the Soviets outside the Lion's Den, precipitating two days of intense fighting.[56]

After repulsing the enemy at a cost of 13 Arab lives and reoccupying the Lion's Den, bin Laden's unit continued to repulse further Soviet assaults and held out under sustained bombardment by Soviet aircraft and artillery.[57] On 13 June 1987, Soviet forces withdrew from the fighting, failing to capture the Lion's Den, and leaving the mountains around Jaji firmly in Arab hands. Throughout the battle, bin Laden incited his men to greater acts of tenacity and defiance by leading from the front and engaging in intense hand-to-hand combat with the enemy.[58]

The fighting around Jaji did not end with the Soviet defeat of 13 June. In August 1987, bin Laden reportedly renewed his efforts to improve his unit's combat capabilities, executing more attacks on Soviet forces around Jaji after receiving new recruits eager for combat experience. In his splendid biography *Osama bin Laden*, Michael Scheuer states that this second round of vicious fighting at Jaji erupted on 17 August 1987 and raged for "about three weeks."[59] The battle's duration and ferocity appear to be confirmed by the scholar Gregory Johnsen, citing a conversation between Azzam and the North Yemeni jihadi cleric Shaykh Abd al-Wahhab al-Daylami, the father of a slain volunteer.[60]

Bin Laden's refusal to withdraw from battle even after suffering from low blood pressure, inhaling napalm, and sustaining injuries in combat reportedly inspired his men to fight harder.[61] In the end, the Arabs successfully held their ground despite not capturing any Soviet bases and repulsed the attackers after sustaining and inflicting heavy losses. *Al-Raya*, the black banner flown by Salafi jihadi groups throughout the world, continued to wave over the Lion's Den base in Jaji's towering mountaintops.[62]

During the fierce fighting at Jaji, bin Laden seized an AKS-74U submachine gun from a Soviet commando that he killed in hand-to-hand combat.[63] Reserved for elite units, this weapon fires a 5.45mm bullet known for creating severe internal injuries and wide exit wounds and made its Afghan debut in 1985 with Gorbachev's escalation and deployment of *Spetsnaz* troops.[64] Bin Laden subsequently carried the weapon until the day of his death, sleeping with it at his side, and displaying it during interviews in the 1990s as a reminder of Islam's victory over the Soviet superpower.[65] Other key participants in the Jaji fighting included the Yemenis Jamal al-Hadhi and Obadah al-Wadihi, and the

Saudi Hamza al-Ghamdi. The first two men subsequently worked closely with bin Laden and the Yemeni Salafi cleric Shaykh Abd al-Majid al-Zindani to support the anti-communist Yemeni Islamists between 1990 and 1994. A skilled wrestler, al-Ghamdi rose quickly in al-Qaeda's ranks, recruiting fighters from Yemen and Saudi Arabia into groups bound for Tajikistan in the 1990s, and serving as a close confidant of bin Laden.[66]

The victory at Jaji following the long months of "vicious battles against the Russians", as bin Laden described them, boosted the morale of the Arab fighters and served as further combat training for the veterans of the initial engagements and the inexperienced new recruits alike.[67] In a December 1993 interview with British journalist Robert Fisk, bin Laden described a 120mm Soviet shell crashing down in front of him but not exploding. Perceiving the episode as an instance of divine intervention, bin Laden remained determined to fight on, and recalled experiencing a feeling of *saqinah* or tranquility even as Soviet troops searching for him closed in on his position.[68]

Bin Laden's performance at the Battle of Jaji appears to have provided an immense propaganda boost, reportedly serving as an inspiration for the veterans of the fighting and new recruits alike. A lightly trained and outnumbered Arab band had held its ground against the elite forces of a superpower, despite superior enemy numbers, equipment, and total domination of the skies. Despite not capturing any Soviet bases, bin Laden's unit had executed successful guerrilla ambushes and played a key role in helping the insurgents remain in control of Jaji's vital arms-smuggling routes.[69]

Bin Laden's leadership during the battle greatly inspired his men to persevere and is documented by several biographers and eyewitnesses.[70] In his excellent 2006 book *The Osama bin Laden I Know: An Oral History of al-Qaeda's Leader*, Peter Bergen describes an interview with Egyptian journalist Isam Darraz, a witness of the Jaji engagement.[71] Throughout the interview, Darraz notes bin Laden's bravery and refusal to withdraw even while suffering from low blood pressure and sustaining battle wounds.[72]

Shaykh Musa al-Qarni, bin Laden's former religious mentor, also participated in the brutal fighting at Jaji. In a March 2006 interview, al-Qarni describes bin Laden as fearless in combat and leading from the front, providing the example of an ideal holy warrior for his men to follow.[73] Al-Qarni states that throughout the battle, even as the fighting grew in intensity, bin Laden's leadership inspired his comrades to hold their ground and repulse the enemy.[74]

In *The Bin Ladens: An Arabian Family in the American Century*, Steve Coll describes bin Laden's combat performance at Jaji as exemplary.[75] Michael Scheuer emphasizes the importance of the Battle of Jaji in propelling bin Laden to leadership in the mujahid ranks. Citing the interviews of al-Qarni, Darraz, and other former comrades of bin Laden, Scheuer highlights the practical benefit the Arabs gained from their successful resistance to far superior forces.[76] Calling attention to the subsequent admiration for bin Laden in Saudi Arabia, Scheuer states that the example of a wealthy bin Laden heir wounded in action alongside his men became an immense propaganda victory.[77]

While not a strategic victory for the insurgents, the Battle of Jaji provided a major propaganda and psychological boost for both the Arab volunteers and Islamist militants throughout the world. Bin Laden stated that the battle served as modern proof of God's promise to come to the aid of the faithful Muslims standing firm and resisting infidel invasion and occupation. He later wrote that "The Soviets acknowledge that at the end of the war, they had spent over US$70 Billion on the Afghan campaign. The outcome of the Battle of Jaji was what prompted the Soviet Prime Minister, Mikhail Gorbachov [sic] to withdraw his troops from Afghanistan."[78] Following the battle, bin Laden and Azzam launched an intense media campaign aimed at emphasizing the victory at Jaji and inspiring greater numbers of non-Afghan jihadi volunteers to join the insurgency.[79]

In a sense, the victory over the odds at Jaji served as a microcosm of the overall struggle between the Islamist insurgents and the Soviet invaders. For jihadis throughout the world, the victory symbolized the renewal of Allah's divine favor and promise of victory to those fighting in His name.[80] Bin Laden and Azzam publicized the battle in *Al-Jihad*, motivating thousands of young volunteers to join the holy war. The men opened more training camps for the volunteers, reportedly training more than 15,000 militants answering the call to holy war according to bin Laden's recollections.[81]

As the insurgent ranks continued to grow, bin Laden began thinking of ways to organize the men into a global organization to channel their fighting experience to train, inspire, and assist local Islamist groups in driving those that he and many Arab fighters regarded as infidel occupiers from Muslim lands, such as his ancestral home of South Yemen. On 10 September 1988, after chairing a series of meetings in his Peshawar guest house, bin Laden established al-Qaeda or "the Base" with 14 comrades, including his fellow Jaji veterans Abu Ubaydah, Abu Hafs, and Hamza al-Ghamdi.[82] Emphasizing the organization's goal of inspiring devout Muslims to take up arms against "infidel" regimes and support them with training, financing, advising, and battle-seasoned guerrilla cadres, the men modeled al-Qaeda after the Afghan insurgent groups that they had fought alongside.[83]

Between 1987 and 1989, bin Laden's unit continued to grow in numbers and combat skills as it engaged Soviet troops in other battles throughout Afghanistan.[84] While detailed accounts of these engagements are sparse, bin Laden's participation in them is described by his associates.[85] His actions during these battles reflect the documented bravery that he displayed at Jaji, often providing machine gun cover fire with two or three guerrilla comrades during necessary tactical withdrawals, and refusing to personally withdraw until others had done so.[86]

During this late period of the Soviet-Afghan War, war correspondent Eric Margolis observed bin Laden as both men paid a visit to a local guerrilla commander near Jalalabad.[87] According to Margolis, bin Laden sat calmly with some of his men as they refitted on the far side of a large room. Margolis recalls that despite his modest dress and demeanor, the Saudi mujahid stood out due to his height and the respect that he commanded from his men as he spoke with them quietly.[88]

Bin Laden's first wife Najwa and their son Omar recall his detailed planning of military campaigns during brief visits home following the Battle of Jaji. Najwa recounts her husband returning home covered in large red welts following a fierce battle and mentions bin Laden acquiring the ability to fly captured Soviet helicopters.[89] Omar describes his father pouring over maps of Afghanistan, carefully studying every detail and preparing for future battles.[90] During these visits between 1987 and 1989, bin Laden also continued taking his sons on long hikes in the Saudi desert, teaching them to go without water for days, and declaring that all Muslims should learn to prepare for desert warfare.[91]

As the Arab fighters continued growing in discipline, fighting experience, and numbers, their presence alongside the Afghan insurgent groups began presenting less of a problem. Totaling only a small number in comparison to the Afghan fighters averaging between 175,000 and 250,000 men, the Arab jihadis contributed little to the war effort in comparison to their hosts.[92] While the private funding provided by wealthy Arab individuals contributed significantly to the mujahedin victory, the military actions of the Arab fighters played no strategic role in the Soviet defeat.[93]

Yet the eager participation of the Arab fighters in combat that expanded after bin Laden's successful repulse of the Soviet troops at Jaji continued training them tactically in guerrilla warfare, enabling the seasoned veterans to train new recruits. One Afghan mujahid veteran described the Arabs' tenacity in combat, stating that while Afghan fighters sought to avoid close encounters with the enemy, the Arabs tended to dig their trenches very close to the frontlines. As the Soviet and Afghan regime troops advanced, the Arab fighters reportedly patiently waited in their trenches until the enemy drew in closely. They then leaped from their positions to confront and kill their surprised adversaries in close quarters fighting.[94]

In speeches and interviews, bin Laden regularly gave credit for the Soviet defeat first and foremost to Allah, and secondly to the Afghan warriors, acknowledging only a minor role played by the Arab contingent.[95] While praising the Afghans for their resilience and perseverance against the odds, bin Laden offered thanks to God for allowing the Arab fighters to play a part in the anti-Soviet struggle.[96] Bin Laden frequently described the Arab role in the anti-Soviet jihad as a blessing for the Arabs rather than the Afghans.[97] The Soviet invasion created a unique opportunity for the jihadis to fight alongside their brethren and master insurgency combat skills while facing far greater forces.

As al-Qaeda fighters continued to face Soviet troops in engagements throughout 1987 and 1988, they practiced evasion tactics during helicopter ambushes.[98] Bin Laden recounted one such episode in battle training in a conversation with his oldest sons during a visit home in this period. As the fighters organized outside a mountain cave complex, a Soviet helicopter appeared and began firing at them. The Arabs reportedly responded by running in a zigzagging pattern, making it difficult for the Soviet pilot to concentrate his fire.[99]

Bin Laden also stated that the Arab fighters mastered the ability to shoot down Soviet helicopters by aiming their grenade launchers at helicopter tail rotors from a high perch. Arab successes in downing Soviet helicopter gunships further reinforced the view of militant Salafists worldwide that they could defeat a superpower by fighting with faith. In his memoir, Nasser al-Bahri recalls the euphoria and inspiration that he and other Saudis experienced after hearing these accounts from Saudi guerrillas returning from the frontlines.[100] Comparing the encounters to meeting a companion of the Prophet in modern times, al-Bahri states that these firsthand accounts inspired his personal journey to join the holy warrior ranks at the age of 16 in 1988.[101]

In his 2010 autobiography, the former Taleban ambassador to Pakistan, Abdul Salam Zaeef, describes the ferocity of the fighting in the final years of the Soviet-Afghan War. Fighting in the ranks of several independent, fundamentalist guerrilla factions, many mullahs refused to lay down their arms and reportedly managed to drive the Soviets from several villages in the Kandahar region. Zaeef describes losing 50 of his 58 men in an assault on Kandahar Airport in the summer of 1988 as the Soviets and Afghan communist militiamen fought fiercely to escape capture by the Islamists.[102] Such hard-won victories over the invaders at enormous costs in manpower and civilian lives further galvanized the most militant Afghan Islamists, such as those mujahedin resistance factions that later formed the Taleban in 1994, and increased their determination to seize power and shield Afghanistan from perceived hostile outside forces and their native collaborators.[103]

In his memoir, Abdullah Anas describes the Soviets' final offensive in the Panjshir Valley. Embedded with Massoud's forces in northern Afghanistan, Anas states that the Soviet Air Force bombed and strafed rebel positions throughout the valley for an entire month leading up to the withdrawal from Afghanistan.[104] Anas recalls that even at the Soviets launched this intense final barrage, he and other Arab fighters experienced a sense of euphoria bordering on disbelief. Despite the most favorable circumstances possible for an invader, a superpower had tasted defeat at the hands of lightly armed and determined Muslims fighting with faith.[105]

On 15 February 1989, Soviet forces completed their retreat from Afghanistan.[106] While Gorbachev's generals portrayed the event as a peaceful and flawless exit, some of the 40th Army's units maintained a constant barrage on insurgent positions before completely withdrawing.[107] Even as Soviet cameramen presented the world an image of brotherly friendship between the Soviet Army and Afghan people, Soviet tanks and aircraft reportedly struck Afghan villages on their way out of the country.[108]

In his 2011 memoir *Killing the Cranes: A Reporter's Journey Through Three Decades of War in Afghanistan*, Edward Girardet recalls that he and Steve McCurry visited the frontlines near Jalalabad in early 1989 and observed Soviet Mi-24 gunships flying in support of regime forces engaged in a sporadic artillery exchange with the guerrillas.[109] As they arrived, the two Westerners spotted a series of trenches flanking a hill occupied by bin Laden and his Arab guerrillas as they appeared to be gathering in preparation to join the rebel artillerists.[110] Bin Laden held a conversation in English with Girardet for almost an hour, explaining that the Westerners had no business in a Muslim country and that the conflict represented a holy war for the true believers seeking to aid their brethren. As the men parted ways, bin Laden reportedly threatened to kill Girardet and his crew if he encountered them a second time.

Girardet recalls returning to Jalalabad several weeks later after the 40th Army's commanders had completed their withdrawal from Afghanistan, and witnessing a field littered with the bodies of Afghan regime troops. Locals explained to Girardet that the Arab fighters had slaughtered the captured men by slitting their throats, a practice that bin Laden later forbade as counterproductive to al-Qaeda's cause. Girardet again encountered bin Laden during this visit and the Saudi jihadi threatened his life once again. An armed standoff between al-Qaeda fighters and Girardet's Afghan escorts ensued, and the journalist again agreed to leave the area.[111]

Bin Laden's perception that the "poor, barefooted Afghans" had "smashed and pulverized" the world's strongest army with minimal assistance from the outside world steeled his resolve to continue training Arab fighters in preparation to help local Islamists overthrow corrupt regimes.[112] The U.S., U.K., and Saudi governments did provide an enormous amount of material aid to the Afghan Islamists through Pakistan's ISI during the war. Yet the physical presence and generosity of Azzam, bin Laden, and the Saudi Salafi NGOs ensured a growing local support structure for the aspiring Arab jihadis regardless of their hostility to the West. Compounded by small but frustrating delays in the arms pipeline through Pakistan during crucial moments in the fighting, many guerrilla commanders seconded bin Laden's perception that only God's divine help and Afghan blood had repelled the Soviets.[113]

Following the Soviet defeat, Gorbachev continued supplying the Afghan communist regime of former secret police chief Mohammad Najibullah with enormous sums of financial and material assistance.[114] On 5 March 1989, Afghan insurgent leaders based in Pakistan launched a semi-conventional assault on the communist military garrison in the city of Jalalabad close to Jaji.[115] Abdul Haq argued against the offensive, fearing a needless massacre of his men and massive bombing by the Soviet Air Force. Massoud expressed similar fears and refused to commit his forces to a drive on the city from the north.[116]

Despite having no experience in conventional warfare, the insurgents advanced quickly, seizing key military outposts in their advance on the city. By the middle of March, Islamist rebels under Hekmatyar and Sayyaf appeared poised for victory.[117] Refusing to work together and coordinate their attacks, the insurgent leaders began quarreling and fighting against each other even as their men invested Jalalabad.[118] Following a massacre of captured regime troops by Arab fighters, the garrison commander in Jalalabad refused to surrender and intense fighting continued into the summer months as Soviet Ilyushin IL-2 transport planes ensured a steady flow of supplies.[119]

Returning to Peshawar from a fundraising tour in Saudi Arabia, bin Laden learned of the mujahedin offensive and quickly rushed to aid the Arab contingent fighting alongside the Afghans, establishing field clinics and purchasing 4x4 Toyota trucks to rush fighters to the frontlines.[120] Successful in these tasks, bin Laden then organized his Arab unit to support the drive into the city. Al-Qaeda fighters seized the apron of the Jalalabad airport in July 1989, temporarily disrupting the flow of supplies for the garrison flown in by enormous, white Soviet IL-76 aircraft.[121] As at the Battle of Jaji, bin Laden received combat injuries and inspired his men to redouble their efforts, returning to the fighting despite his wounds, and reportedly remaining calm and unflinching as a Soviet R-300 "Elbrus" Scud missile came crashing down and exploded close to him.[122] His example also inspired the Afghan fighters, and he persisted in his attempts to persuade them to overcome their differences and work together.[123]

Despite bin Laden's efforts, the Afghan commanders refused to cooperate, and the guerrillas were eventually driven back. Exploiting rebel disunity and infighting, the regime forces successfully concentrated their heavy artillery and airpower on the insurgents' positions, driving them back after fierce fighting.[124]

Citing the disunity that he regarded as the reason for the rebels' repulse at Jalalabad, bin Laden urged his men to beware of spies seeking to sow tensions in their ranks. He also reportedly continued to defer to his more experienced subordinates, Abu Ubaydah and Abu Hafs, during the fighting, apparently attempting to set an example by encouraging the Arab fighters to brush aside national and ethnic differences and fight as a cohesive unit in contrast to their disunited Afghan comrades.[125] Another veteran of the brutal fighting around Jalalabad, the Yemeni fighter Tariq al-Fadhli forged a strong bond with bin Laden and subsequently worked with him to overthrow South Yemen's Marxist regime.[126]

National Geographic photographer Steve McCurry returned to Afghanistan following the insurgent assault on Jalalabad. In an interview with Peter Bergen, McCurry recounts observing the al-Qaeda leader during a brief respite in the fighting at night. McCurry sighted the tall, thin Saudi in a bombed-out house, surrounded by his men and speaking calmly as he addressed them. As he approached the building, McCurry caught the group's attention. Brandishing a pistol, one fighter ordered him to leave as bin Laden watched quietly, showing little interest in the uninvited American.[127]

Bin Laden's actions at the Battle of Jalalabad demonstrate his success in improving al-Qaeda's combat capabilities in the two years following the Battle of Jaji. The victory of his largely inexperienced force in that earlier battle, regarded as an instance of Allah's divine intervention, triggered a boost in jihadi recruitment efforts and the birth of al-Qaeda.[128] Steeled in battle and strengthened in numbers, the al-Qaeda unit continued to grow in combat experience with Soviet forces, demonstrating improved offensive capabilities at Jalalabad in 1989.[129]

Following the Battle of Jalalabad, bin Laden urged his men to avoid the trap of disunity that had caused the Afghans' temporary setback.[130] Emphasizing the positive results of the fighting, he then pointed out that the Arab fighters displayed a significant improvement in their overall use of small arms and guerrilla tactics.[131] This practical training, acquired in battle, gave bin Laden and his lieutenants invaluable experience as they launched al-Qaeda as a trained insurgent organization capable of assisting Islamist insurgencies in other parts of the world.

In his memoir, Nasser al-Bahri describes the immense arsenal of Soviet weaponry used by the Arab jihadis in Afghanistan between the time of the Soviet defeat and the 9/11 attacks.[132] In his role as bin Laden's chief bodyguard between 1997 and 2000, al-Bahri experienced al-Qaeda's intense training program firsthand, eventually working as a trainer and commander in several of the camps himself.[133] He provides a detailed list of Soviet, Western, and Israeli small arms in al-Qaeda's arsenal including Dragunov sniper rifles, RPG-

7 grenade launchers, Uzi submachine guns, M-16s, and AKS-74Us, bin Laden's personal favorite weapon.[134] In a technique called *kasat al-ganabel* or, "grenade spout," al-Qaeda fighters learned to attach prepared hand grenades to their AK-47 assault rifles before firing blanks, propelling the grenades 300 meters out from their position before exploding.[135]

Al-Bahri also states that al-Qaeda's technicians successfully adapted Soviet conventional weaponry for usage in guerrilla warfare. In the al-Qaeda training camps, the men successfully converted 30mm Narenjack grenade launchers into infantry weapons capable of carrying and firing 75 grenades.[136] By comparison, these weapons were originally mounted on Soviet helicopters and capable of carrying only 30 grenades. Camp trainees also practiced operations involving Soviet cluster bombs, SAM-7 surface-to-air missiles, U.S. Stinger missiles, and Toyota pickup-mounted Soviet Katyusha 120mm multiple rocket launchers, "ideal for guerrilla warfare."[137] Due to the Stinger's late and limited introduction into Afghanistan during the war against the Soviets, al-Qaeda lacked spare batteries for many of these missiles but managed to smuggle several of them into Saudi Arabia along with several SAM-7 missiles.[138]

Former French intelligence operative Omar Nasiri infiltrated al-Qaeda in 1994 and experienced intense training in bin Laden's Afghan camps. Nasiri describes al-Qaeda fighters driving Soviet T-55 tanks and practicing mobile operations in the open desert regions of Afghanistan.[139] He also provides a detailed assessment of Soviet and Western weaponry filling al-Qaeda weapons caches in the camps and the training methods used by guerrilla volunteers in the camps.[140] These accounts strongly emphasize the impact of the Soviet-Afghan War on al-Qaeda's emergence as a well-trained guerrilla vanguard for spearheading Islamist insurgencies worldwide.

Bin Laden and his lieutenants entered the Soviet-Afghan War inspired by a desire to help their Afghan coreligionists despite lacking a clear plan as to the method of accomplishing this goal. They left the war equally motivated by the deep convictions that had propelled them to action in the beginning and were further galvanized by their Afghan war experience to support struggling Muslims in other parts of the world. Although lightly trained and small in numbers compared to their Afghan colleagues, they had played a supporting role in facing the mechanized might of the Soviet superpower's army with its preponderance of airpower, armor, and Special Forces. Bin Laden's steadfastness and courage under fire had transformed him into a holy war hero capable of commanding the respect and admiration of other militants and inspiring them to bear arms against the perceived foes of their faith and brethren.[141]

CHAPTER 5

South Arabia's model insurgency and its global ramifications, 1989-1994

Bin Laden's determination to preserve the international jihadi movement generated by Moscow's invasion of Afghanistan and export it to the wider Muslim world did not end with the 40th Army's defeat or the Afghan factional infighting. Even before the Soviet retreat, the al-Qaeda leader had begun preparing with his Yemeni mujahid compatriots to apply their battle-honed guerrilla war tactics against South Yemen's Soviet-backed communist regime. His eventual success in this quest attests to the growth of al-Qaeda's combat capabilities as a result of the Soviet-Afghan War, as well as Yemen's central importance to the Salafi jihadi movement.[1]

As the fighting intensified between the rival Afghan leaders, with the reported exception of bin Laden's comrade Yunis Khalis, the al-Qaeda leader turned his attention back to his native land and returned to Saudi Arabia with his growing family following the setback at Jalalabad.[2] Witnessing his former Afghan hosts falling victims to the very disunity warned against by the Prophet Muhammad and the scholar Ibn Khaldun, bin Laden persisted in his efforts to persuade the insurgent leaders to work together and forge solidarity.[3] He also urged al-Qaeda members to avoid exacerbating the problem by trapping themselves in, "the political games of the Afghans."[4] Bin Laden's persistence in advising unity between the rival factions brought him and al-Qaeda into their first conflict with the Saudi regime and GID, as Prince Turki sought to pit rival Afghan groups against each other. Extending his guerrilla war into his ancestral homeland of Yemen ignited the next stage of conflict between bin Laden and the Saudi regime before the arrival of U.S. troops in 1990 triggered outright hostility.[5]

Beginning in 1962 with the outbreak of fighting between minority Shia and secular nationalist forces in North Yemen, various factions continued fighting for control of all sections of the country.[6] As noted in this book's first chapter, the bloodshed that continued following Britain's defeat eventually resulted in a dictatorial Marxist regime seizing power in the south, while a Saudi-backed military republic rose to power after defeating the royalists in the north.[7] Unable to fully assert its authority in the country's vast tribal regions, the southern Marxist central government largely relied on the aid of Soviet, Cuban, and East German troops to maintain control in its capital, Aden. In an eerie foreshadowing of events in Afghanistan, South Yemen's rulers reportedly arrested some members of the country's devout Sunni Muslim clergy suspected of opposition and attempted to suppress religious dissent in areas under government control.[8]

As Azzam and bin Laden expanded the combat role of Arab fighters in Afghanistan, Yemeni volunteers began steadily flocking to the guerrilla ranks in significant numbers with the staunch support of Salafi clergy and North Yemen's president, General Ali Abdullah Saleh.[9] Ultimately, only the Saudi contingent in Afghanistan outnumbered the Yemeni fighters, and often shared tribal and ethnic kinship with them. Most of the Yemeni jihadis also shared a commitment to the militant Salafism of their Saudi brethren and sought to apply the battlefield experience that they had acquired fighting the Soviets against the South Yemeni regime forces.[10]

Even as he assisted the Afghan guerrillas in their war against the Soviet troops, bin Laden consistently turned his thoughts to South Yemen as the next and most immediate target in the anti-Soviet defensive jihad. According to Islamic tradition, Yemen is the homeland of the original Arab people, known as *Qahtanis* or "South Arabians." Bin Laden's paternal and maternal roots lie deep in Yemen's Hadramut region and much of Saudi Arabia's tribal population hails from *Qahtani* origins as well.[11]

In addition to this deep motivation to liberate their brethren from the oppression of the communist infidels, Saudi and Yemeni Salafists seethed with resentment at the atheist nature of communist policy. Bin Laden often cited the *sunnah* or verified tradition of Muhammad in which the Prophet declared that only Muslims should be allowed to rule in Arabia and pointed out that the saying referred to the entire Arabian Peninsula, including Yemen, as Muslim holy land. The perceived Islamophobic policies of the communist regimes in Afghanistan and South Yemen constituted an act of aggression against Muslims and an attempt to force their conversion to a rival belief system that spurned all faith in God.[12]

From the traditional Salafi perspective, the communists were enforcing their atheist policies on Islam's holiest land, the Arabian Peninsula, and had further violated the Prophet's *sunnah* by inviting infidel forces in the form of Warsaw Pact troops into Yemen. Bin Laden often spoke of the early and solid embracing of Islam by the tribes of Yemen and viewed his ancestral home as a land of self-respecting tribes armed with a warrior culture ideal for supporting the restoration of *Shariah*.[13] In addition, the Aws and Khazraj tribes of Medina that converted to Islam and provided shelter to Muhammad and his early followers hailed from Yemeni origins, having immigrated to the Hejaz region only a century before.[14]

Communism in South Yemen had already begun falling apart in the middle of the 1980s, even as Gorbachev escalated the Soviet Army's campaign in Afghanistan with no immediate intention to withdraw.[15] On 13 January 1986, top politicians in the Yemeni Socialist Party turned against each other over ideological differences, splitting their party into two rival factions and launching a brief and bloody civil war that lasted for 11 days. Most of the experienced Yemeni communist leaders were killed during the fighting, and talks of reunification with North Yemen began shortly afterwards.[16]

On 22 May 1990, North and South Yemen were reunified as the Republic of Yemen, in a power-sharing arrangement between the two former ruling parties, following a May 1988 reunification agreement that occurred as Warsaw Pact forces withdrew from Aden.[17] Peace did not last as tensions ran high between Socialist Vice President Ali Salim al-Bid and Nationalist Party President General Saleh, the former ruler of North Yemen and a staunch supporter of inciting Yemeni jihadis to fight the Soviets in Afghanistan. Cautiously optimistic about the national reconciliation process, bin Laden prepared al-Qaeda to support the Yemeni warriors in their insurgency to drive the communists from power.[18]

Bin Laden subsequently financed and worked with Yemeni cleric Shaykh Abd al-Majid al-Zindani to organize the militant Salafist *Al-Islah* party to inspire and support the growth of the Sunni Islamist resistance movement in Yemen. As al-Qaeda grew in strength and numbers between 1988 and 1989, prominent Yemeni jihadis with Afghan battlefield experience, Tariq-al-Fadhli, Jamal al-Hadhi, Obadah al-Wadihi, and Mukbel al-Wadihi began working closely with bin Laden and al-Zindani to train Yemeni fighters at the al-Qaeda camps.[19] While the first three men earnestly sought bin Laden's help in overthrowing the Yemeni communists, Mukbel al-Wadihi, trained as a Salafist cleric in Saudi Arabia, eventually turned against the al-Qaeda chief after pocketing about 25,000,000 riyals, or about U.S. $6,500,000, from him.[20]

Fearful of a strong and united republic on their southern doorstep, the al-Saud family and North Korea's dynastic communist regime reportedly reached out and offered support to the Yemeni Socialist Party in hopes of creating further obstacles to Yemen's national reunification.[21] Bringing their Afghan battlefield exploits to the table, bin Laden, al-Fadhli, al-Hadhi, and the al-Wadihi brothers established three guerrilla training camps in northern Yemen at Sadaa, Waulia, and Marib, and several others in the southern provinces of Abyan and Shabwah. Bin Laden also spoke in Yemeni mosques and reportedly met with insurgent leaders in the cities of Sadaa and Sanaa, and in the rural mountains of Abyan and Shabwah provinces, urging resistance to the communists.[22] He also reportedly financed a successful assassination campaign directed and executed by al-Fadhli targeting top communist officials between 1990 and 1994. Nasser al-Bahri recalls meeting large numbers of his young Yemeni compatriots passing through Jeddah during this period to meet with the al-Qaeda chief in between training sessions at the camps.[23] Bin Laden's successful campaign, enabled by his experience in the Soviet-Afghan War, exacerbated tensions with the Saudi royal family and sowed the seeds of his 1996 declaration of war on their U.S. and U.K. allies.[24]

Since returning from Afghanistan in 1989, bin Laden had been repeatedly warning Saudi authorities of the possibility that Iraqi Baathist (national socialist) dictator Saddam Hussein may invade Kuwait, a prediction that became a reality in August 1990. U.S. and Western troops quickly arrived in Saudi Arabia as King Fahd rebuffed the al-Qaeda leader's offer to organize an insurgency led by jihadis with Afghan battle experience to repulse a potential Iraqi invasion.[25] The story of the al-Qaeda chief's subsequent house arrest, clever escape to Pakistan, and final break with the al-Saud royal family has been documented thoroughly in other works. After remaining in Pakistan for nearly a year, bin Laden relocated his family and fighters to Sudan at the invitation of the country's Islamist president, Dr. Hasan al-Turabi, in December 1991.[26]

Resentful of the al-Saud's invitation of Western infidels onto the Arabian Peninsula and their support for the Yemeni communists, bin Laden remained undeterred in his initial goal of aiding the Yemeni mujahedin before focusing on the Americans and the West.[27] Based in the al-Riyadh district of the Sudanese capital, Khartoum, he continued financing al-Fadhli's assassination campaign and growing tribal insurgency in Yemen's southern province of Abyan. He also continued financing al-Qaeda's guerrilla training camps in Afghanistan and Yemen as they continued producing seasoned fighters trained by veterans of the battles against the Soviets.[28] Bin Laden also organized the Advice and Reform Committee (ARC) in early 1994 to communicate with *Sahwa* scholars in Saudi Arabia and publish their critiques of the regime. While the al-Qaeda leader managed the ARC from Khartoum, he financed an office in London that published his speeches and those of Islamic Awakening scholars in Saudi Arabia following the Saudi regime's crackdown in early 1994.[29]

On 4 February 1994, a takfiri group in Sudan led by the Libyan extremist Muhammad al-Khulayfi had attempted to assassinate the al-Qaeda leader at his office in Khartoum. Takfiris are a minority and truly extremist sect within Sunni Islam, unrelated to the Wahhabis and Salafists, and are distinguished by their labeling of almost all other Muslims as insufficiently Islamic.[30] Al-Khulayfi and his takfiri organization had judged bin Laden as a false Muslim and launched the first of many unsuccessful assassination attempts on the al-Qaeda chief by takfiri groups in Sudan and Afghanistan.[31]

Bin Laden and his eldest son Abdullah managed to outflank and repulse the attackers in a vicious gun battle that led to the injury of several of his guards, including Jamal al-Hadhi.[32] Two months later, the Saudi government revoked bin Laden's citizenship, froze his assets in the Kingdom, and pressured his family to denounce him publicly. Uninjured and undeterred, bin Laden interpreted these events as obstacles that God intended him to surmount and spared no effort in furthering al-Qaeda's support for the group's Yemeni compatriots.[33]

Launching operations from his group's mountain strongholds in the southern tribal lands of his father, the last Sultan of Abyan, al-Fadhli began dispatching teams of fighters to infiltrate the urban strongholds of the socialist leaders.[34] Al-Fadhli's men executed guerrilla ambushes on socialist army convoys and leaders, as the Socialist Vice President of the fragile republic, Ali Salim al-Bid, ordered assassins to strike Saleh's loyalists in the north. As tensions with his rival mounted, Saleh began calling on his traditional allies in Yemen's rural tribes and jihadi groups, now battle-seasoned with Afghan fighting experience, for aid against the communists.[35]

Securing financing from bin Laden, al-Fadhli's veteran fighters continued to expand their local guerrilla war and assassination campaign across the south, while Saleh received the support of exiled tribal leaders based in Saudi Arabia and al-Zindani's *al-Islah* party.[36] On 27 April 1993, Saleh's nationalist party won an overwhelming majority of votes in the national elections with the support of al-Zindani and *al-Islah*, increasing tensions with al-Bid's southern socialists. Following the combined nationalist and Sunni Islamist victory in a parliamentary election reportedly certified as the Arab world's most fair, free, and representative by most international observers, al-Bid angrily flew to the United States for an unannounced meeting with U.S. Vice President Al Gore as an affront to Saleh.[37]

On the election's anniversary in 1994, fighting broke out across the country as tensions erupted into bloodshed, with al-Bid's socialist supporters seeking secession and control of the southern provinces in the seventh outbreak of civil war in Yemen since 1962.[38] Perceiving this as a desperate last-ditch communist effort to retain power on the Arabian Peninsula, Islam's holiest land, bin Laden and al-Qaeda quickly came to the aid of the Yemeni jihadis fighting alongside Saleh's nationalists against the Yemeni Socialist Party.[39] Strengthened by their Afghan war experience, militants led by bin Laden's anti-Soviet colleagues Tariq al-Fadhli, Jamal al-Hadhi, and Shaykh Abd al-Majid al-Zindani conducted a successful guerrilla campaign. Al-Zindani and his former anti-Soviet colleague, Abd al-Wahhab al-Daylami, issued *fatwas* or religious rulings declaring jihad against al-Bid's socialists.[40]

On 4 May 1994, al-Bid's jet fighter-bombers struck Saleh's capital at Sanaa, and he followed up the attack with a Scud missile barrage on the city several days later. Saleh's top commander and a brother-in-law of al-Fadhli, General Ali Muhsin, struck quickly towards Aden, advancing on the southern port from army bases in the northern mountains.[41] Recently released from a sham house arrest in Sanaa, al-Fadhli immediately returned to Abyan, rallying his veteran jihadi fighters and tribal allies, and advancing towards Aden from the east while a second jihadi group based in Shabwah province struck al-Bid's forces in a diversionary attack from the rear. Led by Abu Ali al-Harithi, another guerrilla veteran of the Afghan battlefields sent back to Yemen by bin Laden, a separate group of jihadi fighters advanced toward Aden, successfully helping al-Fadhli to isolate al-Bid's forces.[42]

As the guerrillas advanced in close cooperation with Saleh's conventional forces, a situation described as the ideal evolution of an insurgency by Mao Zedong, they consistently received reinforcements as bin Laden dispatched veteran cadres of Yemeni jihadis from Sudan.[43] As the fighting in Yemen continued throughout late May and into June, Saudi, Kuwaiti, and North Korean leaders launched a desperate final effort to save al-Bid's socialists, reportedly rushing weapons to them while urging the United Nations (UN) to issue a resolution supporting a ceasefire.[44] Yet as Gregory Johnsen points out in his excellent book *The Last Refuge: Yemen, al-Qaeda, and America's War in Arabia*, the Western world's attention had only just begun focusing on the horrors of the Rwandan Genocide in the spring and summer of 1994. As in the case of Soviet-occupied Afghanistan during much of the previous decade, the raging bloodbath in South Arabia appears to have captured only limited public interest and media attention in many non-Muslim countries in comparison to other international crises.[45]

As the jihadis, their tribal allies, and Saleh's northern armies continued to advance, top socialist politicians began abandoning the struggle and defecting to the growing insurgency. Sensing imminent defeat, al-Bid fled into exile across the Omani border under the protective shield of a loyal military convoy. On 7 July 1994, the jihadi fighters assisted in the capture of Aden, the last bastion of the Yemeni Socialist Party, burning down the country's only brewery in a sign of defiance to the last reminder of communist influence on Islam's sacred soil. President Saleh subsequently reunified the country under his rule, thanking the Islamists for their support by providing them with jobs and limited influence in his new regime.[46]

As an Arab nationalist, Saleh opposed the establishment of an Islamist regime in Yemen, and several allies of al-Qaeda, including Mukbel al-Wadihi, turned against their former comrades, succumbing to financial bribes and positions of power offered by Saleh. Despite Saleh's preemption of an Islamist takeover, jihadi influence remained strong in Yemen and al-Qaeda's loyal local wings burrowed deep into the country's tribal infrastructure. Bin Laden's uncompromising support for the Yemeni Islamists between 1990 and 1994 and the solid bonds that he had built working with them during the war against the Soviets greatly strengthened al-Qaeda's position in the country.[47]

As he prepared for al-Qaeda's war against the West throughout the 1990s, bin Laden continued to cultivate his relationships patiently and persistently with jihadi fighters and tribal leaders in Yemen.[48] His close connections with many Yemeni tribes and guerrilla colleagues such as al-Fadhli, al-Zindani, and others paid off immensely, producing thousands of volunteer recruits for al-Qaeda and a solid base for the group's expanding presence on the Arabian Peninsula.[49] Following bin Laden's death in May 2011, his former anti-Soviet colleague al-Fadhli mourned and voiced respect and admiration for the al-Qaeda chief while reminiscing about their experience fighting the Soviets in Afghanistan.[50]

Following the Soviet Army's defeat in Afghanistan, al-Qaeda fighters continued to hone and spread their martial skills acquired in battle by training new recruits in the group's growing number of insurgent camps. Even after returning briefly to Saudi Arabia, bin Laden maintained the financing and upkeep of the Afghan camps, entrusting close subordinates and fellow guerrilla veterans with the training of new fighters. In the early 1990s, al-Qaeda fighters conducted insurgency support operations for emerging Islamist organizations throughout the former Soviet Union and Eastern Bloc countries.[51]

In 1991, al-Qaeda fighters operating in Afghanistan began transporting trained guerrillas to the border of Tajikistan before and after the collapse of Soviet rule in that country. Nasser al-Bahri later rose to prominence in a group of Saudi and Yemeni jihadis fighting alongside Muslim rebels against Serbian troops in 1994 and 1995.[52] Following the expulsion of the Arab fighters from Bosnia, al-Bahri and a close friend and al-Qaeda veteran of the Soviet-Afghan War, Mohanad al-Jadawi, joined a band of Saudi and Yemeni compatriots heading for Afghanistan. Under the leadership of Jaji veteran Hamza al-Ghamdi, the group infiltrated Tajikistan through the Afghan border to participate in the Tajik Islamists' resistance to the country's Russian-backed regime.[53] From 1989 forward, al-Qaeda fighters began appearing to inspire and support local jihadi groups in Kashmir, Chechnya, and Mindanao as well.[54]

Following his return to Afghanistan on 18 May 1996, bin Laden's reputation as a holy warrior helping the Afghans to oust the Soviet occupiers eventually earned him the protection of Taleban chief Mullah Muhammad Omar and his adviser, Mullah Jalil.[55] This legitimacy in the eyes of Sunni Islamist groups from West Africa to Southeast Asia persuaded Omar and many of his subordinates of the need to protect the al-Qaeda chief from infidel powers at any cost. Turning the al-Qaeda leader over to the United States or any foreign power demanding him also contradicted the Pashtun tribal code of *melmastia* or "hospitality" to guests, especially one regarded as a holy warrior defending beleaguered Muslims.[56]

Between May 1996 and October 2001, al-Qaeda fighters continued honing their deadly talents in the tradition of the jihadi group's founders, receiving physical and psychological training in the guerrilla training camps and joining the Taleban in battle against Ahmed Shah Massoud's forces.[57] Bin Laden had never expressed displeasure with Massoud during the war against the Soviets, preferring instead to promote Islamist solidarity by example. As the ethnic Tajik commander forged closer ties with France, Russia, Iran, and other regimes perceived as Islam's foes, opposition to him became a practicality as well as a religious duty.[58]

In 2006, Shaykh Musa al-Qarni recalled that many of his fellow Saudi Salafist clerics had long declared Massoud a traitor to Islam following his temporary 1983 truce with the Soviet Army.[59] As mentioned earlier, this truce had allowed Soviet forces to concentrate and inflict far heavier losses on the uncompromising Afghan Islamist groups fighting on despite the odds. These actions also made him untrustworthy and unworthy of CIA and GID aid from the perspective of Pakistan's ISI. Led by Arab veterans of the Soviet-Afghan War, young al-Qaeda fighters engaged in fierce battles with Massoud's troops throughout the late 1990s and into 2001, improving their combat capabilities and training new recruits as their forefathers had done.[60]

While Massoud also led experienced men, the al-Qaeda fighters met them with a lethal combination of veteran guerrilla cadres and tenacity, launching fearless attacks seeking martyrdom as Arab mujahedin had done from the birth of Saudi Arabia to the Soviet-Afghan War and Yemen's 1994 Civil War. This militant battle drive, enhanced by previous experience from fighting a superpower, created major problems for Massoud. Roy Gutman states that Northern Alliance troops often fought well against Taleban units until al-Qaeda fighters arrived on the battlefield.[61] Nasser al-Bahri recalls that the presence of seasoned al-Qaeda fighters often resulted in the turning point of many local engagements.[62]

Unafraid of death by fire, Arab fighters in al-Qaeda charged enemy positions and employed flamethrowers against their foes, causing Massoud's troops to flee due to a traditional Afghan belief in avoiding such a fate. Many Taleban fighters once shared this fear, a factor that has gradually changed with the increase of Salafist influence among the group's members.[63] Gutman points out that despite holding out in northeastern Afghanistan and securing large amounts of material aid from Moscow, Tehran, and Paris, Massoud struggled militarily and could not manage to defeat the Taleban units supported by al-Qaeda fighters or independent al-Qaeda units.[64]

Bin Laden continued using the Taleban's religiously permissible war against Massoud as a training ground for new al-Qaeda recruits just as he and his small but determined Arab band had honed their fighting skills by helping the Afghan

Islamists in their war against the Soviet troops. This tried and tested method served al-Qaeda well until the group assassinated Massoud on 9 September 2001 and struck the United States in New York, Washington, D.C., and a field near Shanksville, Pennsylvania two days later.[65] Bin Laden's successful luring of the United States, Britain, and their NATO allies into Afghanistan enabled the lightly trained militants of al-Qaeda's newest generations to acquire fresh combat experience against a superpower.[66]

Fighting the Soviets in Afghanistan had provided bin Laden and his colleagues with a blueprint for training jihadi fighters against the world's mightiest armies in the hope of applying this experience in battle against their main enemies, the secular Middle Eastern regimes that they regarded as tyrannies. The West's post 9/11 Afghan campaign enabled new generations of Islamist militants to inherit this intense training regimen, facing the U.S. and NATO troops in battles for nearly 20 years and allowing the Taleban to emerge as the perceived victor over a second superpower.[67]

Bin Laden and his lieutenants organized and launched al-Qaeda as a guerrilla organization not to embark on an impractical war of conquest to convert the entire world to Islam, but to incite and support Islamist insurgencies against perceived Islamophobic regimes. The civil war in Yemen, the ancestral land of bin Laden and the great bulk of al-Qaeda's veteran fighters, served as a demonstration of the organization's battle-honed combat capabilities. Even before the collapse of the southern communists, bin Laden and his Yemeni colleagues had successfully established several key guerrilla strongholds, steadily building a solid base of operations for al-Qaeda.[68]

After the defeat of the South Yemeni communists in July 1994, al-Qaeda's influence continued to grow in the reunified country from which the group's local leadership and foot soldiers executed powerful attacks against the United States and its allies.[69] Large numbers of Yemeni tribesmen had fought the Soviets alongside bin Laden at the Battles of Jaji, Jalalabad, and the engagements in between, and eagerly tested their combat experience against South Yemen's Moscow-backed regime.[70] Reminding the Yemeni tribal chiefs of their warriors' key role in the Afghan resistance against the Soviets, bin Laden secured their staunch support while expanding al-Qaeda's presence in the country throughout the 1990s.[71] Following up this campaign of focusing heavily on recruiting al-Qaeda fighters from the Arabian Peninsula, the al-Qaeda chief secured even greater support in his ancestral homeland through marriage to his fourth, final, and favorite wife, Amal al-Sadah, in early 2000.[72]

Bin Laden correctly calculated that his marriage to Amal, a young woman from a tribe native to the Taez region, enabled him to further expand al-Qaeda's presence in a country already tightly connected to the organization. In his memoir, Nasser al-Bahri explains bin Laden's reasoning, pointing to a tribal "cult of revenge" as central to traditional Yemeni warrior culture.[73] Bin Laden's focus on recruiting fighters from his ancestral homeland has since benefitted al-Qaeda tremendously, as contemporary history continues to demonstrate. As al-Qaeda operatives on board a raft packed with explosives struck and nearly sank the USS *Cole*, a naval vessel docked for refueling in Aden, killing 17 American sailors and injuring 37 others on 12 October 2000, several of the 9/11 "muscle hijackers," those trained to subdue the plane passengers, crews, and pilots, landed in Afghanistan to begin training for their mission.[74] In February 2006, 23 Yemeni al-Qaeda fighters, extradited from Iran after fleeing there from Afghanistan after the December 2001 Battle of Tora Bora, escaped from a prison operated by the Yemeni regime's intelligence service in Sanaa. Following bin Laden's management example and led by his talented former bodyguard and personal secretary, Nasser al-Wahayshi, also known as Abu Bashir al-Yemeni, the men quickly rose to leadership in the local al-Qaeda unit and transformed the group into the global organization's strongest international wing.[75]

Under al-Wahayshi's management, AQAP seized large swathes of land across Yemen, challenging government forces, executing terror attacks on U.S. interests, and fighting the reportedly Iranian and North Korean-backed royalist Shia Houthi movement while defending Salafi *madrassa* students in the city of Taez from their attacks.[76] U.S. forces killed al-Wahayshi in a June 2015 CIA drone strike, and his associates continue to lead AQAP, but the warrior's legacy continues to inflict damage in a manner not unlike that of his close comrade and role model, bin Laden.[77] Al-Wahayshi's success stemmed in large part from his close work with the late al-Qaeda chief, remaining at his side every morning in his office at al-Qaeda's Tarnak Farm compound in Afghanistan.[78] Emulating bin Laden's leadership example and management style, al-Wahayshi closely studied the guerrilla tactics that al-Qaeda's first generation acquired in combat against the Soviet troops.[79]

Al-Wahayshi and his colleagues adhered to bin Laden's plans, utilizing their training to build the group's Yemeni wing into a lethal global threat, strengthening its entrenched presence in the South Arabian nation, and killing three U.S. naval aviators in Pensacola, Florida as late as December 2019.[80] Since al-Wahayshi's 2015 death, the organization has continued to thrive under the leadership of his successors, most recently Qasim al-Raymi and his successor Khalid Said Batarfi, a Saudi fighter of Yemeni origin sometimes known to his comrades as Abu al-Miqdad al-Kindi.[81] Yet had thousands of Yemeni warriors not flocked to the mujahid ranks following the opportunity presented by Moscow's Afghan debacle, the successes resulting from this crucial combat experience may have taken far longer to achieve. The Soviet invasion of Afghanistan created unlimited opportunities for bin Laden and the al-Qaeda top brass, motivating thousands of Islamic zealots to gather in South Asia with a target to focus on and the objective of obtaining practical combat experience for later struggles. Under bin Laden's leadership, these militants succeeded in their quest and formed an organization to rid the Muslim world of infidel influences, beginning with the holy land of Arabia.

EPILOGUE:
The inspirer

My goal in writing this book has been to provide readers with an easily accessible and original work on how bin Laden's life and actions in the Soviet-Afghan War propelled his rise to prominence in the international jihadi movement and trained al-Qaeda in guerrilla warfare. I have not sought to portray him as any sort of legendary Muslim Robin Hood, although to the growing Sunni Islamist movement worldwide he most certainly is that and so much more. Rather, I have sought to explain and clarify the impact of his wartime actions and leadership on training and organizing al-Qaeda for a protracted global struggle by producing the first book to do so.

I also freely admit to being fascinated by him from a historical standpoint, and by the cultural and religious convictions that propelled him to act and lead others in battle following Moscow's perceived aggression against Muslims in Afghanistan. These militant convictions only deepened and intensified as bin Laden led his small but determined Arab guerrilla band into battle against the Soviet troops, experiencing their "brutality" in combat firsthand.[1] This arduous course in facing the forces of a superpower in combat served as intense battlefield training, preparing bin Laden and al-Qaeda for insurgency support operations on a global scale. As has been shown, they subsequently channeled their seasoned combat capabilities acquired in Afghanistan in helping local Islamists to oust Yemen's lingering Marxist officials from power.

The refusal of many Saudi clerics to join the insurgent ranks during the war while inciting their younger compatriots to do so appears to reflect the desire of the Arab regimes to placate domestic Islamists while sending the guerrillas to their deaths at the hands of the Soviets. From bin Laden's perspective, Allah foiled these plots by helping His warriors to vanquish the Soviets and permitting the non-Afghan fighters to return home battle-seasoned and fully trained for later struggles. In addition to this practical experience, bin Laden also believed that Allah had provided a blueprint for defeating another government that he perceived as Islam's foe, the United States, a second superpower that he already regarded as an inevitable enemy due to U.S. foreign policy.[2]

As al-Qaeda remains entrenched in South Asia, the Arabian Peninsula, and elsewhere more than a decade after bin Laden's death and continues to pose a lethal, global threat to the West as he seems to have expected, understanding the sources of the group's strength and the impact of its founder's actions remains crucial.³ If the definition of insanity is taking the same course of action repeatedly and expecting a different outcome, then common sense dictates that U.S. forces and their allies remain withdrawn from Afghanistan and decline to entertain future prolonged interventions to safeguard a regime of the West's choice. Undeterred by massive manpower losses that are quickly replenished by jihadi recruitment efforts driven by Washington's military presence, the Taleban and al-Qaeda have enjoyed two more decades of honing their martial skills against a superpower's forces since 9/11.

NATO's 20-year campaign in Afghanistan has supplemented the decade of training that the Afghan Islamists and their Arab allies obtained while fighting the Soviets with combat experience fighting the American superpower and led to the creation of Taleban and al-Qaeda Special Forces. In the late 2010s, Taleban "Red Units" reportedly began operating regularly throughout Afghanistan, posing an increasingly lethal threat to the U.S. and NATO-backed regime's security forces and its foreign backers.⁴ Al-Qaeda terror attacks such as the January 2015 Paris attacks by the organization's Yemeni wing have also assumed the characteristic hallmarks of professional and lethal Special Forces operations.⁵ In that instance, three militants dressed in gloves and masks aimed at specific targets with deadly precision, forcing a response by more than 90,000 French military, intelligence, and police personnel in the heart of one of the world's major urban environments.⁶

The beginning of wisdom, then, should be to deny these vicious and determined enemies of the West any further opportunity to improve their fighting skills by facing a superpower's forces in a prolonged conflict such as the Soviet and more recent U.S.-NATO campaigns in Afghanistan. By fighting only in necessary instances and conducting brief, tornado-like punitive campaigns focused solely on decisively defeating the enemy rather than remaining as perceived occupiers propping up embattled regimes, the West can hope to avoid future quagmires that ultimately strengthen the Islamists. By rapidly executing such punitive actions in the rare event that they become necessary and refusing to engage in further attempts at exporting and enforcing their preferred style of government in traditional Muslim countries, Western leaders can reduce and redirect the threat posed by the militant Islamists, forcing them to eventually confront the local regimes that remain their primary targets.⁷

Those expressing reservations about the recent U.S. and NATO troop withdrawal from Afghanistan should recall that historian Rodric Braithwaite reportedly found that many Afghans he encountered while researching his 2011 book *Afgantsy: The Russians in Afghanistan 1979-89* expressed favorable views of the Soviet occupation in comparison to the more recent Western one. Concluding that while some of these positive recollections may constitute a historical "travesty," likely influenced by memories of the post-Soviet Afghan Civil War that led to the Taleban's October 1994 formation, Braithwaite states that they nevertheless appear to reflect the reality that Washington's leaders fared no better than their Soviet counterparts in stabilizing the Kabul regime of their choice.[8] While both superpowers enjoyed limited local successes in their respective military interventions, the major decision-makers of each campaign also appear to have overlooked the power of tribal and religious opposition to minority central governments perceived as urban-dominated for much of Afghanistan's turbulent history.[9]

The scholar's responsibility is not to decide foreign policy, however, that job lies entirely in the hands of government leaders entrusted by their constituents with the proper authority for making such decisions. The role of the historian is to present the facts openly, honestly, and accurately, and for my part, I can only say that I have done my very best to accomplish this goal here. As has been shown, a careful examination of the historical facts reveals that the futile efforts of Soviet leaders to impose the central government of their choice on Afghanistan prolonged what they intended to be a short campaign for a decade, providing the founding fathers of al-Qaeda with the training that they required for later struggles and to train new generations.

Bin Laden's example proves that individuals willing to seize the initiative and act, even being outside of state power, can alter the course of history for better or worse. Collectives relying on consensus however, cannot. Had bin Laden chosen the life of a follower and taken the path of those inciting others to holy war from the safety of the sidelines, he may not have emerged as the leader and the lethal threat that he became to those that he deemed Islam's foes. His decision to abandon a billionaire's luxuries and embark on a Spartan journey earned him the respect of his jihadi colleagues and enhanced his image as a veteran holy warrior and an inspiring leader of men.

The same cannot be said of the authoritarian al-Zawahiri, his loyal Egyptians, and others, many of whom look down on both their colleagues from the Arabian Peninsula and non-Arabs alike with scorn and contempt, as documented by the al-Qaeda chief's contemporaries and reluctant defectors. By fighting in the Muslim world only in rare necessary cases, the West can exploit these regional and ethnic tensions to widen the cracks in al-Qaeda, now led by the recently killed-in-action al-Zawahiri's successors, and its international wings by denying ideal training opportunities to the Islamists and splitting their unity. Doing so may play a small role in reversing some of the damage resulting from bin Laden's effective managerial skills and his success in promoting Islamist solidarity during his almost quarter-century career as the al-Qaeda leader.

The Soviet invasion and subsequent war in Afghanistan provided a key window of opportunity for bin Laden and his jihadi colleagues to forge international connections and acquire intense combat training by facing the forces of a superpower. Gorbachev's generals and the world's strongest army served as their unwitting instructors, forcing the Arab fighters to master the tactical art of guerrilla warfare against overwhelming odds. While available accounts provide little evidence of CIA aid to al-Qaeda, the organization benefitted immensely from practical experience fighting the Soviet invaders. Having completed their arduous journey fully trained and steeled in combat, bin Laden and al-Qaeda emerged from the Soviet-Afghan War capable of inspiring and supporting Islamist insurgencies throughout the world.

AUTHOR'S AFTERWORD TO THE SECOND EDITION: U.S.-U.K. Perceptions of Osama's 1994 South Arabian guerrilla war – a conclusion

> Like many other Muslim young men, some Islamists in Egypt gained military experience in the Afghan mojahedin [c]amps. These conditions [secular Arab dictatorships] forced some to take such positions in their countries to defend their religion and themselves.... What I said about Egypt I say about Yemen, which I believe is one of the best Arab and Muslim countries in terms of adherence to traditions and the faith. Nevertheless, its citizens have been subjected to murder and religious persecution. So it is natural for reactions to take place, even if some of Yemen's sons do train in Afghan [guerrilla] camps.
>
> Osama bin Laden during an interview with Al-Quds Al-Arabi newspaper, 9 March 1994[1]

As indicated above, bin Laden spoke these words on 9 March 1994, the day before his 37th birthday and the date on which he granted an interview to journalists from the London-based newspaper *Al-Quds Al-Arabi*. Consistent with many of his other interviews, written letters, and public statements that are cited throughout this book, bin Laden hid neither the reasons for his and al-Qaeda's motivations to resist and repulse those they deemed the foes of Muslims nor his perception that Salafist militants could attain eventual victory given the proper application of the battle-honed guerrilla tactics that they had acquired fighting the Soviets.[2] Rather, he openly and consistently emphasized the invaluable, tactical guerrilla war experience that he perceived that Allah had provided to Salafi jihadi fighters on the Afghan battlefields and the importance of applying this practical combat experience in gradually wearing down the dictatorial, infidel-backed regimes that he regarded as oppressing Muslims. Emphasizing his and al-Qaeda's role as a guerrilla vanguard that he prayed could inspire and train generations of new recruits and tactically spearhead their larger insurgency combat operations, bin Laden subsequently channeled his battle-honed leadership skills in playing a key supporting role in the decisive defeat of the Yemeni Socialist Party (YSP).[3]

As emphasized throughout this book, particularly in Chapter 4, the rugged, rural parts of eastern Afghanistan, dotted by steep, white-capped, snowy mountains and lush green, thickly wooded hills on which bin Laden and his multinational Arab guerrilla band faced and fought the Soviet occupation forces served as the launch pads that catapulted him to leadership and trained al-Qaeda's founding generation.[4] Bin Laden and his senior guerrilla comrades and associates, most of whom shared his ethnic *Qahtani*, or South Arabian, origins, subsequently channeled their newly acquired combat skills in tactically spearheading the Yemeni Salafists' war of resistance to the YSP and ousting it from power in their ancestral land as emphasized in Chapter 5. Yet while al-Qaeda and the global Salafi jihadi movement continue benefitting from bin Laden's 1994 success in contributing to the YSP's defeat, the late Saudi zealot's impact on the 1994 Yemeni Civil War's outcome, like his earlier accomplishing of his goals in fighting the Soviets, appears to continue eluding many experts.[5]

As this book's final draft prepared to go to press and after its publication in early 2022, two other biographies appeared in which the authors, in line with much of the traditional, popular historiography on bin Laden's life, portray the al-Qaeda leader as a failure. Written by truly accomplished, commendable, and expert scholars, these two works, *The Rise and Fall of Osama bin Laden* by Peter Bergen and *The Bin Laden Papers: How the Abbottabad Raid Revealed the Truth about Al-Qaeda, Its Leader and His Family* by Nelly Lahoud, nevertheless appear to overlook much of bin Laden's lasting lethal legacy by overemphasizing his alleged failures.[6] Yet this approach, while somewhat understandable considering the al-Qaeda chief's ruthless actions in prosecuting his war with the West, continues to dangerously blindside scholars to his actual motivations and considerable achievements and the reasons for which his legacy remains deadly and threatening a dozen years after his death.[7]

While bin Laden's involvement in the Yemeni Civil War of 1994 has yet, at the time of writing, to receive book-length treatment, there are several excellent biographies within the existing scholarship on the al-Qaeda chief that briefly discuss this interesting and important episode of his life. To date, a significant gap in the existing historiographical scholarship appears to be the lack of detailed discussion on bin Laden's wartime involvement and the contemporary U.S.-U.K. perceptions of its results. Conversely, a key similarity is that most accounts focus largely on the conventional warfare fought between the conflict's primary belligerents, President Ali Abdullah Saleh's Nationalists and Vice President Ali Salim al-Bid's YSP. Peter Bergen dedicates several pages to this topic in his 2001 bestseller *Holy War, Inc.: Inside the Secret World of Osama bin Laden*, briefly mentioning bin Laden's comradeship with Tariq al-Fadhli and Shaykh Abd al-Majid al-Zindani. Regarding the impact of bin Laden and al-Fadhli's guerrilla years in the Soviet-Afghan War on their successful efforts to help Saleh's Nationalist northern forces defeat al-Bid's Socialist southern armies, Bergen says little more after stating that, "here was another happy opportunity to attack the godless communists."[8]

In his 2021 biography *The Rise and Fall of Osama bin Laden*, Bergen again makes brief mention of bin Laden's desire to act before the 1994 Yemeni Civil War by stating that the al-Qaeda chief desired to help Yemen's anti-communist guerrillas, but explores the topic no further after concluding, "All of bin Laden's jihadist projects in the early 1990s in Afghanistan, Saudi Arabia, and Yemen were flops."[9] In somewhat of a contrast to Bergen, Michael Scheuer appears to view bin Laden's role in the outcome of Yemen's 1994 Civil War as being of at least some significance. Scheuer appears to have become the first scholar to identify bin Laden's role in sponsoring the assassinations of many key YSP leaders between 1990 and 1994 in his 2002 book *Through Our Enemies' Eyes: Osama bin Laden, Radical Islam, and the Future of America*. In this book, Scheuer devotes several paragraphs to bin Laden's role in financing and building guerrilla training camps for al-Fadhli and al-Zindani's fighters in Yemen and the part that these actions played in the al-Qaeda chief's final break with the Saudi royal family.[10]

Scheuer expands somewhat on his analysis and discusses the topic on several pages in his 2011 biography *Osama bin Laden*, briefly mentioning the Yemeni guerrillas being led by al-Fadhli and other experienced Yemeni Soviet-Afghan War veterans while saying little else on the matter.[11] In addition to the excellent biographies of bin Laden authored by Bergen and Scheuer, Gregory Johnsen delves a bit further into the al-Qaeda leader's support for the anti-communist Yemeni guerrillas in his 2013 book *The Last Refuge: Yemen, al-Qaeda, and America's War in Arabia*. Johnsen devotes an insightful chapter to discussing the 1994 Civil War and profiles several key al-Qaeda commanders, such as Jamal al-Hadhi and Abu Ali al-Harithi, whose efforts boosted Saleh's war effort against the YSP's larger armies.[12]

While these splendid books by Bergen, Scheuer, and Johnsen all discuss bin Laden's role in Yemen's 1994 Civil War to varying extents, few other works mention the al-Qaeda chief's involvement at the time. Many of these texts, however, mention in parts the supporting role played by the Islamist militants and tribal militiamen that supported Saleh's conventional forces, yet most of them remain focused on the conventional warfare fought between the northern and southern armies. Though horrific and destructive, the war ended quickly, which is, perhaps, one explanation as to why the 1996 book *The Yemeni War of 1994: Causes and Consequences* edited by Jamal S. al-Suwaidi remains, to date, the only major published work focusing exclusively on the conflict.[13] Like Johnsen's *The Last Refuge*, Ginny Hill's more recent 2017 book *Yemen Endures: Civil War, Saudi Adventurism and the Future of Arabia* devotes a chapter to the 1994 conflict. Yet while Hill's work provides a brief, insightful description of the "naval bridge" that bin Laden established to smuggle weapons between Yemen and Sudan in 1996, the book, in contrast to Johnsen's, makes little mention of bin Laden's role in the 1994 Civil War.[14]

While the works by Hill, al-Suwaidi, Johnsen, Scheuer, and Bergen all discuss jihadi involvement in the 1994 Yemeni Civil War and the latter three authors all make at least some mention of bin Laden and al-Qaeda's wartime support for President Saleh's forces, this Afterword closely focuses on how bin Laden's practical and tactical guerrilla war training during the Soviet-Afghan War helped Yemen's Salafi fighters to boost the Nationalist armies' fortunes.[15] In contrast to these previous works, it also emphasizes the contemporary U.S.-U.K. perceptions of the wartime events to which bin Laden's staunch allies and guerrilla comrades in Yemen contributed as they channeled their Afghan battle experience to help the northern armies triumph over the odds. The reader should not, therefore, interpret this section of the book as an attempt to portray al-Qaeda's veteran jihadi fighters as the main force opposing the southern secessionists, but rather as a close examination of their tactical impact on assisting and hastening the victory primarily achieved by Saleh's conventional armies. Bin Laden and his South Arabian guerrilla brethren could not have aided Saleh and applied their guerrilla tactics effectively without the practical combat training that they received courtesy of the unwitting Soviets and Afghan Army during the preceding decade, and an explanation of how they did so is the purpose of this section.[16]

While Chapter 5 of this book emphasizes Yemen's overall importance to the international Salafi jihadi movement and the impact of bin Laden's successful quest in battling the Soviets on his support for the anti-communist Yemeni mujahedin, this Afterword to the second edition of *The Holy Warrior: Osama Bin Laden and His Jihadi Journey in the Soviet-Afghan War* closely examines the significance of his actions, and the contemporary U.S.-U.K. perceptions of them, during his involvement in his South Arabian ancestral homeland's 1994 Civil War. As discussed in Chapters 1 and 5, consecutive U.K. governments had retained control of the key Arabian Sea port city of Aden since 1839 and, together with the Saudi, Israeli, and Jordanian governments, Whitehall had supported the Shia monarchist forces against the Egyptian-backed, Soviet-armed nationalists in North Yemen's Civil War between 1962 and 1967.[17] As mentioned, the Saudi regime subsequently switched its support to the nationalists after they took power and installed a military regime following the defeat of Nasser's armies, and a Moscow-backed communist clique seized power in South Yemen's capital, Aden, several years after Britain's withdrawal.[18]

As the global Cold War heated up throughout the late 1970s and well into the 1980s, culminating in the Soviet Politburo's reluctantly but brutally executed invasion and occupation of Afghanistan, the respective U.K. and U.S.

administrations of Prime Minister Thatcher and President Reagan cautiously observed developments in South Arabia. While their concerns may appear obsessively and, perhaps, irrationally fearful of South Yemen's Soviet, Cuban, and East German backers in hindsight, scholars must bear in mind the *zeitgeist* of the era in which Reagan, Thatcher, and their respective congressional and parliamentary allies lived and worked to defend Western security interests while averting a nuclear war.[19] The Kremlin's Brezhnev doctrine had militarily strengthened the Soviet Union's global strategic position by assisting in the rise of communist regimes across Asia, Africa, and Latin America, and Moscow's stationing of Warsaw Pact troops in Aden did little to calm their fears that the Eastern Bloc could threaten North Yemen, Saudi Arabia, and Oman, particularly after executing Operation *Storm-333*, the December 1979 Soviet invasion of Afghanistan.[20]

On 1 May 1985, Michael Armacost, the U.S. Under Secretary of State for Political Affairs, delivered a lecture on the Reagan administration's national defense policies at the United States Air Force Academy near Colorado Springs, Colorado. Addressing General Secretary Gorbachev's recent rise to power and his temporary but bloody escalation of the 40th Army's Afghan campaign, Armacost pointed out that the Kremlin continued to maintain its, "brutal occupation of Afghanistan.... while bullying Pakistan" through the Soviet Air Force's frequent bombing raids across the Afghan-Pakistani border as the Soviet High Command persisted in its relentless interdiction strikes against the insurgents.[21] While emphasizing the continued Soviet occupation of Afghanistan and the Reagan White House's determination to maintain its support for the rebels while preventing a full-scale Soviet invasion of Pakistan or nuclear escalation, Armacost also called attention to South Yemen's contemporary position as yet another of Moscow's regional, "outposts of influence" that the Kremlin's Brezhnev doctrine had pulled into its orbit.[22]

CIA Director Bill Casey similarly emphasized his, Reagan's, and Armacost's perceptions of Yemen's importance to the global Cold War struggle and their efforts to combat Moscow's aggressive Brezhnev doctrine, to which Gorbachev's Kremlin would no longer adhere after a few years into his rule, in his public speeches. In an early example of the Reagan administration's concerns regarding this perceived threat from the Kremlin, Casey addressed the members of the U.K. Special Forces Club in London on 23 October 1981, long before Gorbachev assumed power, citing South Yemen, Libya, Cuba, and Syria as key locations from which Soviet forces could threaten and intimidate neighboring states due to their, "large stockpiles of heavy arms" in each respective country.[23] Several years later, in a 25 February 1986 address at New York City's Fordham University, Casey stated, "We recently witnessed a sudden and dramatic display of Gorbachev's application of the Brezhnev Doctrine in its South Yemen satrapy" after calling attention to the Kremlin's redoubling of its, "efforts to crush the valiant *mujahedeen* who have resisted communist aggression in Afghanistan for more than six years."[24] Pointing to South Yemen's recent bloody Civil War of January 1986, in which the YSP leadership had split into two rival factions, Casey emphasized Moscow's forceful rhetoric and threats against the North Yemeni and Ethiopian governments should they try to intervene, and its deployment of, "Soviet fliers, using MiG-21s given to the South Yemen government, to pound beleaguered [less pro-Moscow] government forces."[25]

As mentioned in Chapter 2, Prime Minister Thatcher directed Britain's MI-6 to begin arming the Afghan resistance fighters shortly after the 40th Army's airpower-backed troops and tanks surged across the Afghan frontier in the last days of December 1979.[26] A series of declassified archival documents from Whitehall's Foreign and Commonwealth Office authored between 1979 and 1982 reveal that Thatcher and her Cabinet aides, such as Secretary of State for Foreign and Commonwealth Affairs Lord Peter Carrington, the diplomat Sir Christopher Mallaby, and U.K. Ambassador in Moscow Sir Curtis Keeble, assessed the Politburo's reluctant but, from their perspective, alarmingly sudden and brazen decision to invade Afghanistan as a potential threat to Western interests on the Arabian Peninsula and elsewhere. In a 3:00 p.m. conversation with Soviet Ambassador Nikolai Lunkov at Number 10 Downing Street on the afternoon of 3 January 1980, Thatcher expressed her concern over the presence of, "[Soviet] proxies and surrogates elsewhere e.g. the East Germans in South Yemen and the Cubans in Angola and Ethiopia" while voicing Britain's opposition to the 40th Army's seemingly sudden and aggressive Afghan incursion.[27]

After returning to Britain from talks with his counterparts in Saudi Arabia, Oman, Pakistan, India, and Turkey on 19 January 1980, Lord Carrington advised Prime Minister Thatcher that, "We [Britain] should increase Western and Saudi/Omani influence in the YAR [Yemen Arab Republic/North Yemen]" to help safeguard President Saleh's military regime in Sanaa from covert subversion or overt aggression from Aden's Marxists.[28] A week later, Thatcher informed U.S. President Carter in a letter to the White House that, "We shall do what we can to increase Western influence in the Yemen Arab Republic, and encourage the Saudis and Omanis to be more active there as well: the threat of Soviet subversion leading to an amalgamation of the two Yemens cannot be ignored, and this would represent a further major gain by the Russians" following Carrington's announcement of Whitehall's plans in a 24 January House of Lords debate.[29] Officials from Britain's East European and Soviet Department subsequently expressed their alarm in a 31 January memorandum that, "From their established base in South Yemen they [the Soviet leaders] already are making efforts in the Yemen Arab Republic."[30]

On the following day, Sir Mallaby reflected on a meeting with U.K. diplomat Sir Ewen Fergusson from two days prior in which the two Whitehall officials concluded that while London must firmly demonstrate its commitment to defending Saudi, North Yemeni, and Omani national sovereignty, it could not afford to preemptively act to undermine the perceived threat from Moscow's puppet regime in Aden. Reiterating their findings that, "There was little use in backing insurgency in the PDRY [People's Democratic Republic of Yemen/ South Yemen]," Mallaby and Fergusson appear to have wisely advised that London's regional involvement remain minimal and thereby allow the Soviets to discover, to their detriment, the potential consequences of their colonial overreach in South Arabia's fiercely independent, devout, and largely tribal lands, concluding that, "This was a country of venal, untrustworthy intriguers and attempting to influence them was a lottery. The Russians might find this too."[31] In a meeting with Prime Minister Thatcher at 10 Downing Street on 25 February 1980, West German Chancellor Helmut Schmidt likewise voiced his concern that the Kremlin perceived Western weakness and timidity in resisting its global advances, assessing the Carter administration's response to *Storm-333* as tepid. Stating that, "The object now was to get the Russians out of Afghanistan and prevent them trying the same thing again," Chancellor Schmidt dismissed Carter's boycott of the 1980 Olympic games in Moscow as an ineffective, "pinprick," arguing that, "What was necessary was to make it clear beyond doubt that if the Russians were, for instance, to move against the Yemen Arab Republic, something serious would happen."[32]

Before continuing with this Afterword's focus on U.S.-U.K. perceptions of bin Laden's key tactical and financial support for Yemen's anti-communist guerrillas in 1994, a brief elaboration on some of the reasons for which bin Laden and his small but growing al-Qaeda unit did not appear threatening to Western leaders during the 1980s may be appropriate and helpful. At the time of President Reagan's 11 February 1985 speech commending Saudi King Fahd on Riyadh's support for the Afghan insurgents and refugees, a speech in which the 40th U.S. president, as pointed out by Steve Coll, appears to have implied his awareness and appreciation of bin Laden's ongoing humanitarian aid work along the embattled Afghan frontier, neither bin Laden nor his mujahid compatriots had yet attacked U.S. or U.K. interests.[33] Nor did bin Laden and his largely inexperienced Arab guerrilla unit pose an immediate threat to Western security interests as they faced Soviet troops, tanks, armored cars, and planes in battle during the 1987 Jaji engagements and the subsequent skirmishes that tactically trained them and transformed them into seasoned guerrilla fighters.[34] Despite displaying an intense and militant anti-Western outlook at the time, including expressing documented threats or hostility against U.S. and U.K. journalists such as Edward Girardet and John Simpson, bin Laden wisely and skillfully persuaded his Salafist comrades to focus on the Soviets' perceived greater threat to Muslims while obtaining the combat experience to train new recruits and assist them in later guerrilla campaigns.[35]

While doing so, bin Laden consistently lectured his sons and closest jihadi comrades on the need for Muslims to prepare for a guerrilla war against the Western invasion of Saudi Arabia that he consistently forecasted on the horizon as he expressed his growing resentment of the U.S. government and its Anglo-French allies for their perceived exploitation of, "Muslim energy resources" on the Arabian Peninsula at the expense of the devout Saudi people, both *Adnani* Arabs and those sharing his *Qahtani* or South Arabian origins.[36] According to his son Omar, Osama conditioned himself physically and psychologically to go without water for days, a factor that may have contributed to his low blood pressure that served as his only major physical ailment other than occasional larynx trouble from inhaling Soviet napalm at Jaji, as he led his sons and closest guerrilla comrades on arduous desert hikes and lectured them on the need to prepare for a defensive holy war against a future Western occupation of the Arabian Peninsula.[37] Yet as emphasized by Omar bin Laden and Nasser al-Bahri in their memoirs and by bin Laden biographer Michael Scheuer, Osama also appears to have sought to avoid such conflicts, if possible, and advised his men to focus on fighting the Soviet occupation forces and their Afghan Army clients in the 1980s while expressing his hope that dialogue could prevent unnecessary future conflicts, even against Western infidels.[38]

Displaying neither the fanatical democracy-hatred, anti-Semitism, and national socialism of takfiris such as Abu Musab al-Zarqawi and the secular Arab politicians and Palestinian terrorists nor an agreement with Shia Iran's Ayatollah Khomeini and the Egyptian Wahhabi Said Qutb's irrational calls for an offensive jihad against Western values and beliefs, bin Laden rather rejected such views and called for a closely focused adherence to traditional Salafism's Koranic-based defensive war approach to resisting Islam's perceived foes.[39] Combating Soviet attempts to sow disinformation and disunity within the mujahid ranks and working to forge the solidarity advised by Ibn Khaldun, bin Laden is said to have rejected and forbidden criticism of the Saudi royals at his Arab guerrilla base. In 1986 after King Fahd accepted a British medal resembling a Christian cross, bin Laden reportedly commanded his men in his persuasive, poetic Arabic, "For God's sake, don't discuss this subject. Concentrate on your mission. I don't permit anyone to discuss this issue here," despite his discomfort at the al-Sauds' employment of French Special Forces to help crush al-Utaybi's failed November 1979 uprising at Mecca's Grand Mosque.[40] Bin Laden also reportedly expressed his hope that dialogue could prevail and prevent further fighting between Yemen's rival factions, despite his resentment of the YSP's record of oppressing Yemen's Muslims, before opening his South Arabian guerrilla war, and the al-Qaeda leader is also said to have expressly forbidden and prevented attacks on Jewish civilians in Yemen and Israel during the 1990s, emphasizing the key differences between peaceful innocents and Zionist militants that he regarded as implacably Islamophobic.[41]

Bin Laden and his lightly trained Arab guerrilla band, in short, neither attacked nor declared war on the Western powers during the Soviet-Afghan War, and while they appear to have militantly resented the U.S.-U.K. governments at the time, they nevertheless focused on their holy warrior mission to resist the Soviet enemy while acquiring rich, tactical fighting experience in the process. In doing so, they did not pose a threat to Western security interests at that time, and, even had they been somewhat aware of bin Laden's actions and his battlefield exploits from the spring of 1987 forward, Reagan, Thatcher, and their respective heads of the CIA and MI-6 naturally and logically concluded that Soviet forces and their clients remained the far greater threat to Washington and London's own clients on the Arabian Peninsula and in the wider region.[42] During the years following the Soviet invasion of Afghanistan, Saudi, North Yemeni, and Omani officials likewise expressed growing concern and unease over the presence of a hostile government backed by Eastern Bloc troops in Aden, and Thatcher's diplomats continued to express Britain's support for the regimes that the West deemed crucial to regional stability on the Arabian Peninsula.[43]

In his biography *Osama bin Laden*, Michael Scheuer, the Dean of what may be called "Bin Laden Studies," states that bin Laden worked to lure the United States and its European allies into Afghanistan by executing terror attacks on U.S. interests following his 1996 and 1998 declarations of war.[44] As Scheuer convincingly explains, the exiled al-Qaeda chief sought to drag U.S. and U.K. forces onto Afghanistan's topographically challenging combination of mountainous and desert battlefields on which the Afghan and Arab fighters had doggedly resisted, outlasted, and gradually worn down the Soviet 40th Army's conventional armor, airpower, and Special Forces assaults via attritional guerrilla warfare.[45] Bin Laden appears to have begun mastering this tactical approach during the guerrilla war against the Soviet troops as he labored alongside his men at Jaji to build his Lion's Den mountaintop base and fortified the nearby hills onto which he hoped and prayed that the occupiers could be lured and confronted in a major battle to help the Arab fighters effectively acquire combat experience.[46]

Bin Laden is said to have explained his contemporary reasoning in conversations with his late brother-in-law, Muhammad Jamal Khalifa, Azzam and his son-in-law Abdullah Anas, and others that tried unsuccessfully to dissuade him from risking his life and limbs alongside the guerrillas during the fierce, heavy snowstorms and ice storms that frequently swept over his Arab guerrilla base on Jaji's steep mountain heights between the fall of 1986 and the spring of 1987.⁴⁷ Patiently and repeatedly explaining that "We [the Arab mujahedin] came to be in the front," bin Laden remained undeterred in the face of the criticism and doubts expressed by Khalifa, Azzam, Anas, Sayyaf, and others voicing uncertainty over his decision to form an Arab guerrilla unit, and his persistence paid off as the Soviet planes, troops, and armored forces were lured that spring onto the fortified mountains and hills on which the young Saudi zealot and his men had long prepared to fight them.⁴⁸ Bin Laden subsequently applied this tactical approach once more as he and his senior lieutenants carefully recruited and prepared al-Qaeda's vanguard resistance fighters in Yemen to tactically spearhead the guerrilla campaign against the YSP that the al-Qaeda leader reportedly sought to avoid, if possible, but for which he effectively planned as he forecasted another civil war in his South Arabian ancestral land, the seventh since 1962 at that time, on the horizon. Like a South Arabian black leopard stealthily stalking its prey, bin Laden calculatingly prepared key tactical fighting positions in Yemen's topographically mountainous areas near the cities of Marib, Sadaa, and Waulia in the north, and in Abyan and Shabwah Provinces in the south onto which his guerrilla comrades lured al-Bid's troops, allowing al-Qaeda fighters to viciously ambush and maul the enemy's forces as he helped organize and train new recruits at the guerrilla bases that he and his Yemeni Salafist compatriots established between 1990 and 1994.⁴⁹

Bin Laden appears to have effectively applied the judo skills that he reportedly acquired while earning a blackbelt as he patiently prepared for the day on which he could finally face the Soviet troops in battle with permission from his Afghan hosts, not only as he fought the occupiers in hand-to-hand combat at Jaji in 1987, but on the international stage and in his tactical and strategic planning as well.⁵⁰ Judo is a martial art in which practitioners learn to turn an attacking opponent's momentum against the aggressor and channel it to the advantage of the defender. The judo psychology that bin Laden appears to have absorbed while training alongside Saudi Arabia's national judo team between 1980 and 1984, as discussed in Chapter 2, seems to have helpfully supplemented his subsequent tactical approach as he and his mostly inexperienced Arab guerrilla comrades received their battle baptism at the hands of the Soviet troops.⁵¹

To be sure, bin Laden does not appear to have applied his judo training in the literal sense of fighting the more powerful enemy forces on even terrain as is traditionally done in martial arts tournaments. Bin Laden's training potentially aided him, however, in recognizing the value of fortifying key mountaintop sites from which the Arab fighters could lure the Soviets, as they first attempted by executing the Operation *17 Shaban* and *17 Ramadan* guerrilla raids on 16 April and 15 May 1987 respectively, into fighting on somewhat disadvantageous terrain, a classic guerrilla tactic.[52] Bin Laden's absorption of judo's approach to self-defense by blunting an attacking opponent's momentum appears, therefore, to have somewhat helped him and his lieutenants in obtaining a practical understanding of the classic guerrilla tactic of maneuvering an otherwise stronger enemy, to the extent possible, into a less advantageous position. By selecting a mountaintop location on which to build his Arab guerrilla base at Jaji, bin Laden displayed not only the risk-taking character traits that he had earlier demonstrated as a wounded-in-action guerrilla engineer risking life and limb digging trenches during heavy bombing raids by Soviet jet planes and helicopter gunships, but an ability to skillfully apply the guerrilla tactics that he gradually mastered in luring the enemy onto rugged terrain that he had selected and prepared for battle.[53]

After baffling the Soviets by resisting them doggedly and unexpectedly from their fortified, tactical fighting positions at the Jaji engagements from the spring of 1987 forward, bin Laden and his fellow South Arabian guerrilla comrades again applied this tactic as they lured the YSP's conventional, Warsaw Pact-armed forces onto mountainous terrain dominated by Yemen's rural, religious warrior tribes, many of which had contributed numerous jihadi recruits during the Soviet-Afghan War and eagerly and voluntarily sought to apply their battle-seasoned combat skills against al-Bid's infidel communist army.[54] Far from being one his alleged, "flops" described by Bergen, bin Laden's tactical approach to and involvement in the Yemeni Civil War of 1994 appears to have been, for him and al-Qaeda, a spectacular success story that continues benefitting the international Salafi jihadi movement as al-Qaeda remains active and entrenched in Yemen and appears to continue enjoying a significant degree of tribal and religious support.[55] Neither bin Laden nor his Yemeni guerrilla comrades rushed to install an Islamist regime and hoist *al-Raya*, al-Qaeda's black banner, over Sanaa after attaining their immediate objective in ousting the Riyadh and Pyongyang-backed YSP forces. Rather, further attesting to bin Laden's wartime reputation as a skilled, effective leader and rational actor, they carefully and patiently played the long-term strategic game in Yemen by further strengthening al-Qaeda's already potent and entrenched presence among the South Arabian country's devout, fiercely independent tribesmen and their chieftains.[56]

As many contemporary newspaper reports and numerous other sources emphasize, the primary belligerents involved in the 1994 fighting in Yemen were President Saleh and Vice President al-Bid's respective conventional armies. To be sure, as discussed in much of the previous scholarship on Yemen's brief but bloody 1994 Civil War, Saleh's tribal allies and bin Laden and al-Fadhli's Salafi jihadi fighters played a smaller role in comparison to the northern conventional armies whose actions and surprising victories dominated most contemporary reporting and later works on the conflict alike.[57] Yet bin Laden, al-Fadhli, al-Zindani, and their local tribal supporters played a key supporting role, and, while the part that they played in Saleh's overall military campaign against the YSP may appear minor, their key tactical contribution to the northern forces' victories in numerous local engagements appears to have been significant.[58]

As emphasized by scholars such as Michael Scheuer and Gregory Johnsen, bin Laden and his fellow anti-Soviet guerrilla veteran al-Fadhli played a key part in applying their battle-seasoned guerrilla tactics in steadily wearing down the YSP well before the 1994 Civil War's official outbreak on 4 May that year.[59] As Scheuer and Peter Bergen have stated, bin Laden, clandestinely via his supporters in Saudi Arabia, remained capable of recruiting fighters and raising funds for al-Qaeda's insurgency support operations even after the Saudi government revoked his citizenship, froze his assets in the Kingdom, and pressured his family to publicly denounce him and his activities in April 1994.[60] Bin Laden's holy warrior mission in Yemen between 1990 and 1994, on which he reportedly embarked only after being urged by al-Fadhli, al-Zindani, and others to help them fight the YSP according to his former bodyguard Nasser al-Bahri, seems to have played a part in gradually weakening al-Bid's forces by the time that the two major fighting forces, the Nationalist and Socialist armies, finally clashed.[61]

After being initially reluctant to fully open a guerrilla war in his parents' South Arabian homeland, bin Laden appears to have spared no effort in channeling his and al-Qaeda's battle-seasoned insurgency combat skills and guerrilla tactics as his battlefield comrades such as al-Fadhli rallied and led their fighters in support of Saleh's war effort.[62] The jihadi fighters trained by many of bin Laden's fellow anti-Soviet guerrilla brethren at the training camps in Yemen's rural mountains began operations against the YSP even as Saleh and al-Bid briefly feigned unity, steadily bleeding the enemy to death as they had learned during the Soviet-Afghan War. Bin Laden appears to have kept on his mind the lessons of the Afghan battlefields as he reportedly worked to ensure an effective logistical supply network for Yemen's Salafi guerrillas via his continued financing of the training camps on South Arabia's mountain heights.[63] As described in Chapters 2 and 3, bin Laden developed a passion for guerrilla logistical operations early on during the Soviet-Afghan War and remained consistent in purchasing 4x4 Toyota pickups for his Arab guerrilla band and the Afghan Islamists until the end of the war.[64]

As theorized by the scholars Andrew Mitzcavitch and Don D. Chipman, bin Laden's thinking appears to reflect Mao Zedong's in his emphasis on establishing key guerrilla bases before attacking to maintain a steady logistical flow of supplies to the fighters in the field.[65] Citing Mao's theory, Mitzcavitch and Chipman each explain that this can enable otherwise disadvantaged resistance fighters such as bin Laden and his Arab guerrilla band at Jaji to remain on the offensive in small but numerous tactical attacks that gradually wear down and bleed-to-death a more powerful enemy.[66] By steadily recruiting and preparing al-Qaeda's fighters in Yemen at the guerrilla training camps that he and al-Fadhli established between 1990 and 1994, bin Laden appears to have applied the lessons that he learned as a practicality while fighting the Soviets at Jaji. Bin Laden's careful preparation for the anti-YSP jihad appears to have subsequently helped Yemen's Salafi fighters to continue prosecuting their guerrilla ambushes and raids on al-Bid's military convoys by ensuring that the militants had key base areas on which they could rely for training, regrouping, and refitting.[67]

On 10 September 1991, militants killed Managing Director of Rural Development Husayn al-Huraybi and wounded Professor Omar al-Jawi in a, "shooting incident" in Sanaa that Saleh's General People's Congress (GPC) and al-Bid's YSP jointly condemned as an effort to, "stir up political strife."[68] In a 17 March 1992 attack, jihadi assassins killed YSP politician Muhammad Loutf Massoud, while officials blamed bin Laden's ally al-Zindani and his *al-Islah* Party for inciting violent clashes between rival northern and southern football team supporters in Sanaa and Aden as rioting struck both cities on 22 and 23 March.[69] On 28 March, police in Djibouti intercepted and confiscated a shipment of 7,000 pistols on discovering the contents of the Yemen-bound vessel as bin Laden continued supplying al-Fadhli's guerrilla fighters and assassins from his base in neighboring Sudan.[70] Two days later, assassins killed YSP official Muslah al-Shahwani in Sanaa, and in April, the Salafist militants also shot and injured YSP Justice Minister Abd al-Wasia Ahmed Sallam and detonated a bomb at the home of deputy YSP leader Salim Saleh Muhammad.[71]

Similar incidents continued throughout the year and into 1993 and 1994 as bin Laden and al-Fadhli's men targeted and assassinated leading YSP politicians such as Politburo members Dr. Yasin Said Nu'man and Ali Saleh Abbad Muqbil, and military leaders such as Colonels Haytham Ali Muhsin and Abd al-Qawi Saleh al-Qahm.[72] The jihadis also bombed the U.S. and U.K. embassies, but reportedly inflicted little damage on them, on 23 September 1992 and 10 March 1993, respectively. On 29 December 1992, "Culprits believed to be Afghan-trained Muslim militants" inadvertently killed an Australian tourist and a hotel employee in a failed terror attack on U.S. Marines staying at Aden's Movenpick Hotel in al-Qaeda's second attempt to strike U.S. interests.[73]

Bin Laden, al-Fadhli, al-Zindani, and their local jihadi brethren and tribal allies continued ruthlessly pressing their attacks well into 1994 as their fighters killed two YSP majors and three of their soldiers in Yemen's southern Lahej Province on 4 January. The jihadi fighters followed this successful operation by assassinating YSP leader Abd al-Karim Saleh al-Gahmi on 7 January 1994, killing seven other YSP officials in a vicious firefight in Ibb on 3 March, stabbing YSP politician Haydar Abdullah Ghalib near Sanaa University on 25 March, and shooting YSP official Ahmad Khalid Sayf in the Taez Governorate's Najdah region on 4 April.[74]

On 18 January 1994, Yemen's Political Forces Dialogue Committee, the rapidly faltering front organization of the coalition government that included representatives from Saleh's Nationalist Party, al-Bid's YSP, and Shaykhs al-Zindani and al-Daylami's *al-Islah*, published "The Document of Pledge and Accord" in the English-language Yemeni newspaper, *Yemen Times*.[75] A sham attempt at unity on the part of the rival governing factions even as bin Laden continued inciting and financing his guerrilla comrades' local-level war of resistance and assassination campaign targeting YSP officials and relations further soured between Saleh and al-Bid, the document purported to demonstrate cooperation within the government against, "the Persons Accused of Disturbing the Security of the Nation," while mentioning neither bin Laden nor his senior lieutenants by name.[76] Rather than directly accusing the al-Qaeda chief and his mujahid comrades such as al-Fadhli, Obadah al-Wadihi, Jamal al-Hadhi, and Abu Ali al-Harithi of subversive activity, the Dialogue Committee threatened harsh penalties for, "persons involved in terrorism or sabotage."[77] The document further pledged that the ruling coalition intended to follow and implement all the *Shariah* laws in Yemen as a sop to al-Zindani and *al-Islah* while punishing those that audaciously escaped the YSP's torture chambers, statements that bin Laden subsequently and sarcastically denounced as he emphasized the communists' history of suppressing religious dissent and helped to facilitate al-Hadhi and al-Harithi's escape to Sudan before later dispatching them back to Yemen to fight al-Bid's forces.[78]

In a 7 April 1994 report for the U.K. newspaper *The Guardian*, Brian Whitaker called British readers' attention to the depth to which the increasingly tense relations between Yemen's rival factions had sunk as Saleh and al-Bid publicly refused to meet and bin Laden's ongoing financing of guerrilla bases and his rhetorical incitement of Yemeni jihadis to fight the YSP ensured continued resistance against and assassinations of Socialist officials in the countryside.[79] Calling attention to the government's perceived ineptness at implementing effective unity even after issuing the Document of Pledge and Accord in January and the, "countless tribal militias" that included many jihadi veterans of the Soviet-Afghan War, Whitaker emphasized the role of Saudi Arabia, the United

States, and Britain in the ongoing diplomatic attempts to preserve the Republic of Yemen's collapsing unity.[80] Questioning whether U.S. officials and, by extension, their U.K. and Saudi counterparts, genuinely preferred the South Arabian country to remain united, Whitaker emphasized the level of Washington, D.C.'s perceived intervention in the matter due to its regional oil interests, a point that bin Laden repeatedly raised in the letters he authored at roughly the same time, quoting local Yemenis with whom he spoke as saying, perhaps sarcastically, perhaps sacrilegiously, "*'Ma sha Clinton.'* Not God's will, but Clinton's."[81]

As the Republic of Yemen's governmental unity continued to crumble with the ruling factions edging closer to civil war and bin Laden and al-Fadhli's guerrilla fighters and assassins stalking al-Bid's deputies in both the countryside and urban centers, reportedly assassinating more than 150 YSP officials between 1990 and 1994, U.K. parliamentarians accordingly observed developments in the South Arabian nation with caution. In an 18 April 1994 debate on the floor of Britain's House of Lords, Lord Michael Brougham and Vaux, inquiring about London's official stance on the developing and increasingly volatile situation in South Arabia, asked Minister of State, Foreign and Commonwealth Office Baroness Lynda Chalker of Wallasey, "What is the current situation in Yemen?"[82] Replying that, "We fully support all the people of Yemen in their efforts to overcome the political crisis current[ly], facing the country," Baroness Chalker suggested that Whitehall's primary interest lay in the Republic of Yemen's stability regardless of the tensions flaring between the government's rival factions, emphasizing that, "We urge all parties to engage in dialogue and to work together for a peaceful and stable future for the people of Yemen."[83]

Yemen's already fragile internal stability tottered further towards total collapse in late April as bin Laden's Salafist guerrilla brethren, trained at the bases that he had helped establish in the South Arabian country's northern and southern mountains, continued ruthlessly executing their tactical ambushes and raids on the YSP's military convoys. They also their continued assassinating YSP officials even as Saleh briefly placed al-Fadhli under house arrest in Sanaa in a sham attempt at maintaining unity with al-Bid's Socialists.[84] By the time of the Civil War's official outbreak on 4 May 1994 that followed the intensified fighting that erupted on the 1993 parliamentary election's anniversary on 27 April, al-Bid complained that, "more than 150" YSP politicians had fallen to assassins, "in the last four years" according to a 6 May 1994 newspaper report by Ian Black and Brian Whitaker for *The Guardian* and an 8 July 1994 article by Robert Hurd and Greg Noakes in *Washington Report on Middle East Affairs*.[85] Al-Bid's complaint that he voiced even as he refused to return to Sanaa from Aden and after having already angered Saleh by refusing to recognize the parliamentary election results and meeting with U.S. Vice President Gore without permission, appears to attest to bin Laden's successful recruitment and incitement of Yemen's holy warriors to resist the YSP and his manipulation of the situation to al-Qaeda's advantage.[86] From his guerrilla war room across the Red Sea in the al-Riyadh district of the Sudanese capital, Khartoum, bin Laden, true to his al-Qaeda pseudonym "the Director," skillfully manipulated his portrait of al-Bid's YSP as Islam's foe that Yemen's faithful Muslims must resist, a skill that he had effectively mastered while fighting the Soviet occupation forces and their PDPA clients. Bin Laden's propaganda and incitement campaign further exacerbated and inflamed the inter-regime tensions, even after his anti-Soviet guerrilla comrades in al-Zindani and al-Daylami's *al-Islah* Party had already frustrated the Socialists by winning a much larger number of parliamentary seats in an election that most contemporary international observers reportedly certified as the Arab world's most free and fair.[87]

As the sporadic, intense fighting already afflicting much of Yemen officially exploded into Civil War in early May 1994, al-Bid, like Brezhnev and most Soviet officials regarding their invasion of Afghanistan, is said to have vainly and overconfidently expected to win a quick and relatively bloodless victory due to the larger size and Warsaw Pact-supplied military arsenal that his Socialist Army and Air Force boasted.[88] Yet the YSP vice president appears to have vastly underestimated the resentment that his party had incurred among Yemen's devout and defiant tribal majority due to its perceived record of brutally suppressing Islam and killing devout Yemeni clergymen in the few parts of the country over which it wielded actual control. Consequently, he also seems to have underestimated the key psychological and tactical impact of bin Laden's local guerrilla war and assassination campaign across territories that the YSP claimed as its own between 1990 and 1994. The al-Qaeda leader's key financial, organizational, and recruitment efforts helped to train and prepare Yemen's Salafi fighters to gradually wear down the large, Saudi and North Korean-supplied Socialist armies and slay some of their commanders.[89]

As the fighting between the northern and southern armies began on 4 May and Saleh released al-Fadhli to rally his tribal supporters in Abyan, al-Bid, reportedly emboldened by al-Fadhli's brother-in-law General Ali Muhsin's temporary abandonment of Sanaa to attack YSP troops in Dhamar, pulverized the northern capital with his Eastern Bloc-issued jet aircraft followed by a Scud missile bombardment. Yet al-Bid's forces quickly suffered a series of resounding rebuffs after fierce fighting at Dhamar, Amran, and Sadaa, the last of the three hosting one of several important mountaintop tactical vantage points on which bin Laden and his anti-Soviet comrades had earlier established key guerrilla bases that continued producing trained jihadi fighters to doggedly resist and repulse the YSP.[90] According to Black and Whitaker, Saleh's forces under Muhsin's command, "routed and dispersed" al-Bid's 3rd Armored Brigade at

Amran within a matter of days.[91] Simultaneously, the Nationalist president's Republican Guard, an elite northern unit trained by Saddam Hussein's Iraqi regime, "wiped out" the southern forces at Dhamar in a well-coordinated assault by artillery and rocket fire supported by tanks.[92]

An 8 May 1994 newspaper report by Nora Boustany on the pages of *The Washington Post* discussed the surprisingly rapid advance of Saleh's northern forces as citizens of Western countries and other foreign nationals scrambled to flee the war-ravaged South Arabian country. In her article, Boustany emphasized the divisions caused by the tensions in Sanaa's 301-member Parliament that led to the war, assigning blame to both sides and conveying a sense of shock at Saleh's northern armies' seemingly rapid rout of the YSP's initial offensives that appears to have been boosted by the key assistance of Saleh's, "tribal and conservative [Sunni Salafist] allies."[93] As bin Laden's staunch jihadi allies in Yemen such as al-Fadhli, al-Wadihi, and al-Harithi applied the deadly skills that they had honed on the battlefields at Jaji, Jalalabad, and the smaller, intervening engagements that they fought against the Soviet troops and Afghan Army, Saleh's conventional forces, the main fighting force in the war against the YSP, continued to benefit.[94]

Saleh proceeded to confidently call on the, "secessionist leadership" in Aden to lay down its arms, stating, "Remember that the blood that you are spilling is Yemeni blood and surrender will spare the lives of the remaining (southern) units of the armed forces."[95] Boustany's report, like others, suggests that while Saleh's "conservative allies" continued to play a lesser military role than his conventional northern armies overall, they nevertheless contributed to the fighting in numerous local engagements that gradually added up to help wear down the larger enemy, just as bin Laden had earlier argued that the Arab fighters could do if properly trained as he led his men into battle at Jaji.[96] Bin Laden had earlier deferred to the more militarily experienced Abu Hafs and Abu Ubaydah in executing the guerrilla ambushes that helped the Arab fighters outflank the large Soviet force at Jaji, and he helped al-Fadhli's men by sending several more experienced fighters and commanders such as al-Harithi and Jamal al-Hadhi back to Yemen.[97]

As the Arab fighters had learned to do under lethal Soviet fire and bombing at Jaji in the spring of 1987 and in the smaller engagements that followed, these men helped to lead a series of successful diversionary operations and guerrilla raids on the enemy while Saleh's conventional armies surged onward to Aden in May and June of 1994. Al-Fadhli's tribal brethren in the mountains of Abyan and Shabwah simultaneously struck the YSP troops from the rear, further distracting and dividing al-Bid's forces and inciting mutinies in their ranks.[98] Bin Laden and his senior lieutenants learned to adapt to training and fighting in the rugged, mountainous terrain in eastern Afghanistan on which they built the Lion's Den and other guerrilla bases from which to resist the Soviets. While resisting the Soviet *Spetsnaz* forces and an armored assault at Jaji in late May 1987, bin Laden and a handful of men had engaged the enemy in diversionary attacks that distracted them with sniper fire, allowing his Egyptian lieutenants Abu Ubaydah and Abu Hafs to lead the Arab guerrilla unit's main body of fighters around the opposite side of the mountain on which they were fighting to outflank the enemy on several occasions.[99] In preparing to resist the YSP's armies, bin Laden's anti-Soviet comrades al-Fadhli, al-Wadihi, al-Hadhi, and al-Harithi again applied this tactical approach as they established several key guerrilla bases in Yemen's northern and southern mountains. The jihadi fighters led by al-Fadhli and bin Laden's fellow Jaji veteran al-Wadihi reportedly swept the enemy from the northern mountains around Sadaa, Waulia, and Marib in series of engagements that erupted on the 1994 Civil War's official outbreak on 4 May, helping to pave the way for the advance of Saleh's conventional forces.[100]

Simultaneously, al-Fadhli, after being released immediately by Saleh from his sham house arrest in Sanaa as mentioned in Chapter 5, applied the battle-honed combat and command skills that he had earned while fighting in bin Laden's Arab guerrilla unit at Jalalabad in the spring of 1989.[101] Rallying his tribal supporters in executing a series of diversionary raids on al-Bid's forces that they executed from the jihadis' guerrilla bases in his native Abyan Province, al-Fadhli struck and mauled the enemy from the south and east, tying down some of their forces while Saleh's conventional northern armies advanced. As General Muhsin's troops swept down from their Nationalist army bases in the north in a rapid advance towards Aden, their flanks remained largely secure as the jihadi fighters under al-Wadihi and al-Hadhi fought the enemy elsewhere.[102] Bin Laden simultaneously dispatched his fellow Jaji veteran al-Harithi back to Yemen from Sudan, and the wounded-in-action guerrilla led a separate group of jihadi fighters in helping Muhsin's main force and al-Fadhli's tribesmen to isolate Aden in mid-June 1994, while reportedly walking with a pair of makeshift crutches and urging his men forward as described by Gregory Johnsen.[103]

In a 16 May 1994 news article for *The New York Times*, Chris Hedges emphasized the confusion at the northern armies' surprise advance that reportedly afflicted al-Bid's stupefied generals as Saleh's troops fought their way towards Aden, advancing on the villages of Dhala and Marqula about 60 miles north of the YSP capital, as the Nationalist leadership in Sanaa accused its secessionist rivals of seeking, through UN resolutions, "to blackmail world opinion and waste [sic, stall for] time."[104] Hedges's newspaper report also indicated the tactical impact of bin Laden's al-Qaeda guerrilla cadres on the fighting in many local engagements, describing the YSP troops facing the determined, tenacious zealots as, "wary and demoralized."[105] YSP Lieutenant Hassan Muhammad Hassan cited, "intervention from Sudan, Iraq and Eritrea" while complaining to Hedges that, "They [Saleh's forces] have foreigners helping them with this advance. They attack with ferocity."[106] Yet most of the supposedly non-Yemeni warriors that bin Laden consistently deployed to the battlefields from across the Red Sea in Sudan and from the southern, fiercely independent rural parts of Saudi Arabia appear to have been, like the exiled al-Qaeda chief himself, Saudi guerrillas of Yemeni origin fighting with the same, "indifference to death" that the Russian General Staff had attributed to the Afghan Islamists and their small numbers of Arab jihadi allies in its postwar after-action report on the Soviet-Afghan War.[107]

As emphasized by Jamal al-Suwaidi and Gregory Johnsen in their respective works on Yemen's 1994 Civil War, bin Laden's staunch Salafist allies al-Zindani and al-Daylami continued issuing their calls for a defensive jihad and inciting Sunni Islamist resistance to the YSP as the war raged.[108] While these zealots cannot be said to have won the 1994 Civil War, their wartime support for Saleh's Nationalist Party forces helped to ensure that jihadi fighters continued attacking al-Bid's troops and ensuring resistance in their rear areas as several southern army units mutinied and joined the insurgents. Far from being the main factor in Saleh's victory over al-Bid, bin Laden's wartime actions and those of his guerrilla comrades during Yemen's 1994 Civil War nevertheless served Sanaa's war effort in a supporting role as he intended and helped entrench al-Qaeda deeper in its key South Arabian strongholds.[109]

In an 18 May 1994 newspaper article for *The Washington Post*, Nora Boustany quoted Nationalist General Muhammad Sanabani as declaring Aden's fall to his northern armies as being, "just a question of time."[110] The report proceeded to emphasize the advance of Saleh's northern armies on Anad air base located roughly 40 miles from Aden on the previous day, as well as the retreat of the, "gaunt, dazed and shell-shocked" southern forces that reportedly fled after briefly resisting a relentless artillery barrage from Sanabani's rapidly approaching troops.[111] Several days earlier, northern forces had quickly seized the town of Qarsh to Aden's northwest after pulverizing local YSP cadet conscripts with a ruthless artillery assault while al-Bid's, "gunboats and Soviet-made MiG fighters" briefly delayed another Nationalist armored offensive near the strategic Bab el-Mandeb strait between the Gulf of Aden and the Red Sea.[112]

In a second newspaper report for *The New York Times* on 29 May 1994, Chris Hedges again acknowledged the various combat roles of Sanaa's conventional forces and their tribal and jihadi allies and the impact that this appeared to have on the increasingly demoralized YSP troops. Emphasizing General Muhsin's ongoing conventional military advance on Aden and his armored brigades' hard-won and surprising victories that began at the war's outset,

Hedges insightfully elaborated that, "What Yemen entered, even before the south formally seceded, is a struggle not only between the regular armies of north and south, but among the tribes, militias, clans and families that rule patches of territory as if there were no federal government – as if the Middle Ages had never ended."[113] Through its emphasis on the sporadic fighting that gradually began in Yemen even before the 1994 Civil War's official start, Hedges's report alludes to bin Laden and al-Fadhli's support for their Yemeni jihadi brethren via their prewar financing and tactical guerrilla war training, an effort made possible by their experiences fighting the Soviets.[114] Hedges proceeded to call his readers' attention to the importance of Yemen's tribes, arguing that no central government could remain in power without genuine and staunch tribal support, a key point also raised by Marieke Brandt in her book *Tribes and Politics in Yemen: A History of the Houthi Conflict*.[115]

As the fighting raged across Yemen and the UN vainly continued to issue resolutions for a ceasefire even as the Saudi, Kuwaiti, and North Korean regimes continued arming al-Bid's YSP forces and bin Laden persistently rushed veteran al-Qaeda guerrilla commanders and fighters back to Yemen from his tactical command post across the Red Sea in Sudan, U.S. Assistant Secretary of State for Near Eastern Affairs Robert H. Pelletreau, Jr. delivered a congressional testimony on Washington D.C.'s official position to the U.S. House of Representatives.[116] Speaking at a hearing of the Subcommittee on Europe and the Middle East of the House of Representatives Committee on Foreign Affairs during the second session of the 103rd U.S. Congress on 14 June 1994, Pelletreau delivered his testimony to Chairman Lee H. Hamilton (D-IN), stating, "The current situation in the Republic of Yemen, Mr. Chairman, reminds us that even as the region inclines toward peace, the international community must remain vigilant to prevent, to the extent possible, local rivalries from flaring into violence."[117] Continuing, Pelletreau indicated the Clinton administration's support for the Saudi regime's diplomatic initiative, in effect backing Riyadh's support for the YSP from bin Laden's militant Salafist perspective, emphatically stating that, "The United States shares the special concerns of Yemen's neighbors over the adverse consequences of continued fighting for the stability of the Arabian Peninsula. We are opposed to the imposition of unity by force, just as we are opposed to an act of secession in the midst of war. That is why we support the passage of Security Council Resolution 924 with its clear call for an immediate cease-fire, a resumption of political dialogue, and a halt to the supply of arms to the parties from the outside."[118]

Congresswoman Jan Meyers (R-KS) then asked Pelletreau to clarify the Clinton White House's position on, "whether there should be one or two Yemens?," to which the Assistant Near Eastern Affairs Secretary replied that the United States had supported the 22 May 1990 unification agreement between

Sanaa and Aden and continued to urge, "political reconciliation and dialogue" between the rival factions.[119] Towards the conclusion of Pelletreau's congressional testimony before the House Subcommittee, Chairman Hamilton pointedly inquired, "Does the United States have any foreign policy interests in what happens in Yemen?"[120] In a further indication of Washington, D.C. and London's perceived desire for the protection of Western oil interests on the Arabian Peninsula, Pelletreau replied to the Indiana representative that, "We would not want to see Yemen become a source of instability in its region [South Arabia]."[121] After Hamilton further inquired as to whether, "the North has been the least interested in enforcing a cease-fire" Pelletreau informed the Indiana congressman that, "The longer it [Yemen's Civil War] goes on, the more it calls into question the bona fides and good intentions of the northern leadership," effectively condemning Sanaa's prosecution of the war as Saleh and his tribal and jihadi allies sought and fought to attain total, outright, and unquestioned military victory even as Riyadh, Kuwait City, and Pyongyang likewise fueled South Arabia's raging inferno by pouring in weapons to al-Bid's Socialist armies.[122]

On the day after Pelletreau's congressional testimony before the House of Representatives, Brian Whitaker noted in a 15 June 1994 report on the pages of *The Guardian* that military developments in Yemen had historically, "confounded many outside observers."[123] Observing that Saleh's forces continued to defy outsiders' expectations by sweeping onward to victory despite the assumptions of foreign commentators predicting their swift, inevitable collapse at the hands of al-Bid's vaunted military machine, Whitaker commented, insightfully, that, "Yemen has long been regarded as a graveyard for military ambitions."[124] Bin Laden's recruitment and incitement campaign continued to pay off as the fighting raged in mid-June 1994 and his Salafist guerrilla comrades ruthlessly executed their attritional war of resistance, ousting the YSP's forces entirely from the jihadis' tribal strongholds in the countryside and infiltrating the Socialists' embattled, struggling last bastions in the coastal Arabian Sea ports of Aden and Mukalla, the latter being the capital of bin Laden's ancestral Hadramut Province, even before Saleh's conventional armies besieged the two cities.[125] Under the command of bin Laden's faithful guerrilla comrades al-Fadhli, al-Harithi, al-Wadihi, and others, al-Qaeda fighters and propagandists appear to have successfully incited and supported armed resistance to al-Bid's swiftly collapsing authority in Aden itself, prompting Whitaker to note in his 15 June newspaper article that, "there are reports of unrest [in the city] caused by Islamic militants."[126]

As Saleh's northern armies surged forward towards Aden with the key help of al-Fadhli's tribal allies and bin Laden's seasoned, veteran al-Qaeda guerrilla cadres playing a key supporting role by channeling their Soviet-Afghan War battle experience to strike and maul al-Bid's forces in tactical ambushes and diversionary raids on their flanks and rear positions, U.K. lawmakers voiced their concerns in a 1 July 1994 debate on the floor of Britain's House of Commons.[127] During the debate, House of Commons MP Tony Worthington asked U.K. Secretary of State for Foreign and Commonwealth Affairs Douglas Hogg, "what international action is being taken to protect and care for civilian casualties of the Yemeni war in Aden?"[128] Somewhat mirroring Pelletreau's comments on the Clinton administration's approach to Yemen's raging Civil War during his congressional testimony, Secretary Hogg replied, "The Security Council of the United Nations adopted on 29 June a second resolution, No. 931, expressing its deep concern at the humanitarian situation and requesting the Secretary-General to urgently address the needs of those affected by the conflict, in particular the inhabitants of Aden. The International Committee of the Red Cross is active in Yemen, including Aden, and we have responded to its appeal for donations."[129]

Yet the implicit support that officials in London and Washington, D.C. appear to have voiced for Riyadh's diplomatic UN initiatives to implement and enforce a ceasefire in Yemen, even as the al-Sauds reportedly joined with the Kuwaiti royals and North Korea's rulers in shipping arms to the YSP's armies, failed to prevent bin Laden from executing his mujahid mission in support of Yemen's anti-communist guerrillas as the resistance fighters continued their advance alongside Saleh's forces after repulsing al-Bid's troops in numerous local, tactical engagements.[130] An Associated Press (AP) report for *The New York Times* on 8 July 1994 states that while al-Bid's retreating forces had accused Saleh's northern troops and their tribal and jihadi allies of committing, "massacres, killings and destruction" on entering Aden, the evidence on the ground indicated otherwise as, "there was no sign of slaughter, only looting by civilians" as the northern forces, "encountered no resistance in downtown Aden."[131] As they entered the former Socialist, secessionist capital on the previous day, Saleh's soldiers and their allies reportedly captured more than 3,000 YSP troops, 10 MiG-21 and MiG-29 jet aircraft, and six gunboats.[132] The AP report further states that, "Soldiers of the northern Amalqa Brigade – known for the Muslim fundamentalists among its ranks – stopped cars loaded with looted liquor…. They shot the bottles to pieces and sometimes set fire to the liquor."[133] This outcome, enabled in part by bin Laden's steady propaganda and recruitment efforts that had gradually helped weaken the YSP's hold on the city and opened it to infiltration by the jihadis, resulted in the decisive defeat of al-Bid's superior conventional military forces as the ousted Socialist leader fled to Oman as the insurgents advanced and many of his subordinates readily switched sides. One local citizen named Khaled Mahmoud reportedly exclaimed to the AP reporters, "Thank God! Everything is perfect. We are one nation."[134]

AUTHOR'S AFTERWORD TO THE SECOND EDITION

Three days after Aden's fall and Saleh's victory in the 1994 Civil War, an outcome enabled by bin Laden and his Yemeni mujahid compatriots such as al-Fadhli and al-Zindani, U.K. Prime Minister John Major briefly condemned Sanaa's prosecution of the war in defiance of UN Resolutions 924 and 931.[135] While attending the G7 summit in Naples, Italy on 10 July 1994, Prime Minister Major held a press conference on international affairs at which he stated, "In Yemen we have just seen a particularly brutal civil war, less publicly perhaps than other conflicts, but nonetheless a very serious conflict. What in practice has happened is that North Yemen has used force to suppress the south and a new humanitarian problem has been created within Yemen."[136] After criticizing Saleh's war effort and, by extension, his wartime tribal and mujahid allies, Major continued, "We propose to pay very close attention to developments there, we would like to see reconciliation, we would like to see dialogue, we do not wish to see repression within Yemen and we do wish to see Yemen living at peace with her neighbours, Saudi Arabia, Oman and other countries with whom we have a long and very deep relationship."[137]

Acting quickly to avert the Sunni Islamist takeover that he, al-Bid's Saudi, Kuwaiti, and North Korean backers, and the U.S.-U.K. leaders appear to have feared, Saleh reportedly forgave all but 16 members of the YSP's "untouchables" and invited them to return to their governmental posts in Sanaa's GPC.[138] As pointed out by Brian Whitaker in a 22 July 1994 newspaper report for *Middle East International*, Saleh's GPC also included, naturally, al-Zindani and al-Daylami's *al-Islah*, whose zealous fighters had, after all, been instrumental in securing the combined Nationalist-Salafist victory over the YSP, thereby guaranteeing that bin Laden's staunch allies remained influential members of Yemen's newly reunified government.[139] Satisfied that his and al-Qaeda's wartime actions had helped to ensure and strengthen the position of devout Salafist representatives in Sanaa's reunited parliament, bin Laden, reflecting his rational, pragmatic approach rather than the irrationality of a true fanatic, worked patiently and persistently to further solidify his guerrilla vanguard's local support networks in Yemen. As he had done since recruiting jihadi fighters for the Soviet-Afghan War and the 1994 Civil War via an effective combination of his personal modesty and his consistent rhetorical flattery of Yemen's devout tribal chieftains and their warriors, bin Laden cultivated a respectable *jah*, or reputation. This is a key tool for winning allies in Yemeni society as explained by Gregory Johnsen, and it helped bin Laden to command a strong, enduring following in his parents' South Arabian homeland.[140]

From bin Laden's Salafist perspective, as implied in the al-Qaeda chief's contemporary letters that he authored at his ARC office in Khartoum, faxed to the Saudi opposition office that he financed in London, and clandestinely distributed via his followers in Saudi Arabia, Prime Minister Major's comments, like those of his and President Bill Clinton's senior officials, served as further confirmation of the West's opposition to Muslims resisting their oppressors. In Yemen's case, bin Laden identified these oppressors as the atheistic YSP, and criticized the West's perceived interest in exploiting the Arabian Peninsula's oil wealth at the expense of its people.[141] Arguing that the American and Anglo-French governments were, through their support of the corrupt al-Saud dynasty, essentially plundering the profits from the Saudi Kingdom's oil wealth that rightfully belonged to the people of Saudi Arabia, half of them hailing from the country's staunchly Salafist tribes of ethnic Yemeni (*Qahtani*) origin, bin Laden rhetorically sniped at Saudi King Fahd for his perceived sell out of Yemen's Muslims to al-Bid's dictatorial YSP.[142] Bin Laden alleged that the monarch sought to serve the West's interests in maintaining regional stability and low oil prices by subsidizing the socialist regime. Cleverly seasoning his poetic, classical Arabic with potent doses of stinging sarcasm in reference to the al-Saud dynasty's perceived tyranny, bin Laden, having fully concluded the anti-Soviet struggle that he regarded as being provoked by Moscow through its unacceptable perceived assault on Muslims more than 15 years earlier, began preparing al-Qaeda to refocus on fighting the United States, Britain, and their allies.[143] Pleased by the outcome in Yemen that resulted from the YSP's decisive defeat, bin Laden contented himself with further entrenching al-Qaeda's presence among South Arabia's fiercely independent and pious tribes rather than impatiently attempting to force an Islamist regime on the nation. This, in turn, helped him to steadily strengthen the Salafi jihadi group's already solid, local support structure as he prepared his 23 August 1996 declaration of war on the United States, Britain, and Israel.[144]

Bin Laden implicitly alluded to the comments that Pelletreau and Hogg respectively delivered before the U.S. House of Representatives and the U.K. House of Commons in his ARC letters emphasizing the American and British governments of President Clinton and Prime Minister Major as being concerned for South Arabia's stability solely out of a desire to protect their countries' regional oil interests. Bin Laden subsequently wrote in his letters that the U.S.-U.K. governments had, therefore, since Yemen's May 1990 unification, pressured their al-Saud puppets in Riyadh to switch their support to al-Bid's Socialists.[145] Bin Laden then emphasized that the Riyadh-backed YSP's leaders had, in line with their atheistic communist ideology, slaughtered many devout Sunni Muslim clergymen in Yemen and systematically persecuted the Salafist Islamic Awakening in the South Arabian nation.[146] The concerns for peace, stability, and civilian casualties in Aden that were voiced by these senior officials in Washington, D.C. and London came at a time in which Saleh's northern armies stood on the verge of victory. Crucially, they do not appear to have expressed such concerns regarding local civilian casualties after al-Bid's Eastern Bloc-supplied Scud missiles and attack jets struck Sanaa as the Civil

War began.¹⁴⁷ As the U.S.-U.K. governments appeared, from bin Laden's militant Salafist perspective, to be concerned only with safeguarding their oil interests and in assuming Moscow's former interventionist role by preserving and protecting the YSP, through their al-Saud regime clients, they unwittingly gave the exiled al-Qaeda leader more rhetorical ammunition with which to further feed his jihadi recruitment efforts. This subsequently helped bin Laden to further entrench his guerrilla vanguard group in Yemen and strengthen its already solid and growing support structure in his South Arabian ancestral land.¹⁴⁸

In some ways, perhaps, Yemen's 1994 Civil War appears to have served as a South Arabian microcosm of bin Laden and al-Qaeda's earlier wartime experience in the Soviet-Afghan War. The communists in Aden, like their Kabul counterparts, represented a hated, urban elite that most of Yemen's traditional Muslims regarded as forcing their imported, infidel-backed paganism on the country. The southern Marxists boasted a conventional military machine that appeared fearsome on paper, and they were further bolstered by the flow of arms and ordnance delivered by the Saudi, Kuwaiti, and North Korean regimes. Yet the YSP's reputed armed might gradually collapse as bin Laden's guerrilla war efforts from 1990 forward appear to have boosted the Yemeni warriors in their war of resistance, helping them to wear down al-Bid's large army.¹⁴⁹ As mentioned, the Salafi fighters executed their protracted, attritional struggle that contributed to Saleh's victory from their bases on mountainous, rugged terrain on which they channeled their zealous battle drive in training and preparing effectively before taking the battle to their hated enemy's doorstep and vanquishing the Socialists in July 1994.¹⁵⁰

While the unexpected advances of Saleh's conventional, Nationalist army dominated most contemporary newspaper reports and captured the ire and concerns of representatives in the U.S. Congress and U.K. Parliament at the time, bin Laden and al-Fadhli's Salafi guerrillas and their tribal allies had played a key supporting role that appears to have significantly hastened the northern forces' hard-fought victory. Indeed, few of the contemporary U.S.-U.K. newspaper reports and congressional and parliamentary debates failed to include brief discussions on the presence of, "Muslim fundamentalists," "Islamic militants," and, "foreigners" fighting alongside Saleh's conventional forces.¹⁵¹ As with bin Laden's earlier recruiting and Afghan battle experience in command of his Arab guerrilla band, while the al-Qaeda chief also managed to dispatch a diverse range of jihadi volunteers to Yemen from all parts of the Sunni Muslim world, most of the anti-communist Yemeni mujahedin were, like bin Laden himself, Yemenis and Saudis of Yemeni origin.¹⁵²

Bin Laden's earlier experience in the Soviet-Afghan War that he obtained while fighting in the guerrilla ranks and trenches alongside his Yemeni comrades al-Fadhli, al-Zindani, al-Hadhi, and al-Harithi, helped him and al-Qaeda to play a key supporting role in gradually wearing down the YSP's forces.[153] This, in turn, helped render Yemen's 1994 Civil War considerably shorter than Afghanistan's 1980s' conflict that preceded it. The exiled al-Qaeda leader and his jihadi comrades appear to have effectively channeled their battle-seasoned guerrilla war tactics in contributing to al-Bid's decisive defeat and Saleh's victory in 1994, for which the Nationalist Party president rewarded the Salafists while retaining his grip on power and preventing an Islamist takeover by placating *al-Islah's* leaders and secular politicians alike, including former YSP members, many of whom had, after all, mutinied against the Socialists.[154] Applying the lessons that he learned during the Soviet-Afghan War from observing the first Arab volunteers rushing impatiently into battle and the Afghan Islamists' infighting and their failed semi-conventional assault on Jalalabad in 1989, bin Laden neither attempted to incite an insurgency against Saleh's reunified government nor rushed to raise al-Qaeda's black banner over Sanaa.[155]

Rather, attesting to his willingness to learn from past mistakes and his adherence to Ibn Khaldun's teachings on solidarity, bin Laden labored patiently and persistently in further strengthening his and al-Qaeda's already solid tribal relationships and recruiting strongholds in Yemen. He appears to have been satisfied that South Arabia's holy warriors had faithfully flocked to the guerrilla ranks and rallied to the black flag of jihad.[156] Bin Laden's calculated, razor-sharp focus on strengthening al-Qaeda's presence in the country paid off as he prepared his Salafi jihadi comrades for the protracted, multigenerational struggle ahead while advising against the counterproductive sectarian strife and factional infighting that he regarded as having caused the Afghan insurgents' temporary but avoidable setback at Jalalabad in 1989.[157] Satisfied that he and al-Qaeda's veteran fighters had played a key part in helping al-Fadhli and the Yemeni warriors to fatally fell the YSP and vanquish it decisively, bin Laden consistently advised his men against executing any unnecessary attacks in South Arabia. Bin Laden and his senior lieutenants continued patiently, steadily strengthening their guerrilla vanguard's already entrenched presence in the region, repeatedly emphasizing his perception that, "Yemen is our greatest supporter; it protects us and allows our troops free passage."[158]

On 10 July 1996, less than two months after returning to Afghanistan from Sudan, bin Laden again implicitly alluded to the importance of Yemen and, by extension, the Yemeni tribal parts of rural Saudi Arabia, to him and al-Qaeda during his second interview with British journalist Robert Fisk for the U.K. newspaper *The Independent*. Flanked by his sons Omar and Saad bin Laden, the latter of whom is said to have been a zealous, committed jihadi and faithful al-Qaeda fighter, Osama reportedly sat calmly as he cautioned Fisk that U.S.

service personnel and their Anglo-French allies on the Arabian Peninsula faced imminent danger unless their governments withdrew them immediately.[159] According to Fisk, bin Laden and several of his nearby jihadi fighters reportedly, "burst into laughter" at the U.K. journalist's suggestion that, "Afghanistan was the only place" from which, "he could campaign against the Saudi government."[160] Bin Laden is said to have quietly replied, "There are other places.... There are several places where we have friends and close brothers – we can find refuge and safety in them" in a statement consistent with his previous letters and comments on South Arabia's significance as a key stronghold in which he and al-Qaeda enjoyed deep and staunch tribal and religious support.[161] Cautioning Fisk that the Anglo-French governments should neither doubt the sincerity of his words nor underestimate al-Qaeda's ability to strike their forces in Saudi Arabia, bin Laden warned *The Independent's* readers that, "Not long ago, I gave advice to the Americans to withdraw their troops from Saudi Arabia. Now let us give some advice to the governments of Britain and France to take their troops out – because what happened in Riyadh and Khobar [terror attacks on U.S. military bases] showed that the people who did this have a deep understanding in choosing their targets. They hit their main enemy, which is the Americans. They killed no secondary enemies, nor their brothers in the army or the police of Saudi Arabia... I give this advice to the government of Britain."[162]

In another 1996 interview, bin Laden repeated his perception that the U.S.-U.K. governments and their alleged al-Saud puppets in Riyadh had, beginning in the period leading to the 1994 Yemeni Civil War, sought to replace the Soviets by supporting the YSP against Yemen's faithful Muslims. Stating sarcastically that, "People are supposed to be innocent until proven guilty .... Well, not the Afghan ['Afghan Arab'] fighters. They are the 'terrorists' of the world," bin Laden warned *TIME* magazine's Scott MacLeod that, "pushing them against the wall will do nothing, except increase the terrorism."[163] Bin Laden subsequently spoke again of Yemen's importance to al-Qaeda during a 27 November 1996 interview with *Al-Quds Al-Arabi* Editor Abdel Bari Atwan in Afghanistan. Replying to Atwan's questions regarding the Saudi government's freezing of his financial assets in Saudi Arabia and its pressuring of his family to denounce him, bin Laden implied that al-Qaeda nevertheless managed to prosecute its holy war against Islam's perceived foes. Stating, "we continued to cooperate with them [Yemen's anti-communist mujahedin] against the leaders of atheism in the Socialist party," bin Laden implicitly alluded to his and Tariq al-Fadhli's assassination campaign targeting YSP officials in the leadup to Yemen's 1994 Civil War as explained by Michael Scheuer.[164]

In an interview with Steve Coll for his book *The Bin Ladens: An Arabian Family in the American Century*, al-Fadhli credited bin Laden with enabling his and al-

Zindani's mission to overthrow the YSP, which had exiled the then-three-year-old al-Fadhli and his family to Saudi Arabia after taking power in 1970. Recalling that, "He [bin Laden] funded everything," al-Fadhli credited the founding al-Qaeda chief with helping him return to the homeland of his father, the last Sultan of Abyan, and ousting the communists that had deposed and exiled him during the Cold War.[165] In his February 2010 interview with T*he New York Times*, al-Fadhli again credited bin Laden and al-Qaeda with playing a key supporting role, although not the primary military role, in Saleh's 1994 victory over al-Bid.[166] In a possible attempt to portray himself and bin Laden as being far too chronically peaceful, al-Fadhli also attempted to distance himself from the al-Qaeda chief's tactics, claiming, "When I fought with Osama Bin Laden [against the Soviets and PDPA] in Afghanistan there were no bombings of [enemy] civilians, and I would never have supported them" even though such actions are, after all, reportedly deemed permissible but regrettable acts during wartime in the Salafist interpretation of Sunni Islamic law.[167]

While al-Qaeda has in many ways been eclipsed by the rise of the Islamic State (IS) Islamist insurgent group since the mid-2010s, bin Laden's overall legacy and the results of his wartime actions in aiding Yemen's Salafi guerrillas during their country's 1994 Civil War appear to continue benefitting the Salafi jihadi movement in some ways. As convincingly argued by authors such as Michael Scheuer, Peter Bergen, and Steve Coll, bin Laden appears to have neither expected to live to see final victory over the Middle Eastern regimes that he regarded as tyrannical, nor did he build al-Qaeda to achieve this goal on its own.[168] Rather, acknowledging himself as being just one Salafi guerrilla leader with a small organization, bin Laden frequently identified his goal for al-Qaeda as serving as a guerrilla vanguard group to inspire and tactically support other Muslims to drive the interventionist powers from the region before focusing on gradually toppling the Arab regimes.[169]

From bin Laden's Salafist perspective, Allah had provided a blueprint on how the faithful Muslims could, over time, bleed and ultimately defeat their oppressors as demonstrated by the example of the Afghan mujahedin persevering against the Soviet occupiers in the 1980s. Although the PDPA regime persisted for several more years with Soviet support, its 1992 collapse, followed by the YSP's 1994 defeat at the hands of Saleh's armies with the local-level aid of veteran al-Qaeda guerrilla cadres, led bin Laden to conclude that the Muslim world's hated apostate rulers could, in the absence of a superpower's support, be vanquished with time so long as the Islamic guerrillas persevered on the battlefield.[170] Bin Laden reportedly gave no indication that he sought for al-Qaeda to achieve this objective either swiftly or alone, and he appears to have consistently worked to build an organization that he expected to far outlive him.[171] As Barnett Rubin states in *Afghanistan: What Everyone*

Needs to Know, "The death of bin Laden in 2011 changed little" regarding al-Qaeda's continued presence in the jihadi group's traditional strongholds and the ability of his successors to continue his legacy.[172]

Yet al-Qaeda, while still functioning as a ruthless, resilient guerrilla vanguard in Yemen and several parts of other diverse and devout Sunni Muslim countries, may in some ways no longer be a necessary unit in terms of executing bin Laden's long-term plans. As described by David Wasserstein in *Black Banners of ISIS: The Roots of the New Caliphate*, while the founders of IS splintered away from al-Qaeda during the 2010s and embarked on an independent jihadi journey, the newer, more vicious jihadi group's roots should not be forgotten.[173] While both IS and al-Qaeda may appear less threatening than before at the time of writing (summer 2023), today's leaders and scholars should not take this relative silence for granted. Bin Laden neither spoke loudly nor boasted about his and al-Qaeda's attack capabilities during his jihadi career, telling an interviewer for the Pakistani newspaper *Ummat Karachi* on 28 September 2001 that, "Our silence is our real propaganda. Rejections, explanations, or corrigendum only waste your time, and through them, the enemy wants you to engage in things which are not of use to you. These things are pulling you away from your cause.... Terror is the most dreaded weapon in [the] modern age and the Western media is mercilessly using it against its own people. It can add fear and helplessness to the people of Europe and the United States"[174]

It appears, then, that scholars should not encourage today's leaders to lower their guard, but rather help them learn all that they can about the Salafi jihadi movement's sources of strength in assessing the shared history of al-Qaeda and IS, irrespective of which group poses the greater contemporary threat. As stated by Scheuer, "Bin Laden, in short, meant to light a fuse."[175] While al-Qaeda's flame may not appear as a raging inferno at the time of writing, its embers continue to burn brightly in parts of the Sunni Muslim world in which Western and Eastern interventions inadvertently help local Islamist groups to recruit jihadi fighters while manipulating the image of outside powers as aggressors in an Osama-esque manner, keeping his legacy alive and threatening.[176] Bin Laden consistently described his mission as being to incite resistance, whether executed by al-Qaeda or other Sunni Islamist groups, to Islam's perceived foes, stating, "I must say that my duty is just to awaken the Muslims."[177] As Pakistani journalist Hamid Mir explained during an interview shortly after U.S. forces killed bin Laden, "Yes, bin Laden is dead, but al-Qaeda and its allies are not dead, and their biggest strength is their hatred against America in many parts of the world, including Afghanistan and Pakistan."[178] Mir interviewed bin Laden on three different occasions between March 1997 and November 2001, and recent news reports seem to confirm his 2011 warning to the United States and other countries in the crosshairs of IS's resurgent local wings and the somewhat diminished, but still operating, post-bin Laden al-Qaeda.[179]

As pointed out by Professor Fawaz Gerges, while the U.S. military's February 2022 killing of its leader Ibrahim al-Hashimi al-Qureshi in Idlib, Syria certainly inconvenienced IS, the jihadi group's leadership appears to have prepared numerous successors well in advance and continues to operate, a legacy of its al-Qaeda roots.[180] In April 2023, IS insurgents reportedly seized and briefly held the village of Khirbat al-Muqman and repulsed a Syrian regime military offensive backed by Russian mercenary forces, remaining in control of two key mountains overlooking the city of al-Kawm.[181] Recent terror attacks executed by IS fighters on Russian and Chinese targets in Afghanistan likewise seem to indicate that bin Laden and al-Qaeda's consistent emphasis on fighting these regimes, in addition to the United States, Britain, and their allies, remains a feature of Salafi jihadi motivations to resist and strike governments whose policies the Sunni fundamentalists have historically regarded as Islamophobic.[182] A 5 July 2023 *Critical Threats* report concludes that Russia's ongoing intervention in Mali, "will almost certainly continue fueling the Sahel's Salafi-jihadi insurgency."[183] The report further states that Afghanistan's Taleban rulers remain, "caught between satisfying hard-liners, who support continuing ties to Salafi-jihadi groups, and engaging with foreign countries to seek economic support and international recognition. Islamic State Khorasan Province (ISKP) will likely exploit this tension to try to recruit disaffected Taliban hard-liners alienated by the Taliban's ties to foreign governments."[184]

In Yemen, meanwhile, bin Laden's wartime actions in the 1994 Civil War and the solid support network that he continued cultivating with South Arabia's devout, Salafist tribes appears to continue benefitting al-Qaeda's resilient regional wing as AQAP remains a potent fighting force at the local level. The jihadi group's current leader, Khalid Said Batarfi, released a video statement via AQAP's propaganda media outlet *Al-Malahem* on 29 April 2023. Extending his Ramadan greetings to Yemen and Saudi Arabia's devout Sunni tribal majorities on the *Eid al-Fitr* holy day, al-Batarfi urged them to follow the Taleban's example for inspiration and fight the "agents of Iran and U.S."[185] Throughout late 2022 and early 2023, Batarfi's fighters translated his words into actions, killing more than 20 soldiers from Yemen's rival Southern Movement faction in a single attack, kidnapping a UN worker in the South Arabian country, and displaying increased adeptness at the employment of unmanned drones and roadside bombs in warfare, killing a high-ranking enemy commander in Shabwah on 18 May 2023.[186] While somewhat diminished and relatively quiet on the international stage as a whole at the moment, al-Qaeda appears to remain firmly entrenched in Yemen and capable of vicious, determined resistance. Bin Laden's wartime actions and the legacy that he left behind, while rendering neither him nor the movement that he led and inspired an unassailable, seven-headed hydra, nevertheless appear, at present, to be keeping AQAP lethal and functioning in South Arabia.[187]

Having succeeded spectacularly first in acquiring command and battle experience in his supporting role while assisting the Afghan warriors in ousting the Soviet occupiers and their PDPA regime clients and next in tactically spearheading his Yemeni mujahid comrades' victorious guerrilla war against the YSP, bin Laden appears to have yet again applied his judo training in successfully luring the United States, Britain, and their NATO allies into Afghanistan.[188] Bin Laden's carefully calculated strategic maneuver, executed tactically via terror attacks and protracted, attritional guerrilla warfare, with his emphasis on the former as being a means by which to attain and execute the more desirable latter, continues to pay dividends for al-Qaeda and the global Salafi jihadi movement with the Taleban and, by extension, their allied al-Qaeda guerrilla cadres at the local, tactical level, having emerged as the perceived victors over a second superpower as mentioned briefly in Chapter 5.[189] Bin Laden's calculated, skilled application of the guerrilla war tactics and judo psychology that he mastered during the anti-Soviet jihad appears to have benefitted al-Qaeda and its militant Salafist allies in not only achieving their goals in Yemen's 1994 Civil War, but in later targeting and luring a second superpower onto ground familiar to the jihadi fighters. Bin Laden's skilled application of judo psychology in battle appears, then, to have served him and al-Qaeda well as they effectively channeled it as a key part of their tactical guerrilla war in luring their foes to attack them on rugged terrain unfavorable to the infidel assailants, first at Jaji in 1987, secondly throughout Yemen between 1990 and 1994, and once again in drawing the Americans and their NATO allies into Afghanistan between 1997 and the 9/11 attacks.[190]

Osama's mujahid mission, lethal legacy, and enduring impact on history

As mentioned in this book's Prologue, Karl Marx emphasizes the key role of individuals in history in his scholarly 1852 text *The Eighteenth Brumaire of Louis Bonaparte*, stating, "Men make their own history, but they do not make it just as they please; they do not make it under circumstances chosen by themselves, but under circumstances directly encountered, given and transmitted from the past."[191] Born to devout, hardworking Muslim immigrant parents of Yemeni origin on 10 March 1957 in the al-Maz district of the Saudi Arabian capital, Riyadh, Osama bin-Muhammad bin-Awad bin Laden grew up to eventually shape and leave his mark on history, perhaps even more so than Napoleon III, the subject of Marx's book 105 years before Osama's birth.[192] Bin Laden neither held nor aspired to hold public office or governmental authority, yet throughout his life, beginning with his formative years as a frontline guerrilla engineer, foot soldier, and tactical commander in the Soviet-Afghan War, he nevertheless rose to threaten and strike ruthless blows against those he deemed the foes of Muslims without wielding the conventional power of a head of state.[193] Bin Laden, in short, encountered situations that he could not control and that were often created by politicians, whether Western, Soviet, or Muslim, yet he embraced a supporting role to participate in these world-changing events, enabling him to rise to leadership and win the respect of his comrades, gradually taking control of the situation through his patience and perseverance.[194]

Bin Laden's careful, calculating approach to rising to leadership in the guerrilla ranks and applying the practical and tactical experience that he and his senior al-Qaeda lieutenants obtained fighting the Soviets in Afghanistan in his anti-U.S. strategy appears to have played a considerable part in his success at drawing U.S.-U.K. forces into the South Asian country to enable new jihadi generations to replicate the process.[195] Bin Laden's life and actions seem to serve as strong confirmation of Marx's 1852 theory that risk-taking individuals seizing key windows of opportunity, even those that, to somewhat paraphrase the *Eighteenth Brumaire* author, may appear to their foes as insignificant ants, can overcome the obstacles over which they wield no direct control to effectively manage the situation immediately before them to emerge as lions, and make an impact on history.[196] As explained throughout this book, while bin Laden entered a wartime atmosphere created by politicians in Moscow, Kabul, Islamabad, Riyadh, Washington, D.C., London, and Sanaa, he managed to surmount the hurdles placed before him, winning the Afghan insurgent leaders' respect and appreciation and their permission to form an Arab guerrilla unit and acquire the crucial combat and command experience that he and other Arab fighters had sought since the beginning of the Soviet invasion.[197]

Bin Laden's successful quest seems to have been largely enabled by his patience, determination, and willingness to temporarily defer to his more experienced comrades to grow as a leader and learn to channel the momentum of Islam's perceived foes to his and al-Qaeda's advantage. These traits, in some ways, appear to further attest to his effective mastery of judo skills, guerrilla war tactics, and psychology. To be sure, he did not apply his skills in the sense of fighting the enemy on even ground as in a traditional judo tournament. Rather, he seems to have applied them in his tactical approach to finding a way to help Salafi fighters to somewhat "even the odds" by forcing their superpower enemies into a confrontation on rugged terrain of his and al-Qaeda's choosing.[198]

As mentioned previously, bin Laden appears to have adopted this approach based on his Arab guerrilla unit's experiences fighting the Soviets, and the judo tactic of using an attacking opponent's momentum against them appears to have somewhat enhanced his understanding of the classic guerrilla tactic of luring a stronger opponent into a disadvantageous position.[199] Bin Laden appears to have implied this to be the case in his interview that he granted to the former Egyptian military intelligence officer and journalist Isam Darraz, an eyewitness of the 1987 Jaji engagements. During his post-Jaji interview with Darraz, bin Laden admitted that neither he nor most of the men in his Arab guerrilla band had ever enjoyed the benefits of professional military training, stating, "we not military persons [before the Battle of Jaji], we were civilians."[200] In this regard, the judo blackbelt that he reportedly earned in preparation to fight the Soviets may have somewhat compensated for his lack of professional military training in helping him to grasp the importance of classic guerrilla tactics such as luring the enemy into a trap, and he appears to have applied this in practice under heavy Soviet fire and bombardment at Jaji.[201]

As stated in this book's Preface and Epilogue, I have sought neither to praise nor excessively vilify bin Laden, but to emphasize the ways in which he effectively took control of the situation presented to him by cleverly building on the momentum provided by the prolonged Soviet military occupation of Afghanistan to build a following and rise to leadership. In doing so, I have sought to produce a more scholarly and nuanced historical portrait of bin Laden and his actions in the Soviet-Afghan War and Yemen's 1994 Civil War to help clarify for scholars the reasons for which he became a lethal threat to those he regarded as the oppressors of Muslims. By calling the reader's attention to the nuances surrounding bin Laden's life, actions, and motivations that many authors appear to have largely overlooked or perhaps lightly touched on, I have sought to make this book serve as a nonfiction cautionary tale offering crucial lessons from history regarding the detrimental impact that prolonged military interventions, such as the Soviet and U.S.-NATO occupations of Afghanistan, can have on aiding Salafi fighters in honing their combat skills while inspiring, recruiting, and training new generations.[202]

I have also attempted in this book to restore agency to bin Laden by emphasizing his own role, rather than that of outsiders such as the CIA, KGB, MI-6, GID, GRU, or ISI in transforming him into the deadly, implacable foe that he became for those he deemed Islamophobic aggressors against Muslims.[203] Bin Laden's ability to exercise personal agency and acquire command and battle experience of his own accord, while acting on his personal motivations and convictions, has been largely disregarded, whether consciously or not, by those arguing that President Reagan's CIA or Prime Minister Thatcher's MI-6 somehow, "created" him and al-Qaeda during the Soviet-Afghan War through their support of the Afghan resistance.[204] Those parroting this misinformed talking point appear to assume that no Muslim guerrilla, let alone a devout

Sunni Salafist and ethnically South Arabian man such as bin Laden, could possibly exercise personal agency and emerge as a skilled, effective leader and vicious opponent capable of resisting and outwitting a superpower's forces. As has been shown in Chapter 3, this far-fetched myth, which I hope this book has played a small part in demolishing, began with deliberate and relentless Soviet disinformation during the 1980s as Brezhnev, Andropov, Gorbachev, and their generals and KGB and GRU officials arrogantly asserted the Afghan warriors to be incapable of resisting their 40th Army of occupation without Western, Saudi, or Pakistani-supplied arms and ordnance.[205] As stated previously, the words of bin Laden's closest associates and reluctant defectors, such as Nasser al-Bahri, Tariq al-Fadhli, Najwa and Omar bin Laden, Musa al-Qarni, and others, in addition to his documented threats to kill John Simpson and Edward Girardet, appear to contradict the notion that the al-Qaeda chief enjoyed a relationship with the CIA, MI-6, or any intelligence agencies, save for Saudi Arabia's GID, during the Soviet-Afghan War.[206]

While their decision to intervene militarily in Afghanistan in December 1979 had been a reluctant one at which they arrived only after much deliberation, hesitation, and debate within the Politburo, the Soviet leadership's repeatedly prolonged occupation of the traditional Muslim country in the name of ensuring, in the well-intentioned manner of Joseph Rudyard Kipling's White Man's Burden, that its government remained a Kremlin-approved communist one, served as the key window of opportunity that helped bin Laden and his al-Qaeda lieutenants to connect with the Afghan Islamists, obtain superpower-provided combat experience, and recruit and train new generations of jihadi fighters in guerrilla warfare.[207] Although limited and temporary in nature, the Soviet 40th Army's occupation also appears to have been brutally executed in many parts of Afghanistan, and while the Soviet High Command, Politburo, and consecutive general secretaries all desired a withdrawal from the country as quickly as possible, their repeated delaying of an exit played into the hands of the resistance. The 40th Army's merciless interdiction campaigns and heavy bombing raids on the guerrillas during its prolonged occupation of Afghanistan combined with the Eastern Bloc's support for South Yemen's communist regime to serve as the canvas on which bin Laden skillfully painted, shaped, and manipulated his portrait of the Soviet occupiers as Islam's foes that sought to kill and oppress all traditional Muslims or forcibly convert them to the Kremlin's official, state-sponsored atheism.[208]

And while the Soviet leaders did not seek to dominate and colonize Afghanistan or annex the country into the Soviet Union, they nevertheless presided over a campaign that appeared aggressive and colonialist enough to many contemporary Afghans from the country's rural, religious Pashtun tribes whose support of the resistance appears to have been galvanized as the

Kremlin escalated its campaign before withdrawing. While the documentary collections on the Politburo sessions between June and October 1979 held by the *Bukovsky Archives* and the *Wilson Center Digital Archive* demonstrate that the Soviet leaders, including hardline KGB men such as Andropov, had few designs on Afghanistan other than ensuring that its government remained firmly in the hands of pro-Moscow communists, they also reveal that Soviet Army officers, KGB advisers, and GRU agents were, in fact, operating in the country in support of the PDPA regime well before the Kremlin launched *Storm-333* that December.[209] And while Gorbachev and many of his generals, like their predecessors, wished for and actively sought to order a pullout, their continued efforts to interdict the steady stream of guerrilla recruits and supply caravans entering from Pakistan kept their troops actively supporting the PDPA's military offensives even as they prepared to execute their phased withdrawal that began on 15 May 1988.[210]

According to a 1989 report published by *Amnesty International*, Soviet troops operating in support of an Afghan Army unit captured the village of Kolagu in Paktia Province and bound together 12 guerrillas that they had taken prisoner inside a local mosque before filling it with explosives that they then detonated, "by means of a cable" on 16 January 1988, barely four months before General Gromov's phased withdrawal began.[211] The report proceeds to quote both, "survivors and eyewitnesses" as stating that nine of the 12 captive fighters were killed along with seven children whose nearby home collapsed from the shockwaves resulting from the explosion that ravaged the Muslim house of worship.[212] To be sure, such atrocities were by no means representative of the actions of all or even most of the 40th Army's combat personnel, just as the battlefield savagery sometimes displayed by the Afghan Islamists and their small numbers of Arab allies cannot be attributed to all of the resistance fighters. Yet those that the occupiers are said to have committed can only have played further into bin Laden's hands, boosting his propaganda and recruitment efforts as he and his non-Afghan Salafi comrades launched al-Qaeda as an experienced, seasoned guerrilla vanguard for recruiting and training Islamist militants to resist the perceived apostate regimes at home and their infidel backers abroad.[213]

Bin Laden skillfully and effectively manipulated this propagandized portrait of the Soviet occupiers to the psychological and recruitment benefit of the Afghan Islamist insurgent groups and the small but growing numbers of non-Afghan Salafi fighters flocking to the ranks of his Arab guerrilla unit. Bin Laden later stated, "The Russians are known for their brutality," emphasizing the Soviet Air Force's frequent, heavy bombing raids that he first witnessed while working as a frontline guerrilla engineer during merciless strafing assaults by swarms of enemy Mi-24 gunships and recalled the Soviet helicopters deploying napalm to incinerate the thick, jungle-like foliage to deny ambush positions to the Arab guerrillas during the Battle of Jaji, recalling, "I was subjected to this [napalm inhalation]."[214] Yet bin Laden, writing, "credit must be given where it is due," rightly and repeatedly commended the Soviet soldiers on their outstanding fighting qualities, while equally praising the hard-fighting Afghan warriors for their battlefield tenacity and defiance of the enemy's far superior conventional forces, attesting to his rational appraisal of friends and foes alike.[215] Bin Laden does not appear to have exaggerated the military role that he and his lightly trained al-Qaeda unit played in the Soviet-Afghan War, repeatedly emphasizing his perception that only God's divine favor and the Afghan insurgents' perseverance had vanquished the 40th Army while allowing the Arab fighters to play a small part and emerge as battle-seasoned guerrillas.[216]

As U.S.-U.K. forces prepared to assault bin Laden's fortified mountain redoubt at Tora Bora in eastern Afghanistan's Spin Ghar, or White Mountain range, on 29 November 2001, Afghan insurgent veterans Haji Din Mohammad and Commander Sair ur-Rahman recalled their observations of the most hunted man on the planet in action during the Soviet-Afghan War in an interview with journalists from *The Irish Times* newspaper. At the time of the interview, Din Mohammad's brother had just become the governor of Jalalabad working for the post-Taleban Afghan regime of Hamid Karzai that the U.S. and NATO forces had installed.[217] Yet he unhesitatingly commended bin Laden's unflappable steadfastness in battle that he witnessed, stating that, "a lone soldier remained standing, refusing to surrender. That man was Osama bin Laden," as the al-Qaeda chief rallied his men to doggedly defy the Afghan Army's heavy artillery bombardment and attempt to capture, "a hill known as Parkan Post" south of Jalalabad as Soviet combat forces were withdrawing from the country at the beginning of 1989.[218] Din Mohammad recalled that while many insurgents fell to the enemy's merciless assault and the rebels' situation appeared hopeless, "the communists never got to capture that place [Parkan Post]. Bin Laden never gave in and did not allow them to make ground. They never took the hill."[219]

Commander ur-Rahman, a former Afghan insurgent leader that fought alongside bin Laden's staunch wartime ally, Yunis Khalis, likewise recalled of the exiled Saudi jihadi that, "He [bin Laden] was very patient and very calm and did not speak very loudly."[220] Ur-Rahman proceeded to recount to the *Irish Times* reporters bin Laden's 18 May 1996 return to Afghanistan from Sudan that Khalis had helped to facilitate, and the newspaper report states that, "At the meeting, bin Laden was sitting very relaxed, with a Kalashnikov rifle [sic, his AKS-74U submachine gun] standing between his knees."[221] Crucially, while both men reportedly stated that, "We don't care if he [bin Laden] is captured.

We want to solve our [local Afghan] problems," neither Din Mohammad nor ur-Rahman attempted to deny the al-Qaeda chief's record of bravery in battle and readily acknowledged the qualities that helped catapult him to leadership in the mujahid ranks.[222]

As discussed throughout this book, bin Laden's actions and the lethal legacy that he left behind do not appear to reflect those of a true and irrational fanatic or takfiri such as the Jordanian militant Abu Musab al-Zarqawi and the Syrian intellectual Abu Musab al-Suri. Nor do his life and actions resemble those of a secular, national socialist, Muslim-in-name-only "Islamofascist" tyrant in the mold of Hussein, Muammar Qaddafi, or Hafiz and Bashir al-Assad. Rather, bin Laden's life and actions appear to have been those of a calculating, skilled, and ruthless adversary meriting serious scholarly study rather than blind hatred, contempt, and ridicule. Rather than the popular but misinformed and Manichaean caricature of him as a white-turbaned, South Arabian Jack the Ripper, bin Laden appears to have been a rational, pragmatic operator, inspiring leader, and cogent guerrilla tactician and thinker whose legacy continues to inflict physical and psychological harm on those he regarded as Islam's foes.[223]

Bin Laden, while a ruthless and implacable opponent of those he deemed the foes of Muslims, does not appear to have automatically sought conflict with those whose views somewhat differed from his personal convictions and beliefs. He reportedly praised his close anti-Soviet comrade Yunis Khalis as a tenacious, "tiger" defending Muslims from infidel aggression and occupation in his propaganda poetry in which the al-Qaeda leader repeatedly commended the Afghan insurgent leaders for their victory over the Soviet superpower.[224] As mentioned previously, Khalis helped enable bin Laden's May 1996 return to Afghanistan from Sudan, and, together with another of the al-Qaeda leader's anti-Soviet comrades, Commander Jalaluddin Haqqani, offered the exiled Saudi zealot his protection as the Taleban and al-Qaeda's Arab fighters initially mistrusted each other.[225]

Even though Khalis did not share the traditional Salafism that bin Laden embraced but rather subscribed to mystical Sufism and prayed at the shrines of Islamic saints, a practice rejected by the Wahhabis and Salafis, bin Laden, reflecting his pragmatism and adherence to the Salafist inclination to live and let live unless threatened, consistently expressed appreciation and gratitude to his former anti-Soviet comrade.[226] As explained in Chapter 1 and this book's Glossary, scholars such as Professors Khaled Abou El Fadl and Quintan Wiktorwicz convincingly argue that while Salafists and Wahhabis share many similarities in their fundamentalist interpretations of Sunni Islamic law, and both hail from the same Hanbali school of orthodox Sunni Islam, there are key differences that separate the two closely related sects.[227] While many members of the Saudi regime's official religious establishment and groups such as Egyptian Islamic Jihad (EIJ), such as bin Laden's recently killed-in-action successor and former second-in-command Ayman al-Zawahiri and al-Zawahiri's possible successor Saif al-Adel, adhere to Wahhabism and tend to shun or otherwise look down on non-Arab and non-Sunni Muslims, Salafists such as bin Laden reject such an approach as counterproductive.[228]

To be sure, militant Salafists such as bin Laden and many of his senior lieutenants hailing from the grassroots Salafist Islamic Awakening movement that historically attracted followers in Yemen, Saudi Arabia, and elsewhere, certainly regard it as their duty to ruthlessly battle to the death Islam's perceived foes. Salafi jihadis such as bin Laden, however, also cautiously adhere to the concept of waging a defensive war, rather than seeking to attack and convert others to their interpretation of Sunni Islamic law by force or coercion as emphasized by Professor Rudolph Peters.[229] Bin Laden, in accordance with traditional Salafist custom rather than the vengeful urges of the Wahhabis and takfiris, reportedly rejected the notion that the al-Saud royal family and other Arab rulers merited immediate execution once they were eventually overthrown.[230]

Rather, bin Laden appears to have consistently advised al-Qaeda members that the perceived tyrants should be brought before, "the Islamic judiciary" after being deposed in line with Salafist teaching and, in contrast to Wahhabis such as al-Zawahiri and al-Adel, "considered it of some value that they [Arab government leaders] were actually Moslems."[231] While mandating the execution of vicious, determined resistance to Islam's perceived foes, bin Laden's militant Salafist outlook remains focused on the traditional Koranic approach to warfare and the prevention of counterproductive sectarianism advocated by men such as al-Zawahiri, al-Zarqawi, and al-Adel.[232] Bin Laden founded al-Qaeda in 1988 not for the unrealistic purpose of aggressively exporting his and his men's fundamentalist ideology to countries in which Islam has historically not been the dominant faith, but as a small, ruthless guerrilla vanguard to help local Islamists gradually topple, over the course of decades, the regimes to which they remained opposed.[233]

Bin Laden's organizational tactics that he utilized in seeking to gradually weaken the foundations of the hated Arab regimes, as mentioned in this book's Prologue, somewhat resembled his fellow exiled zealot Vladimir Lenin's approach to gradually undermining Czarist Russia's monarchy.[234] Yet due at least in some part to his adherence to traditional Salafism, bin Laden sought to tactically assist, via a multigenerational guerrilla war, local Salafists in executing a Sunni Islamist restoration, rather than a Lenin-style revolution, in Muslim countries.[235] Nor does bin Laden appear to have shared Lenin's reputed thirst for vengeful regicide that the founding Soviet leader appears to have conveyed through his regime's ruthless execution of Czar Nicholas II and his Romanov royal family in July 1918. Rather, bin Laden appears to have sought to absorb and utilize others' tactics and skills that he regarded as useful while remaining committed to traditional Salafism's historical approach to warfare that, while permitting vicious attacks on those regarded as Islam's foes, remains defensive in nature, rendering him a deadly and pragmatic opponent.[236]

As al-Qaeda continued striking U.S. interests abroad throughout the 1990s and Clinton administration officials imposed economic sanctions on the Taleban with the UN's backing, Mullah Omar, after demanding on several occasions that bin Laden take his men and leave Afghanistan, increasingly found himself reversing his decisions and permitting the Arab jihadis to continue their independent holy war against the Americans and their allies. In contrast to his Foreign Minister *Mawlawi* Wakil Ahmad Mutawakil, Mullah Omar's Political Advisor Mullah Abdul Jalil reportedly maintained a favorable view of bin Laden and the Arab fighters, and, as U.S. and UN pressure mounted on the Taleban regime during the late 1990s, the Deobandi cleric grew increasingly defiant towards those demanding that he surrender the al-Qaeda chief.[237] On 7 August 1998, after bin Laden had twice declared war on the United States, Britain, and Israel, al-Qaeda fighters truck-bombed the U.S. embassies in Kenya and Tanzania, and President Clinton subsequently retaliated with an ineffective Cruise missile attack on the jihadi group's training camps in Afghanistan on 20 August 1998.[238]

Later that day, Clinton announced the strike against, "the network of radical groups affiliated with and funded by Osama bin Laden," in a speech in which the 42nd U.S. president asserted that, "The groups associated with him [bin Laden] come from diverse places, but share a hatred for democracy, a fanatical glorification of violence, and a horrible distortion of their religion to justify the murder of innocents. They have made the United States their adversary precisely because of what we stand for and what we stand against."[239] Overlooking bin Laden's previously and consistently expressed grievances against specific U.S. and Western policies in the Muslim world rather than Western freedoms and values as the reasons that the al-Qaeda leader listed for his declaration of war on the United States and its European allies, Clinton continued, "This will be a long, ongoing struggle between freedom and fanaticism; between the rule of law and terrorism.... America is and will remain a target of terrorists precisely because we are leaders; because we act to advance peace, democracy, and basic human values; because we're the most open society on Earth; and because, as we have shown yet again, we take an uncompromising stand against terrorism."[240]

Clinton subsequently dispatched U.S. Secretary of Energy and Ambassador to the UN Bill Richardson to meet with Mullah Omar's officials and pressure them to surrender bin Laden and evict al-Qaeda from Afghanistan, even though Washington refused to recognize the Taleban regime over its refusal to implement the Western world's 1990s' interpretations of women's rights and even as al-Qaeda fighters promptly rebuilt their damaged insurgent camps.[241] Richardson's visit and his attempt to pressure the Taleban on 24 August 1998 appears to have boomeranged harmfully as Mullah Omar, reflecting his firm devotion to the Pashtun tribal code of *melmastia* or "hospitality" to guests, especially one regarded as a veteran holy warrior seeking shelter, and his dedication to preserving the Taleban's image as the Muslim world's sole contemporary Islamic Emirate, resented Washington's perceived threat.[242] Regarding Clinton and Richardson's demands as both insulting to his and the Taleban's Pashtun tribal honor and Deobandi religious convictions, even as they continued, through the UN, to impose sanctions on Afghanistan over the Islamists' rejection of 1990s' Western-style women's rights, Omar reportedly grew closer to Mullah Jalil's pro-al-Qaeda faction within the Taleban and repeatedly reversed his demands that bin Laden leave Afghanistan.[243]

Bin Laden and his senior al-Qaeda lieutenants, all devout, militant Salafists, did not agree entirely with the Taleban's Deobandi interpretation of Sunni Islamic law regarding the status of Muslim women in an apparent supreme irony considering the West's refusal to hold dialogue with the Afghan Islamists over this key issue. At al-Qaeda's main Afghan headquarters at Tarnak Farm near the Taleban's stronghold of Kandahar, bin Laden reportedly permitted the female relatives of al-Qaeda members to receive an education and opened a, "girls' school" for them to pursue, "higher education" after reaching a certain age.[244] Naturally, al-Qaeda women and female teachers ran the school in accordance with the jihadi group's Salafist interpretation of *Shariah*, and bin Laden is even said to have listened patiently to the angry complaints of one his lieutenant's wives before asking the man to address the problem.[245] Bin Laden reportedly opened the school in defiance of the Taleban's opposition to, "[all] girls going to school," daringly siding with the considerable number of women at al-Qaeda's living quarters rather than his Afghan Islamist hosts.[246] One of bin Laden's four wives, Khairiah Sabar, is said to have held a Ph.D. in Islamic Studies, and the al-Qaeda chief reportedly deferred to her regularly on matters relating to Islamic law and tradition, permitting women to teach Arabic, Koranic Studies, and other subjects at al-Qaeda's girls' school even as Washington unwittingly drove the Taleban leadership closer to its Arab guests over its demands that the group surrender the exiled Saudi zealot and immediately conform to contemporary Western views of gender equality.[247]

Bin Laden, in contrast to both the Afghan Islamists with whom he forged close comradeship and his unapproachable, authoritarian, Wahhabi-oriented Egyptian colleague Ayman al-Zawahiri alike, is also said to have refused to engage in criticism of the northern Afghan commander Ahmed Shah Massoud during the Soviet-Afghan War. Rather, he gratefully accepted into al-Qaeda's ranks experienced Arab volunteers that had fought alongside the ethnic Tajik commander, such as his close comrades, the Egyptians Abu Hafs and Abu Ubaydah, as emphasized by Michael Scheuer, despite respectfully disagreeing with Azzam's insistence that Arab fighters should fight primarily alongside Massoud's forces and in Afghan units only.[248] Reflecting the character traits that he appears to have developed during his youth, bin Laden reportedly rejected and rebuffed the calls of some of Azzam's intolerant Wahhabi or takfiri contemporaries from North Africa and the Levant calling for Massoud's death due to the Afghan insurgent leader's alleged hosting of a swimming pool for Western women and his supposed harboring of non-fundamentalist views.[249]

Yet despite his apparent rejection of other militants' wartime anti-Massoud gossip while fighting the Soviets, it has sometimes been suggested that bin Laden always hated the ethnic Tajik insurgent leader, an assertion that appears to be belied by the al-Qaeda chief's initial trusting of the Northern Alliance commander over the Taleban in 1996 despite the fact that Saudi Salafist clerics had long before declared the northern Afghan commander a foe of Islam since his 1983 truce with the Soviets.[250] Azzam's Algerian son-in-law Abdullah Anas, a former close comrade of Massoud's, contributes to this misperception in his 2019 memoir while condescendingly mocking and underestimating the, "guerrilla warfare, hit and run strikes" that bin Laden and his men gradually mastered while battling the Soviet occupation forces between 1987 and 1989.[251] And even the brilliant and renowned scholar, Professor Mark Galeotti, a leading and highly respected international authority on the Soviet-Afghan War and Russian security matters, errs in his portrayal of bin Laden as a chronic Massoud-hater in his nevertheless excellent 2021 book *The Panjshir Valley 1980-86: The Lion Tames the Bear in Afghanistan*, stating of post-Soviet, 1990s' Afghanistan that, "The instability also allowed the al-Qaeda jihadist terror network under Osama bin Laden (who had long disliked Massoud) and Ayman al-Zawahiri to establish itself in Afghanistan, under the wing of the Taliban, from 1996."[252]

Rather than exhibiting the behavior of the irrational, bloodthirsty madman that he has often been caricatured as, bin Laden appears to have displayed character traits like those of other historical figures whose actions, whether subjectively positive or negative, rendered them revered and respected leaders of diverse groups and causes throughout history. Bin Laden reportedly studied the lives and tactics of such great figures as he consistently sought to improve his leadership and management skills and al-Qaeda's resilience as a guerrilla vanguard organization for tactically spearheading and supporting Islamist insurgencies.[253] The al-Qaeda chief is said to have closely read the autobiographies, speeches, and other books authored by men such as British Field Marshal Bernard Law Montgomery, U.S. President Franklin D. Roosevelt, U.S. President Richard M. Nixon, North Vietnamese revolutionary and President Ho Chi Minh, and French Brigadier General and President Charles de Gaulle.[254] As mentioned, Don Chipman and Andrew Mitzcavitch both theorize that bin Laden closely studied and absorbed the lessons of Mao Zedong's *The Red Book of Guerrilla Warfare* during the Soviet-Afghan War.[255] As discussed throughout this book, bin Laden also earned a judo blackbelt before temporarily moving to Pakistan in 1984 in preparation to fight the Soviets and, according to his former bodyguard Nasser al-Bahri, closely studied, "several books" on and sought to master the guerrilla tactics utilized by Israel's Irgun fighters during their war of resistance against the British colonial forces.[256]

Bin Laden neither automatically dismissed nor disregarded the practical teachings of others, whether nominal Muslims or infidels, based on their national or ideological origins.[257] Rather, he appears to have wisely applied the practical principle often attributed to the legendary martial arts grandmaster Bruce Lee that an effective warrior must learn to absorb useful information while ignoring distractions and rejecting counterproductive ideas. Bin Laden, after all, is said to have greatly enjoyed Lee's action films, even as a devout, young Salafist during his teenage years in Saudi Arabia, according to his childhood friend, Dr. Khaled al-Batarfi. He appears to have applied the martial arts master's wisdom and practical, common sense approach in selecting weaponry and tactics that he believed could help both himself and al-Qaeda fighters to improve their skills and become a greater threat to their foes.

This appears to be further attested to by his choice of Soviet, Israeli, Western, and other types of arms and ordnance at the jihadi group's guerrilla training camps in Afghanistan, Yemen, and elsewhere.[258] Bin Laden, in short, appears to have embraced neither the irrational path of a takfiri nor that of a less fanatical but still intolerant Wahhabi, such as actual extremists from the Levant, North Africa, and within the Saudi regime's religious establishment as described in Chapter 1 and this book's Glossary.[259] Nor does bin Laden appear to have subscribed to the hateful, anti-Semitic "Islamofascism," or, more accurately, national socialism (Baathism), of tyrannical rulers such as Hussein, Qaddafi, the al-Assads, and the Egyptian and Algerian generals, a secular ideology that appears to have been exported and bolstered by both the Western and Eastern Blocs during and after the Cold War as Moscow, Washington, and their respective allies backed their preferred Arab client regimes to which the founding al-Qaeda chief's Salafi jihadi brethren remain militantly opposed. Rather, bin Laden staunchly and zealously embraced the path of a traditional but militant Salafist like most of his closest guerrilla comrades and followers hailing from the grassroots sectors of Saudi and Yemeni society and other devout and diverse parts of the Sunni Muslim world.[260]

Yet the popular but inaccurate and far-fetched caricature of bin Laden, al-Qaeda, and the global Sunni Islamist movement overall that appears to have been influenced, in many ways, by the Soviets' disinformation campaign against the Afghan and Arab fighters in the 1980s appears to have reappeared in some ways with President Clinton's 20 August 1998 speech. It seems to persist with a stubbornness reminiscent of both Osama's persistence in digging frontline guerrilla trenches and Moscow's backing of the PDPA's attempts to gradually convert the rural, religious Pashtuns into Kremlin-approved communists.[261] With the U.S.-NATO military occupation of Afghanistan having lasted nearly twice as long as the Soviet one, untold numbers of Islamist militants are likely to have received at least some degree of combat experience to channel in inspiring and training others, an outcome for which bin Laden appears to have consistently hoped, planned, and prayed.[262]

Repeating the Clinton White House's historical miscalculations between 1998 and 2001 that further entrenched bin Laden and al-Qaeda in Afghanistan and strengthened their ties with the Taleban's pro-al-Qaeda factions and other local Sunni Islamist groups, U.S. President Joseph R. Biden's team again risks further incurring and amplifying anti-U.S. resentment in the region and abroad. As recent reports indicate, this comes at a time in which the Taleban leadership faces internal challenges from the increasingly lethal and resilient ISKP insurgency, whose veteran fighters also appear to have honed their combat capabilities in battle with the U.S. and NATO troops for the better part of a decade between the group's formation of its local wing in the mid-2010s and NATO's August 2021 withdrawal.[263] In the wake of Washington's poorly executed and badly botched but long overdue Afghan pullout, Taleban fighters continued demonstrating their improved combat skills that 20 years of a superpower's military presence helped them to hone. They reportedly quickly seized and held the Panjshir Valley, Massoud's former stronghold, within a matter of weeks and during a raging, global pandemic, a feat that neither the Taleban's less-experienced founders in the 1990s nor the Soviet 40th Army and PDPA regime in the 1980s accomplished over the course of entire decades.[264]

Yet the ISKP fighters now appear determined to challenge the Taleban's rule through protracted, attritional insurgency combat, motivated, in part, by the latter group's reputed forging of relations with the Chinese and Russian governments.[265] Bin Laden and al-Qaeda long ago denounced these regimes' policies as Islamophobic and oppressive towards Muslims, and ISKP's attacks are likely to increase in lethality as their ranks doubtlessly include many seasoned guerrilla cadres capable of determined and vicious resistance, a legacy of IS's historical origins as a wing of al-Qaeda based in Iraq.[266] ISKP's recruitment efforts are likely to be boosted by the jihadi group's emphasis on the Taleban's perceived sell out to the Chinese and Russian regimes that were, together with New Delhi's allegedly fundamentalist Hindu rulers, consistently denounced by bin Laden as the foes of Muslims from at least 1996 forward.[267]

As mentioned, the Taleban's perceived victory over the U.S.-NATO forces and rapid toppling of their puppet regime in Kabul have greatly enhanced its image as Islam's defenders in Sunni Islamist circles worldwide.[268] Yet the ISKP leadership remains capable of challenging this perception to its advantage while being inadvertently aided by Western and UN sanctions that are likely to further fuel resentment and push local Islamists, including many Taleban veterans, into joining and lending their battle-seasoned fighting skills to ISKP.[269] Rather than further alienating the Taleban leadership's more locally-focused factions and inadvertently empowering those that have historically been pro-Salafist and supportive of the Arab jihadis, whether bin Laden's al-Qaeda or today's IS, Western officials should learn from the Clinton team's counterproductive, Wilsonian 1990s' approach. The Clinton team's approach appears to have led Mullah Omar to fully close ranks with bin Laden and failed to coerce Afghanistan's devout, rural Pashtuns into becoming democratic, Westernized secularists just as the Soviets and PDPA failed in their progressive crusade to convert them into atheistic communists.[270]

Yet history's mistakes regarding U.S. Afghan policy appear to fall to the background as other international developments seem to captivate most Western officials. Barely a month after the publication of this book's first edition, a new global security crisis seemed to erupt onto the world stage with the outbreak of the current war in Ukraine, a conflict that has been raging in that country's embattled eastern regions since 2014.[271] While much international attention has been focused on the Russian Federation's military intervention and the ongoing fighting, still current and with no apparent end in sight at the time of writing, it has come to my attention that this book, now in its second edition for which I am deeply grateful, may still offer important lessons regarding a somewhat more hidden threat to the West that seems to escape the attention of many current analysts, observers, and commentators. Like the Soviet-Afghan War, the early 2020s conflict in Ukraine presents a window of opportunity for aspiring, secular "holy warriors" of a sort, even in a non-Salafist sense of the word, to acquire battle and command experience and inspire, recruit, and train others in a truly Osama-esque manner.[272]

To be sure, prolonged, destructive conflicts do not automatically produce Osama bin Ladens, and historians cannot predict the future, nor is it our place to decide policy. Yet in applying history's lessons, scholars can, and should, however, seek to advise those in positions of power on the potential ramifications of their policies and how they can attempt to avoid replicating past catastrophes. To prevent potential militants from seizing the initiative and emerging as lethal, lasting threats, Western leaders should cautiously observe developments in Ukraine as resistance or paramilitary leaders on both sides may decide to don the field green, semi-military, combat half-uniforms of guerrilla fighters and commanders while rhetorically portraying their respective forces as the valiant victims fighting to repel either Western or Russian aggression. Such tactics can assist potential militants in shaming their allies and supporters into committing more finances, arms, or manpower to the struggle, essentially replicating Osama's mujahid example, even if in a non-fundamentalist sense, while acquiring the key combat and command experience to recruit and train new fighters and prosecute later wars.[273] While much attention seems to be focused on the conventional military battles being fought between the Ukrainian and Russian armies, less seems to be known about the clashes that doubtlessly rage daily between rival insurgent or mercenary bands on both sides.[274]

Whether such militant groups hail from local origins or from the ranks of foreign volunteers fighting on one side or the other, both Western powers and other countries supplying weaponry to either belligerent should remain mindful and proceed with caution regarding whose hands may be receiving the arms and ordnance flooding onto Ukraine's battlefields and the motives of those obtaining them and firing them in battle. Yet few U.S. lawmakers at present – save perhaps, for notable exceptions such as Senator Rand Paul (R-KY) – appear to display such a pragmatic, common sense concern regarding the potential for the ongoing deliveries of lethal weaponry being intercepted by hostile factions or falling into the wrong hands. Likewise, the Russian, Iranian, and North Korean rulers, no less than their Western counterparts, would be wise, for once, to absorb history's lessons and consider how the Soviet leadership, by repeatedly prolonging the 40th Army's occupation of Afghanistan to bolster the central government of Moscow's choice, unwittingly trained and prepared bin Laden and al-Qaeda for guerrilla recruitment and tactical operations in support of their Salafi jihadi brethren on a global scale.[275] The recent U.S.-NATO defeat in Afghanistan serves as another relevant example, with the Taleban emerging more battle-hardened and equipped by foreign weaponry than ever, and, crucially, as the perceived victor among Sunni Islamist groups worldwide over a second superpower as mentioned previously.[276] Yet just as the Biden administration seems eager to again provoke the Afghan Islamists and repeat the mistakes of the 1990s, the war in Ukraine continues to rage, increasing the likelihood that an anti-Western leader could, by utilizing Osama-esque tactics, learn to manage and manipulate the situation and hone his or her leadership and combat skills. Considering Osama's actions during the Soviet-Afghan War, it seems possible that such militants, while going largely unnoticed at the present time, could someday emerge on the world stage to threaten and ruthlessly strike deadly blows against the perceived enemies of their people and philosophical convictions.[277]

There are, of course, key differences between the currently ongoing Russo-Ukrainian War and the Soviet-Afghan War that trained bin Laden and al-Qaeda's founding generation in the tactical art of guerrilla warfare, helping them to subsequently export their battle-honed fighting skills to their militant Salafist brethren in Yemen and elsewhere. To be sure, the current war in Ukraine is a young conflict at this time, and neither diplomats nor scholars can predict how the results of the fighting may play out as each day seems to present fresh developments. Yet as explained throughout this book, bin Laden's rejection of other Arab volunteers' desire to rush into battle impatiently and untrained appears to have led him to embark on a pragmatic approach to organizing his Arab guerrilla band for the purpose of acquiring the battle experience necessary to apply in more effectively aiding the Islamist insurgents.[278] Other conflicts also provided such opportunities for Salafi jihadi fighters to obtain battle experience during the 1990s. Key al-Qaeda fighters and commanders such as Soviet-Afghan war veteran Mohanad al-Jadawi and his friend Nasser al-Bahri fought against Serbian troops in 1994 and 1995 during the war in Bosnia-Herzegovina as mentioned in Chapter 5.[279]

As pointed out by Nir Arielli in his 2018 book *From Byron to bin Laden: A History of Foreign War Volunteers*, wars throughout history have attracted foreign fighters to adhere to various ideologies for centuries. Citing the modern conflicts in Syria and Ukraine, Arielli calls attention to Chechen Islamist militants such as Abdulvakhid Edelgiriyev that fought alongside al-Qaeda or IS before traveling to Ukraine to attack Russian separatists there in 2015, as well as the case of Ruslan Starobudov, a veteran Russian soldier lending his experience in support of pro-Moscow separatists at roughly the same time.[280] Kurdish groups in Iraq and Syria have likewise employed foreign military volunteers, some of whom reportedly volunteered for combat in Ukraine.[281] The recent demonstration of tensions bordering on open conflict between Russian mercenary soldiers and their government appears to indicate that neither the West nor the East can fully control such groups any more than outside forces could control the Afghan and Arab guerrillas during or after the Soviet-Afghan War.[282] By no means do these facts alone render the current Russo-Ukraine conflict any more like the Soviet-Afghan War than those occurring elsewhere. Rather, they appear to render the war yet another brutal struggle in which protracted conflict, like the ongoing fighting in Yemen, Syria, and Mali, could potentially allow those seeking to inflict long-term harm on their perceived adversaries to follow bin Laden's deadly example in patiently acquiring the fighting experience to do so.[283]

AUTHOR'S AFTERWORD TO THE SECOND EDITION

As mentioned in this book's Prologue, bin Laden, like General Robert E. Lee during the American Civil War (1861-1865), managed to inflict severe psychological and physical damage on the United States and its closest allies in a way that no Soviet leader did in nearly a half-century of the costly, dangerous Cold War. It should also be noted here that like General Lee, bin Laden also inspired his men, and his courage and risk-taking actions, from digging guerrilla trenches under lethal Soviet fire and bombing to inhaling Soviet helicopter napalm and sustaining yet more combat wounds at Jaji in 1987 and Jalalabad in 1989, commanded their admiration and respect as they prepared with him in luring a second superpower into the mountainous Afghan deathtrap.[284] As with bin Laden more than a century later, Lee likewise rejected a true fanatic's path, and while he led the Confederacy's Army of Northern Virginia into battle in its rebellion against the United States, he also appears to have later rejected the urges of his subordinates to wage a postbellum guerrilla war against the North, wisely opting to surrender to the equally chivalrous and determined Union General Ulysses S. Grant and his Army of the Potomac in April 1865 and commanding his men to again become loyal U.S. citizens and fight no more.[285]

Lee's example, like bin Laden's for many of his militant Salafist brethren from the spring of 1987 until his killed-in-action, 2 May 2011 death, prevented futile, sectarian-like bloodshed, and during the last five years of the former Confederate commander's life, he is said to have led by example, just as he and bin Laden had done on the battlefield, in helping to calm resentment and reunite the republic, reportedly becoming the first white man to kneel and take communion alongside an elderly Black American man at St. Paul's Church in Richmond, Virginia.[286] While such actions cannot be said to render Lee any sort of humanitarian hero or ideal abolitionist in the mold of MP William Wilberforce, Frederick Douglass, or Senator Charles Sumner (R-MA), they certainly appear to distinguish him from being a truly fanatical "fire-eater" or antebellum pro-slavery figurehead along the lines of Edmund Ruffin, Representative Preston Brooks (D-SC), or MP George Hibbert. By the same token, bin Laden ruthlessly prosecuted his war with the West from the time of his 23 August 1996 declaration of war on the United States, Britain, and Israel forward, yet his firm, steady adherence to a pragmatic approach and rejection of sectarian violence indicates his faithful, staunch adherence to traditional Salafist custom and philosophical thought rather than that of a murderous, takfiri fanatic.[287]

Bin Laden, no less than Giuseppe Garibaldi, appears to have inspired his men, commanded their respect, and served as a present, approachable leader whose steadfastness under pressure and readiness to admit to and learn from his mistakes motivated them to fight harder in the face of seemingly insurmountable odds.[288] Just as Garibaldi is said to have inspired, recruited, and fought alongside his fellow volunteer Italian "Redshirts" in guerrilla wars in Brazil and Uruguay before returning to the Italian Peninsula battle-seasoned and prepared for leadership, bin Laden also led his lightly-trained and mostly inexperienced men, many of them sharing his ethnic *Qahtani* (South Arabian) origins, to fight tenaciously against the far superior Soviet troops and Special Forces, backed by aircraft and armor, at Jaji in 1987 and the Soviet-backed Afghan Army and Air Force at Jalalabad in 1989.[289] No less than Garibaldi's successes in militarily spearheading Italy's *Risorgimento* during the country's Wars of Independence and Unification fought between 1848 and 1871, bin Laden's battlefield exploits appear to have propelled him to leadership in the global Salafi jihadi movement and holy war hero status among his Saudi countrymen, stimulating recruitment and al-Qaeda's September 1988 birth as a deadly, battle-seasoned guerrilla vanguard group.[290]

Garibaldi's enemies, such as the French and Austrian army commanders occupying parts of disunited, mid-nineteenth-century Italy, naturally sought to defeat his movement, yet they recognized the lethal threat that he and his patriotic ideals, battle and command experience, and dynamic leadership example posed to their continued domination of parts of the Italian Peninsula.[291] Likewise, today's leaders and decision-makers can learn from the failures of their predecessors to recognize and develop a healthy respect for bin Laden as a worthy adversary and the reasons for which the al-Qaeda chief remains a threat long after his death. While he may have been physically consigned to become fish food somewhere beneath the Arabian Sea's waves more than a dozen years ago, courtesy of U.S. troops in Pakistan and the CIA's intelligence warriors, bin Laden, in spirit form, appears to have good reason to look back on his lethal legacy and smile his quiet, shy smile.[292]

Additional acknowledgments and concluding remark

Before adding to this book my concluding remark on bin Laden's life, actions, and place in world history, a topic that has fascinated me since my teenage years, I wish to thank here several people whose names I was unable to include in the Acknowledgements section when the first edition came out. I could not mention these wonderful people at the time because I had already written the Acknowledgements section and had not yet had the pleasure of meeting several of them or telling the ones who have known me my whole life about my project, as I wanted to be sure that its publication was, indeed, a reality before informing them. My Aunt, Karen Treadway, more than merits special mention here, as she is a wonderful, caring, and thoughtful person who, like my loving, entrepreneurial mother Rebecca, has never failed to express her support for my efforts and those of my beautiful, brilliant, Brazilian-born bride, Grazi.

Together with my heroic, late grandfather, James Harold Treadway, the greatest storyteller I have ever known, my wonderful, loving grandmother, Wanda Mae Treadway, read often to me as a child and inculcated in me a deep interest in and lifelong respect for history. I am also deeply and forever grateful to Dr. Blanca Caro Duran, Commissioning Editor at Vernon Press, for being absolutely kind, professional, and excellent to work with. Dr. Caro's willingness to accept my proposal to submit this detailed Afterword and publish with Vernon Press a second edition of *The Holy Warrior* made it possible for me to further improve my life's work, and without her approachability and kindness, this book would not now be in readers' hands. I also want to sincerely thank this book's peer reviewer, a true scholarly ace who is still anonymous to me at the time of writing, for helping me to improve my work through their extremely helpful suggestions and constructive criticism, which helped me to sharpen the book's key points and transform it into the masterpiece that I envisioned.

As the great medieval Muslim historiographer Ibn Khaldun wrote in the concluding remarks to his scholarly 1377 text *The Muqaddimah*, "Perhaps some later (scholar), aided by the divine gifts of a sound mind and of solid scholarship, will penetrate into these problems in greater detail than we [sic, I] did here."[293] Be that as it may, and while some readers may neither agree with nor appreciate my conclusions in this book, I can only express my sincerest hope that the book has served as the nonfiction cautionary tale and a more nuanced biographical portrait of bin Laden that I have intended it to be by calling attention to the need for scholars to understand his historical significance, lasting appeal, and the reasons for which he remains a potent threat a dozen years after his death. In this regard, I cannot agree more with Ibn Khaldun, as the North African-born scholar of Yemeni origin wrote, "You, student, should realize that I am here giving you useful (hints) for your study. If you accept them and follow them assiduously, you will find a great and noble treasure. Man's ability to think is a special natural gift that God created exactly as He created all His other creations."[294] It is a statement with which I completely concur, and I hope that this book, made possible by the 287 indispensable primary, secondary, and archival sources that I have consulted and cited in researching it, has helped the reader to understand that there remains no excuse to persist in believing the Manichaean myths that portray bin Laden as a mere madman, as the deadly threat that he posed lies rooted in history that remains dangerous to ignore.[295]

Yet history offers lessons on how the West can hope to decisively defeat the still growing and increasingly resilient post-9/11 global Sunni Islamist movement, and it appears that today's leaders must wisely begin, in Osama-esque fashion, to demonstrate a willingness to admit and learn from their past mistakes, and those of their predecessors, by refraining from policies that continue to draw Western military forces into traditional Muslim lands as perceived occupiers backing hated, minority central governments for prolonged periods.[296] On the rare occasions on which genuine U.S. or Western security interests are truly served by such military interventions, the campaigns must be conducted swiftly, perhaps no longer than a 12, 15, or 18-month period, and remain strictly focused on killing-in-action as many jihadi fighters and insurgent leaders as possible before executing a successful, victorious withdrawal. History's lessons appear to demonstrate that remaining to subsidize governments of the West's, or the East's, choice to vainly ensure that devout, tribal Muslim societies can produce spitting images of the latest pop culture celebrities will only result in the further recruitment and practical guerrilla war training of Salafi fighters for many generations.[297] In the unlikely event that such a hurricane-force, punitive effort becomes necessary, the mission must remain strictly military in its focus and objectives, and cannot be accomplished solely by CIA drone strikes, law enforcement efforts, and Elite Special Forces raids backed by carrier-based, U.S.-U.K. naval airpower. Valiant though such efforts are, the West's post 9/11 experience demonstrates that they are supplementary tools and are not war-winners in and of themselves, and such a mission is only likely to succeed with the full, unrestrained aid of the junior officers and enlisted men and women warriors of the U.S. Army and Marine Corps and their tenacious European and Canadian sisters and brothers serving in their counterpart military branches of NATO.

Finally, in beginning to tackle bin Laden's lethal legacy, scholars advising today's decision-makers and teaching tomorrow's leaders can consult the example of a former U.S. president whose actions, like bin Laden's later, catapulted him to hero status and distinguished him as a leader of men.[298] In a 10 April 1899 speech in Chicago, Illinois, New York Governor Theodore "Teddy" Roosevelt, the man after whom the teddy bear is said to have been named, urged those aspiring to leadership to embrace, "the strenuous life" of the rugged outdoorsman.[299] Like bin Laden, whose well-documented Spartan lifestyle reveals his staunch and militant adherence to Ibn Khaldun's teachings that warriors must abhor and resist luxuries and injustice while embracing nature and the outdoors to toughen themselves and forge solidarity with their people while leading by example, Roosevelt walked the walk of leadership rather than merely talking the talk, and resigned his position as U.S. Assistant Secretary of the Navy the year before his famous speech to recruit and organize in Texas the 1st United States Volunteer Cavalry, or "Rough Riders," to oust Spain's colonial forces from Cuba.[300]

Like bin Laden's al-Qaeda, the men that served in the ranks of Roosevelt's Rough Riders, or fought alongside them against the Spanish troops in Cuba, are said to have hailed from diverse ethnic, racial, cultural, and socioeconomic origins and reportedly included men from several American Indian nations, Ivy League alumni, Black and Hispanic American "buffalo soldiers" and cowboys, Texas Rangers, and frontiersmen. The *zeitgeist* in which Roosevelt and his Rough Riders lived and fought alongside each other rendered their exploits as a cohesive fighting unit even more remarkable and unlikely. Yet they fought together as comrades under his command, just as bin Laden's approachable, indirect management style and leadership example in risking life and limb battling the Soviets alongside his men reportedly helped him to forge the solidarity that Ibn Khaldun emphasized as crucial to warfare and leadership. Despite his imperfections and mistakes, like those inherent to bin Laden and all merely human historical figures, Roosevelt could not be accurately labeled a hypocrite by his critics, and, as he advised his countrymen to reject, "the life of ease" and take up, "the life of strenuous endeavor," there could be little doubt by his allies and opponents alike that he had led by example in wartime.[301]

Rather than continuing to arrogantly and unwisely dismiss bin Laden and those militant Salafists seeking to emulate his example most closely as a minuscule band of irrational, "violent extremists," "Islamofascists," "takfiris," or, in the Politburo of the CPSU Central Committee's misinformative words, "right-wing Muslim opposition," today's leaders can learn from history to avoid repeating the past's errors and handing the Salafi jihadis another 20 years or more to hone their fighting skills in battle with a superpower's forces.[302] Osama bin Laden, like Teddy Roosevelt, made a lasting impact on history, and the ball remains in the West's and the East's respective courts to learn from history how to avoid prolonging counterproductive wars and creating new generations of Osama bin Ladens enjoying the advantages of following in the founding al-Qaeda leader's footsteps. It is for these, and for the many other reasons discussed in this Afterword and in the preceding and succeeding chapters and sections of this second edition of *The Holy Warrior*, including many of the book's 1,057 total endnotes in which I elaborate further on specific key points, that I believe the lessons of history on which this book is closely focused to be equally as important, if not even more so, today, as they were on the date on which its first edition received publication.

James Reagan Fancher, M.A., Ph.D.

Denton, Texas

(Friday, 14 July 2023 A.D.)

ACKNOWLEDGEMENTS

Writing this book and seeing its publication become a reality has been the fulfillment of a lifelong dream for me, a dream that would not have come true without the crucial support of several wonderful people who more than merit special mention here. First, I wish to offer my deepest thanks to Dr. Victoria Echegaray, Assistant Editor at Vernon Press, for her interest and faith in my project. Dr. Echegaray kindly reached out to me after discovering my interest in this topic, and from my perspective her message was the answer to my daily prayers as I had just finished revising this book's first draft and hoped to find the perfect publisher.

I also want to sincerely thank Dr. Ellisa Anslow, Commissioning Editor at Vernon Press, for consistently keeping me informed during the peer review process and working with me to make this book a reality. Dr. Anslow and Dr. Echegaray are absolutely kind, professional, and reliably responsive to every email, keeping me informed of each step along the way. They were both immensely helpful to this first-time book author, and I cannot thank them and the rest of their excellent team at Vernon Press enough for the honor of working with them.

My loving, brilliant, and beautiful wife Graziele, to whom this book is dedicated first and foremost, made this work possible and worthwhile through her endless love, patience, encouragement, and support. My loving mother Rebecca has always encouraged me to pursue my dreams and to never lose hope on seeing them come to pass, and I can only hope that my work here reflects a fraction of the creativity and entrepreneurial drive that she has always sought to instill in me. Through their constant love, encouragement, and prayers, my father-in-law Vanderlei and mother-in-law Suzel Boleli have never wavered in their support for my efforts to make this dream a reality. I also wish to sincerely thank my dear Saudi friend and brother, Eissa Nasraldeen, for his many years of friendship and encouragement to continue pursuing my interest in and research on this topic while generously sharing his culture with me. Eissa's kindness has not only led to a lifelong friendship since our days together as undergraduate and graduate students at ULM but has enabled me to experience a fascinating and rich culture and its history firsthand.

I also want to thank one of my former professors and a brilliant scholar at the ULM History Department, Dr. Jeffrey Anderson, for his encouragement, constructive criticism, and positive words over the years. Dr. Anderson has not only been a true role model and mentor since my time as a history graduate student and assistant at ULM, but he also kindly agreed to proofread my first draft of the manuscript for this book, before revision and correction, in January 2021. He is a wonderful friend whose advice has always been honest, helpful, and encouraging, and I cannot thank him enough for taking the time to share it with me.

Finally, I would also like to sincerely thank the junior officers and enlisted men and women serving in the U.S. Armed Forces and Intelligence Community, particularly those in the U.S. Army, Marine Corps, and CIA. These men and women have found their efforts impaired by rules imposed on them that are not recognized by the Islamists while admirably defending the republic from the growing threat that they have continued to pose in the decades since 9/11. Like the Soviet troops before them, their achievements have also been obstructed by a similar desire by their collective leadership to remain militarily for an extended period to bolster besieged central governments while inadvertently allowing their jihadi adversaries to hone their skills in combat against them. These brave young people have persevered beyond measure despite witnessing their hard-won victories being constantly hamstrung by Washington's bipartisan bureaucrats whose apparently endless thirst for counterproductive wars continues to galvanize the holy warrior ranks and train new generations of jihadi recruits faster than those currently in the field can be killed.

Since receiving my M.A. in History in December 2017, I have had the great honor and privilege of teaching several of these outstanding warriors serving in the U.S. military about the martial origins of bin Laden and al-Qaeda in my World History survey courses. I have found many of them to be highly receptive to new information and having a healthy respect for and interest in the republic's Islamist foes as well as a determination to utterly defeat them. This mindset is crucial if Americans and their allies wish to avoid the fate of the arrogant Soviets by learning from past errors and denying further practical training to new generations of Salafi fighters patiently applying history's lessons to grow stronger in both victory and defeat.

GLOSSARY

Note: I have not sought to make this book's glossary exhaustive but to include in it only the major terms encountered frequently in the main body of text relating to religion, organizations, and some of the weapons relating to our topic that readers may be unfamiliar with. It therefore does not include every term that the reader may encounter while reading this book.

***Adnanis*-** According to Islamic tradition, these are the "Arabized Arabs" or "North Arabians" descended from Ishmael, brother of Isaac and son of the Biblical patriarch Abraham and Hagar, his servant. They therefore share partial ethnic heritage with the ancient Hebrews through Abraham and the ancient Egyptians through Hagar and adopted the Arab cultural identity, thus becoming "Arabized," following Ishmael's marriage to a Yemeni woman and the birth of their son, Adnan. Muhammad, the Prophet of Islam, hailed from this branch of the Arab peoples, as do the al-Saud royal family, their official religious establishment, known as the Al Ash Shaykh family, and the majority of Arabs from the Levant region, North Africa, and the northern part of the Arabian Peninsula.

AKS-74U- Initially reserved for Soviet special forces, this weapon first entered Afghanistan in 1985 following Mikhail Gorbachev's slightly escalated military campaign involving large numbers of Spestnaz commandos being deployed to the war zone. Firing a 5.45mm bullet known for tumbling through its victims, it is essentially a smaller and lighter variant of the AK-74, a more modern adaptation of the better known and much more common AK-47 assault rifle designed by Mikhail Kalashnikov. Osama bin Laden seized an AKS-74U, known to the Arab fighters as a "Kalakov," after killing the Soviet commando wielding it during fierce hand-to-hand combat at the 1987 Battle of Jaji, and subsequently kept the weapon as his side. It is also reportedly referred to as "the Osama" in jihadi circles.

AQAP- Al-Qaeda on the Arabian Peninsula, the Yemeni wing of the same global organization founded by bin Laden and his senior lieutenants in September 1988 with a growing presence and local wings on at least five continents.

***badal*-** Meaning "revenge," this is a Pashtun tribal concept and a key component of *Pashtunwali* promising that warriors will fight fiercely to avenge the deaths or dishonoring of their loved ones or fellow tribesmen by slaying their killers or oppressors. Like the Pashtuns, the Yemeni tribes live by an identical warrior code of revenge as a key component of their tribal law or *urf*.

BM-21- Known to Soviet troops as *Grad* or "Hail," these truck-mounted 122mm multiple rocket launchers saw action in the Soviet-Afghan War where they were used by the Soviet troops who brought them to Afghanistan and the Afghan and Arab fighters who managed to capture them.

Brezhnev Doctrine- Aggressive Soviet Cold War foreign policy of supporting the advance of communist forces on a global scale adopted in the 1970s by Soviet General Secretary Leonid Brezhnev and his KGB Chairman and immediate successor in the Kremlin, Yuri Andropov. Under this doctrine, Soviet leaders committed themselves to dramatically increasing covert and overt aid to communist regimes and insurgencies in Asia, Africa, and Latin America, ultimately leading them into the reluctant decision to invade Afghanistan and the resulting war against the Islamic guerrillas for which they were unprepared.

CIA- Central Intelligence Agency of the United States. Contrary to popular perceptions, CIA directors answer directly to the White House as the agency serves as the U.S. president's personal intelligence service.

cluster bombing- Considered to be especially effective against guerrilla fighters, this is a form of aerial bombardment in which attacking aircraft drop large bombs each of which then open to release and scatter hundreds of smaller "bomblets" over a wide area, creating multiple explosive "ripple effects" over enemy targets. During the Soviet-Afghan War, Soviet planes engaged in intense cluster bombing to strike the guerrillas in their mountain bases and interdict their supply routes along the Afghan-Pakistani border.

CPSU- Communist Party of the Soviet Union.

Deobandism- A puritanical minority sect within the Hanafi school of Sunni Islam originating in the Indian subcontinent. The movement is named after the northern Indian city of Deoband where it emerged in an Islamic seminary as a reaction against British rule in the eighteenth century. The Deobandis of the Taleban share many customs with the Salafi jihadis of al-Qaeda, yet there are key differences, such as the Taleban's traditional opposition to women's education and their practice of praying at the graves of fallen martyrs.

Eid al-Fitr- A holy day for Muslims marking the end of Ramadan and the ending of the daily dawn to dusk fast or *sawm* performed during the holy month.

GLOSSARY

Faridat al-Jihad - A defensive jihad, historically referring to a holy war of resistance, following an invasion of a Muslim country by those perceived as occupiers. For non-Muslim Westerners and peoples of the former Soviet republics, it may be useful to think of such a trigger event as having the psychological impact and galvanizing effect of the Pearl Harbor attack or the Nazi invasion of the Soviet Union in stimulating a grassroots response by Islamist militants rallying to defend their besieged faith and brethren. In such an event, such as the Soviet invasion of Afghanistan, militant Salafists believe that it is the responsibility of every able-bodied Muslim to support his or her brethren in the country under attack or occupation, and not merely of those living in the afflicted country. This support may come in the form of financing the resistance fighters and their war effort or participating in frontline combat as a mujahid depending on the request for aid from the Muslim population under attack.

fajr - The dawn prayer performed by Muslims. Osama bin Laden was said to be particularly inspired for battles and other actions by performing the dawn prayer.

FIM-92 - Known as the "Stinger," this is a heat-seeking missile developed by the United States in the 1980s and eventually supplied by the CIA to the Afghan Islamist insurgents beginning in late September 1986. While far from a war winner in and of itself, the weapon proved very effective in shooting down Soviet planes and helicopters and provided a tremendous morale boost to the mujahedin fighters.

GID - Saudi Arabia's General Intelligence Directorate intelligence agency. Bin Laden worked closely with GID, but was not a member himself, during the Soviet-Afghan War of the 1980s.

Grand Mosque - Islam's holiest site located in the holy city of Mecca in Saudi Arabia.

GRU - Soviet and modern Russian military intelligence agency responsible for Special Forces *(Spetsnaz)* operations.

hijra - A term referring to the Prophet Muhammad's journey from Mecca to Medina, then known as Yathrib, to escape his unbelieving Quraish tribe that sought to kill him and his followers, the first Muslims. In reference to this example of leaving a place of unbelief for a place of relief, the Saudi Ikhwan warriors referred to their communal agricultural colonies as *hujar*, the plural of *hijra*.

Ikhwan - Tribal religious militia representing the first modern Salafi jihadi movement in early twentieth-century Arabia. The Ikhwan hailed from almost all tribes on the Arabian Peninsula and helped establish the Kingdom of Saudi Arabia before conflict broke out between the movement and the Saudi King, Ibn Saud.

ISI - Inter-Services-Intelligence, the Pakistani military intelligence agency.

al-Islah - Yemeni Salafist opposition movement founded by bin Laden and Shaykh Abd al-Majid al-Zindani to help organize resistance against South Yemen's communist regime.

Islamism - Ideological movement of Islamic fundamentalists (Islamists) from both denominations and all Muslim sects seeking the restoration of *Shariah* (Islamic law) in Muslim countries.

KGB - Soviet intelligence agency, the Committee for State Security.

KhAD - Intelligence agency of the Afghan PDPA regime.

Kifayat al-Jihad - Known as "preemptive" jihad, this is an act of military aggression and can only be declared by a *caliph*. After being declared, only Muslims serving in the armed forces of the country at war are required to participate in such a conflict of expansion.

Koran/*Quran* - The holy book of Islam.

madrassa - An Islamic religious seminary, often connected to a mosque.

***Makhtab al-Khadamat* (MK)** - Meaning "Services Bureau," this was an organization established by Abdullah Azzam, Abdullah Anas, and Osama bin Laden in 1984 to help recruit non-Afghan volunteers from throughout the Muslim world but primarily from Arab nations to support the Afghan insurgents through financing, humanitarian aid work, or frontline combat participation as guerrilla fighters, transforming the anti-Soviet Afghan jihad into a global holy war. Modeled after the Saudi non-governmental organizations (NGOs) assisting the Afghan warriors and refugee families in Pakistan, MK operated between 1984 and Azzam's death in November 1989. Bin Laden financed the group's operations, propaganda activities, and recruitment efforts until after the official establishment of al-Qaeda as a separate and independent organization in September 1988.

***melmastia*-** Meaning "hospitality," this is a Pashtun tribal concept and a key component of *Pashtunwali* promising shelter for refugees and exiles, especially those perceived as holy warriors fighting in the path of God against Islam's perceived foes. Yemeni tribal law or *urf* also mandates the protection of such guests seeking shelter.

MI-6- Britain's foreign intelligence agency, known as Secret Intelligence Service.

Mikoyan MiG-27- Known as "Flogger," this is a powerful Soviet ground attack plane and fighter-bomber rarely deployed outside the Soviet Union but introduced in Afghanistan beginning in 1987 to support ongoing counterinsurgency operations, often dropping cluster bombs over insurgent strongholds, as Gorbachev's generals desperately sought to crush the resistance.

Mil Mi-24- Designed and produced by the Soviet helicopter factory Mil, this helicopter gunship, code-named "Hind" in NATO military circles but known as the "flying tank" and *krokodil* by Soviet pilots, saw constant action throughout the Soviet-Afghan War. The world's best attack helicopter at the time, it contained 128 rocket and four missiles and also served as a low-capacity troop transporter to insert Soviet Special Forces commandos, or *Spetsnaz*, in assaults on guerrilla positions. These powerful weapons of war could also carry and fire up to 30 grenades, launch the notorious Soviet PFM-1 "butterfly mines," and deploy napalm, a highly flammable incendiary substance, as well. They remained a menacing presence in the skies throughout the war, inflicting massive casualties on the mujahedin fighters even after the resistance began acquiring U.S. Stinger missiles.

mosque/*masjid*- An Islamic house of worship, where services are presided over by an *imam* or prayer leader.

***mufti*-** A Muslim theological and legal expert who can issue a religious juridical decree or *fatwa*.

***mujahid*-** A resistance fighter participating in a defensive jihad as a "holy warrior" following an act of foreign aggression against Muslims. Groups of these resistance fighters are collectively known as *mujahedin*. A woman may participate in combat only if Muslim women in the country under attack have begun to do so in self-defense, a condition that did not occur during the Soviet-Afghan War but has since changed in other embattled regions such as Chechnya and Russia's North Caucasus region.

mullah- A Muslim theological and legal expert who can also lead prayers as an *imam*. The term is widely used in Sunni Muslim communities throughout South Asia.

National Security Decision Directive (NSDD)- A type of presidential directive used during Ronald Reagan's presidency in which he issued instructions to his advisers and assistants on matters relating to U.S. national security and defense.

NATO/Western Bloc (est. April 1949)- An acronym for the North Atlantic Treaty organization, NATO was initially formed as an alliance between the United States and Western European countries to counter aggressive Soviet expansion in Europe. Several key NATO member states, particularly the United States, Britain, and France, also undertook efforts to counter communist expansion on a global scale by supporting local allies or independent anti-communist resistance groups in Asia, Africa, and Latin America, leading to increased involvement by these countries in the Muslim world, and growing Sunni Islamist resentment over the perceived threat posed by the West's support for the unpopular regimes in the region.

Pashtuns/Pathans- These people are the ethnic majority in Afghanistan as well as the largest minority group in Pakistan. Pashtuns also comprise most of the core members of the Taleban, although the movement has increasingly been recruiting members of other ethnic groups throughout Afghanistan into its ranks in recent years.

Pashtunwali- This is the tribal legal code of the Pashtun tribes in Afghanistan and Pakistan, sometimes compared to *Shariah* law, and resembling it in many ways while also remaining distinct.

PDPA- People's Democratic Party of Afghanistan, the Afghan Communist Party further divided between the rival *Khalq* and *Parcham* factions.

PFM-1- Known as the "butterfly mine" due to their distinctive shape, these Soviet-made mines were employed by the 40th Army during its occupation of Afghanistan throughout the 1980s. Soviet troops planted millions of land mines in Afghanistan during the war, making it the world's most mined country, and Soviet helicopters sometimes fired them in huge numbers to ensure their wide distribution in fields and villages, hoping to cripple the insurgency by creating large numbers of wounded fighters and civilians. As the butterfly mine is designed to injure rather than kills its victims, the Soviets hoped to create havoc

GLOSSARY 149

in the insurgent ranks as caring for an injured man sapped more enemy manpower than burying a dead one.

Politburo- The executive committee of the Communist Party of the Soviet Union (CPSU) answering to the General Secretary of the CPSU.

qabili- Meaning "tribesman," this is Yemen's traditional warrior class, although the country's ancient imamate caste system was officially abolished in 1962. As the tribes represent Yemen's majority population, the *qabili* ousted the British colonial troops from Aden, repulsed an invasion by Egypt's Soviet-backed Nasser regime, and flocked to the mujahid ranks during and after the Soviet-Afghan War. The term *qabili* is derived from the root word *qabila* meaning "tribe."

Qahtanis- According to Islamic tradition, these are the original Arab people also known as "South Arabians." Known as the Arabs of Yemeni origin, they are the indigenous people of South Arabia, a historical region covering modern Yemen, the Saudi provinces of Najran, Jazan, and Asir, and the Dhofar region of western Oman. They trace their ancestry to the Biblical figure Joktan, known in Arabic as Qahtan, a great-great grandson of Shem, son of Noah. The medieval scholars Al-Kindi and Ibn Khaldun hailed from this branch of the Arab peoples, as do the sultans of Oman and several important Saudi business families of Yemeni origins including the bin Mahfouz, al-Amoudis, Baroum, and bin Ladens.

al-Raya- Meaning, "the Banner" and popularly known in much of the West as the "black flag of jihad," this flag was flown by the Prophet Muhammad and his companions when they were forced to resort to armed resistance against Islam's enemies during the religion's early history. Emulating the Prophet's example, the Saudi Ikhwan warriors also rallied around it in early twentieth-century Arabia, and various Afghan insurgent groups and al-Qaeda revived its use for the same reasons during the Soviet-Afghan War. While the flag comes in several variations, it always features a black background in a sign of mourning, as war is not to be celebrated. The version used by Osama bin Laden also includes a large white *shahada*, the Muslim profession of faith, emblazoned in Arabic script across the front, reading from right to left, "There is no god but Allah (God) and Muhammad is His Rasul (Prophet)."

R-300 "Elbrus"- Known in NATO military circles as Scud, these tactical ballistic missiles acquired a fearsome reputation in Afghanistan, like the Mi-24 helicopter gunships, after being introduced by the Soviets prior to their withdrawal in early 1989.

Reagan Doctrine- Cold War foreign policy adopted by U.S. President Ronald Reagan and CIA Director Bill Casey to counter the Soviet Union's aggressive Brezhnev Doctrine by supporting anti-communist resistance fighters actively engaging communist regimes or Soviet occupation forces in their countries. Through this policy, Reagan and his top officials sought to repulse Soviet aggression while avoiding outright war with Moscow and the resulting nuclear devastation of Europe and North America by actively supporting those already resisting dictatorial communist regimes and Soviet aggression in Afghanistan and elsewhere.

RPG-7- Soviet-designed rocket-propelled grenade launcher popular with the Afghan and Arab fighters who captured and used them in battle as antitank weapons.

salaf- Meaning "pious ancestors." Refers to the Prophet Muhammad, his companions, and the first three generations of Muslims.

Salafism- A puritanical minority sect within the Hanbali school of Sunni Islam originating on the Arabian Peninsula and focused on a literal interpretation of the Koran, the *sunnah* (or *hadith*), and the practices of the *salaf*.

Salafi jihadis- Militant Salafists advocating a war of resistance against perceived enemies of Islam, whether infidel powers or nominal Muslim rulers, to purify Islam, restore *Shariah* law in Muslim countries, and reconquer lands taken from Muslims by force, from southern Spain to Mindanao. The movement led by these men emerged following the Soviet invasion of Afghanistan in late 1979. They are a minority within Salafism, which is a minority sect within Sunni Islam, yet a legitimate and growing minority due to their focus on the traditions of the Koran and *sunnah* and the growing perception among Sunni Muslims that the U.S. government and other foreign powers seek to dominate Muslims by supporting corrupt and dictatorial regimes in their countries.

Shariah- Sunni Islamic law.

Shia/Shi'ite Muslims- Followers of the minority denomination of Islam, comprising some 15% of Muslims worldwide. Following Muhammad's death, the Shia declared that only one of his relatives could be worthy of leading the global Muslim nation or *ummah*, supporting his nephew and son-in-law, Ali. They therefore became known as the *Shi'at Ali* or "Party of Ali," hence the term "Shia."

***Shura* Council**- A "consultative council" or "advisory council" chaired by a traditional Muslim ruler or military commander in which he allows debate, listens to various opinions, seeks advice, and weighs all options before deciding on a specific course of action. Both Osama bin Laden and Taleban leader Mullah Muhammad Omar chaired *Shura* Councils in their respective organizations, even after bin Laden's 1998 oath of allegiance or *bayat* to Mullah Omar.

***Spetsnaz*-** Elite special forces commandos in the Soviet and modern Russian armies, closely linked with military intelligence (GRU) operations.

Sukhoi Su-25- Known as *Grach* or "Raven" to Soviet pilots but "Frogfoot" in NATO military circles, these close air support jet aircraft played a major role in Soviet counterinsurgency operations in Afghanistan, often dropping cluster bombs on the insurgent strongholds.

***sunnah/hadith*-** The collection of the verified traditions and sayings of the Prophet Muhammad.

Sunni Muslims- Followers of the majority denomination of Islam, comprising some 85% of Muslims worldwide. Devout Sunnis reject the notion that a *caliph* or successor to Muhammad must be descended from him by blood relation. Within Sunni Islam, there are numerous minority sects with distinctive customs, such as the Salafists on the Arabian Peninsula and the Deobandis in South Asia.

***ulema*-** A collective body of Muslim religious scholars and legal experts.

Tajiks- An ethnic Iranian people forming the majority of inhabitants of the Central Asian nation of Tajikistan, they are also found in northern Afghanistan where they form a local majority while remaining a national minority. The Afghan insurgent commander Ahmed Shah Massoud was a strong leader of Afghanistan's ethnic Tajiks.

takfiris- These truly radical and extreme individuals are a miniscule and largely shunned minority in the Muslim world. They differ greatly from Salafists and Wahhabis by displaying a fanatical obsession with declaring all other Muslims to be insufficiently Islamic and take it upon themselves to target these individuals, whether Shia Muslims or Sunnis of other sects, resulting in sectarian violence. The Jordanian militant Abu Musab al-Zarqawi is one example of a takfiri.

***ummah*-** The international community of Muslim believers. The concept transcends tribal and ethnic differences, nationalities, class divisions, and other social factors, emphasizing unity as one family of the faithful.

Wahhabism- While Wahhabism shares the same theological origins as Salafism, deriving from the same Hanbali school of Sunni Islam, Wahhabis are differentiated by their general shunning of non-Arab Sunni Muslims and are far less tolerant of the diversity in customs and thought within the other Sunni Muslim sects, an outlook not shared by the traditional Salafists.

Warsaw Pact/Eastern Bloc (est. May 1955)- A political and military alliance between the Soviet Union and the communist regimes that it backed in Eastern Europe. Led by the Soviet Union, several other Warsaw Pact countries including East Germany, Bulgaria, and Czechoslovakia, together with the communist regimes of Cuba and Vietnam, also supported the unpopular Marxist regimes in Afghanistan, South Yemen, and elsewhere by sending troops to bolster the oppressive regimes against these countries' domestic Sunni Islamist resistance groups and their devout and fiercely independent tribal supporters.

Yemeni Socialist Party (YSP)- The official name of the Communist Party of South Yemen that ruled the country between 1970 and 1990 with Soviet and Warsaw Pact support and shared power with Yemeni nationalists between national reunification in 1990 and the party's defeat in the 1994 civil war.

NOTES

PREFACE

[1] Abd al-Rahman Ibn Khaldun, *The Muqaddimah – An Introduction to History: The Classic Islamic History of the World*, ed. N.J. Dawood, trans. Franz Rosenthal, (Princeton: Princeton University Press, 2015), 459.

[2] Peter L. Bergen, *Holy War, Inc.: Inside the Secret World of Osama bin Laden* (New York: Simon & Schuster, 2002), 57-58.

[3] Bergen, *Holy War, Inc.*, 34; Yossef Bodansky, *Bin Laden: The Man Who Declared War on America* (New York: Random House, 2001), 3, 101.

[4] Bergen, *Holy War, Inc.*, 226-227.

[5] Peter L. Bergen, *The Osama bin Laden I Know: An Oral History of al-Qaeda's Leader* (New York: Free Press, 2006), 54-55.

[6] Steve Coll, *Ghost Wars: The Secret History of the CIA, Afghanistan, and bin Laden, From the Soviet Invasion to September 10, 2001* (New York: The Penguin Press, 2004), 74-75.

[7] Abdullah Anas and Tam Hussein, *To the Mountains: My Life in Jihad from Algeria to Afghanistan* (London: C. Hurst & Co., 2019), 63; Steve Coll, *The Bin Ladens: An Arabian Family in the American Century* (New York: Penguin Books, 2009), 256, 377, 381; Rob Schultheis, *Hunting bin Laden: How al-Qaeda is Winning the War on Terror* (New York: Skyhorse Publishing, 2008), 54-55; Lawrence Wright, *The Looming Tower: Al-Qaeda and the Road to 9/11* (New York: Vintage, 2007), 100, 116, 138.

[8] Coll, *The Bin Ladens*, 302.

[9] Michael Scheuer, *Osama bin Laden* (New York: Oxford University Press, 2012), 1-2.

[10] Scheuer, *Osama bin Laden*, 48-49, 52-54.

[11] Ibid., 112-113.

[12] Coll, *The Bin Ladens*, 256, 377, 381; Scheuer, *Osama bin Laden*, 63-64; Wright, *The Looming Tower*, 100, 116, 138.

[13] Coll, *Ghost Wars*, 204; and Scheuer, *Osama bin Laden*, 4-5, 189n5.

[14] Scheuer, *Osama bin Laden*, 4-8, 182-183.

[15] Anas and Hussein, *To the Mountains*, 63.

[16] Schultheis, *Hunting bin Laden*, 54-55.

[17] Ibid.

[18] *The Bukovsky Archives*, "Communism on Trial," "The Situation in the Democratic Republic of Afghanistan and possible measures for its improvement," 29 June 1979, https://bukovsky-archive.com/2016/07/09/29-june-1979-pb-156ix/.

[19] Robert D. Kaplan, *Soldiers of God: With Islamic Warriors in Afghanistan and Pakistan* (New York: Vintage Books, 2001), 10-11; David B. Ottaway, "Agreement on Afghanistan Signed in Geneva," *The Washington Post*, 15 April 1988, https://www.washingtonpost.com/archive/politics/1988/04/15/agreement-on-afghanistan-signed-in-geneva/c7288c64-6764-4e73-9bc5-7eeb48f7827d/.

[20] Osama bin Laden, "Open Letter for Sheikh Bin Baz," Advice and Reform Committee (ARC) communiques, 1994-1998, 29 December 1994, and OBL, "Open message to King

Fahd," ARC, 3 August 1995, *Combating Terrorism Center at West Point*, https://ctc.usma.edu/wp-content/uploads/2013/10/Letter-from-Bin-Laden-Translation.pdf; Scheuer, *Osama bin Laden*, 76-77.

[21] Omar Nasiri, *Inside the Jihad: My Life with al-Qaeda* (New York: Basic Books, 2008), 149.

[22] At the time of writing, Afghanistan and Yemen continue to serve as examples of this boomerang effect, with the Taleban and al-Qaeda growing increasingly resilient as foreign powers continue supporting one side or another, each apparently disregarding the lessons of history and generating resentment among the fiercely independent, religious, and tribal populations in these countries that largely remain militantly opposed to perceived infidel invaders and those regarded as their local, apostate client rulers. It is little wonder then that the Taleban, like their Afghan mujahedin forebears, have fought a second superpower to a standstill and al-Qaeda on the Arabian Peninsula (AQAP), the global organization's Yemeni wing, has been considered the most dangerous and resilient branch of the group for more than a decade, nearly bombing Northwest Airlines Flight 253 as it approached Detroit Metropolitan Airport on Christmas Day 2009 and striking inside the United States at a Pensacola, Florida Naval Air Station a decade later in December 2019. See, for example, Samy Magdy, "Al-Qaida in Yemen claims deadly shooting at Florida's Naval Air Station Pensacola," *Navy Times*, 2 February 2020, https://www.navytimes.com/news/your-navy/2020/02/02/al-qaida-in-yemen-claims-deadly-shooting-at-floridas-naval-air-station-pensacola/; Mujib Mashal, "How the Taliban Outlasted a Superpower: Tenacity and Carnage," *The New York Times*, 26 May 2020, https://www.nytimes.com/2020/05/26/world/asia/taliban-afghanistan-war.html; Reuters Staff, "Bin Laden claims U.S. plane bombing attempt," *Reuters*, 24 January 2010, https://cn.reuters.com/article/instant-article/idUKTRE60N0L920100124; and Eric Tucker, "FBI: Shooter at Pensacola Navy Base coordinated with al-Qaida," *Military Times*, 18 May 2020, https://www.militarytimes.com/news/your-military/2020/05/18/official-fbi-finds-link-between-pensacola-gunman-al-qaida/.

PROLOGUE

[1] Bergen, *The Osama bin Laden I Know*, 54-55.

[2] Lawrence Malkin, "Reagan and the End of the Cold War," *The New York Times*, 14 June 2012, https://www.nytimes.com/2012/06/15/opinion/reagan-and-the-end-of-the-cold-war.html.

[3] Ibn Khaldun, *The Muqaddimah*, 67, 107, 109, 114-115, 227. An early pioneer of historiography, the study of historical writing and research methods, Ibn Khaldun discusses the alleged corrupting and weakening influence of luxuries and material comforts most clearly and eloquently on these pages but returns to the topic repeatedly throughout the book. The first authors to identify Ibn Khaldun's influence on bin Laden and the way that he organized al-Qaeda appear to be Malise Ruthven and Michael Scheuer. Both authors point to the great Arab scholar's impact on the personal lifestyle and leadership example of the al-Qaeda chief. As a dedicated student of management and economics, despite abandoning his college studies to fight the Soviets, bin Laden likely studied the teachings of Ibn Khaldun from the time of his youth in Saudi Arabia, as the medieval scholar devotes considerable space to these topics and bin Laden's modest lifestyle is described in nearly all primary accounts, particularly those by Najwa and Omar bin Laden, the al-Qaeda leader's childhood friend, Khaled al-Batarfi, and his

former chief bodyguard Nasser al-Bahri. For two excellent scholarly analyses of this topic see Malise Ruthven, "The eleventh of September and the Sudanese mahdiyya in the context of Ibn Khaldun's theory of Islamic history," *International Affairs*, Vol. 78, Issue 2 (April 2002), 339-351, https://academic.oup.com/ia/article-abstract/78/2/339/2434744?redirectedFrom=fulltext.; and Michael Scheuer, *Osama bin Laden* 17, 37-38; and for several detailed firsthand accounts of bin Laden's modest and Spartan daily living despite his family's immense wealth, see Najwa bin Laden, Omar bin Laden, and Jean Sasson, *Growing Up bin Laden: Osama's Wife and Son Take us Inside Their Secret World* (London: OneWorld Books, 2016), 25, 53, 166; Dr. Khaled M. al-Batarfi, "Growing up with Osama: 2 youths took different paths," *Seattle Times*, 6 January 2007, https://www.seattletimes.com/nation-world/growing-up-with-osama-2-youths-took-different-paths/; and Nasser al-Bahri and Georges Malbrunot, *Guarding bin Laden: My Life in al-Qaeda*, ed. and trans. Susan de Muth, (London, Thin Man Press, 2013), 76, 206-208.

[4] Al-Bahri and Malbrunot, *Guarding bin Laden*, 210-211; Scheuer, *Osama bin Laden*, 77-78.

[5] Osama bin Laden, "Jihad Against Jews and Crusaders: World Islamic Front Statement," 23 February 1998, https://fas.org/irp/world/para/docs/980223-fatwa.htm; Lewis, "License to Kill: Usama bin Ladin's Declaration of Jihad," *Foreign Affairs* (November/December 1998), https://www.foreignaffairs.com/articles/saudi-arabia/1998-11-01/license-kill-usama-bin-ladins-declaration-jihad.

[6] John Miller, "Greetings America. My Name is Osama bin Laden," *Esquire*, 1 February 1999, http://www.esquire.com/news-politics/a1813/osama-bin-laden-interview/; The Middle East Forum, "Usama bin Ladin: 'American Soldiers are Paper Tigers,'" *Middle East Quarterly*, Vol. 5 No. 4 (December 1998), 73-79, https://www.meforum.org/435/usama-bin-ladin-american-soldiers-are-paper-tigers. Bin Laden does not appear to have claimed that he or al-Qaeda, being just one Arab Muslim guerrilla and a small organization, could hope to defeat the United States militarily, but reportedly expressed his hope to Miller and others that they could inspire their militant compatriots to take up arms or contribute financial donations to help bleed the Americans economically through guerrilla warfare just as the Soviet economy had been drained to an extent by the insurgency in Afghanistan. Miller also discusses the arduous living conditions that bin Laden shared with his men and contrasts this with previous experiences interviewing Cuban President Fidel Castro and Libyan ruler Colonel Muammar Qaddafi. According to Miller, bin Laden served meals and provided transportation and travel arrangements for his journalistic guests but also expected them to temporarily tolerate the same Spartan living conditions that he and his men endured daily, while Castro and Qaddafi appear to have indulged in luxuries and treated visiting journalists to extravagant hotel accommodations.

[7] Elizabeth Brown Pryor, *Reading the Man: A Portrait of Robert E. Lee Through His Private Letters* (New York: Penguin, 2007), 172-174, 231, 323-325.

[8] Brown Pryor, *Reading the Man*, 172-174, 231, 323-325.

[9] Ali Abd-al-Karim and Nur Ahmad al-Nur, "Interview with Saudi businessman Usama bin Ladin," *Al-Quds al-Arabi*, 9 March 1994, https://scholarship.tricolib.brynmawr.edu/bitstream/handle/10066/4733/OBL19940309.pdf; Miller, "Greetings America. My Name is Osama bin Laden."

[10] Karl Marx, *The Eighteenth Brumaire of Louis Bonaparte* (New York: International Publishers, 1994), 5-7.

[11] Vladimir I. Lenin, *Essential Works of Lenin*, ed. Henry M. Christman (Mineola, NY: Dover Publications, 1987), 116-117, 120, 173-175.
[12] Marx, *The Eighteenth Brumaire*, 5-7.
[13] Coll, *The Bin Ladens*, 57; Scheuer, *Osama bin Laden* 195n9.
[14] Marx, *The Eighteenth Brumaire*, 5-7, 126-128.

CHAPTER 1

[1] John Lewis Gaddis, *The Landscape of History: How Historians Map the Past*, 52-54, 65 (New York: Oxford University Press, 2004.
[2] Gaddis, *The Landscape of History*, 52-54, 65.
[3] Albert Hourani, *A History of the Arab Peoples* (Cambridge, MA: Harvard University Press, 2002), 144, 179-180.
[4] Delong-Bas, Natana J., *Wahhabi Islam: From Revival and Reform to Global Jihad* (New York: Oxford University Press, 2004), 4, 21; Scheuer, *Osama bin Laden*, 42-43.
[5] Scheuer, *Osama bin Laden*, 42-43.
[6] Abdel Bari Atwan, *The Secret History of al-Qaeda* (Berkeley: University of California Press, 2008), 220; Delong-Bas, *Wahhabi Islam*, 54-56.
[7] Atwan, *The Secret History of al-Qaeda*, 220; Richard A. Gabriel, *Muhammad: Islam's First Great General* (Norman: University of Oklahoma Press, 2007), 218. Some scholars tend to lean heavily on the popular claim that jihad refers to personal and societal improvement rather than warfare. In this sense they are partially correct in stating that holy war may not be the literal translation of jihad. The term *harb* means "war" in the Arabic language, and there is a Saudi tribe of Yemeni origin called the Harb or "War" tribe. In historical literature however, *qital fi sabillillah*, or "fighting in the path of God" is often understood as relating to warfare, or at the very least an act of resistance, whether one is fighting against temptation, false teachings, or physical infidel aggression. A good comparison is the tendency of U.S. public officials to refer to a "war on drugs" or "war on poverty." While this may not mean a literal declaration of war and the inflicting of violence on drugs or the causes of poverty, it is understood as a serious resistance effort to resolve these problems and the harm that they bring to individuals and society. In the same manner, jihad has historically been understood to define a resistance effort, sometimes referring to self-improvement, but often relating to warfare in defense of the faith and brethren. The medieval scholar Ibn Khaldun, among many others, explicitly referred to such armed resistance efforts to defend Muslims and their faith as being literally defined as, "the holy war" and, "holy and just wars" mandated by, "the religious law [*Shariah*]." While some scholars may continue debating the literal terminology relating to jihad, the West's foremost enemies in the Salafi jihadi movement suffer from no confusion regarding the historical facts. Bin Laden's former chief bodyguard Nasser al-Bahri and the al-Qaeda leader himself consistently referred to their armed struggle as, "Holy War" and those waging it against Islam's perceived foes as, "Holy Warriors." See also Ibn Khaldun, *The Muqaddimah*,158, 180-183, 223-224; al-Bahri and Malbrunot, *Guarding bin Laden*, 16-17, 106; Bin Laden, bin Laden, and Sasson, *Growing Up bin Laden*, 219-221; and Scheuer, *Osama bin Laden*, 112.
[8] Geoffrey Hindley, *Saladin: Hero of Islam* (Barnsley, South Yorkshire: Pen & Sword, 2015), 21, 34-35; James Reston, Jr., *Warriors of God: Richard the Lionheart and Saladin in the Third* Crusade (New York: Anchor Books, 2002), 37-38, 128-128.

[9] Nasiri, *Inside the Jihad*, 149; Scheuer, *Osama bin Laden*, 44.
[10] Nasiri, *Inside the Jihad*, 149.
[11] Atwan, *The Secret History of al-Qaeda*, 220.
[12] Abd-al-Karim and al-Nur, "Interview with Saudi businessman Usama bin Ladin,"; OBL, "Open Letter for Sheikh Bin Baz," ARC, 29 December 1994. For example, as late as a 19 May 2011 speech, two weeks after ordering and overseeing the operation by U.S. troops that killed bin Laden in Pakistan, President Barack Obama continued echoing the claims of his White House predecessors by dismissing the al-Qaeda chief and his followers as a limited number of irrational, bloodthirsty fanatics with a miniscule following and motivated only by, "violent extremism" and a blind hatred of Western freedoms, popular culture, and secular democracy. Former CIA Director John O. Brennan, the Obama administration's top Terrorism Czar, had previously characterized bin Laden and al-Qaeda in this way in a 6 August 2009 speech addressing the continued threat posed by the jihadi group. Similarly, as late as early January 2019, while concluding that the Afghan Islamists' attritional guerrilla war had damaged the Soviet economy, President Donald Trump reportedly stated that the Kremlin had been, "right" to invade Afghanistan as, "terrorists" based there had been raiding into the Soviet Union, even though neither the Afghan or non-Afghan Salafi fighters such as bin Laden received the necessary practical training to incite and support an Islamist insurgency in Soviet Central Asia until after the Soviet invasion, an event that provided them with both a target to unite against and the battle experience that trained them for later insurgency support operations. See Peter Baker, "Why Did the Soviets Invade Afghanistan? Documents Offer History Lesson for Trump," *The New York Times*, 29 January 2019, https://www.nytimes.com/2019/01/29/us/politics/afghanistan-trump-soviet-union.html; John O. Brennan, "A New Approach to Safeguarding Americans," *Foreign Policy*, 6 August 2009, https://foreignpolicy.com/2009/08/06/a-new-approach-to-safeguarding-americans/; and President Barack Obama, "Obama's Mideast Speech – Text – The New York Times," *The New York Times*, 19 May 2011, https://www.nytimes.com/2011/05/20/world/middleeast/20prexy-text.html.
[13] Bin Laden regularly repeated his and al-Qaeda's motives and war aims from the time of their August 1996 declaration of war on the United States until his May 2011 death at the hands of U.S. forces. See, for example, Osama bin Laden, "Full transcript of bin Ladin's speech," *Al-Jazeera*, 1 November 2004, https://www.aljazeera.com/news/2004/11/1/full-transcript-of-bin-ladins-speech; Mark McDonald, "New Message Reported From bin Laden," *The New York Times*, 14 September 2009, https://www.nytimes.com/2009/09/15/world/15tape.html.
[14] Abdul Salam Zaeef, *My Life with the Taliban*, ed. Alex Strick van Linschoten, trans. Felix Kuehn (London: Hurst & Company, 2010), 10.
[15] Alexei Vassiliev, *The History of Saudi Arabia*, (New York: New York University Press, 2000), 75, 80-82.
[16] Delong-Bas, *Wahhabi Islam*, 21; Vassiliev, *The History of Saudi Arabia*, 75, 77.
[17] Hourani, *A History of the Arab Peoples*, 257-258.
[18] Quintan Wiktorwicz, "Anatomy of the Salafi Movement," *Studies in Conflict and Terrorism*, Vol. 29, Issue 3 (August 2006), 207-239.
[19] Wiktorwicz, "Anatomy of the Salafi Movement," 215; Scheuer, *Osama bin Laden*, 174-175.
[20] John L. Esposito, *The Oxford History of Islam* (New York: Oxford University Press, 1999), 280-281; Scheuer, *Osama bin Laden*, 42-43.

21 Al-Bahri and Malbrunot, *Guarding bin Laden*, 105-106, 206-208.

22 Despite bin Laden's public pronouncements against "Crusaders and Jews," he frequently overruled al-Zawahiri and others advocating the deliberate targeting of Jewish, Christian, Shia, and other non-Salafi and non-Wahhabi Muslim civilians, reportedly describing such attacks as unnecessary and counterproductive distractions potentially damaging to al-Qaeda's cause. Nasser al Bahri quotes the al-Qaeda leader as regularly advising his men against such sectarian acts and advising al-Qaeda fighters to focus on killing their enemy Christian and Jewish combatants in battle but to try avoiding civilian casualties. That bin Laden accepted civilian deaths, Muslim or not, as an unfortunate but unavoidable result of all warfare, guerrilla or conventional, Islamic or Western, is true. Bin Laden's deliberate targeting of U.S. civilians in al-Qaeda terror attacks designed to draw the United States into Afghanistan after 1997 is equally true and religiously permissible from his ruthless Salafi jihadi perspective due to his frequent citing of U.S. President Bill Clinton's and UK Prime Minister Tony Blair's enforcement of UN sanctions on Iraq from Western military bases, that is, infidel military bases, in the Prophet's homeland on the Arabian Peninsula. However, he also appears to have urged al-Qaeda members to avoid being drawn into sectarian violence and the deliberate targeting of Muslim and non-Muslim civilians that he viewed as highly counterproductive, un-Islamic, and damaging to al-Qaeda's cause, especially in Muslim countries in which he and al-Qaeda benefitted from strong tribal connections and support such as Yemen and Saudi Arabia. Relating several episodes from the late 1990s, al-Bahri recalls that bin Laden turned down a group of, "Yemeni extremists" seeking his blessing to execute simultaneous attacks on the embassies of the United States, Britain, Italy, Cuba, and France in Yemen's capital, Sanaa. Bin Laden immediately rejected their proposals, reportedly stating that al-Qaeda had no quarrel with Cuba and that Yemenis living close to the embassies could also be killed. Considering Castro's prior support of the South Yemeni and Afghan communist regimes, this is an example of bin Laden's cautious adherence to the Koranic tradition of resorting to warfare as a last resort for defensive purposes only, and to live and let live if an infidel invader ceases its perceived aggression against Muslims. Indeed, al-Bahri recalls that the al-Qaeda chief commended Castro and Che Guevara for resisting, "injustice" by fighting against, "colonialism and occupation" in conversations with his closest associates. On another occasion, bin Laden replied to a Palestinian member of the Jordanian extremist Abu Musab al-Zarqawi's group that he, "wouldn't do anything [about Jewish civilians in Israel]," if given the chance to govern a recaptured Palestine. Bin Laden reportedly proceeded to explain that Jewish people had lived close to Muslims in Palestine peacefully for centuries and emphasized his conviction that each person should be treated as an individual, according to his or her preference for peace or war with Muslims, and not as automatic members of an enemy group. Al-Bahri states that on each occasion al-Zawahiri encouraged the extreme militants to target Jewish and Shia Muslim civilians only to be rebuffed by bin Laden. The former bodyguard also recalls that, "He [al-Zawahiri] didn't dare contradict bin Laden," while Omar bin Laden recalls that despite his abrasive, bullying spirit, the former Egyptian surgeon never spoke without asking bin Laden's permission first, stating, "He would say 'Sheik Osama, may I please speak?' Or 'Sheik Osama, please, may I say something to the men?'" Recalling that neither al-Zawahiri nor his loyal Egyptians spoke out loud without bin Laden's approval, Omar concludes that, "no matter their status in their organizations, none dared utter a single thought without my father's permission."

These recollections, as well as bin Laden's former sister-in-law Carmen's comment that he, "always had a commanding presence," Khaled al-Batarfi's statement that, "Even then [during their teenage years], Osama was a charismatic leader," and Najwa's recollection that, "Despite his serene demeanor, no one ever thought of Osama as weak-willed, for his character was strong and firm [even as a preteen]," appear to contradict Lawrence Wright's claim that al-Zawahiri, a proponent of sectarian violence and an initial supporter of the Jordanian takfiri radical Abu Musab al-Zarqawi, has always been the true leader of al-Qaeda whose example influenced bin Laden's leadership style and not the other way around. See al-Bahri and Malbrunot, *Guarding bin Laden*, 76-77, 105-106, 205, 206-208; al-Batarfi, "Growing up with Osama,"; Bin Laden, bin Laden, and Sasson, *Growing Up bin Laden*, 10, 266-167; Carmen bin Laden, *Inside the Kingdom: My Life in Saudi Arabia* (New York: Grand Central Publishing, 2005), 3-4; and for Wright's statement, see Wright, 148-149.

[23] Khaled Abou El Fadl, "Islam and the theology of power," *Middle East Report*, No. 221 (Winter 2001), 32; Scheuer, *Osama bin Laden*, 174-175; Wiktorwicz, "Anatomy of the Salafi Movement," 227-229.

[24] Scheuer, *Osama bin Laden*, 174-175.

[25] Coll, *Ghost Wars*, 74-75.

[26] Yaroslav Trofimov, *The Siege of Mecca: The 1979 Uprising at Islam's Holiest Shrine* (New York: Anchor Books, 2008), 14-15.

[27] Vassiliev, *The History of Saudi Arabia*, 110-111.

[28] Delong-Bas, *Wahhabi Islam*, 83.

[29] Coll, *Ghost Wars*, 76.

[30] Madawi al-Rasheed, *A History of Saudi Arabia* (Cambridge, UK: Cambridge University Press, 2002), 35, 56.

[31] R. Bayly Winder, *Saudi Arabia in the Nineteenth Century* (New York: St. Martin's Press, 1965), 63-64.

[32] Winder, *Saudi Arabia*, 275-278.

[33] Donald Powell Cole, *Nomads of the Nomads: The Al Murrah Bedouin of the Empty Quarter* (Arlington Heights, IL: AHM Publishing, 1975), 53, 57, 87.

[34] Al-Rasheed, *A History of Saudi Arabia*, 71-72.

[35] Robert Lacey, *Inside the Kingdom: Kings, Clerics, Modernists, Terrorists, and the Struggle for Saudi Arabia* (New York: Penguin, 2010), 14.

[36] John S. Habib, *Ibn Sa'ud's Warriors of Islam: The Ikhwan of Najd and Their Role in the Creation of the Sa'udi Kingdom, 1910-1930* (Riyadh: Mars Publishing, 1997), 35.

[37] Habib, *Ibn Sa'ud's Warriors of Islam*, 36-37; Al-Rasheed, *A History of Saudi Arabia*, 59-60.

[38] Habib, *Ibn Sa'ud's Warriors of Islam*, 36-37; Martin Lings, *Muhammad: His Life Based on the Earliest Sources* (Rochester, VT: Inner Traditions, 2006), 122-125.

[39] Coll, *Ghost Wars*, 76; Al-Rasheed, *A History of Saudi Arabia*, 62.

[40] Habib, *Ibn Sa'ud's Warriors of Islam*, 21-22.

[41] Al-Rasheed, *A History of Saudi Arabia*, 59-61.

[42] Habib, *Ibn Sa'ud's Warriors of Islam*, 69-70, 76.

[43] Lacey, *Inside the Kingdom*, 15-16.

[44] Vassiliev, *The History of Saudi Arabia*, 254-257.

[45] Coll, *Ghost Wars*, 76; Trofimov, *The Siege of Mecca*, 16-17.

[46] Al-Rasheed, *A History of Saudi Arabia*, 59-61.

⁴⁷ Coll, *Ghost Wars*, 76.
⁴⁸ Gabriel, *Muhammad*, 213; Habib, *Ibn Sa'ud's Warriors of Islam*, 94.
⁴⁹ Agha I. Akram, *Khalid bin al-Waleed – Sword of Allah: A Biographical Study of One of the Greatest Military Generals in History*, ed. A. B. al-Mehri (Birmingham, UK: Maktabah Publishers, 2007), 206, 305.
⁵⁰ Habib, *Ibn Sa'ud's Warriors of Islam*, 417-148; Lacey, *Inside the Kingdom*, 15-16.
⁵¹ Habib, *Ibn Sa'ud's Warriors of Islam*, 153-155.
⁵² Lacey, *Inside the Kingdom*, 15-16.
⁵³ Coll, *Ghost Wars*, 76.
⁵⁴ Habib, *Ibn Sa'ud's Warriors of Islam*, 160-162.
⁵⁵ Ibid.; Al-Rasheed, *A History of Saudi Arabia*, 67-69.
⁵⁶ Coll, *Ghost Wars*, 76-77; Lacey, *Inside the Kingdom*, 17-18; Trofimov, *The Siege of Mecca*, 18.
⁵⁷ Al-Rasheed, *A History of Saudi Arabia*, 70, 100-101.
⁵⁸ Scheuer, *Osama bin Laden*, 80, 82; Musa al-Qarni, "Bin Laden's Former 'Mufti' Musa Al-Qarni Talks about the Jihad in Afghanistan and Says Most Mujahideen in Iraq Are Saudis," *MEMRI TV: Middle East Media Research Institute TV Monitor Project*, 17 March 2006, https://www.memri.org/tv/bin-ladens-former-mufti-musa-al-qarni-talks-about-jihad-afghanistan-and-says-most-mujahideen-iraq/transcript.
⁵⁹ Al-Rasheed, *A History of Saudi Arabia*, 131-133; Vassiliev, *The History of Saudi Arabia*, 385.
⁶⁰ Leslie Campbell, "Yemen: The Tribal Islamists," *Wilson Center*, 27 August 2015, https://www.wilsoncenter.org/article/yemen-the-tribal-islamists; Peter Grier, "Soviets bolster an Arab ally. Military buildup in South Yemen worries US officials," *The Christian Science Monitor*, 11 March 1988, https://www.csmonitor.com/1988/0311/ayem.html; Marvine Howe, "Southern Yemen Blends Marxism With Islam and Arab Nationalism," *The New York Times*, 25 May 1979; *Parliamentary Record – House of Commons*, 1ˢᵗ Session (1979), https://www.theyworkforyou.com/debates/?id=1979-03-26a.40.1&s=Afghanistan+1980s#g106.1; Al-Qarni, "Bin Laden's Former 'Mufti' Musa Al-Qarni Talks about the Jihad in Afghanistan,"; Jonathan C. Randal, "Threat to N. Yemen Spurs Saudi Anxiety," *The Washington Post*, 30 March 1979, https://www.washingtonpost.com/archive/politics/1979/03/30/threat-to-n-yemen-spurs-saudi-anxiety/b676aa1b-09e5-48f9-b1a2-3b60cf4c5983/; Al-Rasheed, 131-133.
⁶¹ Al-Qarni, "Bin Laden's Former 'Mufti' Musa Al-Qarni Talks about the Jihad in Afghanistan."
⁶² Victoria Clark, *Yemen: Dancing on the Heads of Snakes* (New Haven: Yale University Press, 2010), 94-95.
⁶³ The New York Times, "SAUDIS SAY U.A.R. BOMBED VILLAGES; Break Relations With Cairo in Dispute Over Yemen," *The New York Times*, 7 November 1962, https://www.nytimes.com/1962/11/07/archives/saudis-say-uar-bombed-villages-break-relations-with-cairo-in.html.
⁶⁴ Al-Bahri and Malbrunot, *Guarding bin Laden*, 12-13; Robert Hurd and Greg Noakes, "North and South Yemen: Lead-up to the Break-up," *Washington Report on Middle East Affairs* 8 July 1994 (July/August 1994), 48, https://www.wrmea.org/1994-july-august/north-and-south-yemen-lead-up-to-the-break-up.html.
⁶⁵ Clark, *Yemen*, 95-97; Hourani, *A History of the Arab Peoples*, 411, 416-417; Howe, "Southern Yemen blends Marxism,"; Hurd and Noakes, "North and South Yemen," 48; Randal, "Threat to N. Yemen,"; Dana Adams Schmidt, "British in Aden Depart as

Egyptians Leave Yemen; Fighting Begun in 1963 Commandos Depart Accord in Geneva 'Good Fortune' Wished Welcome by U.N. Penel," *The New York Times*, 30 November 1967, https://www.nytimes.com/1967/11/30/archives/british-in-aden-depart-as-egyptians-leave-yemen-fighting-begun-in.html.

66 Nick van der Bijl, *British Military Operations in Aden and Radfan: 100 Years of British Colonial Rule* (Barnsley, South Yorkshire: Pen & Sword, 2014), 115, 162-164; Jonathan Walker, *Aden Insurgency: The Savage War in Yemen 1962-67* (Barnsley, South Yorkshire: Pen & Sword, 2015), 50, 53-54, 93; Schmidt, "British in Aden Depart as Egyptians Leave Yemen."

67 Van der Bijl, *British Military Operations*, 140; Walker, *Aden Insurgency*, 52, 57, 93, 127; Schmidt, "British in Aden Depart as Egyptians Leave Yemen."

68 *Parliamentary Record – House of Commons*, 1st Session (1967), https://www.theyworkforyou.com/debates/?id=1967-02-27a.97.0&s=Aden+1967#g172.3.

69 *Parl. Rec. – House of Commons*, 1st Sess. (1967).

70 Ibid.

71 Van der Bijl, *British Military Operations*, 140; Walker, *Aden Insurgency*, 127, 231; Schmidt, "British in Aden Depart as Egyptians Leave Yemen."

72 Hurd and Noakes, "North and South Yemen," 48; Howe, "Southern Yemen Blends Marxism,"; Schmidt, "British in Aden Depart as Egyptians Leave Yemen."

73 Campbell, "Yemen,"; Grier, "Soviets bolster an Arab ally,"; Hurd and Noakes, "North and South Yemen," 48; Howe, "Southern Yemen Blends Marxism,"; John Kifner, "SOVIET SAID TO TRY TO CALM SOUTH YEMEN," *The New York Times*, 17 January 1986, https://www.nytimes.com/1986/01/17/world/soviet-said-to-try-to-calm-south-yemen.html.; Tim Mackintosh-Smith, *Yemen: The Unknown Arabia* (New York: The Overlook Press, 2001), 164-165; Randal, "Threat to N. Yemen,"; Van der Bijl, *British Military Operations*, 206; Walker, *Aden Insurgency*, 296-298.

74 OBL, "Our invitation to Give Advice and Reform," ARC, 12 April 1994; Clark, *Yemen*, 232-234; Hurd and Noakes, "North and South Yemen," 48; Howe, "Southern Yemen Blends Marxism,"; Randal, "Threat to N. Yemen."

75 Al-Bahri and Malbrunot, *Guarding bin Laden*, 12-13; Campbell, "Yemen,"; Tik Root, "A Sheikh's Life: What Tariq al-Fadhli's story says about the mixed-up world of Yemeni politics," *The American Prospect*, 30 April 2013, https://prospect.org/world/sheikh-s-life/; Robert F. Worth, "Ex-Jihadist Defies Yemen's Leader; and Easy Labels," *The New York Times*, 26 February 2010, https://www.nytimes.com/2010/02/27/world/middleeast/27tareq.html.

76 Howe, "Southern Yemen Blends Marxism,"; *Parl. Rec. – House of Commons*, 1st Sess. (1979); Al-Qarni, "Bin Laden's Former 'Mufti' Musa Al-Qarni Talks about the Jihad in Afghanistan,"; Randal, "Threat to N. Yemen."

77 Coll, *Ghost Wars*, 80-82.

78 Kaplan, *Soldiers of God*, 233-236; Zaeef, *My Life with the Taliban*, 65.

79 OBL, "The Banishment of Communism from the Arabian Peninsula: The Episode and the Proof," 11 July 1994, and OBL, "Open message to King Fahd," ARC, 3 August 1995; Scheuer, *Osama bin Laden*, 194n56.

80 Al-Qarni, "Bin Laden's Former 'Mufti' Musa Al-Qarni Talks about the Jihad in Afghanistan."

[81] Al-Bahri and Malbrunot, *Guarding bin Laden*, 12-13. During his years as an al-Qaeda mujahid, al-Bahri answered to the pseudonym or *kunya* Abu Jandal meaning "Father of Death" or "The Killer."

[82] Ibid., 12-13, 14. Al-Bahri's father appears to have desired Arab and Islamic solidarity more than embracing Nasserism itself. This sentiment reflects the attitudes of many of his contemporaries in Saudi society and seems to slightly justify al-Qarni's view that communism remained a potent threat capable of hypnotizing some Muslims and turning them against their faith. Bin Laden also described the takeover of Somalia by the secular military ruler Ziyad Bari, initially backed by Brezhnev's Soviet Union in 1970, as another regional assault on Muslims by the communists. After 10 Islamic scholars pointed out the new regime's perceived anti-religious activities, Bari's secret police reportedly seized them and burned them publicly in downtown Mogadishu. See Osama bin Laden, "Introduction to the Battle of the Lion's Den, Afghanistan, 1987," in Shaykh Abdullah Azzam, *The Lofty Mountain*, 1st Edition, n.d., 77, https://ebooks.worldofislam.info/ebooks/Jihad/The%20Lofty%20Mountain.pdf.

[83] Osama bin Laden, *Messages to the World: The Statements of Osama bin Laden*, ed. Bruce Lawrence, trans. James Howarth, (New York: Verso, 2005), 32; Martin Chulov, "My son, Osama: the al-Qaeda leader's mother speaks for the first time," *The Guardian*, 2 August 2018, https://www.theguardian.com/world/2018/aug/03/osama-bin-laden-mother-speaks-out-family-interview.

[84] Al-Batarfi, "Growing up with Osama,"; Scheuer, *Osama bin Laden*, 34-35.

[85] Atwan, *The Secret History of al-Qaeda*, 41; Coll, *Ghost Wars*, 84-85; Haley Sweetland Edwards and Paul Stephens, "The house bin Laden built," *Agence France-Presse*, 1 January 2010, https://www.pri.org/stories/2010-01-01/house-bin-laden-built; Scheuer, *Osama bin Laden*, 21.

[86] Charles M. Sennott, "Saudi Arabia's Highway 15 Revisited," *GlobalPost*, 6 September 2011, https://www.pri.org/stories/2011-09-06/saudi-arabia-s-highway-15-revisited.

[87] Al-Batarfi, "Growing up with Osama,"; Atwan, *The Secret History of al-Qaeda*, 41; Edwards and Stephens, "The house bin Laden built,"; Coll, *The Bin Ladens*, 138-140.

[88] Atwan, *The Secret History of al-Qaeda*, 41, 41; Scheuer, *Osama bin Laden*, 23-25.

[89] Anas and Hussein, *To the Mountains*, 173-174; Atwan, *The Secret History of al-Qaeda*, 41; Coll, *The Bin Ladens*, 57; and Scheuer, *Osama bin Laden*, 195n9. As explained by Abdullah Anas in this detailed memoir and Michael Scheuer in his excellent biography *Osama bin Laden*, even the bin Laden family is not exempt from the prejudices and stereotypes inherent in all societies and cultures. As a family of ethnic Yemenis, or *Qahtanis*, the bin Ladens were said to have been constantly reminded of their secondary or even tertiary status in the Kingdom. The comment of Prince Turki al-Faisal regarding bin Laden's father, Muhammad, is particularly helpful in clarifying this point. During an interview with Steve Coll, Turki recalled of the bin Laden patriarch, "but he was always the construction man," implying that the royal family considered the bin Ladens to be somewhat lesser than them despite their construction skills, work ethic, and hard-earned fortune resulting from their key role in building the Saudi Kingdom's infrastructure. Coll also emphasizes this in his splendid book *The Bin Ladens: An Arabian Family in the American Century*, comparing the Yemeni bin Laden patriarch to a Sicilian entrepreneur raising a family in the 1950s' United States.

[90] Al-Rasheed, *A History of Saudi Arabia*, 144-145.

[91] Trofimov, *The Siege of Mecca*, 76-77.

⁹² Al-Rasheed, *A History of Saudi Arabia*, 144-145.
⁹³ Trofimov, *The Siege of Mecca*, 239-240.
⁹⁴ Coll, *Ghost Wars*, 23-24; Trofimov, *The Siege of Mecca*, 143.
⁹⁵ Jonathan Randal, *Osama: The Making of a Terrorist* (London: I.B. Tauris, 2012), 60-61; Scheuer, *Osama bin Laden*, 202n107.
⁹⁶ Trofimov, *The Siege of Mecca*, 162, 167.
⁹⁷ OBL, "Saudi Arabia supports the communists in Yemen," ARC, 7 June 1994; OBL, "The Banishment of Communism from the Arabian Peninsula," ARC, 11 July 1994; OBL, "Open Letter for Sheikh Bin Baz," ARC, 29 December 1994; Scheuer, *Osama bin Laden*, 195n56; Trofimov, *The Siege of Mecca*, 246-247.
⁹⁸ Bergen, *The Osama bin Laden I Know*, 59-60; Coll, *The Bin Ladens*, 228-229; Scheuer, *Osama bin Laden*, 51-52.

CHAPTER 2

¹ Mark Galeotti, *Afghanistan: The Soviet Union's Last War* (London: Frank Cass & Co. Ltd, 1995), 9-10; Artemy M. Kalinovsky, *A Long Goodbye: The Soviet Withdrawal from Afghanistan* (Cambridge, MA: Harvard University Press, 2011), 23-24.
² Bergen, *Holy War, Inc.*, 57-58.
³ Ibn Khaldun, *The Muqaddimah*, vii-viii; Abu Yusuf al-Kindi, *The Medical Formulary or Aqrabadhin of Al-Kindi*, ed. and trans. Martin Levey, (Madison: The University of Wisconsin Press, 1966), 4-5; Trofimov, *The Siege of Mecca*, 48-49. Radek Sikorski, *Dust of the Saints: A Journey Through War-Torn Afghanistan* (New York: Paragon House, 1989), 216; Svetlana Alexievich, *Boys in Zinc*, trans. Andrew Bromfield (London: Penguin Modern Classics, 2017), 10-11; Artyom Borovik, *The Hidden War: A Russian Journalist's Account of the Soviet War in Afghanistan* (New York: Grove Press, 2001), 120.
⁴ Kaplan, *Soldiers of God*, 147, 149.
⁵ Galeotti, *Afghanistan*, 4; Kaplan, *Soldiers of God*, 147, 149.
⁶ Galeotti, *Afghanistan*, 4; Kalinovsky, *A Long Goodbye*, 17; Zaeef, *My Life with the Taliban*, 8-9.
⁷ Mark Urban, *War in Afghanistan* (London: MacMillan, 1988), 5.
⁸ Urban, *War in Afghanistan*, 18-19.
⁹ Kaplan, *Soldiers of God*, 168, 216.
¹⁰ Coll, *Ghost Wars*, 38-39.
¹¹ Galeotti, *Afghanistan*, 4; Malkin, "Reagan and the End of the Cold War,"; *Wilson Center Digital Archive, Collection 76*, "Soviet Invasion of Afghanistan," "CPSU CC Politburo Decision on Draft Telegram to the Soviet Embassy in Afghanistan, 7 January 1979," 7 January 1979, digitalarchive.wilsoncenter.org/collection/76/soviet-invasion-of-afghanistan. Malkin points out here that Brezhnev vainly sought to serve the interests of, "the leaders of the [Soviet] military-industrial complex that had advanced his career."
¹² Edward Girardet, *Killing the Cranes: A Reporter's Journey Through Three Decades of War in Afghanistan* (White River Junction, VT: Chelsea Green Publishing, 2011), 90; Kaplan, *Soldiers of God*, 115-117, 174; Kalinovsky, *A Long Goodbye*, 8-9.
¹³ Ahmed Rashid, *Taliban: The Power of Militant Islam in Afghanistan and Beyond* (London: I.B. Taurus, 2010), 22-23.
¹⁴ Zaeef, *My Life with the Taliban*, 9-10.
¹⁵ Ibid., 22-23, 31-32.

[16] Coll, *Ghost Wars*, 40-41; Malkin, "Reagan and the End of the Cold War."
[17] Kaplan, *Soldiers of God*, 115-117.
[18] Galeotti, *Afghanistan*, 7-8; Sikorski, *Dust of the Saints*, 212-214.
[19] Galeotti, *Afghanistan*, 7-8; Coll, *Ghost Wars*, 40-41.
[20] Girardet, *Killing the Cranes*, 91, 94-96.
[21] Ibid.
[22] Ibid.; Paul Kengor, T*he Crusader: Ronald Reagan and the Fall of Communism* (New York: Harper Perennial, 2007), 228-229.
[23] Zaeef, *My Life with the Taliban*, 175, 280n7.
[24] Kaplan, *Soldiers of God*, 152-153.
[25] Zaeef, *My Life with the Taliban*, 39.
[26] Abdullah Azzam, "Sheikh Abdullah Azzam said about Usama Bin Ladin," in Abdullah Azzam, *The Lofty Mountain*, n.d., 151-153, https://ebooks.worldofislam.info/ebooks/Jihad/The%20Lofty%20Mountain.pdf?; OBL, "Introduction," 77; Bin Laden, bin Laden, and Sasson, *Growing Up bin Laden*, 33.
[27] Malkin, "Reagan and the End of the Cold War,"; Sikorski, *Dust of the Saints*, 269.
[28] Seth G. Jones, *In the Graveyard of Empires: America's War in Afghanistan* (New York: W. W. Norton & Company, 2010), 16-17; Coll, *Ghost Wars*, 47, 49; *Wilson Center Digital Archive, Collection 76*, "Transcript of CPSU CC Politburo Discussions on Afghanistan," 17 March 1979.
[29] Coll, *Ghost Wars*, 47, 49; *Wilson Center Digital Archive, Collection 76*, "Transcript of CPSU CC Politburo Discussions on Afghanistan," 17 March 1979.
[30] The Russian General Staff, *The Soviet-Afghan War: How a Superpower Fought and Lost*, ed. Lester W. Grau, trans. Michael A. Gress, (Lawrence: University Press of Kansas, 2002), 60.
[31] Galeotti, *Afghanistan*, 4, 6.
[32] *The Bukovsky Archives*, "The Situation in the Democratic Republic," 29 June 1979.
[33] Ibid.
[34] Ibid.
[35] *The Bukovsky Archives*, "The Situation in the Democratic Republic," 29 June 1979.
[36] Ibid.
[37] Ibid.
[38] Galeotti, *Afghanistan*, 7-8.
[39] Rodric Braithwaite, *Afgantsy: The Russians in Afghanistan 1979-89* (New York: Oxford University Press, 2013), 57; Urban, *War in Afghanistan*, 40-41; *Wilson Center Digital Archive, Collection 76*, "Telegram from East German Embassy in Kabul to Socialist Unity Party (SED) General Secretary Erich Honecker, 17 September 1979," 17 September 1979.
[40] Kengor, *The Crusader*, 228-229; *Wilson Center Digital Archive, Collection 76*, "Excerpt from transcript, CPSU CC Politburo meeting," 20 September 1979.
[41] Kaplan, *Soldiers of God*, 116.
[42] *The Bukovsky Archives*, "The situation in Afghanistan and our policy in this respect," 31 October 1979.
[43] Baker, "Why Did the Soviets Invade Afghanistan?"; Braithwaite, *Afgantsy*, 57; Coll, *Ghost Wars*, 47.
[44] Baker, "Why Did the Soviets Invade Afghanistan?"; Gregory Feifer, *The Great Gamble: The Soviet War in Afghanistan* (New York: Harper Perennial, 2010), 65-67. Brezhnev, Andropov, and many of their Kremlin and Politburo associates' alleged fear of the United

States successfully bringing Afghanistan into Washington's orbit of influence and potentially stationing nuclear missiles in the country reflects their failure, like that of many U.S. and Western leaders, to comprehend the fiercely independent nature of traditional Afghan society by ignoring Afghan history and the ways in which the Pashtun tribes have historically resisted foreign encroachments and invasions.

[45] *The Bukovsky Archives*, "The situation in Afghanistan," 31 October 1979.
[46] Ibid.
[47] Ibid.
[48] Coll, *Ghost Wars*, 49; Feifer, *The Great Gamble*, 65-67; *Wilson Center Digital Archive, Collection 76*, "Personal Memorandum Andropov to Brezhnev," 1 December 1979.
[49] Coll, *Ghost Wars*, 49; Feifer, *The Great Gamble*, 65-67; Malkin, "Reagan and the End of the Cold War,"; *Wilson Center Digital Archive, Collection 76*, "Personal Memorandum Andropov to Brezhnev," 1 December 1979.
[50] Scott R. McMichael, *Stumbling Bear: Soviet Military Performance in Afghanistan* (London: Brassey's (UK), 1991), 7-8; The Russian General Staff, *The Soviet-Afghan War*, 16-18; *Wilson Center Digital Archive, Collection 76*, "Summary of a CC CPSU Meeting," 26 December 1979.
[51] McMichael, *Stumbling Bear*, 8; Urban, *War in Afghanistan*, 44, 46-47; The Russian General Staff, *The Soviet-Afghan War*, 17-18; *Wilson Center Digital Archive, Collection 76*, "Letter from Leonid Brezhnev to Karmal Babrak, Attachment to CPSU Political Protocol # 177," 27 December 1989.
[52] Neamatollah Nojumi, *The Rise of the Taliban in Afghanistan: Mass Mobilization, Civil War, and the Future of the Region* (London: Palgrave MacMillan, 2002), 56-57; The Russian General Staff, *The Soviet-Afghan War*, 17-18; *Wilson Center Digital Archive, Collection 76*, "Letter from Leonid Brezhnev to Karmal Babrak, Attachment to CPSU Political Protocol # 177," 27 December 1989.
[53] Galeotti, *Afghanistan*, 15; Malkin, "Reagan and the End of the Cold War."
[54] The Russian General Staff, *The Soviet-Afghan War*, 35-37.
[55] OBL, "Introduction," 77; The Russian General Staff, *The Soviet-Afghan War*, 57-58, 62-63.
[56] The Russian General Staff, *The Soviet-Afghan War*, 154, 159.
[57] Kaplan, *Soldiers of God*, 16.
[58] Malkin, "Reagan and the End of the Cold War."
[59] Kengor, *The Crusader*, 58.
[60] McMichael, *Stumbling Bear*, 9; The Russian General Staff, *The Soviet-Afghan War*, 17-18.
[61] Kengor, *The Crusader*, 58-59; Robert Pear, "Arming Afghan Guerrillas: A Huge Effort Led by U.S.," *The New York Times*, 18 April 1988, https://www.nytimes.com/1988/04/18/world/arming-afghan-guerrillas-a-huge-effort-led-by-us.html.
[62] Galeotti, *Afghanistan*, 15.
[63] Braithwaite, *Afgantsy*, 84, 86-87, 125, 334; Galeotti, *Afghanistan*, 15.
[64] Braithwaite, *Afgantsy*, 125; Galeotti, *Afghanistan*, 15-16.
[65] Galeotti, *Afghanistan*, 15-16, 18-19.
[66] Ibid.
[67] The Russian General Staff, *The Soviet-Afghan War*, 60.
[68] Kalinovsky, *A Long Goodbye*, 39; The Russian General Staff, *The Soviet-Afghan War*, 23-24.

[69] Braithwaite, *Afgantsy*, 140-143, 272; The Russian General Staff, *The Soviet-Afghan War*, xix, 43-44.

[70] Galeotti, *Afghanistan*, 15; The Russian General Staff, *The Soviet-Afghan War*, 60.

[71] Abdel Bari Atwan, "My weekend with Osama bin Laden: 'Having borne arms against the Russians for 10 years, we think our battle with the Americans will be easy by comparison'," https://www.theguardian.com/world/2001/nov/12/afghanistan.terrorism2; Miller, "Greetings America. My Name is Osama bin Laden."

[72] Atwan, "My weekend with Osama bin Laden,"; Miller, "Greetings America. My Name is Osama bin Laden,"; The Middle East Forum, "Usama bin Ladin," 73-74.

[73] Scheuer, *Osama bin Laden*, 116-117; The Middle East Forum, "Usama bin Ladin," 78-79.

[74] Mohammad Yousaf and Mark Adkin, *Afghanistan – The Bear Trap: The Defeat of a Superpower*, (Barnsley, South Yorkshire: Pen & Sword, 2001), 26, 92.

[75] *Congressional Record – United States Senate*, 100th Congress, 2nd Session (1988), https://babel.hathitrust.org/cgi/pt?id=pst.000013390709&view=1up&seq=1; Henry Kamm, "Afghan Rebels Reported Furious Over Rumors of U.S.-Soviet Deal, *The New York Times*, 24 February 1988, https://www.nytimes.com/1988/02/24/world/afghan-rebels-reported-furious-over-rumors-of-us-soviet-deal.html.

[76] *Congressional Record – United States Senate*, 100th Congress, 2nd Session, pt.2 (1988), https://www.govinfo.gov/content/pkg/GPO-CRECB-1988-pt2/pdf/GPO-CRECB-1988-pt2-8-1.pdf.; Kamm, "Afghan Rebels Reported Furious,"; Abdul Haq, "Afghanistan Won't Be a U.S. or Soviet Puppet," *The New York Times*, 9 June 1989, https://www.nytimes.com/1989/06/09/opinion/l-afghanistan-won-t-be-a-us-or-soviet-puppet-628089.html.; Yousaf and Adkin, *Afghanistan*, 212-213.

[77] Scheuer, *Osama bin Laden*, 85; Rahimullah Yusufzai, "Osama bin Laden: Conversation with Terror," *TIME*, 11 January 1999, http://content.time.com/time/subscriber/article/0,33009,989958-1,00.html.

[78] Yusufzai, "Osama bin Laden."

[79] Gregory Johnsen, *The Last Refuge: Yemen, al-Qaeda, and America's War in Arabia* (New York: W. W. Norton & Company, 2014), 8-10; Rahimullah Yusufzai, "Moments that changed the Middle East: The Soviet invasion of Afghanistan," *Arab News*, 19 April 2020, https://www.arabnews.com/node/1661431.

[80] Peter Schweitzer, *Reagan's War: The Epic Story of His Forty-Year Struggle and Final Triumph Over Communism* (New York: Anchor Books, 2003), 234-235, 238; Yusufzai, "Moments that changed the Middle East."

[81] Scheuer, *Osama bin Laden*, 49.

[82] Bin Laden, bin Laden, and Sasson, *Growing Up bin Laden*, 33.

[83] Ibid.

[84] Scheuer, *Osama bin Laden*, 37-38, 54-56, 206-207n33. Scheuer also calls attention to bin Laden's spectacular poetic skills as a clever propaganda tactic, another strong indication of Ibn Khaldun's possible influence on the al-Qaeda leader due to the scholar's emphasis on the Prophet Muhammad's example and the subsequent use of classical Arabic poetry as a persuasive and eloquent rhetorical device for commanding leadership and respect in much of the Muslim world. See also Gabriel, *Muhammad*, xxvi, for an excellent account of the Prophet's use of poetry in warfare and diplomacy; and Ibn Khaldun, *The Muqaddimah*, 441-443, 443-450.

[85] Scheuer, *Osama bin Laden*, 37-38. In several audiotaped messages addressed to Americans and their leaders, bin Laden expressed disgust at Washington's perceived disinterest in effectively fighting climate change and saving God's Creation, stating, "the White House insists on not observing the Kyoto accord, with the knowledge that the statistic speaks of the death and displacement of millions of human beings because of that, especially in [Muslim majority] Africa," and challenging Washington to work to make a, "rational decision to save humanity from the harmful gases that threaten its destiny" rather than continue expending resources on prosecuting its war with the Islamists. To Scheuer's theory on Ibn Khaldun's influence in this regard, it may be added that the eventual victory of the largely tribal and devout Afghan and Yemeni anti-communist mujahedin over the urban and Moscow-backed Marxist regimes, as discussed in later chapters, could only have reinforced bin Laden's concurrence with the medieval historiographer's conclusions, along with the earlier example of the Saudi Ikhwan's victories over their mostly urban Ottoman foes perceived as tyrannical, decadent, and corrupt. As Scheuer points out, bin Laden certainly shared Ibn Khaldun's view of nature and the outdoors as the purest of God's creations, intended by God to provide man with the means of embracing a Spartan rural life to strengthen and prepare warriors to resist urban tyranny and restore civilization and Sunni Islamic law. Bin Laden's love of the natural world is well documented by his associates. His friend Khaled al-Batarfi recalls bin Laden's rejection of luxuries and fascination with nature even as a teenager in Jeddah, sleeping on the bare sand, "and among horses" at his family's farm in the desert south of the Red Sea port city. Born in 1981, Omar bin Laden describes his father's eyes as, "sparkling" at the sight of his horses at their family farm in Jeddah during the late 1980s and early 1990s, and bin Laden's wife Najwa states that her husband always displayed a deep interest in all things natural, even the smallest insects. Omar later contradicts himself by stating that he and his brothers were horrified to learn that a baby monkey that they played with during bin Laden's time of exile in Sudan had been killed by one of his father's men at the al-Qaeda chief's urging. Omar claims that his father had convinced the unidentified militant that Jewish people were descended from monkeys and that therefore the man believed that he had killed a, "baby Jew." While it serves as an invaluable primary account, Omar and Najwa's memoir is also intended to serve the Saudi and other Arab regimes' interests by sometimes portraying bin Laden as a hateful, bloodthirsty, and un-Islamic fanatic only happy while involved in killing. This seems unlikely, as bin Laden did not forbid his children from playing with the monkey in the first place and, according to Omar, always encouraged them to embrace, "God's natural gifts" as their source of happiness. Indeed, despite his inference, Omar does not explicitly state that his father confessed to ordering the monkey's death and does not elaborate further on his allegation. Bin Laden does not appear to have asked his men to perform actions that he had not personally performed or that he did not condone. His former chief bodyguard, the Yemeni Nasser al-Bahri, also recalls the al-Qaeda chief's love of the outdoors, saying, "he talked about them [shiny, black Arabian horses] almost as he spoke of Islam," and refutes the notion that bin Laden expressed such dehumanizing views of Jewish people in his private conversations, reportedly emphasizing the key differences between peaceful innocents that should be left unharmed and Zionists that he perceived as Islam's implacable foes. Al-Bahri recalls that bin Laden emphatically refused the permission of, "extremists" to target Jewish civilians in Yemen. The point here is that despite his ruthless and uncompromising tactics directed against those that he regarded

as Islam's foes, bin Laden appears to have differed from some of his more bloodthirsty and sectarian-minded associates such as Ayman al-Zawahiri, Abu Musab al-Zarqawi, and Abu Musab al-Suri by not supporting the automatic targeting of civilians based on their religious or ethnic origins. This also serves as an example of his militant but traditional view of jihad as a defensive war to repel, "infidel forces," whether Soviet communists or American capitalists, that he perceived as seeking to impose their will on Muslims rather than a tool for an irrational campaign of forcibly converting Westerners and others to Islam. See Al-Bahri and Malbrunot, *Guarding bin Laden*, 76, 205, 206-208; Al-Batarfi, "Growing up with Osama,"; bin Laden, bin Laden, and Sasson, *Growing Up bin Laden*, 25, 53, 166; Osama bin Laden, "Transcript – ABC News," *ABC News*, 6 September 2007, https://abcnews.go.com/images/Politics/transcript2.pdf; Jonathan Landay, "Bin Laden called for Americans to rise up over climate change," *Reuters*, 1 March 2016 (January 2010 audio recording), https://www.reuters.com/article/us-usa-binladen-climatechange-idUSKCN0W35MS; and Guy Lawson, "Osama's Prodigal Son: The Dark, Twisted Journey of Omar bin Laden," *Rolling Stone*, 20 January 2010, https://www.rollingstone.com/politics/politics-news/osamas-prodigal-son-the-dark-twisted-journey-of-omar-bin-laden-199468/.

[86] Ibn Khaldun, *The Muqaddimah*, 152-154, 351-352.

[87] Ibid.

[88] Scheuer, *Osama bin Laden*, 37-38.

[89] Al-Batarfi, "Growing up with Osama."

[90] Al-Bahri and Malbrunot, *Guarding bin Laden*, 79, 90; Al-Batarfi, "Growing up with Osama,"; Scheuer, *Osama bin Laden*, 37-38.

[91] Bin Laden, bin Laden, and Sasson, *Growing Up bin Laden*, 19; Ibn Khaldun, *The Muqaddimah*, 278-279; Scheuer, *Osama bin Laden*, 37-38.

[92] Scheuer, *Osama bin Laden*, 37-38.

[93] Al-Bahri and Malbrunot, *Guarding bin Laden*, 79, 90. The former bodyguard also describes the atmosphere of the al-Qaeda chief's office in the same way. Regarding Tarnak Farm's former status as a Soviet Army barracks, Robert Kaplan points out that the invaders garrisoned in the Kandahar region and its nearby airport constituted the most southern strongpoint of Soviet troops stationed in South Asia. See Kaplan, *Soldiers of God*, 186-187.

[94] Al-Bahri and Malbrunot, *Guarding bin Laden*, 150-152, 153-154. Al-Bahri also states that bin Laden passed down his family's tradition of hard work, risk-taking, and personal frugality to his sons, giving them allowances, but not raises, and assigning positions of financial and logistical responsibility to his two most committed, reliable, and physically similar sons, Saad, and Muhammad, born in 1979 and 1985 respectively, at al-Qaeda's Afghan headquarters, Tarnak Farm. On one occasion, Saad reportedly approached his father expressing his desire to marry, and bin Laden advised his most financially trustworthy and dedicated son to continue working the plot of land that he had allotted to him beside the group's mosque and to save his own money to pay for the wedding. Saad faithfully obeyed, and later married a Sudanese woman of Yemeni origin, like the bin Ladens, traveling on a Yemeni passport to retrieve his bride and to sell his father's last remaining business interests in Sudan in 1999. Al-Bahri recalls his former boss sitting with his sons on another occasion and quotes him as explaining to them that, "My sons, the millions of dollars you have heard about do not belong to your father. It's money for all the Moslems. I have dedicated it all to God and you are not entitled to a rial [sic]!"

[95] Ruthven, "The eleventh of September and the Sudanese mahdiyya," 341-344.
[96] Ibid., 348-349.
[97] Abd-al-Karim and al-Nur, "Interview with Saudi businessman Usama bin Ladin,"; Scheuer, *Osama bin Laden*, 37-38.
[98] See al-Bahri and Malbrunot, *Guarding bin Laden*, 208-210; and Ibn Khaldun, *The Muqaddimah*, 297-298, 367-371, and 387-388. In this regard, Ibn Khaldun's influence is particularly interesting as it echoes bin Laden's perception that Muslims had caused their own problems by neglecting the religious laws concerning the duty of, "holy war" to defend their faith and brethren. In this militant outlook, God and the Prophet are not responsible for the calamities befalling Muslim populations, rather those refusing to defend their brethren are responsible due to their failure to act.
[99] Scheuer, *Osama bin Laden*, 59-60, 62.
[100] Tayseer Alouni, "Transcript of Bin Laden's October interview," *Al-Jazeera*, 5 February 2002, https://edition.cnn.com/2002/WORLD/asiapcf/south/02/05/binladen.transcript/; Atwan, "My weekend with Osama bin Laden,"; Miller, "Greetings America. My Name is Osama bin Laden."; Scheuer, *Osama bin Laden*, 76-77.
[101] Nida'ul Islam, "Mujahid Usamah Bin Ladin talks exclusively to Nida'ul Islam about the new powder keg in the Middle East," *Nida'ul Islam*, Issue 15, 15 January 1997, https://fas.org/irp/world/para/docs/LADIN.htm; Scott MacLeod, "The Paladin of Jihad: Fearless and super-rich, Osama bin Laden finances Islamic extremism. A TIME exclusive," *TIME*, Vol. 147, No. 19 (6 May 1996), 51-52, https://time.com/vault/issue/1996-05-06/page/51/; Scheuer, *Osama bin Laden*, 76-77; Kenneth R. Timmerman, "This Man Wants You Dead: Osama bin Laden," *Reader's Digest* (July 1998), 50-57, https://www.rd.com/article/this-man-wants-you-dead-osama-bin-laden/.
[102] Yousaf and Adkin, *Afghanistan*, 106.
[103] Martin Smith, "Interview: Dr. Saad al-Fagih," *PBS Frontline Online*, (April 1999), https://www.pbs.org/wgbh/pages/frontline/shows/binladen/interviews/al-fagih.html.
[104] Al-Bahri and Malbrunot, *Guarding bin Laden*, 218; Robert Fisk, "Anti-Soviet warrior puts his army on the road to peace: The Saudi businessman who recruited mujahedin now uses them for large-scale building projects in Sudan," *The Independent*, 6 December 1993, https://www.independent.co.uk/news/world/anti-soviet-warrior-puts-his-army-road-peace-saudi-businessman-who-recruited-mujahedin-now-uses-them-large-scale-building-projects-sudan-robert-fisk-met-him-almatig-1465715.html.
[105] Bergen, *The Osama bin Laden I Know*, 24-25; Scheuer, *Osama bin Laden*, 50-52.
[106] Bin Laden, *Inside the Kingdom*, 111-112; Miller, "Greetings America. My Name is Osama bin Laden."; Nida'ul Islam, "Mujahid Usamah Bin Ladin."
[107] Bin Laden, *Inside the Kingdom*, 111-112; Coll, *The Bin Ladens*, 251; Scheuer, *Osama bin Laden*, 50-52; Al-Qarni, "Bin Laden's Former 'Mufti' Musa Al-Qarni Talks about the Jihad in Afghanistan,"; Mary Anne Weaver, "The real bin Laden," *The New Yorker*, 17 January 2000, 32, https://www.newyorker.com/magazine/2000/01/24/the-real-bin-laden.
[108] Azzam, "Sheikh Abdullah Azzam said about Usama Bin Ladin," 151. Azzam states here that, "he [bin Laden] lives in his house the life of the poor" emphasizing the devout Saudi's modest living and strict avoidance of luxuries despite donating millions of riyals to the mujahid cause. Bin Laden's older sister, Shahira, a neighbor of Nasser al-Bahri's family in Jeddah, also reportedly worked closely with her brother as a staunch supporter of the holy warriors during the war against the Soviets. See al-Bahri and Malbrunot, *Guarding bin Laden*, 26.

109 Fisk, "Anti-Soviet warrior puts his army on the road to peace,"; Scheuer, *Osama bin Laden*, 65, 69.

110 Al-Bahri and Malbrunot, *Guarding bin Laden*, 218; Bergen, *Holy War, Inc.*, 53-54, 59; Isam Darraz, "Impressions of an Arab Journalist in Afghanistan," in Abdullah Azzam, *The Lofty Mountain*, first edition, n.d., 108-109, https://ebooks.worldofislam.info/ebooks/Jihad/The%20Lofty%20Mountain.pdf; Yousaf and Adkin, *Afghanistan*, 109; Zaeef, *My Life with the Taliban*, 28. The Arab fighters under bin Laden's command later favored these vehicles for their flexibility and reliability. Bergen further states that bin Laden also used the trucks in performing mine-clearing operations in eastern Afghanistan's mountainous rural regions with his men.

111 Kaplan, *Soldiers of God*, 184-185, 186-187.

112 Scheuer, *Osama bin Laden*, 21.

113 Nida'ul Islam, "Mujahid Usamah Bin Ladin,"; Peter Arnett, "Transcript of Osama Bin Ladin interview by Peter Arnett," *CNN*, March 1997, http://anusha.com/osamaint.htm; MacLeod, "The Paladin of Jihad," 51-52; Coll, *Ghost Wars*, 156-157; Miller, "Greetings America. My Name is Osama bin Laden."; Timmerman, "This Man Wants You Dead," 51, https://www.rd.com/article/this-man-wants-you-dead-osama-bin-laden/; Scheuer, *Through Our Enemies Eyes: Osama bin Laden, Radical Islam, and the Future of America* (Dulles, VA: Potomac Books, 2007), 104-105.

114 Bergen, *Holy War, Inc.*, 31; Scheuer, *Osama bin Laden*, 69, 166.

115 Al-Bahri and Malbrunot, *Guarding bin Laden*, 70. Al-Bahri recounts an episode from 1998 in which the al-Qaeda chief rushed to judgment after the bodyguard handled an Iraqi translator accompanying *ABC News* journalist John Miller roughly. Bin Laden later summoned al-Bahri and apologized to him in the presence of others including the militant Sorak al-Yemeni. His willingness to admit rash decisions and apologize to his men for committing such errors, another character trait suggesting the influence of Ibn Khaldun's teachings, brought tears to al-Yemeni's eyes and prompted al-Bahri to kiss their leader's forehead while addressing him as *khal* or, "uncle" as a sign of deep respect and in recognition of the Yemeni origins that he and bin Laden shared. For Ibn Khaldun's possible influence on bin Laden's reportedly approachable and relatively representative leadership style and his willingness to admit mistakes, see Ibn Khaldun, *The Muqaddimah*, 152-154; 351-352.

116 Bin Laden, bin Laden, and Sasson, *Growing Up bin Laden*, 33.

117 Scheuer, *Osama bin Laden*, 37-38.

118 Al-Batarfi, "Growing up with Osama."; Ibn Khaldun, *The Muqaddimah*, 152-154, 351-352.

119 Ibn Khaldun, *The Muqaddimah*, 152-154, 351-352. This deep conviction appears to have remained with bin Laden throughout his life. Nasser al-Bahri recalls that during a period of financial constraint following U.S. pressure on the Pakistani authorities and President Bill Clinton's retaliatory Cruise missile barrage after al-Qaeda's 1998 twin truck bombings of the U.S. embassies in Kenya and Tanzania, bin Laden experienced hunger and hardship alongside his men at their Tarnak Farm compound in Kandahar. Al-Bahri states that he approached the al-Qaeda leader with the concern that the fighters were hungry and running out of food. Dipping a piece of bread in a bowl of water, bin Laden reportedly replied that, "millions of people on the planet dream of having a meal like this," reminding al-Bahri of the Prophet Muhammad's example during the difficult days at the beginnings of Islam. Bin Laden often could not pay his men and fared no better

than them during times of financial hardship, frequently citing the Prophet's example to sustain them until funds arrived from wealthy Saudi donors. Encouraged by his example and dedication, many of the fighters remained loyal to bin Laden as they struck U.S. and Western interests throughout the 1990s, while Western officials and successive bipartisan U.S. Terrorism Czars hoped desperately that cutting off the al-Qaeda chief's personal fortune and other sources of funding amounted to victory. This mindset dangerously underestimates the power of faith to psychologically sustain the Salafi fighters of al-Qaeda and its global wings and keep them in the field, just as the group's founders and the Afghan Islamists remained steadfast while facing the Soviet superpower's forces armed with considerable material advantages ranging from armor and airpower to R-300 Scud missiles. Yet in a 19 May 2011 speech, President Obama, mirroring the statements of his White House predecessors, appears to have continued denying the key role of religious fervor in motivating the jihadis' war efforts and perseverance against far superior forces from Afghanistan, to Yemen, to Syria. See Al-Bahri and Malbrunot, *Guarding bin Laden*, 132-133; Mustafa Hamid and Leah Farrall, *The Arabs at War in Afghanistan* (London: Hurst & Company, 2015), 240-241; President Barack Obama, "Obama's Mideast Speech – Text – The New York Times,"; Scheuer, *Osama bin Laden*, viii-ix; and Tim Weiner, "U.S. Hard Put to Find Proof Bin Laden Directed Attacks," *The New York Times*, 13 April 1999, https://www.nytimes.com/1999/04/13/world/us-hard-put-to-find-proof-bin-laden-directed-attacks.html.

[120] Scheuer, *Osama bin Laden*, 49-50.

[121] Abd-al-Karim and al-Nur, "Interview with Saudi businessman Usama bin Ladin,"; Al-Bahri and Malbrunot, *Guarding bin Laden*, 17-18; Scheuer, *Osama bin Laden*, 50.

[122] Anas and Hussein, *To the Mountains*, 63; Coll, *The Bin Ladens*, 256, 377, 381; Schultheis, *Hunting bin Laden*, 54-55; Weaver, "The real bin Laden,"; Wright, *The Looming Tower*, 100, 116, 138. Indeed, Anas appears to undermine his assertion by admitting that he did not participate in any of the battles that bin Laden fought in, contrary to the firsthand accounts by eyewitnesses of and participants in these engagements including Abdullah Azzam, Isam Darraz, Musa al-Qarni, and Tariq al-Fadhli. Yet Lawrence Wright appears to have accepted Anas's claim unquestioningly while apparently disregarding the other primary accounts by these actual eyewitnesses, and his portrayal of the former Algerian jihadi as the most courageous and talented of the Arab holy warriors in the Soviet-Afghan War is potentially erroneous, as pointed out by Steve Coll and Michael Scheuer, considering Anas's reported envy and anger at bin Laden because of the devout Saudi's role in successfully preempting his planned takeover of Azzam's organization and financial connections after his 24 November 1989 assassination. As Coll and Scheuer point out, after later obtaining political exile status in Britain, Anas reportedly continued seeking to improve his image while ranting and raving against bin Laden from London until the al-Qaeda leader's death on 2 May 2011. See also Coll, *Ghost Wars*, 204; and Scheuer, *Osama bin Laden*, 4-5, 189n5.

[123] Darraz, "Impressions," 94; Weaver, "The real bin Laden,"; MacLeod, "The Paladin of Jihad," 51-52; Miller, "Greetings America. My Name is Osama bin Laden."; Scheuer, *Osama bin Laden*, 61; Timmerman, "This Man Wants You Dead," 52-53.

[124] Al-Bahri and Malbrunot, *Guarding bin Laden*, 197. Al-Bahri explains the Salafist perception that one of the, "main conditions for [defensive] jihad" is a request for assistance by the Muslim population in the country under attack. Following such a call for help, it becomes the religious obligation of all committed Muslims to aid their

beleaguered brethren, either through financing, humanitarian aid, or bearing arms against the infidel aggressor, and is no longer the sole responsibility of the besieged faithful living in the occupied land. Initially, the Afghan Islamist groups were in desperate need of financing rather than untrained volunteers, and by honoring their wishes bin Laden displayed a far greater understanding of jihad than many other Arabs and non-Afghan volunteers. As shown in this book's fourth chapter, his patience, persistence, and deference to the Afghan commanders paid off, winning their trust, and eventually allowing him to establish an independent guerrilla base to train and command a small Arab band and acquire rich fighting experience. Once the Arabs acquitted themselves well in battle, they emerged as seasoned warriors and their presence became increasingly welcomed in the Afghan guerrilla units.

[125] Arnett, "Transcript of Osama Bin Ladin interview,"; Coll, *Ghost Wars*, 156-157; MacLeod, "The Paladin of Jihad," 51-52; Miller, "Greetings America. My Name is Osama bin Laden."; Scheuer, *Through Our Enemies Eyes*, 104-105; Timmerman, "This Man Wants You Dead," 54.

[126] Arnett, "Transcript of Osama Bin Ladin interview,"; Coll, *Ghost Wars*, 156-157; MacLeod, "The Paladin of Jihad," 51-52; Miller, "Greetings America. My Name is Osama bin Laden."; Scheuer, *Through Our Enemies Eyes*, 104-105; Timmerman, "This Man Wants You Dead," 55-57. This battle drive and steadiness under pressure appears to have remained with bin Laden. In early 2000, the al-Qaeda chief reportedly joined his men and the Taleban on the frontlines of the Kabul front against Massoud's Northern Alliance troops. Informing his chief bodyguard, Nasser al-Bahri, of his desire to reenergize his commitment to al-Qaeda's jihad by spending time on the battlefield, bin Laden left to fight alongside his men near Kabul for three days, and managed to resolve a crisis within the al-Qaeda group with the help of two Saudi compatriots of Yemeni origin, al-Bahri and Abd al-Rahim al-Nashiri, after the Syrian extremist Abu Musab al-Suri created tensions by trying to force his views on the others and criticizing the Taleban for their customs such as praying at the graves of martyred fighters. See al-Bahri and Malbrunot, *Guarding bin Laden*, 148-149.

[127] MacLeod, "The Paladin of Jihad," 51-52; Timmerman, "This Man Wants You Dead," 55-57.

[128] Miller, "Greetings America. My Name is Osama bin Laden."; Nida'ul Islam, "Mujahid Usamah Bin Ladin." Bin Laden's efforts building tunnels, houses, and roads for the majority Pashtun insurgents and their tribal supporters paid off significantly in several ways during his and al-Qaeda's later war against the West. Nasser al-Bahri recalls Taleban chief Mullah Omar asking bin Laden to leave Afghanistan, once following the U.S. Cruise missile attacks of 20 August 1998 in retaliation for al-Qaeda's bombings of the U.S. embassies in East Africa, and again following the al-Qaeda chief's December 1998 interview with *al-Jazeera*. On both occasions, Mullah Omar reportedly sent his representative, Mullah Jalil, back to bin Laden with a message to disregard the Taleban leader's request that he and al-Qaeda leave Afghanistan and to continue with his independent holy war against the United States. Bin Laden repeatedly offered to leave Afghanistan as U.S. and UN pressure mounted on the Taleban regime, embarrassing and indirectly shaming Omar by implying that despite the al-Qaeda leader's contributions to the Afghan warriors' struggle against the Soviet invaders, the Taleban could not be counted on to fulfill their obligation to provide shelter for a fellow mujahid seeking refuge from the U.S. and Saudi governments. Bin Laden subsequently organized a gathering of

40 Afghan and Pakistani Islamist *ulema* headed by Mullah Nidam al-Deen Shamsi into a *Shura* Council or, "consultative council" like those that he and Mullah Omar each chaired in their respective organizations, asking the scholars to issue a ruling and advise him on his status to remain in Afghanistan. The clerics reportedly concluded that Mullah Omar must defend bin Laden at all costs, even in the event of a foreign attack resulting in Afghan and Pakistani civilian deaths, reminding the Taleban leader of his religious and tribal duty to protect a holy warrior seeking refuge from infidel powers. Bin Laden's solid reputation with the Pashtun tribes in Afghanistan and Pakistan also helped to facilitate his escape from U.S. forces at Tora Bora in 2001, enabling him to fight another decade. Citing bin Laden's son Omar's account, Michael Scheuer points out that in addition to having already thoroughly memorized every trail and tunnel in the mountains, the al-Qaeda leader also knew that the Pakistan Army's soldiers hailed from the local Pashtun tribal populations and obeyed the orders of their tribal chiefs, all staunch supporters of bin Laden demanding that he be allowed to escape, rather than their commanding general in the Pakistan Army. See al-Bahri and Malbrunot, *Guarding bin Laden*, 86, 136-138, 218; Bin Laden, bin Laden, and Sasson, *Growing Up bin Laden*, 214-215, 318; and Scheuer, *Osama bin Laden*, 73, 123-124, 126-128, 131.

[129] Weiner, "U.S. Hard Put to Find Proof."

[130] Bergen, *Holy War, Inc.*, 53; Scheuer, *Osama bin Laden*, 24.

[131] Bin Laden, bin Laden, and Sasson, *Growing Up bin Laden*, 74-75.

[132] Daily Mail Reporter, "I taught judo to Osama bin Laden, claims Taiwanese coach (and here are the pics to prove it)," *Daily Mail*, 7 May 2011, https://www.dailymail.co.uk/news/article-1384682/I-taught-Osama-bin-Laden-judo-claims-Taiwanese-coach.html.

[133] Daily Mail Reporter, "I taught judo to Osama bin Laden."

[134] Ibid.

[135] Nicky Loh and Ben Tai, "Osama bin Laden a serious student, Taiwan judo coach says," *Reuters*, 7 May 2011, https://www.reuters.com/article/idINIndia-56847220110507?edition-redirect=in.

[136] Bin Laden, bin Laden, and Sasson, *Growing Up bin Laden*, 45; Loh and Tai, "Osama bin Laden a serious student." Wu's concern that bin Laden's unusual height could have been an obstacle to judo training appears to contradict Lawrence Wright's statement that the al-Qaeda chief stood only slightly taller than six feet. Further evidence is provided by former *ABC News* journalist John Miller and Canadian freelance cameraman, Rick Bennett. On meeting bin Laden for an interview in Afghanistan in May 1998, Miller and Bennett were immediately struck by the al-Qaeda chief's very thin (about 160 pounds) but very tall physical stature. Miller recalls, "First of all I am shocked, the guy is huge. He is like 6'5"," while Bennett states, "I'm six foot two and he towered above me." Eric Margolis reportedly observed bin Laden on the far side of a room as both men visited an Afghan guerrilla commander near Jalalabad in 1989, stating that he, "noticed him [bin Laden] because of his stature, over 6 feet 5 inches, and his gaunt body," while Nasser al-Bahri recalls his former boss's height as 1.90 meters, a height shared only by his second eldest son, Abdul Rahman, born in 1978, and an unnamed Yemeni jihadi, both sometimes acting as decoys or body doubles for the al-Qaeda leader. See al-Bahri and Malbrunot, *Guarding bin Laden*, 84, 152; Bergen, *The Osama bin Laden I Know*, 214-216; Eric S. Margolis, *War at the Top of the World: The Struggle for Afghanistan, Kashmir, and Tibet* (New York: Routledge, 2002), 84; Miller, "Greetings America. My Name is Osama bin Laden."; and Wright, *The Looming Tower*, 95-96.

[137] Scheuer, *Osama bin Laden*, 46, 53-54.
[138] Steve Coll, *The Bin Ladens*, 295-296.
[139] Arnett, "Transcript of Osama Bin Ladin interview,"; Bergen, *The Osama bin Laden I Know*, 29; Coll, *Ghost Wars*, 156-157; MacLeod, "The Paladin of Jihad," 51-52; "Greetings America. My Name is Osama bin Laden."; Scheuer, *Osama bin Laden*, 60; Timmerman, "This Man Wants You Dead," 52-53.
[140] Owen Bowcott, "UK discussed plans to help Mujahideen weeks after Soviet invasion of Afghanistan," *The Guardian*, 30 December 2010, https://www.theguardian.com/uk/2010/dec/30/uk-mujahideen-afghanistan-soviet-invasion.
[141] Martin Beckford, "National Archives: Britain agreed secret deal to back Mujahideen," *The Telegraph*, 30 December 2010, https://www.telegraph.co.uk/news/worldnews/asia/afghanistan/8215187/National-Archives-Britain-agreed-secret-deal-to-back-Mujahideen.html.
[142] Bowcott, "UK discussed plants to help Mujahideen."
[143] Margaret Thatcher, *The Downing Street Years* (New York: HarperCollins, 2012), 68; UK Prime Minister, "Afghanistan: FCO letter to No.10 ('Afghanistan: Future Action') [response to Soviet intervention] [declassified 2010]," *Foreign and Commonwealth Office*, London, SWIA 2AH, 28 February 1980, *Margaret Thatcher Foundation*, https://c59574e9047e61130f13-3f71d0fe2b653c4f00f32175760e96e7.ssl.cf1.rackcdn.com/C42D7645C94E4A8A8341AD8E9A688D9F.pdf.
[144] *Parliamentary Record – House of Commons*, 1st Session (1980), https://www.theyworkforyou.com/debates/?id=1980-04-28a.995.0&s=Afghanistan+1980s#g1057.0.
[145] Department of the Army, *Soviet Army Operations* (Arlington, VA: U.S. Army Intelligence and Threat Analysis Center, 1978), Part III, 6-1, 6-4, 6-5.
[146] McMichael, *Stumbling Bear*, 8; Wilson Center Digital Archive, Collection 76, "Diary of the events surrounding the September 1981 defection of the 913th Afghan Border Battalion," 25 September 1981.
[147] The Russian General Staff, *The Soviet-Afghan War*, 19-20; Wilson Center Digital Archive, Collection 76, "CPSU CC Politburo Decision on Afghanistan, with report by Gromyko, Andropov, Ustinov, and Zagladin, 7 April 1980," 10 April 1980.
[147] The Russian General Staff, *The Soviet-Afghan War*, 19-20.
[148] Ibid.
[149] Alexievich, *Boys in Zinc*, 10-11; McMichael, *Stumbling Bear*, 14; Wilson Center Digital Archive, Collection 76, "Memorandum of the Bulgarian Department of Foreign Policy and International Relations on Afghanistan," 18 May 1987.
[150] McMichael, *Stumbling Bear*, 14; Wilson Center Digital Archive, Collection 76, "Politburo Decision on Soviet Policy on Afghanistan, with report on proposal by Fidel Castro to Mediate between Afghanistan and Pakistan, and approved letter from L.I. Brezhnev to Fidel Castro," 10 March 1980; Zaeef, *My Life with the Taliban*, 21.
[151] Kalinovsky, *A Long Goodbye*, 39; Kaplan, *Soldiers of God*, 224; Kengor, *The Crusader*, 230.
[152] Department of the Army, *Soviet Army Operations*, Part II, 3-8, 3-9, 3-10.
[153] Ali Ahmad Jalali, *A Military History of Afghanistan: From the Great Game to the Global War on Terror* (Lawrence: University Press of Kansas, 2017), 395-398.
[154] Jalali, *A Military History of Afghanistan*, 398; Kaplan, *Soldiers of God*, 187-188; Nojumi, *The Rise of the Taliban*, 57-59.

[155] Bin Laden, bin Laden, and Sasson, *Growing Up bin Laden*, 217. Another possible example of Ibn Khaldun's influence on bin Laden is the al-Qaeda chief's documented fascination with engaging in dream interpretation, despite neither man basing his decisions on dreams, after performing the *fajr* or dawn prayer with his men, regularly asking them if anyone had had a good dream as recalled by Nasser al-Bahri. Stating, "This is one of the sciences of the religious law [*Shariah*]" and pointing out that the Prophet Muhammad often asked his men about their dreams, "…in order to derive good news from dream visions, which might refer to the victory of Islam and the growth of its power" Ibn Khaldun appears to have contributed to the al-Qaeda leader's love for Islam's Prophet and his psychological Salafist desire to honor and emulate him in yet another profound way. See also al-Bahri and Malbrunot, *Guarding bin Laden*, 177; and Ibn Khaldun, *The Muqaddimah*, 80-83, 367-371.

[156] Al-Bahri and Malbrunot, *Guarding bin Laden*, 113, 158-159.

[157] Zaeef, *My Life with the Taliban*, 8-9.

[158] Kaplan, *Soldiers of God*, 226-227; Scheuer, *Osama bin Laden*, 76-77.

[159] Zaeef, *My Life with the Taliban*, 39.

[160] *Wilson Center Digital Archive, Collection 76*, "A Report by Soviet Military Intelligence," 1 September 1981.

[161] U.S. President, "National Security Decision Directive Number 75: U.S. Relations with the USSR," *The White House*, Washington, D.C. 17 January 1983, *Ronald Reagan Presidential Library & Museum*, https://www.reaganlibrary.gov/public/archives/reference/scanned-nsdds/nsdd75.pdf.

[162] William J. Casey, *Scouting the Future: The Public Speeches of William J. Casey*, ed. and comp. Herbert E. Meyer (Washington, D.C.: Regnery, 1989), 183, 218, 227; Coll, *Ghost Wars*, 600n12; Kengor, *The Crusader*, 165-167; Joseph E. Persico. *Casey: The Lives and Secrets of William J. Casey from the OSS to the CIA*. (New York: Penguin Books, 1991), xi, 13, 17.

[163] Casey, *Scouting the Future*, 119-120, 183; Kengor, *The Crusader*, 169.

[164] *The Bukovsky Archives*, "MEETING OF CPSU POLITBURO 18 January 1983."

[165] *The Bukovsky Archives*, "MEETING OF CPSU."

[166] Ibid.

[167] Kengor, *The Crusader*, 169, 254-256, Schweitzer, *Reagan's War*, 238.

[168] Casey, *Scouting the Future*, 119-120, 186-187; Coll, *Ghost Wars*, 600n17; Rone Tempest, "Sen. Humphrey Visits Kabul, Refuses Talks," *Los Angeles Times*, 15 April 1987, https://www.latimes.com/archives/la-xpm-1987-04-15-mn-247-story.html.

[169] Casey, *Scouting the Future*, 119-120, 144; *The National Security Archive, Vol. II*, "Episode 20 Soldiers of God: Interview with Frank Anderson – August 1997," https://nsarchive2.gwu.edu//coldwar/interviews/episode-20/anderson2.html; Coll, *Ghost Wars*, 600n17; George Crile, *Charlie Wilson's War: The Extraordinary Story of how the Wildest Man in Congress and a Rogue CIA Agent Changed the History of Our Times* (New York: Grove Press, 2003), 325-327, 330-331; Pear, "Arming Afghan Guerrillas."

[170] Yousaf and Adkin, *Afghanistan*, 81-83.

[171] Jack Anderson and Dale van Atta, "Afghan Rebel Aid Enriches Generals," *The Washington Post*, 8 May 1987, https://www.washingtonpost.com/archive/local/1987/05/08/afghan-rebel-aid-enriches-generals/40243b90-55d4-421b-80b7-929c3e4b1075/; Yousaf and Adkin, *Afghanistan*, 85.

[172] Anderson and van Atta, "Afghan Rebel Aid Enriches Generals."

173 Pear, "Arming Afghan Guerrillas,"; Yousaf and Adkin, *Afghanistan*, 84, 98.

174 Anderson and van Atta, "Afghan Rebel Aid Enriches Generals,"; Yousaf and Adkin, *Afghanistan*, 98.

175 Crile, *Charlie Wilson's War*, 390; Hussein Haqqani, *Pakistan: Between Mosque and Military* (Washington, D.C.: Carnegie Endowment for International Peace, 2005), 162-165; Pear, "Arming Afghan Guerrillas,"; Yousaf and Adkin, *Afghanistan*, 81-83.

176 Kengor, *The Crusader*, 58-59; Pear, "Arming Afghan Guerrillas."

177 *Congressional Record – United States Senate*, 97th Congress, 2nd Session (1982), pt.? Government Publishing Office, https://babel.hathitrust.org/cgi/pt?id=mdp.39015011692970&view=1up&seq=1.

178 *Cong. Rec. – United States Senate*, 97th Cong. 2nd Sess. (1982). Stoessel further decried the alleged mass looting of the city by Soviet troops following the Soviet Air Force's prolonged bombing campaign and assessed the dogged resistance of the Afghan fighters as courageous in the face of such seemingly irresistible odds.

179 *Congressional Record – United States Senate*, 98th Congress, 2nd Session (1984), pt. 98-181, Government Publishing Office, https://babel.hathitrust.org/cgi/pt?id=umn.31951d00829084i&view=1up&seq=1; Haq, "Afghanistan Won't Be a U.S. of Soviet Puppet."

180 *Cong. Rec – United States Senate*, 98th Cong. 2nd Sess. (1984) pt. 98-181.

181 *Cong. Rec – United States Senate*, 98th Cong. 2nd Sess. (1984) pt. 98-181. Paul Kengor states that the Soviets planted between 5,000,000 and 10,000,000 land mines in Afghanistan, mines that continue to kill and maim Afghan civilians more than 30 years after Gorbachev's withdrawal of Soviet troops. See Kengor, *The Crusader*, 228-229, 230-232.

182 Ibid.

183 Jones, *In the Graveyard of Empires*, 41; Robert M. Gates, *From the Shadows: The Ultimate Insider's Story of Five Presidents and How They Won the Cold War* (New York: Simon and Schuster, 1996), 431; *National Security Archive, Vol. II*, "Episode 20 Soldiers of God."

184 Crile, *Charlie Wilson's War*, 390; Kengor, *The Crusader*, 230-232; Barnett R. Rubin, *Afghanistan: What Everyone Needs to Know* (New York: Oxford University Press, 2020), 72-73; Tempest, "Sen. Humphrey Visits Kabul."

185 David B. Ottaway, "Afghan Rebels Assured of More U.S. Support," *The Washington Post*, 13 November 1987, https://www.washingtonpost.com/archive/politics/1987/11/13/afghan-rebels-assured-of-more-us-support/ebdbf011-8283-43f8-aba8-88c5c8b540ca/.

186 Haq, "Afghanistan Won't Be a U.S. or Soviet Puppet."

187 Kaplan, *Soldiers of God*, 170-172, 217; *The National Security Archive, Vol. II*, "Episode 20 Soldiers of God,"; Yousaf and Adkin, *Afghanistan*, 106.

188 Kengor, *The Crusader*, 230-232; Ronald Reagan, *An American Life* (New York: Threshold Editions, 2011), 604.

189 Casey, *Scouting the Future*, 119-120, 183; Reagan, *An American Life*, 267.

190 Reagan, *An American Life*, 604; U.S. President, "Remarks on Signing the Afghanistan Day Proclamation," *The White House*, Washington, D.C., 20 March 1987, *Ronald Reagan Presidential Library & Museum*, https://www.reaganlibrary.gov/archives/speech/remarks-signing-afghanistan-day-proclamation.

191 Tempest, "Sen. Humphrey Visits Kabul."

192 Haqqani, *Pakistan*, 162-165; Ronald Reagan, *The Reagan Diaries*, ed. Douglas Brinkley (New York: Harper Perennial, 2009), 128-129; Yousaf and Adkin, *Afghanistan*, 62-63, 81,

120. Yousaf states that the ISI broke this rule only once, in 1987, arranging a trip for Congressman Charlie Wilson across the Afghan border to a guerrilla base against the express orders of Pakistani President Zia but with the silent approval of General Akhtar of ISI. Yousaf also claims that he arranged a for Senator Humphrey to visit a Stinger missile training school run by the ISI in 1987 due to the agency's appreciation of the senator's enthusiastic and crucial support, together with Congressman Wilson, for the Reagan administration and CIA's efforts to arm the mujahedin with Stingers.

[193] Ottaway, "Soviets, Afghan Rebels Pressure U.S. on Arms," https://www.washingtonpost.com/archive/politics/1988/10/02/soviets-afghan-rebels-pressure-us-on-arms/1011636c-7396-4a11-ba7a-35259125c258/.

[194] Ottaway, "Afghan Rebels Assured."

[195] Al-Bahri and Malbrunot, *Guarding bin Laden*, 134-136, 150; Scheuer, *Osama bin Laden*, 102-103, 105-106, 222-223n116-121. Scheuer also emphasizes the dishonesty of Sudan's braggart Islamist ruler, Dr. Hasan al-Turabi, as making bin Laden's return to Afghanistan crucial in addition to the mounting pressure from the U.S. and Saudi governments on the Sudanese regime. Described as a, "plunger" by Jonathan Randal, al-Turabi, a corrupt and arrogant Islamist scholar educated in Britain and France, took advantage of bin Laden's initial deference to trained Islamic scholars by taking the exiled al-Qaeda leader on, "a fund-draining exercise," claiming that all of his investments were being directed to charity. Reportedly expressing hopes that he could help modernize Sudan and ease the economic suffering of its people, bin Laden invested heavily in the country, building infrastructure, funding humanitarian projects, purchasing military and agricultural equipment and crops, and constructing an airport in Port Sudan on the Red Sea coast. Al-Turabi proceeded to live lavishly while reportedly pocketing the funds from bin Laden's investments and although the al-Qaeda chief refused to criticize the Sudanese ruler personally he began reaching out to trusted Afghan comrades such as Yunis Khalis during this period in the mid-1990s to explore the possibility of returning to Afghanistan. Recalling his 1996 interview with bin Laden in Afghanistan in his memoir, the journalist and former *Al-Quds al-Arabi* editor Abdel Bari Atwan states that al-Turabi successfully drained about $300,000,000 from the al-Qaeda chief, while British journalist Mark Huband cites a figure of around $92,000,000. Regardless of the massive financial losses resulting from al-Turabi's deceit, bin Laden managed to gradually recoup enough funds to prosecute al-Qaeda's war with the United States after returning to Afghanistan, sending his faithful son Saad to Sudan on a Yemeni passport in 1999 to sell his last remaining properties in the East African nation, and dispatching him on a similar successful mission about six months later according to Nasser al-Bahri. See Atwan, *The Secret History of al-Qaeda*, 31; Bin Laden, bin Laden, and Sasson, *Growing Up bin Laden*, 139; Coll, *The Bin Ladens*, 653; Fisk, "Anti-Soviet warrior puts his army on the road to peace,"; Mark Huband, *Brutal Truths, Fragile Myths* (New York: Basic Books 2004), 72, 83; MacLeod, "The Paladin of Jihad," 51-52; Randal, *Osama*, 117-120; and Wright, *The Looming Tower*, 224.

[196] *The National Security Archive, Vol. II*, "Episode 20 Soldiers of God,"; Yousaf and Adkin, *Afghanistan*, 90.

[197] Bergen, *Holy War, Inc.*, 57, 73; Coll, *Ghost Wars*, 329; *The National Security Archive, Vol. II*, "Episode 20 Soldiers of God."

[198] Jalali, *A Military History of Afghanistan*, 404-405; Yousaf and Adkin, *Afghanistan*, 71; Kaplan, *Soldiers of God*, 40-41; *The National Security Archive, Vol. II*, "Episode 20 Soldiers

of God,"; *Wilson Center Digital Archive, Collection 76*, "Memorandum of Conversation Between M. S. Gorbachev and General Secretary of the CC NDPA [National Democratic Party of Afghanistan], Chairman of the Revolutionary Council of DRA [Democratic Republic of Afghanistan] B. Karmal," 14 March 1985.

[199] Bergen, *Holy War, Inc.*, 76.

[200] Yousaf and Adkin, *Afghanistan*, 70-71.

[201] Kaplan, *Soldiers of God*, 40-41; *The National Security Archive, Vol. II*, "Episode 20 Soldiers of God."

[202] Yousaf and Adkin, *Afghanistan*, 106.

[203] Ibid., 85.

[204] Ibid.

[205] Kengor, *The Crusader*, 232; Sikorski, *Dust of the Saints*, 267.

[206] Jalali, *A Military History of Afghanistan*, 414-415; Kengor, *The Crusader*, 232.

[207] Kaplan, *Soldiers of God*, 187.

[208] Borovik, *The Hidden War*, 120; Kaplan, *Soldiers of God*, 77, 121; Sikorski, *Dust of the Saints*, 267.

[209] Kaplan, *Soldiers of God*, 186-187.

[210] Ibid., 41, 186-187; James W. Spain, *The Way of the Pathans* (Karachi: Oxford University Press, 1979), 46, 48, 52.

[211] Jalali, *A Military History of Afghanistan*, 416-417; Scheuer, *Osama bin Laden*, 64, 73.

[212] Ottaway, "Agreement on Afghanistan Signed in Geneva."

[213] *Parliamentary Record – House of Commons*, 1st Session (1988), https://www.theyworkforyou.com/debates/?id=1988-03-04a.1280.0&s=Afghanistan+1980s#g1280.3.

[214] Haq, "Afghanistan Won't Be a U.S. or Soviet Puppet."

[215] *Cong. Rec.*, 1st Sess. (1988).

[216] Ibid.

[217] Ibid.

[218] Ibid.

[219] Kaplan, *Soldiers of God*, 189. Contrary to a popular misperception, U.S. and Western officials did not abandon or forget about Afghanistan following the Soviet 40th Army's defeat. Between the retreat of the last Soviet forces on 15 February 1989 and the 9/11 attacks, the Russian, U.S., UK, and German governments appear to have continued to pressure the various mujahedin factions into accepting an interim government including the some members of the hated Afghan communist and royalist parties, both perceived as corrupt and oppressive by many rural Afghans. During this period, the two Bush administrations and the Clinton administration dispatched four successive U.S., "Special Envoys" to Afghanistan, Peter Tomsen, Robert Oakley, Phyllis Oakley, and Zalmay Khalilizad, each in their turn, with the objective of preventing a Sunni Islamist regime from taking power even though these groups appear to have been those that fought the hardest to oust the Soviet invaders. Hoping to pressure Taleban leader Mullah Muhammad Omar to surrender bin Laden in 1998, President Bill Clinton dispatched the U.S. Energy Secretary and UN ambassador Bill Richardson to Afghanistan, threatening to cancel a proposed oil pipeline running through the Kandahar region if the Taleban refused to turn the al-Qaeda leader over to the United States or Saudi Arabia. Refusing to comply, Omar reportedly pointed out that surrendering bin Laden to foreign powers amounted to the betrayal of, "the great Arab mujahid" responsible for providing generous assistance to the Afghan warriors in their struggle against the Soviet troops. Bin Laden

and al-Qaeda subsequently continued building and strengthening their solid local support system among the Afghan and Pakistani Islamist *ulema*, Omar's deputies in the Taleban, and other regional Islamist groups, as counterproductive U.S. threats and UN sanctions stiffened the Taleban leadership's resistance to foreign demands to turn the al-Qaeda chief over to the U.S. or Saudi governments. See Al-Bahri and Malbrunot, *Guarding bin Laden*, 138-139; Roy Gutman, *How We Missed the Story: Osama bin Laden, the Taliban, and the Hijacking of Afghanistan* (Washington, D.C.: United States Institute of Peace Press, 2013), 7; Scott Peterson, "Osama bin Laden is a 'hero' in Afghanistan," *The Christian Science Monitor*, 14 December 1999, https://www.csmonitor.com/1999/1214/p7s1.html; Scheuer, *Osama bin Laden*, 123-124; Weiner, "U.S. Hard Put to Find Proof."

[220] Kaplan, *Soldiers of God*, 36-38; 171-172.

[221] Haq, "Afghanistan Won't Be a U.S. or Soviet Puppet,"; Yousaf and Adkin, *Afghanistan*, 212-213. In an August 1997 interview for *CNN's* documentary on the Soviet-Afghan War, former CIA officer Frank Anderson appears to concur with Haq's conclusion that while the U.S., UK, and Saudi governments played a key role in financing and arming the Afghan resistance, the guerrillas themselves had paid the price in blood that eventually resulted in Moscow's retreat. Formerly in charge of delivering supplies to the Afghan insurgent groups based in Pakistan, Anderson recalls that, "I made the comment [during the war] that 'gratitude in the Afghan's dictionary is gonna be found somewhere after gimme and gotcha'... On the other hand there was a constant current of understanding that while we were providing the means to wage this war, they were waging it and that it is entirely true that this was a war that was fought with our gold but with their blood..." For Anderson's highly informative interview on CIA-mujahedin interactions during the war, see *National Security Archive, Vol. II,* "Episode 20 Soldiers of God."

CHAPTER 3

[1] David Selbourne and Mary Kenny Deal, "Which side were you on in the last Afghan war?" *The Guardian*, 23 October 2001, https://www.theguardian.com/world/2001/oct/23/afghanistan.terrorism6.

[2] *Parliamentary Record – House of Commons*, 1st Session (1986), https://www.theyworkforyou.com/debates/?id=1986-06-18a.1082.0&s=Afghanistan+speaker%3A10123#g1129.0.

[3] *Parl. Rec. – House of Commons*, 1st Sess. (1986); Sikorski, *Dust of the Saints*, 255.

[4] *Parl. Rec. – House of Commons*, 1st Sess. (1986).

[5] Julie Burchill, "Out of the rubble," *The Guardian*, 20 October 2001, https://www.theguardian.com/world/2001/oct/20/september11.usa1.

[6] Burchill, "Out of the rubble,"; Sikorski, *Dust of the Saints*, 256.

[7] Selbourne and Kenny Deal, "Which side were you on in the last Afghan war?"

[8] Ibid.; Sikorski, *Dust of the Saints*, 256.

[9] These arguments are not unlike the popular but incorrect assumption that all Sunni Islamist groups, including al-Qaeda, are waging an endless offensive war to conquer the West due to their hatred of its freedoms. This assertion ignores the words of bin Laden and his associates stating that specific U.S. and Western policies rather than values are the driving force behind their 1996 declaration of war, in the same way that they did not take up arms against the Soviets until the Kremlin's 1979 invasion of Afghanistan. For the stated war motives of bin Laden and al-Qaeda, see OBL, "Jihad Against Jews and

Crusaders,"; Lewis, "License to Kill,"; OBL, "Full transcript of bin Ladin's speech,"; and Rahimullah Yusufzai, "Face to face with Osama," *The Guardian*, 26 September 2001, https://www.theguardian.com/world/2001/sep/26/afghanistan.terrorism3.

[10] Kaplan, *Soldiers of God*, 212.

[11] Ibid.

[12] Ibid.

[13] Scheuer, *Osama bin Laden*, 52-53.

[14] Abd-al-Karim and al-Nur, "Interview with Saudi businessman Usama bin Ladin,"; OBL, "Open Letter for Sheikh Bin Baz," ARC, 29 December 1994; and OBL, "Introduction," 85-86. Bin Laden wrote that, "The whole Muslim World could not believe that it was possible to stand up to the Soviet Union. People had lived in a complete state of fear from this seemingly 'invincible' Soviet military machine. This disease was not only present in the minds of the masses but also amongst the ranks of the scholars. This defeatism and pessimism was such that the scholars would advise any of their students who wished to join the Mujahideen, that the Soviets were impossible to defeat. Even after the Battle of Jaji, when the indicators seemed to suggest a Soviet withdrawal, the Muslims still refused to believe this could happen because of the defeatism and cowardice that had overwhelmed the Muslim minds."

[15] OBL, "Introduction," 85.

[16] Scheuer, *Osama bin Laden*, 204-205n19.

[17] Bergen, *Holy War, Inc.*, 58-59; Coll, *Ghost Wars*, 65-67, 72.

[18] OBL, "Introduction," 85; OBL, ARC, 19 September 1994.

[19] OBL, ARC, 19 September 1994; Scheuer, *Osama bin Laden*, 97.

[20] OBL, "Introduction," 81.

[21] Ibid. Ironically, perhaps due in some part to bin Laden's wartime efforts and the eventual triumph of the Afghan rebels over the odds, the region has increasingly offered safe passage to al-Qaeda fighters and other Sunni Islamist militants passing through in the decades since the Soviet defeat. Nasser al-Bahri recalls that bin Laden sometimes purchased his favorite type of horse, a small breed of black Arabian horse, from Baluchi breeders, stabling 12 of these rare animals at his Tarnak Farm compound in Kandahar, his favorite being, "a stallion called Adham [meaning "shiny black stallion"]" that only the al-Qaeda chief and his second eldest son Abdul Rahman could ride bare-back, despite all of Abdul Rahman's brothers being accomplished horsemen like their father. Several top al-Qaeda leaders and fighters, such as bin Laden's most trusted and faithful son, Saad, the Egyptian Saif al-Adel, and the Yemeni Nasser al-Wahayshi, received support from the Sunni Muslim Baluchi tribes in neighboring Iran, a double minority in that country, to enter Iran and eventually return to fighting for al-Qaeda in Afghanistan or in their native countries. While al-Adel and other Egyptians reportedly remained and enjoyed Tehran's protection, even taking Iranian wives, the Saudis and Yemenis such as Saad bin Laden and Nasser al-Wahayshi received harsh treatment upon discovery by the Iranian authorities, often being subjected to house arrest in Saad's case or extradition for imprisonment in their countries of origin in the case of al-Wahayshi. See al-Bahri and Malbrunot, *Guarding bin Laden*, 76, 150-152, 181, 209-210, for Nasser al-Bahri's detailed account of al-Qaeda's relationship with the Baluchi tribes and the ways in which this relationship enabled the militants to escape both the initial U.S.-NATO invasion and Iranian custody only to return and fight another day in Afghanistan or Yemen. For further details on Saad bin Laden's escape from Iran and subsequent death in a 2009 CIA drone

strike in Pakistan, see Pamela Engel, "Osama bin Laden's son wrote this letter to his wife in 2008 outlining his last wishes," *Business Insider*, 20 May 2015, https://www.businessinsider.com/osama-bin-laden-2008-letter-to-his-wife-2015-5; Reuters Staff, "U.S. says Bin Laden son may be dead," *Reuters*, 23 July 2009, https://www.reuters.com/article/us-binbinladen-saad-sb/u-s-says-bin-laden-son-may-be-dead-idUSTRE56M4Y K20090723; and Eric Schmitt, "U.S. Officials Say a Son of bin Laden May be Dead," *The New York Times*, 24 July 2009, https://www.nytimes.com/2009/07/24/world/asia/24pstan.html.

[22] Abd-al-Karim and al-Nur, "Interview with Saudi businessman Usama bin Ladin,"; OBL, "Introduction," 81, 111-113. Bin Laden described being motivated by both a desire for Arab units to gain combat experience and to persuade the Afghans that they were not alone, as the Afghan communist rulers enjoyed the, "might of the Soviet Army" and its Warsaw Pact allies bolstering their position, a situation that he found to be, "sinful" and essentially, "abandonment" of Islam's cause due to the lack of large numbers of Arab and other non-Afghan volunteers in the guerrilla ranks.

[23] Kaplan, *Soldiers of God*, 82-84.
[24] Ibid., 99-100.
[25] Bergen, *The Osama bin Laden I Know*, 59-60; Scheuer, *Osama bin Laden*, 51-52.
[26] Atwan, "My weekend with Osama bin Laden,"; Bergen, *The Osama bin Laden I Know*, 59-60; Osama bin Laden, "Translation of bin Laden's message," *Al-Jazeera*, 23 October 2007, https://www.aljazeera.com/news/2007/10/23/translation-of-bin-ladens-message; Scheuer, *Osama bin Laden*, 51-52, 204n15.
[27] Chalmers Johnson, *Blowback: The Cost and Consequences of American Empire* (New York: Owl Books, 2001), 8-11.
[28] Johnson, *Blowback*, 8-11.
[29] Robin Cook, "The struggle against terrorism cannot be won by military means," *The Guardian*, July 8, 2005, https://www.theguardian.com/uk/2005/jul/08/july7.development.
[30] Jalali, *A Military History of Afghanistan*, 382-383.
[31] Bergen, *The Osama bin Laden I Know*, 61, 398, 446n20; Michael Moore, "Death, Downtown," michaelmoore.com, 12 September 2001, https://michaelmoore.com/.
[32] Arundhati Roy, "The algebra of infinite justice," *The Guardian*, 29 September 2001, https://www.theguardian.com/world/2001/sep/29/september11.afghanistan.
[33] Chris McGreal, "Fidel Castro claims Osama bin Laden is a US spy," *The Guardian*, 27 August 2010, https://www.theguardian.com/world/2010/aug/27/fidel-castro-osama-bin-laden-us-spy.
[34] Kaplan, *Soldiers of God*, xx-xxi; Yousaf and Adkin, *Afghanistan*, 81-83, 85, 106.
[35] Bin Laden, bin Laden, and Sasson, *Growing Up bin Laden*, 89.
[36] Ibid.
[37] Worth, "Ex-Jihadist Defies Yemen's Leader."
[38] Ibid.
[39] Root, "A Sheikh's Life."
[40] Al-Bahri and Malbrunot, *Guarding bin Laden*, 16-17.
[41] Ibid.
[42] Kengor, *The Crusader*, 230-232; Reagan, *An American Life*, 604.
[43] Bin Laden, bin Laden, and Sasson, *Growing Up bin Laden*, 74-75, 89.
[44] Ibid.
[45] Ibid.

⁴⁶ Root, "A Sheikh's Life,"; Worth, "Ex-Jihadist Defies Yemen's Leader."
⁴⁷ Oren Adaki, "Yemeni tribal leader joins AQAP," *FDD's Long War Journal*, 17 June 2014, https://www.longwarjournal.org/archives/2014/06/yemeni_tribal_leader_joins_aqa.php; Akbar Ahmed and Harrison Akins, "Making enemies in Yemen," *Al-Jazeera*, 5 May 2013, https://www.aljazeera.com/opinions/2013/5/5/making-enemies-in-yemen.
⁴⁸ Adaki, "Yemeni tribal leader joins AQAP,"; Ahmed and Akins, "Making enemies in Yemen." Indeed, as these two newspaper reports state, al-Fadhli zealously embraced his sons' willing participation as guerrillas in the ranks of AQAP and proudly burned the same U.S. flag that he had flown during his February 2010 interview with *The New York Times* in an internet video that he and his tribesmen circulated, citing his staunch resentment of the Obama administration's increased use of CIA drone strikes in Yemen and an alleged 2009 U.S. cluster bombing of a Yemeni village in his native Abyan province that reportedly killed 41 people including 14 women and 21 children.
⁴⁹ Al-Bahri and Malbrunot, *Guarding bin Laden*, 17.
⁵⁰ Ibid.; OBL, "Introduction," 78-79.
⁵¹ For two excellent analyses of the organization's steady growth despite the West's ongoing military and intelligence operations against it, see Bushra al-Maqtari, "The evolution of militant Salafism in Taiz," *Sana'a Center for Strategic Studies*, 29 September 2017, https://sanaacenter.org/publications/analysis/4843; and Mashal, "How the Taliban Outlasted a Superpower."
⁵² Atwan, "My weekend with Osama bin Laden,"; MacLeod, "The Paladin of Jihad," 51-52; Miller, "Greetings America. My Name is Osama bin Laden."
⁵³ Trofimov, *The Siege of Mecca*, 48-49.
⁵⁴ Mikhail Gorbachev, *Perestroika: New Thinking for Our Country and the World* (New York: Harper & Row, 1988), 162-163; Ottaway, "Soviets, Afghan Rebels Pressure U.S. on Arms,"; Yousaf and Adkin, *Afghanistan*, 81-83.
⁵⁵ OBL, "Introduction," 78-79; Grier, "Soviets bolster an Arab ally,"; Howe, "Southern Yemen Blends Marxism,"; Kifner, "SOVIET SAID TO TRY,"; The New York Times, "Afghans Accept Both Losses and Gains in 'Holy War' Against the Russians," *The New York Times*, 31 October 1985, https://www.nytimes.com/1985/10/31/world/afghans-accept-both-losses-and-gains-in-holy-war-against-the-russians.html.
⁵⁶ Bergen, *Holy War, Inc.*, 58-59, 107; Kengor, *The Crusader*, 230-232.
⁵⁷ Pear, "Arming Afghan Guerrillas,"; *Wilson Center Digital Archive, Collection 76*, "A Report by Soviet Military Intelligence," 1 September 1981; Yousaf and Adkin, *Afghanistan*, 106.
⁵⁸ Pear, "Arming Afghan Guerrillas,"; Yousaf and Adkin, *Afghanistan*, 81-83, 105-106.
⁵⁹ Kalinovsky, *A Long Goodbye*, 43; Kaplan, *Soldiers of God*, 176-177; The New York Times, "Afghans Accept Both Losses and Gains."
⁶⁰ Braithwaite, *Afgantsy*, 203-205; Galeotti, *Afghanistan*, 18, 195-196; Kalinovsky, *A Long Goodbye*, 43; The New York Times, "Afghans Accept Both Losses and Gains."
⁶¹ OBL, "Introduction," 77, 80.
⁶² Camille Tawil, *Brothers in Arms: The Story of Al-Qa'ida and the Arab Jihadists*, London: Saqi Books, 2010, 19-20.
⁶³ Sikorski, *Dust of the Saints*, 266.
⁶⁴ Kaplan, *Soldiers of God*, xx-xxi.
⁶⁵ Ibid.
⁶⁶ Yousaf and Adkin, *Afghanistan*, 106.

67 Randal, *Osama*, 80-81.
68 Ibid., *Osama*, 83-84, 116.
69 Anderson and van Atta, "Afghan Rebel Aid Enriches Generals,"; Randal, *Osama*, 85.
70 Anderson and van Atta," "Afghan Rebel Aid Enriches Generals,"; *Wilson Center Digital Archive, Collection 76*, "Soviet Invasion of Afghanistan." 1 September 1981.
71 Kaplan, *Soldiers of God*, 137.
72 Coll, *Ghost Wars*, 40-41; *The National Security Archive, Vol. II*, "Episode 20 Soldiers of God."
73 Crile, *Charlie Wilson's War*, 205-206; Kaplan, *Soldiers of God*, 137; *The National Security Archive, Vol. II*, "Episode 20 Soldiers of God." Senator Percy and Congressman Long both worked as ardent advocates of congressional support for Operation *Cyclone*, the latter after becoming persuaded in a meeting with Congressman Wilson before the November 1984 defeats of both of their reelection campaigns.
74 Tempest, "Sen. Humphrey Visits Kabul,"; The National Security Archive, Vol. II, "Episode 20 Soldiers of God,"; *Wilson Center Digital Archive, Collection 76*, "A Report by Soviet Military Intelligence," 1 September 1981.
75 Gates, *From the Shadows*, 431; Jones, *In the Graveyard of Empires*, 41.
76 Gates, *From the Shadows*, 431.
77 Crile, *Charlie Wilson's War*, 330-331, 370; *The National Security Archive, Vol. II*, "Episode 20 Soldiers of God."
78 *Congressional Record – House of Representatives*, 100th Congress, 1st Session pt.? (1987), https://babel.hathitrust.org/cgi/pt?id=pst.000013351069&view=1up&seq=1.
79 *Cong. Rec. – House of Representatives*, 100th Cong., 1st Sess. (1987).
80 *Cong. Rec. – United States Senate*, 100th Cong. 2nd Sess. (1988).
81 Ibid.; David K. Shipler, "Reagan Didn't Know of Afghan Deal," *The New York Times*, 11 February 1988, https://www.nytimes.com/1988/02/11/world/reagan-didn-t-know-of-afghan-deal.html.
82 *Cong. Rec. – United States Senate*, 100th Cong. 2nd Sess. (1988); Shipler, "Reagan Didn't Know of Afghan Deal."
83 Kaplan, *Soldiers of God*, 171-172, 217; Yousaf and Adkin, *Afghanistan*, 107-108.
84 Kaplan, *Soldiers of God*, 170.
85 Rubin, *Afghanistan*, 72-73; Thatcher, *The Downing Street Years*, 68; UK Prime Minister, "Margaret Thatcher: TV Interview for ITN (Afghanistan)," *No. 10 Downing Street*, London, 13 December 1985, *Margaret Thatcher Foundation*, https://www.margaretthatcher.org/document/106201.
86 Prime Minister Thatcher's MI-6 had begun supplying the mujahedin with the Blowpipe surface-to-air missiles (SAMs) manufactured by the Short Brothers company based in Northern Ireland following Haq's visit to London earlier that year, but the insurgents quickly found them to be of little use against the lightning-fast Soviet ground attack planes, the MiG-27s (between 1987 and 1989) and Su-25s, and the fearsome Mi-24 helicopter gunships. Nevertheless, many commanders gratefully accepted the considerable material aid that they received but sometimes voiced their frustration that the United States and Britain, at the general insistence and consensus of congressional and parliamentary lawmakers rather than the heads of state and intelligence, sometimes received faulty equipment from their supply sources. For example, Ishaq Gailani's fighters reportedly frowned and spoke unfavorably of the Soviet-made SAM-7 missiles supplied by the CIA's arms purchases from the secular Arab and Chinese regimes in a

1985 conversation with Debra Denker of *National Geographic* while Commander Abdul Haq voiced similar frustrations in several conversations with Robert Kaplan. Nevertheless, the Stinger's introduction in late 1986 made a tremendous impact on insurgent morale, serving as the most accurate and effective SAM available at the time, and forcing Soviet planes to fly at higher altitudes and helicopters to sweep in lower in hopes of avoiding a direct hit. As the eyewitness Radek Sikorski points out however, it should also be remembered that had the insurgents not fought doggedly for control of the rural regions, the Stinger's effectiveness may have been greatly diminished. See Debra Denker, *National Geographic*, "Along Afghanistan's War-Torn Frontier," Vol. 167, No. 6, (June 1985), 772-797; David C. Isby, *War in a Distant Country: Afghanistan: Invasion and Resistance* (London: Arms and Armour Press, 1989), 8, 33; Kaplan, *Soldiers of God*, 176-178; Sikorski, *Dust of the Saints*, 268; Rubin, *Afghanistan*, 72-73; Thatcher, *The Downing Street Years*, 68; and UK Prime Minister, "Margaret Thatcher."

[87] Kaplan, *Soldiers of God*, 18, 169.

[88] Ibid., 158, 169; Rubin, *Afghanistan*, 72-73.

[89] Kaplan, *Soldiers of God*, 158, 169; Kengor, *The Crusader*, 230-232.

[90] Persico, *Casey*, 225-227; Yousaf and Adkin, *Afghanistan*, 81-83, 107-108.

[91] Yousaf and Adkin, *Afghanistan*, 107-108. Yousaf relates an encounter with one such Pakistan Army officer in the presence of Charlie Wilson during the congressman's ISI-guided visit across the Afghan border.

[92] Bergen, *Holy War, Inc.*, 150.

[93] Kaplan, *Soldiers of God*, 171-172.

[94] OBL, "Introduction, 77, 80-81; Fisk, "Anti-Soviet warrior puts his army on the road to peace."

[95] Al-Bahri and Malbrunot, *Guarding bin Laden*, 16-17; Bin Laden, bin Laden, and Sasson, *Growing Up bin Laden*, 33, 89; Yousaf and Adkin, *Afghanistan*, 105-106.

[96] Yousaf and Adkin, *Afghanistan*, 105-106.

[97] Girardet, *Killing the Cranes*, 228-230.

[98] Ibid., 254-255.

[99] Ibid.

[100] Yousaf and Adkin, *Afghanistan*, 106.

[101] Ibid.

[102] Bergen, *Holy War, Inc.*, 57.

[103] Ibid., 66-68.

[104] Ibid., 131, 133-134.

[105] Coll, *The Bin Ladens*, 7-8, 10.

[106] Ibid., 11-12.

[107] Schultheis, *Hunting bin Laden*, 52-53.

[108] John Simpson, "Simpson on Sunday: The day that Osama bin Laden out a price on my head," *The Telegraph*, 16 September 2001, http://www.telegraph.co.uk/news/world news/asia/afghanistan/1340688/Simpson-on-Sunday-The-day-that-Osama-bin-Laden-put-a-price-on-my-head.html.

[109] Simpson, "Simpson on Sunday: The day that Osama bin Laden put a price on my head," *The Telegraph*, 16 September 2001. Bin Laden is reported to have wept after this incident out of frustration that his Afghan hosts did not yet perceive the threat that he believed the West posed towards Muslims. His refusal to kill the Westerners himself while offering $500 for his hosts to do so, a characteristically vicious action against a perceived

enemy but a financially generous offer for Afghanistan, reflects his deferral to his hosts on matters of targeting outsiders regardless of his own feelings on the matter. For further examples of bin Laden's indirect confrontational style and refusal to raise his voice towards comrades that disappointed him, see al-Bahri and Malbrunot, *Guarding bin Laden*, 72.

[110] OBL, *Messages to the World*, 86-88.

[111] Ibid.

[112] Al-Bahri and Malbrunot, *Guarding bin Laden*, 207-208; Bin Laden, bin Laden, and Sasson, *Growing Up bin Laden*, 219-221; Girardet, *Killing the Cranes*, 260-262.

[113] Al-Bahri and Malbrunot, *Guarding bin Laden*, 207-208; Bin Laden, bin Laden, and Sasson, *Growing Up bin Laden*, 219-221; Scheuer, *Osama bin Laden*, 142-143.

[114] Al-Bahri and Malbrunit, *Guarding bin Laden*, 207-208; Bin Laden, bin Laden, and Sasson, *Growing Up bin Laden*, 219-221.

[115] Scheuer, *Osama bin Laden*, 116-117.

[116] OBL, "Transcript – ABC News,"; Andrew Hammond, "Bin Laden warns U.S. on Israel ties," *Reuters*, 13 September 2009, https://www.reuters.com/article/us-binladen-tape-idUSTRE58D0CX20090914; McDonald, "New Message Reported From bin Laden,"; Joseph Rhee and Rehab el-Buri, "Osama bin Laden message Surfaces in Wake of 9/11 Anniversary," *ABC News*, https://abcnews.go.com/Blotter/osama-bin-laden-message-surfaces-wake-911-anniversary/story?id=8564631; Scheuer, *Osama bin Laden*, 116-117, 213n94. In a September 2009 audio message, bin Laden states that by remaining in Afghanistan and increasing the U.S. troop presence there, President Barack Obama only continued to exacerbate the economic and military attrition begun by President George W. Bush's 7 October 2001 invasion, warning that unless the 44th president began showing true signs of reversing his White House predecessor's policies, "we will have no choice but to continue our war of attrition [guerrilla warfare] on every front." Echoing a 2007 statement comparing President Bush's refusal to withdraw from Afghanistan with that of Brezhnev's stubbornness on the same issue, bin Laden proceeds to compare the U.S. and Soviet leaders and occupations with both only succeeding in galvanizing devout Muslims against the occupiers and strengthening the resistance through stimulating voluntary recruitment, financial donations, and practical military training in battle against the superpowers' armies.

[117] OBL, "Full transcript of bin Ladin's speech."

[118] Bin Laden, bin Laden, and Sasson, *Growing Up bin Laden*, 74-75.

[119] OBL, "An invitation to Give Advice and Reform," ARC, 12 April 1994; Scheuer, *Osama bin Laden*, 97.

[120] Bergen, *Holy War, Inc.*, 226-227; Lewis, "License to Kill,"; Scheuer, *Osama bin Laden*, 116-117.

[121] OBL, "Full transcript of bin Ladin's speech."

[122] OBL, "An invitation to Give Advice and Reform," ARC, 12 April 1994; OBL, *Messages to the World*, 8.

[123] OBL, "An invitation to Give Advice and Reform," ARC, 12 April 1994; OBL, *Messages to the World*, 8; Robert Fisk, "10 July 1996: Arab rebel leader warns the British: Get out of the Gulf," *The Independent*, 10 July 1996, https://www.independent.co.uk/news/long_reads/robert-fisk-osama-bin-laden-saudi-arabia-afghanistan-war-b1561291.html.

[124] Scheuer, *Osama bin Laden*, 64, 73, 68-69, 212-213n91-93. This appears to contradict the weakly supported but widely held perception of bin Laden and the movement that

he led and inspired as a band of irrational fanatics bent on killing for pleasure or sport. While there are others certainly deserving of this image, such as the late Jordanian extremist Abu Musab al-Zarqawi, and al-Qaeda's current leader, Ayman al-Zawahiri prior to bin Laden's influence on him, it is inapplicable to bin Laden and those closest to him, such as the former jihadi Nasser al-Bahri and his Yemeni compatriot, the late Nasser al-Wahayshi. Indeed, those following bin Laden's example and that of traditional Salafism most closely often appear to realize the un-Koranic and impractical futility of fanatical wars of conquest and although utterly ruthless in combat, they adhere strictly to their belief in defensive warfare against the perceived occupiers. This of course makes them far more dangerous than sectarian-minded takfiris such as al-Zarqawi and others bent on killing or forcibly converting others, because they often earn the respect of their followers and increase the mujahid ranks. Stating that bin Laden managed al-Qaeda and chaired *Shura* or, "consultative council" discussions in a much more representative manner than Saddam Hussein or the al-Assad family in Iraq and Syria, Nasser al-Bahri, recalls that the al-Qaeda leader also frequently overruled the unwise urges of al-Zawahiri and others expressing agreement with al-Zarqawi's insistence on fighting the Arab governments and Shia Muslims without first giving dialogue a chance. Bin Laden appears to have maintained a steady hand on the al-Qaeda leadership's tiller from 1988 forward, regularly chairing *Shura* Council debates within the organization while refusing to approve or support counterproductive terror attacks or sectarian violence against the secular Arab and Muslim regimes, Israel, or the Shia until first driving the United States from the region, consistently citing the example of the Soviet occupiers' defeat in Afghanistan and the subsequent collapse of Moscow's Eastern Bloc puppet regimes as a God-given blueprint for eventual Islamist success, given the right amount of patience, determination, and avoidance of counterproductive sectarian attacks. Al-Bahri adds that bin Laden frequently voiced his displeasure with al-Zarqawi's desire to wage a sectarian war against the Shia, while al-Zawahiri initially supported such proposals. Reading such accounts, the researcher cannot help but marvel at bin Laden's seemingly unlimited degree of patience by tolerating al-Zawahiri, his fellow Egyptian Islamic Jihad (EIJ) member Saif al-Adel, and al-Zarqawi, by permitting but disagreeing with their stubborn arguments in favor of sectarian attacks and other actions that could easily have spelled doom for al-Qaeda. Comparing the Afghan Islamists' eventual triumph over the Soviet Army with al-Qaeda's struggle against the United States in his 1998 interview with *ABC News*, bin Laden told John Miller that, "There is a lesson to learn from this for he who wishes to learn… The Soviet Union entered Afghanistan in the last week of 1979, and with Allah's help their flag was folded a few years later and thrown in the trash, and there was nothing left to call the Soviet Union… You [Americans] will leave [like the Soviets] when the youth send you in wooden boxes and coffins. And you will carry in them the bodies of American troops and civilians. This is when you will leave." Citing Gorbachev's admission to the Soviet Politburo that the Afghan war had struck a fatal economic blow to Moscow's economy, bin Laden also wrote that the Soviet economy had suffered a, "huge economic drain" resulting from the attritional damage inflicted on the Soviet occupiers by the Afghan and Arab fighters' guerrilla war tactics, subsequently describing the Islamists' perseverance against, "the leading idol-power of the time [the Soviet Union]" as Allah's blueprint for victory over infidel occupiers and apostate regimes. See also al-Bahri and Malbrunot, *Guarding bin Laden*, 206, 210-212; Atwan, "My weekend with Osama bin Laden,"; OBL, "Introduction," 77, 79, 86; Abd-al-Karim and al-Nur,

"Interview with Saudi businessman Usama bin Ladin,"; and Miller, "Greetings America. My Name is Osama bin Laden."

[125] Bin Laden, bin Laden, and Sasson, *Growing Up bin Laden*, 89.

[126] Archie Brown, *The Gorbachev Factor*, (New York: Oxford University Press, 1997), 376n203; Bergen, *Holy War, Inc.*, 47; Gorbachev, *Perestroika*, 10; Scheuer, *Osama bin Laden*, 21.

[127] As pointed out by Najwa bin Laden, devout Muslims do not normally celebrate birthdays in the same manner as Westerners, but nor do they fail to acknowledge them, especially in perceived instances of divine favor. In this case of course, Gorbachev's decision to allow four more years of bloody futility in Afghanistan benefitted the Arab jihadis by finally enabling them to participate in the battles and gain the fighting experience that they had sought for so long. See bin Laden, bin Laden, and Sasson, *Growing Up bin Laden*, 91.

[128] Galeotti, *Afghanistan*, 18-19; Kalinovsky, *A Long Goodbye*, 38.

[129] Brown, *The Gorbachev Factor*, 221, 235; Gorbachev, *Perestroika*, 162-163; Kalinovsky, *A Long Goodbye*, 38; *Wilson Center Digital Archive, Collection 76*, "Politburo on Afghanistan," 13 November 1986.

[130] Crile, *Charlie Wilson's War*, 342-344; Isby, *War in a Distant Country*, 35-37; Kalinovsky, *A Long Goodbye*, 38; Kengor, *The Crusader*, 228-230, 232; *Wilson Center Digital Archive, Collection 76*, "CPSU CC Politburo Meeting Minutes (excerpt)," 13 November 1986.

[131] Brown, *The Gorbachev Factor*, 221, 235; Gorbachev, *Perestroika*, 162-163.

[132] Crile, *Charlie Wilson's War*, 342-344; Isby, *War in a Distant Country*, 35-37; Kengor, *The Crusader*, 232; *Wilson Center Digital Archive, Collection 76*, "CPSU CC Politburo Meeting Minutes (excerpt)," 13 November 1986. Of course, these previous interventions bore little to no similarity with the situation in Afghanistan, yet Gorbachev seems to have hoped that the successful careers of these two top generals presented a chance to withdraw quickly after sufficiently crippling the mujahedin. This in turn suggests that he, like his predecessors, potentially refused to acknowledge the indications that the resistance continued to grow in strength and resilience as his generals temporarily escalated the conflict and thereby prolonged the occupation, pushing a greater number of Afghan civilians into the insurgent ranks.

[133] Isby, *War in a Distant Country*, 35-37; Kaplan, *Soldiers of God*, 184-185, 188, 223; Yousaf and Adkin, *Afghanistan*, 164-165.

[134] Jalali, *A Military History of Afghanistan*, 375-376; Kaplan, *Soldiers of God*, 188, 223.

[135] For several firsthand accounts of Soviet slaughters of animals in Afghanistan to deny food or logistical support for the insurgents or their civilian supporters, see Denker, "Along Afghanistan's War-Torn Frontier," 773-774; Kaplan, *Soldiers of God*, 186-187; The New York Times, "Afghans Accept Both Losses and Gains,"; and Zaeef, *My Life with the Taliban*, 25.

[136] Denker, "Along Afghanistan's War-Torn Frontier," 783-785; Kaplan, *Soldiers of God*, 186-187, 188.

[137] Denker, "Along Afghanistan's War-Torn Frontier," 787-788, 794.

[138] Rubin, *Afghanistan*, 76-77.

[139] Galeotti, *Afghanistan*, 18-19; Rubin, *Afghanistan*, 76-77.

[140] Tempest, "Sen. Humphrey Visits Kabul."

141 *Cong. Rec. – United States Senate*, 100th Cong. 2nd Sess. (1988); Abdul Haq, "Afghanistan Won't Be a U.S. or Soviet Puppet,"; Kamm, "Afghan Rebels Reported Furious,"; Ottaway, "Afghan Rebels Assured."
142 *The National Security Archive, Volume II.* "Afghanistan: Lessons from the Last War." February 1987, nsarchive2.gwu.edu/NSAEBB57/us.html.
143 Al-Bahri and Malbrunot, *Guarding bin Laden*, 16; Bergen, *Holy War, Inc.*, 58.
144 Johnsen, *The Last Refuge*, 8-10. The cities of Sanaa, Sadaa, and Taez, as well as much of Yemen overall, North and South, appear to have produced prominent al-Qaeda fighters and leaders, represented by their strong presence in positions of administrative, media, and financial responsibility in the organization and in most of its guerrilla training camps and as members of bin Laden's 12-man bodyguard unit until at least February 2001. See al-Bahri and Malbrunot, *Guarding bin Laden*, 82, 87.
145 Persico, *Casey*, 310-311.
146 Mikhail Gorbachev, *Memoirs* (London: Transworld Publishers, 1997), 216; Kengor, *The Crusader*, 256, Persico, *Casey*, 310-311.
147 U.S. President, "National Security Decision Directive Number 166: U.S. Policy, Programs and Strategy in Afghanistan," *The White House*, Washington, D.C., 27 March 1985, *Ronald Reagan Presidential Library & Museum*, https://www.reaganlibrary.gov/public/archives/reference/scanned-nsdds/nsdd166.pdf.
148 Kengor, *The Crusader*, 232-233; Rubin, *Afghanistan*, 72-73; *The National Security Archives, Vol. II*, "Episode 20 Soldiers of God."
149 Kaplan, *Soldiers of God*, 187-188; Sikorski, *Dust of the Saints*, 268.
150 Reagan, *The Reagan Diaries*, 464; U.S. President, "National Security Decision Directive Number 270: Afghanistan," *The White House*, Washington, D.C., 1 May 1987, *Ronald Reagan Presidential Library & Museum*, https://www.reaganlibrary.gov/public/archives/reference/scanned-nsdds/nsdd270.pdf.
151 Coll, *Ghost Wars*, 160-161; Persico, *Casey*, 543-545; *Wilson Center Digital Archive, Collection 76*, "Conversation between M.S. Gorbachev and Ronald Reagan on Afghanistan (Excerpt)," 9 December 1987. At roughly the same time, Commander Abdul Haq alleged in a conversation with Robert Kaplan that his small amount of allotted aid had been completely discontinued, despite his successful capture of Soviet General Yevgeny Nikolaivich Akhrimiyuk, a relative of Brezhnev and former head of KGB operations in Afghanistan, in 1982. Commander Yunis Khalis' fighters later killed Akrimiyuk after the captured general refused to discuss a prisoner exchange with the insurgent leaders. See Kaplan, *Soldiers of God*, 159-160, 171-172, 217.
152 Kamm, "Afghan Rebels Reported Furious,"; Ottaway, "Afghan Rebels Assured."
153 Ottaway, "Afghan Rebels Assured."
154 Ibid.
155 Kamm, "Afghan Rebels Reported Furious,"; Ottaway, "Afghan Rebels Assured."
156 Bergen, *Holy War, Inc.*, 54; Coll, *Ghost Wars*, 155; Scheuer, *Osama bin Laden*, 54.
157 Abdullah Azzam, "Join the Caravan," 3-4, 15 April 1987, https://ebooks.worldofislam.info/ebooks/Jihad/Join%20the%20Caravan.pdf. Bergen, *Holy War Inc.*, 55; Tawil, *Brothers in Arms*, 17-18.
158 Azzam, "Join the Caravan," 3-4; Bergen, *The Osama bin Laden I Know*, 24; Scheuer, *Osama bin Laden*, 54.
159 Randal, *Osama*, 66, 85-86; Scheuer, *Osama bin Laden*, 54.
160 Scheuer, *Osama bin Laden*, 53-54, 132.

[161] Hamid and Farrall, *The Arabs at War in Afghanistan*, 70, 151; Randal, *Osama*, 87; Scheuer, *Osama bin Laden*, 55.
[162] Azzam, "Join the Caravan," 16-17; Hamid and Farrall, *The Arabs at War in Afghanistan*, 70, 151; Al-Qarni, "Bin Laden's Former 'Mufti' Musa Al-Qarni Talks about the Jihad in Afghanistan."
[163] Scheuer, *Osama bin Laden*, 115-116.
[164] Ibid., 55.
[165] Abd Al-Aziz Al-Muqrin, *Al-Qa'ida's Doctrine for Insurgency: Abd Al-Aziz Al-Muqrin's 'A Practical Course for Guerrilla War'*, trans. Norman Cigar (Dulles, VA: Potomac Books, 2009), 103-105; Scheuer, *Osama bin Laden*, 70.
[166] Anas and Hussein, *To the Mountains*, 42; Al-Qarni, "Bin Laden's Former 'Mufti' Musa Al-Qarni Talks about the Jihad in Afghanistan,"; Smith, "Interview: Dr. Saad al-Fagih."
[167] Azzam, "Join the Caravan," 16-17.
[168] Anas and Hussein, *To the Mountains*, 150, 176-177; Tawil, *Brothers in Arms*, 18. A firmly committed al-Qaeda jihadi, Othman later received specialized military training in bin Laden's Afghan camps and quickly grew into the, "soldier of the family" during his youth in the late 1990s according to Nasser al Bahri, one of his trainers. See al-Bahri and Malbrunot, 150-152.
[169] Anas and Hussein, *To the Mountains*, 150, 176-177; Bin Laden, bin Laden, and Sasson, *Growing Up bin Laden*, 45.

CHAPTER 4

[1] Akram, *Khalid bin al-Waleed*, 417-418; Bergen, *The Osama bin Laden I Know*, 49-50; Gabriel, *Muhammad*, 100-102, 147-149; Hindley, *Saladin*, 134-135; Reston, Jr., *Warriors of God*, 88-90; Lings, *Muhammad*, 153-156, 240-241; Scheuer, *Osama bin Laden*, 30, 132.
[2] Coll, *The Bin Ladens*, 254-255.
[3] Azzam, "Sheikh Abdullah Azzam said about Usama Bin Ladin," 152-153; OBL, "Introduction," 84-85; Darraz, "Impressions," 92-93; Hamid and Farrall, *The Arabs at War in Afghanistan*, 70, 150-151; Scheuer, *Osama bin Laden*, 61. Just as Theodore Roosevelt resigned his post as Assistant Secretary of the Navy to recruit and organize his band of "Rough Riders" and lead them on the frontlines during the Spanish-American War of 1898, bin Laden displayed a similar zeal and militancy in matching his beliefs with actions in stark contrast to the numerous Saudi clerics inciting young recruits to join the fighting while avoiding it themselves, a key factor in winning him the admiration of his comrades and generating broader support for al-Qaeda's activities. For a fine work on the impact of Roosevelt's zeal on his battlefield exploits, see Edward J. Renehan, Jr., *The Lion's Pride: Theodore Roosevelt and His Family in Peace and War* (New York: Oxford University Press, 1999), 3-4, 22, 26-27, 30.
[4] Bergen, *The Osama bin Laden I Know*, 62; Scheuer, *Osama bin Laden*, 61; Anne Stenersen, *Al-Qaida in Afghanistan* (Cambridge: Cambridge University Press, 2017), 17.
[5] Scheuer, *Osama bin Laden*, 61-62; Tawil, *Brothers in Arms*, 18. Tawil points out here that Azzam had already established a training camp for Arab fighters, built by bin Laden, at the Pakistani town of Sada near the Afghan border in 1985, but only for the purpose of dispatching the volunteers in small numbers to the various Afghan insurgent groups, therefore severely limiting the non-Afghan fighters' opportunities for combat experience as they were viewed as a nuisance by the guerrilla commanders. Bin Laden concluded

that the only way to allow the bulk of the Arab fighters to participate in battle lay in forming a separate unit inside Afghanistan an obtaining practical experience in a large battle to apply in future training.

[6] Abd-al-Karim and al-Nur, "Interview with Saudi businessman Usama bin Ladin,"; Anas and Hussein, *To the Mountains*, 178; Bergen, *The Osama bin Laden I Know*, 44; Scheuer, *Osama bin Laden*, 61.

[7] Bergen, *The Osama bin Laden I Know*, 52-53; Coll, *The Bin Ladens*, 290-292; Isby, *War in a Distant Country*, 35-37; Scheuer, *Osama bin Laden*, 61-62.

[8] Bergen, *The Osama bin Laden I Know*, 52-53; Scheuer, *Osama bin Laden*, 210n59.

[9] Darraz, "Impressions," 102.

[10] Ibid.; Scheuer, *Osama bin Laden*, 61-62.

[11] Azzam, "Join the Caravan," 16-17; Bergen, *The Osama bin Laden I Know*, 51.

[12] Scheuer, *Osama bin Laden*, 61-62.

[13] Anas and Hussein, *To the Mountains*, 176-177; Al-Bahri and Malbrunot, *Guarding bin Laden*, 96.

[14] Darraz, "Impressions," 97; Scheuer, *Osama bin Laden*, 63; Tawil, *Brothers in Arms*, 18.

[15] Coll, *The Bin Ladens*, 291-292; Scheuer, *Osama bin Laden*, 61-62.

[16] Don D. Chipman, "Osama bin Laden and Guerrilla War," *Studies in Conflict & Terrorism*, Vol. 26, Issue 3 (2003) 163-170, https://www.tandfonline.com/doi/abs/10.1080/10576100390211400; Andrew Mitzcavitch, "Al Qaeda and Mao Zedong: Analogies of Protracted Warfare," *Counter Terrorist Trends and Analyses*, Vol. 6, No. 4 (May 2014), 14-18, https://www.jstor.org/stable/26351249?seq=1#metadata_info_tab_contents; Mao Zedong, *The Red Book of Guerrilla Warfare* (El Paso, TX: El Paso Norte Press, 2010), ed. Shawn Connors, trans. Samuel W. Griffith and Foreign Language Press, Peking, 52-53.

[17] Scheuer, *Osama bin Laden*, 61.

[18] Darraz, "Impressions," 102-103; Nida'ul Islam, "Mujahid Usamah Bin Ladin,"; Scheuer, *Osama bin Laden*, 61.

[19] Darraz, "Impressions," 95-96; Bergen, *The Osama bin Laden I Know*, 56; Scheuer, *Osama bin Laden*, 62-63.

[20] Nida'ul Islam, "Mujahid Usamah Bin Ladin,"; Darraz, "Impressions," 97.

[21] Scheuer, *Osama bin Laden*, 62-63.

[22] Nida'ul Islam, "Mujahid Usamah Bin Ladin,"; Darraz, "Impressions," 102-103.

[23] Anas and Hussein, *To the Mountains*, 178.

[24] Ibid., 180.

[25] Ibid., 178-179.

[26] Bergen, *The Osama bin Laden I Know*, 51-52; Scheuer, *Osama bin Laden*, 61-62.

[27] Bergen, *The Osama bin Laden I Know*, 51-52; Scheuer, *Osama bin Laden*, 61-62.

[28] Bergen, *The Osama bin Laden I Know*, 53; Girardet, *Killing the Cranes*, 253-254.

[29] Schultheis, *Hunting bin Laden*, 50-51.

[30] Darraz, "Impressions," 101.

[31] Ibid.

[32] Ibid.; Nida'ul Islam, "Mujahid Usamah Bin Ladin."

[33] Nida'ul Islam, "Mujahid Usamah Bin Ladin,"; MacLeod, "The Paladin of Jihad," 51-52; Timmerman, "This Man Wants You Dead," 52-53. Most authors, including Peter Bergen and Steve Coll, list 17 April as the starting date for the fighting, while bin Laden and several associates, using the corresponding date on the Islamic *Hijri* calendar, state clearly that they launched their operation during the evening of 16 April 1987 and even

named it in honor of that date, 17 Shaban. In addition to the Jaji engagements, it is also known that bin Laden's unit fought the Soviets in the Tora Bora region located in Afghan territory on the opposite side of Pakistan's "Parrot's Beak" region following the Jaji engagements, although detailed primary accounts of these engagements remain sparse. See OBL, "Introduction," 101-104, 112; Bergen, *Holy War Inc.*, 60; Jason Burke, "Revealed: Secret hideout of world's most feared terrorist," *The Guardian*, 4 July 1999, https://www.theguardian.com/world/1999/jul/04/osamabinladen.alqaida; Coll, *The Bin Ladens*, 302.

34 Bergen, *Holy War, Inc.*, 58-59; Darraz, "Impressions," 97, 102-103; Flagg Miller, *The Audacious Ascetic: What the bin Laden Tapes Reveal About al-Qa'ida* (London: Hurst & Company, 2015), 83; Scheuer, *Osama bin Laden*, 63-64; Wright, *The Looming Tower*, 115-116. Miller and Wright each state that a single Afghan sniper held off the inexperienced Arab force, yet this is not mentioned in the primary source, Darraz's interview with bin Laden and his veteran comrades from the engagement. While certainly possible, it seems unlikely, as the Arabs attacked in five separate groups with one group remaining lost until midnight due to the confusion sown by the heavy Soviet air and artillery strikes that forced the fighters to withdraw and return to the Lion's Den.

35 OBL, "Introduction," 114; Darraz, "Impressions," 106; Miller, *The Audacious Ascetic*, 83. Miller states that Operation *17 Ramadan* occurred on 22 May, but the date of 17 Ramadan 1407 on the Muslim calendar corresponds to 15 May 1987, meaning that the operation occurred on this day, while three weeks of the heaviest fighting at Jaji began a week later, on 22 May.

36 OBL, "Introduction," 114; MacLeod, "The Paladin of Jihad," 51-52; Timmerman, "This Man Wants You Dead," 55-57.

37 OBL, "Introduction," 114.

38 Darraz, "Impressions," 105-106; OBL, "Introduction," 114-115.

39 Bergen, *The Osama bin Laden I Know*, 54-55; Isby, *War in a Distant Country*, 40-42; Scheuer, *Osama bin Laden*, 64.

40 Darraz, "Impressions," 107-108. Robert Kaplan recalls that the mujahedin regarded hail as, "Allah's mine sweeper" due to the tendency of the crashing ice chunks to detonate the notorious and numerous Soviet, "butterfly mines" and the insurgents almost entirely lacking effective mine-clearing equipment. See Kaplan, *Soldiers of God*, 122.

41 OBL, "Introduction," 114-115; Isby, *War in a Distant Country*, 40-42.

42 Darraz, "Impressions," 108-109.

43 Bergen, *Holy War, Inc.*, 53-54, 59; Darraz., "Impressions," 108-109.

44 Bergen, *The Osama bin Laden I Know*, 54-55; Darraz, "Impressions," 109-110.

45 OBL, "Introduction," 114-115; Scheuer, *Through Our Enemies Eyes*, 110.

46 OBL, "Introduction," 114-115. Bin Laden's comrade Muhammad al-Azman, hailing from Saudi Arabia's Eastern Province, also went by the pseudonym Mukhtar.

47 Ibid.; Darraz, "Impressions," 105; Scheuer, *Through Our Enemies Eyes*, 110. Bin Laden told the Egyptian journalist and former military intelligence officer Isam Darraz, also an eyewitness of the Jaji engagements, that the Arabs had named the hill briefly occupied by the Soviets in honor a beloved Saudi compatriot and, "an excellent brother" from Taif, Ahmad al-Zahrani, the first Arab casualty of Operation *17 Shaban* on the evening of 16 April 1987. During that earlier engagement, a Soviet mortar round felled al-Zahrani as he fired a heavy machine gun at the Soviet troops from his position on the hill.

48 OBL, "Introduction, 115-116; Girardet, *Killing the Cranes*, 260-262.

49 OBL, "Introduction," 115-116.

[50] Darraz, "Impressions," 109-110.
[51] OBL, "Introduction," 116.
[52] Darraz, "Impressions," 110-111; Tawil, *Brothers in Arms*, 19-20; Stenersen, *Al-Qaida in Afghanistan*, 18-19.
[53] Darraz, "Impressions," 110-111, Fisk, "Anti-Soviet warrior puts his army on the road to peace,"; Scheuer, *Through Our Enemies Eyes*, 110.
[54] OBL, "Introduction," 116-117; Miller, "Greetings America. My Name is Osama bin Laden."
[55] OBL, "Introduction," 116-117; Darraz, "Impressions," 109-110; Miller, "Greetings America. My Name is Osama bin Laden."; Stenersen, *Al-Qaida in Afghanistan*, 18-19.
[56] Darraz, "Impressions," 119. Bin Laden's childhood friend Khaled al-Batarfi describes the al-Qaeda leader as being particularly inspired by performing the dawn prayer with his friends and comrades. See al-Batarfi, "Growing up with Osama,"; Randal, *Osama*, 60-61; and Scheuer, *Osama bin Laden*, 41.
[57] Bergen, *The Osama bin Laden I Know*, 54-55; OBL, "Introduction," 117; David C. Isby, "Four Battles in Afghanistan: Mujahideen Destroy Myth of Soviet Invincibility," *Soldier of Fortune* (April 1988), 32-34, https://archive.org/details/soldieroffortunemagazine/Soldier%20of%20Fortune%20%5B1988%2704%5D/page/n31/mode/2up; Stenersen, *Al-Qaida in Afghanistan*, 18-19.
[58] Azzam, "Sheikh Abdullah Azzam said about Usama Bin Ladin," 152; Fisk, "Anti-Soviet warrior puts his army on the road to peace," Scheuer, *Osama bin Laden*, 63-64.
[59] Scheuer, *Osama bin Laden*, 64; Stenersen, *Al-Qaida in Afghanistan*, 18-19; Washington Post Staff, "Afghan Rebel Gains Against Soviets Reported by U.S. Aide," *The Washington Post*, 6 July 1987, https://www.latimes.com/archives/la-xpm-1987-07-06-mn-1274-story.html.
[60] Azzam and al-Daylami recount the death of the latter's son, an inexperienced Yemeni recruit named Hisham bin Abd al-Wahhab al-Daylami, on 1 September 1987. Participating in bin Laden's operations against the Soviets, the zealous 19-year-old reportedly attempted to fire a rocket with no barrel, killing himself and two nearby Yemeni compatriots. The slain fighter's father and brothers received news of his battlefield death almost two weeks later, on 12 September 1987, in a phone call to the family's home in Sanaa. The two-week delay between al-Daylami's death and the phone call to his family in Sanaa indicates that the fighting had continued for a considerable period after the young recruit's death and had likely been going on for some time before the incident as he had been in the thick of a fierce battle. Moreover, the elder al-Daylami recalls hearing of the Lion's Den and the operation being executed under bin Laden's command, justifying the statements of Michael Scheuer and Isam Darraz that by the end of the Jaji engagements the Saudi zealot had grown considerably in prominence and leadership. See Darraz, "Impressions," 113; Johnsen, *The Last Refuge*, 4-6; Scheuer, *Osama bin Laden*, 64.
[61] Al-Bahri and Malbrunot, *Guarding bin Laden*, 74; Bergen, *The Osama bin Laden I Know*, 59; Miller, "Greetings America. My Name is Osama bin Laden,"; Scheuer, *Osama bin Laden*, 63-64.
[62] Stenersen, *Al-Qaida in Afghanistan*, 18-19; Tawil, *Brothers in Arms*, 19-20.
[63] Azzam, "Sheikh Abdullah Azzam said about Usama Bin Ladin," 152-153; Nida'ul Islam, "Mujahid Usamah Bin Ladin,"; Bergen, *Holy War, Inc.*, 18; Tawil, *Brothers in Arms*, 19-20.
[64] Sikorski, *Dust of the Saints*, 152; Yousaf and Adkin, *Afghanistan*, 92, 135.

[65] Alouni, "Transcript of Bin Laden's October interview,"; Atwan, "My weekend with Osama bin Laden,"; Nida'ul Islam, "Mujahid Usamah Bin Ladin,"; MacLeod, "The Paladin of Jihad," 51-52; Miller, "Greetings America. My Name is Osama bin Laden."

[66] Alouni, "Transcript of Bin Laden's October interview,"; Al-Bahri and Malbrunot, *Guarding bin Laden*, 22-23, 50, 53; Campbell, "Yemen,"; Hamid and Farrall, *The Arabs at War in Afghanistan*, 200-202; Johnsen, *The Last Refuge*, 30-31; Scheuer, *Osama bin Laden*, 80.

[67] Alouni, "Transcript of Bin Laden's October interview,"; Miller, "Greetings America. My Name is Osama bin Laden."; Nida'ul Islam, "Mujahid Usamah Bin Ladin,"; Weiner, "U.S. Hard Put to Find Proof."

[68] Fisk, "Anti-Soviet Warrior puts his army on the road to peace." Bin Laden's remarkable ability to remain silent for extended periods of time, whether during personal confrontations or international crises, served as one of his most spectacular skills and greatest rhetorical weapons, causing his opponents to give up the chase or lower their guard by assuming that he had already died or somehow no longer posed a threat, as his Soviet pursuers appear to have erroneously done in this instance. This characteristic, documented by several of bin Laden's closest associates, seems to fully justify Michael Scheuer's conclusion that, "Osama has always held his cards close to the vest, and would later demonstrate an almost preternatural ability to use the power of silence to avoid creating new enemies while driving his existing foes – especially non-stop-talking Westerners – to distraction, as well as encouraging them to draw absurd conclusions." See Al-Bahri and Malbrunot, *Guarding bin Laden*, 72; Al-Batarfi, "Growing up with Osama,"; Bergen, *The Osama bin Laden I Know*, 12-15; Bin Laden, bin Laden, and Sasson, *Growing Up bin Laden*, 10; and Scheuer, *Osama bin Laden*, 46, 133-135.

[69] Bergen, *The Osama bin Laden I Know*, 54-55; MacLeod, "The Paladin of Jihad," 51-52; Scheuer, *Osama bin Laden*, 64; Timmerman, "This Man Wants You Dead," 54.

[70] Bodansky, *Bin Laden*, 19-20. Bodansky's work is a courageous and splendid early biography of bin Laden. He appears to err, however, in referring to Shaban as an actual location inside of Afghanistan, apparently confusing the Muslim month with a physical location from which bin Laden mounted operations against the Soviets. This confusion is easily explained after a careful check of the primary sources relating to the Battle of Jaji, bin Laden's "Introduction" and Darraz's "Impressions."

[71] Bergen, *The Osama bin Laden I Know*, 13, 55.

[72] Bergen, *The Osama bin Laden I Know*, 13, 55.

[73] Al-Qarni, "Bin Laden's Former 'Mufti' Musa Al-Qarni Talks about the Jihad in Afghanistan."

[74] Ibid.

[75] Coll, *The Bin Ladens*, 302.

[76] Scheuer, *Osama bin Laden*, 64-65.

[77] Ibid.

[78] Alouni, "Transcript of Bin Laden's October interview,"; Bergen, *Holy War., Inc.*, 60; OBL, "Introduction," 85-86, 117; Bodansky, *Bin Laden*, 19-20; Scheuer, *Osama bin Laden*, 64. Bin Laden's statement refers not only to his unit's successful defiance of the Soviets at Jaji but to the larger series of offensive operations launched by the Soviets on 20 May 1987 involving about 10,000 Soviet troops against the Afghan Islamist insurgent strongholds in the Jaji region at the time. While only a small part of an overall larger battle, the dogged resistance of the small Arab band at the Lion's Den served as a major morale boost for the

Arab and Afghan fighters alike, propelling bin Laden to leadership and demonstrating that the Arab fighters, if properly led and disciplined, could successfully channel their religious zeal into acquiring battle experience and emerge as well-trained and effective guerrilla fighters. By successfully holding their ground against the Soviets that attacked the Lion's Den, the Arabs played a key role by remaining in control of the base and bin Laden's string of guerrilla fortifications in the mountains immediately surrounding it. Returning from the war zone after the intense fighting at Jaji, U.S. defense expert David Isby reported in an article for *Soldier of Fortune* Magazine that the Jaji engagements may have been, "The most important battle of 1987 – perhaps of the entire war," while a *Washington Post* article described the Soviets as losing 120 *Spetsnaz* commandos killed in the late May engagements with between 250 and 300 more killed in the fighting during the first two weeks of June 1987 and 15 Soviet aircraft shot down by the rebels in the region during the same period. As Anne Stenersen points out, the Arabs at the Lion's Den did not have Stinger missiles at the time and did not acquire them until after the Soviet defeat as the Afghan insurgent commanders refused to trade or sell the precious few Stingers that they owned, yet they still managed to repulse the Soviet attacks on their base, reinforcing bin Laden's conviction that God had guided His holy warriors to victory over a materially stronger foe. See also Isby, "Four Battles in Afghanistan," 32-34; Stenersen, *Al-Qaida in Afghanistan*, 18-19; and Washington Post Staff, "Afghan Rebel Gains Against Soviets Reported by U.S. Aide."

[79] OBL, "Introduction," 85-86; Scheuer, *Osama bin Laden*, 64; Yusufzai, "Face to face with Osama."

[80] Scheuer, *Osama bin Laden*, 64.

[81] OBL, *Messages to the World*, 76; MacLeod, "The Paladin of Jihad," 51-52; Scheuer, *Osama bin Laden*, 48-49, 212. Bin Laden described his Afghan battle experience, and the guerrilla training camps as a, "university" and the graduates of the camps and battles against the Soviets as, "students" in a May 1996 interview with Scott MacLeod of *TIME* Magazine. There is perhaps no better description of bin Laden's arduous wartime education, as the fighting experience that he and his lieutenants obtained in battles against their unwitting Soviet teachers enabled them to teach the skills that they acquired to thousands of new recruits, many of whom subsequently trained others to maintain the momentum generated by Moscow's invasion and channel their combat experience to support their struggling brethren fighting Islamist insurgencies throughout the world.

[82] Bergen, *The Osama bin Laden I Know*, 81; Hamid and Farrall, *The Arabs at War in Afghanistan*, 200-202.

[83] Scheuer, *Osama bin Laden*, 73-74.

[84] Burke, "Revealed: Secret hideout of world's most feared terrorist."

[85] Ibid.; Al-Qarni, "Bin Laden's Former 'Mufti' Musa Al-Qarni Talks about the Jihad in Afghanistan."

[86] Scheuer, *Osama bin Laden*, 64.

[87] Margolis, *War at the Top of the World*, 84-85.

[88] Ibid.

[89] Bin Laden, bin Laden, Sasson, *Growing Up bin Laden*, 40-41.

[90] Ibid., 56.

[91] Bergen, *The Osama bin Laden I Know*, 26; Bin Laden, bin Laden, and Sasson, *Growing Up bin Laden*, 64, 74-76. Bin Laden maintained a home in Peshawar between 1984 and 1989, but his family only stayed there for three months during the summers because his

older sons were enrolled in school in the holy city of Medina by the middle and late 1980s. These desert hikes took place during bin Laden's brief visits to his home in Saudi Arabia during the period.

[92] Bergen, *The Osama bin Laden I Know*, 49-50; Scheuer, *Osama bin Laden*, 48-49, 212; Tawil, *Brothers in Arms*, 20.

[93] Tawil, *Brothers in Arms*, 20.

[94] Azzam, "Sheikh Abdullah Azzam said about Usama Bin Ladin," 152-153; Darraz, "Impressions," 126-128.

[95] Abd-al-Karim and al-Nur, "Interview with Saudi businessman Usama bin Ladin,"; Alouni, "Transcript of Bin Laden's October interview,"; Fisk, "Anti-Soviet Warrior puts his army on the road to peace,"; Scheuer, *Osama bin Laden*, 74-75; Yusufzai, "Face to face with Osama."

[96] Alouni, "Transcript of Bin Laden's October interview,"; Atwan, "My weekend with Osama bin Laden,"; Osama bin Laden, *Osama bin Laden: America's Enemy in His Own Words*, ed. and trans. Randall B. Hamud (San Diego: Nadeem Publishing, 2005), 72; OBL, *Messages to the World*, 147; Miller, "Greetings America. My Name is Osama bin Laden."

[97] Arnett, "Transcript of Osama Bin Ladin interview,"; Osama bin Laden, "Fight the allies of the devil," *The Guardian*, 12 February 2003, https://www.theguardian.com/world/2003/feb/12/alqaida.terrorism2 ; Osama bin Laden, "Exposing the New Crusader War – Bin Laden – Statement -February 2003," *Terrorisme.net* (11 February 2003), https://www.terrorisme.net/pdf/newcrusaderwar.pdf; Miller, "Greetings America. My Name is Osama bin Laden."; Fisk, "10 July 1996: Arab rebel leader warns the British,"; Scheuer, *Osama bin Laden*, 76-77, 208n43.; Yusufzai, "Osama bin Laden: Conversation with Terror."

[98] Bin Laden, bin Laden, and Sasson, *Growing Up bin Laden*, 43.

[99] Ibid.

[100] Al-Bahri and Malbrunot, *Guarding bin Laden*, 16.

[101] It is important to note here that due to disagreements with his father, a Bin Laden Company employee but a strong supporter of secular Arab causes, al-Bahri failed in his quest until 1994. Pointing to the notable absence of Salafist clerics on the Afghan battlefields with the young men that they incited to holy war, al-Bahri's father temporarily prevented his son from beginning his jihadi journey. Despite this, however, al-Bahri admits to participating clandestinely in the Islamic Awakening movement at the time, inspired by the seminars hosted and paid for by Azzam, bin Laden, and the latter's two anti-Soviet colleagues, the Saudi cleric Shaykh Musa al-Qarni and the Yemeni cleric Shaykh Abd al-Majid al-Zindani. The substantive importance here is al-Bahri's determination to act on his beliefs, inspired by the accounts of his Saudi and Yemeni compatriots at the front, and his eventual success in defying his father in a culture that discourages sons from doing so. See al-Bahri and Malbrunot, *Guarding bin Laden*, 16-17.

[102] Zaeef, *My Life with the Taliban*, 47-49.

[103] Ibid.

[104] Anas and Hussein, *To the Mountains*, 103-104.

[105] Ibid. 105.

[106] Bin Laden, bin Laden, and Sasson, *Growing Up bin Laden*, 91; Jones, *In the Graveyard of Empires*, 35-37; Zaeef, *My Life with the Taliban*, 47.

[107] Gutman, *How We Missed the Story*, 7.

[108] Ibid.; Sikorski, *Dust of the Saints*, 264-265.

[109] Edward Girardet, "Afghan Rebels Take Hold. KUNAR: A HINT OF THE FUTURE?" *The Christian Science Monitor*, 14 February 1989, https://www.csmonitor.com/1989/0214/okun.html.

[110] Girardet, *Killing the Cranes*, 255-257.

[111] Ibid. To be sure, in the Salafist interpretation of *Shariah*, killing and plundering the wealth and property of fellow Sunni Muslims actively serving infidel occupiers or apostate regimes is religiously permissible as such an act of treason against God's *ummah*, the global Muslim nation, nullifies a believer's profession of faith, thereby removing the protection that it normally affords. During the jihad against the Soviets, Sunni Islamist *ulema* throughout the world, including the clergy of Pakistan, Saudi Arabia, and North Yemen, ruled the killing of the Afghan troops fighting for the Soviet occupiers to be a religiously permissible act, as their perceived actions against Muslims nullified their profession of faith. Adhering strictly to these religious rulings, bin Laden did not forbid al-Qaeda members from killing their fellow Sunni Muslims working in the service of Islam's perceived foes while in battle, but rather advised al-Qaeda commanders and guerrillas fighting the U.S.-backed regimes in Iraq, Afghanistan, and elsewhere to do so with bullets rather than decapitation to avoid abhorring and alienating Muslim civilian populations by behaving like intolerant and highly unpopular takfiris. Bin Laden also pointed out that while he and al-Qaeda sought to avoid and minimize Muslim civilian casualties, enemy soldiers had to be killed in battle, even those claiming to be Muslims but fighting for the perceived apostate regimes, as not taking such practical measures prevented the mujahedin from fighting in God's path and liberating His people from their oppressors. In this regard, the al-Qaeda chief's thinking reflects the practical outlook and tactical approach of any effective guerrilla commander determined to defeat a more powerful occupation force and accepting the possibility of both civilian casualties and the killing of one's own coreligionists on the opposing side as unfortunate but necessary to achieving victory. For example, after executing a rocket attack on the Soviet embassy in Kabul on 13 September 1984, Afghan Commander Abdul Haq reportedly told UK Defense Correspondent Mark Urban that, "Their target is not the civilians. But if I hit them I don't care… If my family lived near the Soviet embassy I would hit it. I wouldn't care about them. If I'm prepared to die, my son has to die for it and my wife has to die for it." Bin Laden later expressed disgust at the perceived hypocrisy of the official Saudi scholars for ruling against Yemen's anti-communist mujahedin by arguing that the Yemeni communists were Muslims and should not be killed, despite their record of suppressing Islam in Yemen. In a 1994 letter addressed to Saudi Grand *Mufti* Shaykh Abdul bin Baz, reportedly a former supporter of inciting young Saudis to fight the Soviets in Afghanistan, bin Laden wrote, "These apostate rulers who wage war on God and his Messenger have neither legitimacy, nor sovereignty over Muslims," and "When were the communists ever Muslims? Aren't you the one who previously issued a *fatwa* (juridical decree) on their apostasy and the necessity of killing them in Afghanistan? Or is there a difference between Yemeni communists and Afghan communists?" See, OBL, "Open Letter for Sheikh Bin Baz," ARC, 29 December 1994; OBL, *Messages to the World*, 8; Al-Jazeera, "Bin Laden urges end to Gaza closure," *Al-Jazeera*, 19 May 2008, https://www.aljazeera.com/news/2008/5/19/bin-laden-urges-end-to-gaza-closure; Lawson, "Osama's Prodigal Son,"; Haroon Siddique, "Bin Laden urges uprising against Musharraf," *The Guardian*, 20 September 2007, https://www.theguardian.com/world/

2007/sep/20/alqaida.pakistan; Scheuer, *Osama bin Laden*, 144, 245n34; and for Haq's comment, see Urban, *War in Afghanistan*, 152-153.

[112] OBL, "Introduction," 86; Scheuer, *Osama bin Laden*, 65-66.

[113] OBL, "Introduction," 80, 81-82. Bin Laden later explained the meaning of the Soviet-Afghan War to him, writing, "The Soviet Prime Minister at the time of the Afghan invasion was Brezhnev, who decided to play his leading card by invading Afghanistan… Hence, Brezhnev gave the command and Soviet forces invaded Afghanistan; a fateful move, which would prove to have a disastrous effect on the Soviet empire… The Afghans were able to repel the largest invasion in recent times, by the forces of disbelief against Islam. We ask Allah to reward them with the best of rewards."

[114] Anas and Hussein, *To the Mountains*, 103; Jones, *In the Graveyard of Empires*, 35-37; *Wilson Center Digital Archive, Collection 76*, "CPSU CC Memo, excerpt from Protocol # 163/44, 22 July 1989," 22 July 1989; Zaeef, *My Life with the Taliban*, 48-49; *The Bukovsky Archives*, "Measures linked to the forthcoming withdrawal of Soviet troops from Afghanistan," 24 January 1989.

[115] Jalali, *A Military History of Afghanistan*, 429; Yousaf and Adkin, *Afghanistan*, 227-228.

[116] Coll, *The Bin Ladens*, 7-8; Kaplan, *Soldiers of God*, 166-167; Yousaf and Adkin, *Afghanistan*, 220.

[117] Jalali, *A Military History of Afghanistan*, 431.

[118] Ibid.

[119] Coll, *The Bin Ladens*, 342-343; Yousaf and Adkin, *Afghanistan*, 230.

[120] Bergen, *The Osama bin Laden I Know*, 53; Coll, *Ghost Wars*, 193-195; Scheuer, *Osama bin Laden*, 65, 69.

[121] Coll, *Ghost Wars*, 193-195; Jalali, *A Military History of Afghanistan*, 430; Scheuer, *Osama bin Laden*, 65.

[122] Bergen, *Holy War, Inc.*, 126; Margolis, *War at the Top of the World*, 84, 95; Yousaf and Adkin, *Afghanistan*, 230. Enduring and learning to evade such sustained bombardment by Soviet Scud missiles and other heavy artillery through guerrilla dispersion tactics like those that they employed to minimize casualties from the Mi-24 gunships psychologically trained bin Laden and his lieutenants such as Hamza al-Ghamdi to endure the 1998 U.S. Cruise missile strikes and the 12 days of bombardment that they endured before escaping to Pakistan at the Battle of Tora Bora in December 2001. See al-Bahri and Malbrunot, *Guarding bin Laden*, 182; Hamid and Farrall, *The Arabs at War in Afghanistan*, 240-241; Scheuer, *Osama bin Laden*, 118, 120; and the excellent firsthand account by former CIA officer Gary Berntsen and journalist Ralph Pezzullo, *Jawbreaker: The Attack on bin Laden and al-Qaeda: A Personal Account by the CIA's Key Field Commander* (New York: Crown Publishers, 2006), 261-262, 275-276.

[123] Bergen, *The Osama bin Laden I Know*, 87-88; Scheuer, *Osama bin Laden*, 66.

[124] Kaplan, *Soldiers of God*, 139, 222; Yousaf and Adkin, *Afghanistan*, 230.

[125] Scheuer, *Through Our Enemies' Eyes*, 112-113.

[126] Adaki, "Yemeni tribal leader joins AQAP,"; Ahmed and Akins, "Making enemies in Yemen,"; Root, "A Sheikh's Life,"; Worth, "Ex-Jihadist Defies Yemen's Leader,"; Scheuer, *Osama bin Laden*, 80.

[127] Bergen, *The Osama bin Laden I Know*, 88-89.

[128] Bergen, *Holy War, Inc.*, 60; Coll, *The Bin Ladens*, 303-304; Scheuer, *Osama bin Laden*, 66-67.

[129] Scheuer, *Osama bin Laden*, 66-67.

[130] Ibid.
[131] Al-Bahri and Malbrunot, *Guarding bin Laden*, 94-95; Bergen, *The Osama bin Laden I Know*, 88-89; Scheuer, *Osama bin Laden*, 66-67.
[132] Al-Bahri and Malbrunot, *Guarding bin Laden*, 110-113.
[133] Ibid., 34-37.
[134] Ibid.,76-77, 107-108; Bergen, *Holy War, Inc.*, 18; Tawil, *Brothers in Arms*, 19. The significant presence of Israeli Uzis in al-Qaeda's arsenal in the Afghan training camps again reflects bin Laden's practical approach to life, weapons, and warfare, especially as compared to many of his and al-Qaeda's foes in the secular Arab regimes and rival organizations, by not disregarding an effective weapon, like an effective fighter, based on national origin or place of manufacture. In his memoir, Pakistani ISI Brigadier Mohammad Yousaf states that, "I had no idea that Israel was a source [of captured Soviet weaponry purchased by the CIA to supply the Afghans] until quite recently, as, had it been known, there would have been considerable trouble with the Arab nations [the Egyptian and Saudi regimes]. It would not have been acceptable to wage a Jehad with weapons bought from Israel." Bin Laden again demonstrated his pragmatic approach, a trait that rendered him an effective leader and vicious opponent, in stark contrast to the secular Arab regimes, takfiri groups, and al-Zawahiri's EIJ comrades, in his choice of weaponry for al-Qaeda's guerrilla training camps, viewing any weapon as useful, whether Israeli, American, British, or Soviet, if wielded in battle by a properly trained and committed al-Qaeda jihadi. Al-Bahri adds that bin Laden applied this same practical logic to tactics and strategy, recalling that, "He had also read Viet-Cong leader Ho Chi Minh's speeches against the Americans and several books about the guerrilla tactics employed by the Zionist terror group, the Irgun gang, until the establishment of the state of Israel in 1948." Bin Laden, in short, appears to have consistently rejected the irrational outlook of a true fanatic like al-Zarqawi and always sought to improve his and al-Qaeda's leadership and combat skills, displaying an interest in acquiring knowledge or ordnance from any valuable source, Muslim, Western, or otherwise, and applying such lessons and weaponry to practical training to strengthen al-Qaeda and its supporting role for Islamist insurgencies worldwide. For Yousaf's comment, see Yousaf and Adkin, *Afghanistan*, 83-84.
[135] Al-Bahri and Malbrunot, *Guarding bin Laden*, 108-110.
[136] Ibid.
[137] Ibid., 106, 108-110, 111; Bergen, *Holy War, Inc.*, 103. Al-Bahri reports that the Taleban also used the Soviet cluster bombs, occasionally deploying them in their war against Massoud's forces in northern Afghanistan.
[138] Al-Bahri and Malbrunot, *Guarding bin Laden*, 106, 108-110; Bergen, *Holy War, Inc.*, 103. Indeed, the Saudi authorities arrested a large number of militants planning to use them in an attack in the holy city of Mecca, but foreign planes, that is, infidel planes, are not permitted to fly over the holy city, so only Saudis and Muslims could have been targeted. Al-Bahri recalls that after hearing of the plotters being captured, bin Laden expressed horror that the men apparently intended to use the weapons against fellow Muslims and Saudis in Islam's holiest city and knelt to pray and thank God that the unsanctioned operation had been foiled.
[139] Nasiri, *Inside the Jihad*, xi, 206-207.
[140] Ibid., 209-210.

[141] Fisk, "Anti-Soviet Warrior puts his army on the road to peace,"; Miller, "Greetings America. My Name is Osama bin Laden." Nida'ul Islam, "Mujahid Usamah Bin Ladin."

CHAPTER 5

[1] Coll, *Ghost Wars*, 221-222; Scheuer, *Osama bin Laden*, 80.
[2] OBL, "Introduction," 77, 80-81; Bin Laden, bin Laden, and Sasson, *Growing Up bin Laden*, 96-98; Scheuer, *Osama bin Laden*, 105-106.
[3] Abd-al-Karim and al-Nur, "Interview with Saudi businessman Usama bin Ladin."
[4] Bergen, *The Osama bin Laden I Know*, 29; Scheuer, *Osama bin Laden*, 54. The Afghan warriors eventually succeeded in overthrowing Najibullah's communist regime in 1992 even while fighting each other, yet the continued infighting between rival Islamist factions raged on until the Taleban successfully conquered most of the country in the late 1990s. Bin Laden remained uninvolved in the civil war that raged throughout the decade, but continued financing the al-Qaeda training camps in the country, leaving his trusted comrades and veterans of the fighting against the Soviets to manage the training of new recruits until his return to Afghanistan and subsequent alliance with Taleban leader Mullah Omar in 1996.
[5] OBL, *Messages to the World*, 8.
[6] Clark, *Yemen*, 232-234; Mackintosh-Smith, *Yemen*, 164-165; The New York Times, "SAUDIS SAY U.A.R. BOMBED VILLAGES."
[7] Clark, *Yemen*, 232-234; Howe, "Southern Yemen Blends Marxism,"; Hurd and Noakes, "North and South Yemen," 48; Mackintosh-Smith, *Yemen*, 164-165; Randal, "Threat to N. Yemen,"; Schmidt, "British in Aden Depart as Egyptians Leave Yemen,"; Walker, *Aden Insurgency*, 296-298.
[8] OBL, "Introduction," 78-79; Grier, "Soviets bolster an Arab ally,"; Howe, "Southern Yemen Blends Marxism,"; Kifner, "SOVIET SAID TO TRY,"; *Parl. Rec. – House of Commons*, 1st Sess. (1979); Randal, "Threat to N. Yemen,"; Van der Bijl, *British Military Operations*, 206.
[9] Johnsen, *The Last Refuge*, 8-10.
[10] Bergen, *Holy War, Inc.*, 176-177; Coll, *The Bin Ladens*, 373-374.
[11] Ibn Khaldun, *The Muqaddimah*, vii-viii; Al-Kindi, *The Medical Formulary or Aqrabadhin*, 4-5. In addition to Yemen, the three southwestern provinces of Saudi Arabia, Najran, Jazan, and Asir, and the far western Dhofar region of Oman are traditionally considered to be part of the historical South Arabia region of the Arabian Peninsula, also known as Greater Yemen, as these regions have also historically been populated by indigenous *Qahtanis* with close tribal links to their ancestral land. See Glossary for further details as well as Yaroslav Trofimov's fine book *The Siege of Mecca: The 1979 Uprising at Islam's Holiest Shrine*, 48-49.
[12] Bergen, *Holy War, Inc.*, 176-177; OBL, *Messages to the World*, 8.
[13] Al-Bahri and Malbrunot, *Guarding bin Laden*, 201-202; Scheuer, *Osama bin Laden*, 37-38.
[14] Hourani, *A History of the Arab Peoples*, 17; Lings, *Muhammad*, 111-112.
[15] Johnsen, *The Last Refuge*, 20-21; Kifner, "SOVIET SAID TO TRY,"; *Wilson Center Digital Archive, Collection 76*, "Notes from Politburo Meeting, 21-22 May 1987 (Excerpt)," 22 May 1987.

[16] Clark, *Yemen*,126-128; Kifner, "SOVIET SAID TO TRY,"; Van der Bijl, *British Military Operations*, 206.

[17] Clark, *Yemen*, 130-131; Johnsen, *The Last Refuge*, 20-21.

[18] Al-Bahri and Malbrunot, *Guarding bin Laden*, 22-23.

[19] Ibid.; Scheuer, *Osama bin Laden*, 80.

[20] Al-Bahri and Malbrunot, *Guarding bin Laden*, 22-23; Coll, *The Bin Ladens*, 373-374. Al-Bahri explains that while Obadah al-Wadihi had fought fiercely alongside bin Laden against the Soviets, his brother Mukbel, the founder of a Salafist *madrassa* in Sadaa, displayed much less enthusiasm for liberating their Yemeni compatriots from the clutches of communism, preferring to oppose the local Shia Muslim minority instead, and lied to the al-Qaeda chief about wanting to establish a guerrilla training camp, pocketing his share of the allotted funds while the others recruited and trained fighters at the camps. Bin Laden also initially expressed uncertainty about opening a guerrilla war in his ancestral homeland, no doubt fearing a loss of Yemeni civilian lives, a concern that he is said to have brought up repeatedly as the leader of al-Qaeda. Once the Yemeni jihadis expressed their deep desire to turn their Afghan war experience against South Yemen's communists however, the al-Qaeda chief reportedly wasted no time and spared no effort in supporting their holy war to banish Marxism from its sole outpost on Islam's holiest land, the Arabian Peninsula.

[21] OBL, "The Banishment of Communism from the Arabian Peninsula," ARC, 11 July 1994; Johnsen, *The Last Refuge*, 24-25; Samuel Ramani, "North Korea's Balancing Act in the Persian Gulf," *HuffPost*, 17 August 2015, https://www.huffpost.com/entry/north-koreas-balancing-ac_b_7995688; Jamal S. Al-Suwaidi, Michael Hudson, Paul Dresch, Charles Dunbar, Robert Burrowes, and Mark Katz, *The Yemeni War of 1994: Causes and Consequences* (London: Saqi Books, 1996), 87-88.

[22] Al-Bahri and Malbrunot, *Guarding bin Laden*, 22-23; Johnsen, *The Last Refuge*, 33-34; Scheuer, *Osama bin Laden*, 80.

[23] Al-Bahri and Malbrunot, *Guarding bin Laden*, 22-23; Atwan, "My weekend with Osama bin Laden,"; Scheuer, *Through Our Enemies Eyes*, 122.

[24] Abd-al-Karim and al-Nur, "Interview with Saudi businessman Usama bin Ladin,"; OBL, ARC, 19 September 1994.

[25] Bin Laden, bin Laden, and Sasson, *Growing Up bin Laden*, 102-103; Coll, *The Bin Ladens*, 372-373.

[26] Bin Laden, bin Laden, and Sasson, *Growing Up bin Laden*, 113; Scheuer, *Osama bin Laden*, 87-88.

[27] OBL, "Saudi Arabia supports the communists in Yemen," ARC, 7 June 1994; OBL, "Open Letter for Sheikh Bin Baz," ARC, 29 December 1994; and Scheuer, *Osama bin Laden*, 97, 221n89. Bin Laden claimed that by supporting the Yemeni Socialist Party's leaders despite the fact that the communists reportedly, "had enslaved" and, "killed" the people of Yemen and many devout members of the country's Sunni Muslim clergy, the al-Sauds had willingly placed themselves in the same trenches as God's enemies, while also emphasizing Saudi King Fahd's earlier financial support, "to the Soviet Union prior to its collapse at the hands of the mujahidin."

[28] Atwan, "My weekend with Osama bin Laden,"; Coll, *The Bin Ladens*, 373-374; Scheuer, *Osama bin Laden*, 80, 87-88.

²⁹ Abd-al-Karim and al-Nur, "Interview with Saudi businessman Usama bin Ladin,"; Atwan, "My weekend with Osama bin Laden,"; OBL, "Our invitation to Give Advice and Reform," ARC, 12 April 1994; Scheuer, *Osama bin Laden*, 93-94.

³⁰ Bin Laden, bin Laden, and Sasson, *Growing Up bin Laden*, 154-155; Hamid and Farrall, *The Arabs at War in Afghanistan*, 145-146; Johnsen, *The Last Refuge*, 35-38; Scheuer, *Osama bin Laden*, 88.

³¹ Bin Laden became the target of assassination attempts by takfiri groups and Arab regimes on at least two other occasions following his return to Afghanistan in May 1996. Michael Scheuer points out that bin Laden broke off relations with Algeria's Armed Islamic Group (GIA) in late 1995 after its representative in Khartoum, Redouane Makudor, threatened to slit his throat in the event that al-Qaeda acted independently of GIA in Algeria. Scheuer also points out that in October 1998 the Taleban arrested a Saudi from a Tajik immigrant family in the Kingdom hired by GID to kill bin Laden, while in March 1999 the same takfiri group that had targeted the al-Qaeda chief in Sudan again tried to take his life after accusing bin Laden of being an, "infidel" and CIA agent, receiving a series of resounding repulses after engaging in fierce firefights with al-Qaeda fighters in Afghanistan. Nasser al-Bahri states that on another occasion in the summer of 2000, three Afghan attackers, allegedly hired by the U.S. Army and acting under the pretense of performing humanitarian work with the United Nations' Afghan mission, attempted to overtake bin Laden, organizing into a triangular formation around the al-Qaeda leader's small convoy as he enjoyed a rare drive in his car the day after marrying his young Yemeni bride, Amal al-Sada. Bin Laden radioed his small number of bodyguards, including al-Bahri and Saif al-Adel, allowing them to block the three assailants, knocking one off his motorbike and capturing the other two before turning all the captives over to the Taleban. Another possible attempt by takfiris to assassinate the al-Qaeda leader is the late 1998 visit to bin Laden's compound by a Sudanese extremist named Abu Ashatha. A fellow veteran of the anti-Soviet jihad, Ashatha arrived one day for an impromptu visit with bin Laden, and the al-Qaeda chief sat separately from his bodyguards and courteously listened to the fanatic's ravings and complaints against al-Bahri's better wishes. Bin Laden reportedly remained calm, true to his character even under Soviet fire, while maintaining a steady grip on his AKS-74U submachine gun, preparing for self-defense as Ashatha's agitation and railings grew in intensity. After the arm-flailing extremist appeared poised to seize bin Laden by his chest-length beard, al-Bahri intervened, almost killing Ashatha with a well-placed knee strike to the fanatic's solar plexis. Bin Laden urged al-Bahri to desist, forgiving his failed assassin on the spot, and handing him, "a bundle of dollars" for his trouble. Bin Laden appears to have committed few major errors over the course of his jihadi journey, but those that he did commit almost proved to be fatal to him and al-Qaeda. Yet every risky undertaking that bin Laden successfully engaged in, from his refusal to stop working even under lethal Soviet fire, to the hard-won victory over the Soviets at Jaji in 1987, to his survival of takfiri assassination attempts and U.S. Cruise missile strikes in the 1990s and his successful evasion of the U.S. and NATO forces for a decade after 9/11 enhanced his perception across the Sunni Muslim world as a genuine holy warrior fighting in God's path against His enemies, boosting al-Qaeda's fortunes and damaging U.S. and Western security interests in ways that may have proved to be impossible had he not taken such risks. See Atwan, "My weekend with Osama bin Laden,"; al-Bahri and Malbrunot, *Guarding bin Laden*, 10-11, 130-131, 210-211; OBL, "Our invitation to Give Advice and Reform," ARC,

12 April 1994; Lawson, "Osama's Prodigal Son,"; and Scheuer, *Osama bin Laden*, 87-88, 108-110, 132-133; 166, 218-219n41, 226n18-25.

32 OBL, "Saudi Arabia supports the communists in Yemen," ARC, 7 June 1994; Johnsen, *The Last Refuge*, 35-38. Previously implicated in al-Qaeda's first attack on U.S. Marines at two hotels in Aden, Yemen in December 1992 and imprisoned by al-Bid's socialists in a notorious prison known for its use by the Marxists as a torture chamber for jihadis, al-Hadhi had escaped with several compatriots and joined bin Laden in Khartoum, serving as one of his top bodyguards at the time.

33 Abd-al-Karim and al-Nur, "Interview with Saudi businessman Usama bin Ladin,"; OBL, "The Banishment of Communism from the Arabian Peninsula," ARC, 11 July 1994; Scheuer, *Through Our Enemies Eyes*, 122.

34 Root, "A Sheikh's Life,"; Worth, "Ex-Jihadist Defies Yemen's Leader."

35 Bergen, *Holy War, Inc.*, 177-178; Johnsen, *The Last Refuge*, 30-31.

36 Campbell, "Yemen,"; Hurd and Noakes, "North and South Yemen," 48; Johnsen, *The Last Refuge*, 32; Scheuer, *Through Our Enemies Eyes*, 122.

37 Nora Boustany, "Civil War in Yemen Heightens Worries of Wider Instability," *The Washington Post*, 18 June 1994, https://www.washingtonpost.com/archive/politics/1994/06/18/civil-war-in-yemen-heightens-worries-of-wider-instability/94dcbfa8-7655-4659-b8f5-d989c1ee7571/; Johnsen, *The Last Refuge*, 38-39; Al-Suwaidi et al., *The Yemeni War of 1994*, 83; The Associated Press, "Yemen Claims Victory in Civil War After Seizing Rebel City," *The New York Times*, 8 July 1994, https://www.nytimes.com/1994/07/08/world/yemen-claims-victory-in-civil-war-after-seizing-rebel-city.html.

38 Boustany, "Civil War in Yemen,"; Clark, *Yemen*, 133-134; Hurd and Noakes, "North and South Yemen," 48; Johnsen, *The Last Refuge*, 38-39; Al-Suwaidi et al., *The Yemeni War of 1994*, 81; The Associated Press, "Yemen Claims Victory."

39 Bergen, *Holy War, Inc.*, 177-178.

40 Al-Bahri and Malbrunot, *Guarding bin Laden*, 22-23; Campbell, "Yemen,"; Johnsen, *The Last Refuge*, 40-41.

41 Boustany, "Civil War in Yemen,"; Johnsen, *The Last Refuge*, 40-41; The Associated Press, "Yemen Claims Victory."

42 Adaki, "Yemeni tribal leader joins AQAP,"; Ahmed and Akins, "Making enemies in Yemen,"; OBL, "Saudi Arabia supports the communists in Yemen," ARC, 7 June 1994; Boustany, "Civil War in Yemen,"; Johnsen, *The Last Refuge*, 42-43. Johnsen points out here that al-Harithi, like bin Laden, led his men from the front and rallied them in their attacks on al-Bid's forces, marching ahead fearlessly with makeshift crutches after receiving combat wounds in the fighting.

43 Boustany, "Civil War in Yemen,"; Chipman, "Osama bin Laden and Guerrilla War," 163-170; Mitzcavitch, "Al Qaeda and Mao Zedong," 14-18; Zedong, *The Red Book*, 52-53; 64-65.

44 OBL, "The Banishment of Communism from the Arabian Peninsula," ARC, 11 July 1994; Johnsen, *The Last Refuge*, 43-44; Ramani, "North Korea's Balancing Act,"; Al-Suwaidi et al., *The Yemeni War of 1994*, 87-88.

45 Johnsen, *The Last Refuge*, 43-44; The Associated Press, "Yemen Claims Victory." Bin Laden is said to have later cited the Rwandan Genocide, in addition to the UN sanctions and U.S.-UK bombings of Iraq from military bases in Saudi Arabia, as partial justification for al-Qaeda's August 1998 bombings of the U.S. embassies in Kenya and Tanzania in private conversations with Nasser al-Bahri and other al-Qaeda members protesting the

operatives' timing of the attack and selection of the embassies as targets due to the large number of nearby civilians killed and injured. Bin Laden reportedly countered immediately, replying that U.S. leaders had unhesitatingly struck Hiroshima and Nagasaki with atomic bombs despite large numbers of civilians being killed, and claimed that al-Qaeda had to demonstrate an ability to retaliate against those perceived as aggressors against Muslims, a point that he had previously emphasized in his May 1998 interview with John Miller, while also alleging the involvement of the CIA's regional base at the U.S. embassy in Nairobi in the Rwandan massacres, a popular theory with Sunni Islamists worldwide, and pointed out that the al-Qaeda leadership had issued multiple warnings for civilians to avoid the areas around the U.S. East African embassies. Bin Laden also reportedly employed his persuasive poetic skills during such debates, concluding that, "when your voice is not listened to in dialogue, you will have to take up your gun." See Al-Bahri and Malbrunot, *Guarding bin Laden*, 118-119, 203, 204-205; OBL, ARC, 7 May 1998; and Miller, "Greetings America. My Name is Osama bin Laden."

[46] Bergen, *Holy War, Inc.*, 177-178; OBL, "The Banishment of Communism from the Arabian Peninsula," ARC, 11 July 1994; Johnsen, *The Last Refuge*, 44-45; The Associated Press, "Yemen Claims Victory."

[47] Al-Bahri and Malbrunot, *Guarding bin Laden*, 22-23, 163-164; OBL, "The Banishment of Communism from the Arabian Peninsula," ARC, 11 July 1994; Clark, *Yemen*, 162, 165.

[48] OBL, "The Banishment of Communism from the Arabian Peninsula," ARC, 11 July 1994; Campbell, "Yemen."

[49] Adaki, "Yemeni tribal leader joins AQAP,"; Ahmed and Akins, "Making enemies in Yemen,"; Al-Bahri and Malbrunot, *Guarding bin Laden*, 210-212.

[50] Root, "A Sheikh's Life,"; Worth, "Ex-Jihadist Defies Yemen's Leader."

[51] Al-Bahri and Malbrunot, *Guarding bin Laden*, 50, 53; Scheuer, *Osama bin Laden*, 73, 82.

[52] Al-Bahri and Malbrunot, *Guarding bin Laden*, 50, 53.

[53] Ibid.

[54] Hamid and Farral, *The Arabs at War in Afghanistan*, 200-202; Scheuer, *Osama bin Laden*, 73, 97, 221n90. Bin Laden subsequently denounced the al-Sauds' support for the UN initiatives in the Balkans that he described as Islamophobic as another betrayal of Islam by the Saudi regime, stating that the UN had intentionally, "surrendered [the Bosnian Muslims] to the Serbian monster," by cooperating with the UN to expel the Arab mujahedin from the region. See OBL, ARC, 11 August 1995.

[55] Al-Bahri and Malbrunot, *Guarding bin Laden*, 136-137, 138-140; Scheuer, *Osama bin Laden*, 105, 123-124, 126-128. Bin Laden initially opposed al-Qaeda fighters participating in the Taleban's war against Massoud, as the ethnic Tajik's men had spread rumors that the Taleban were former communists and that the cities that they had captured were now again being controlled by communist forces. Taleban means "students" and this is likely the source of the initial confusion, allowing Massoud to portray the religious militia as communist scholars. Bin Laden quickly recognized this error in judgment, subsequently playing a key role in financing the Taleban's advance on Kabul in September 1996, persuading other Afghan Islamist commanders to stand aside and allow the Taleban to approach the city, and permitting his Arab fighters to participate and acquire combat experience in the fighting against Massoud, while further reinforcing the Taleban units with seasoned al-Qaeda veterans from the war against the Soviets. In any case, bin Laden's initial mistrust of the Taleban's true motives and ideological loyalties must have

surely been erased after the group burst into the UN compound in Kabul and seized the former communist secret police chief Najibullah, the Soviets' final Afghan puppet ruler, and eagerly executed him by hanging after horrendously torturing him as described by Robert Kaplan. See Kaplan, *Soldiers of God*, 237.

[56] Kaplan, *Soldiers of God*, 136; Peterson, "Osama bin Laden is a 'hero' in Afghanistan,"; Spain, *The Way of the Pathans*, 47-48, 52.

[57] Gutman, *How We Missed the Story*, 203-204.

[58] Al-Qarni, "Bin Laden's Former 'Mufti' Musa Al-Qarni Talks about the Jihad in Afghanistan,"; Scheuer, *Osama bin Laden*, 124, 127.

[59] Al-Qarni, "Bin Laden's Former 'Mufti' Musa Al-Qarni Talks about the Jihad in Afghanistan."

[60] Gutman, *How We Missed the Story*, 203-204; Jalali, *A Military History of Afghanistan*, 404-405; Kaplan, *Soldiers of God*, 40-41; Yousaf and Adkin, *Afghanistan*, 71.

[61] Gutman, *How We Missed the Story*, 203-204; Scheuer, *Osama bin Laden*, 124, 127.

[62] Al-Bahri and Malbrunot, *Guarding bin Laden*, 113, 159-159.

[63] Ibid.

[64] Gutman, *How We Missed the Story*, 203-204; Scheuer, *Osama bin Laden*, 124, 127.

[65] Al-Bahri and Malbrunot, *Guarding bin Laden*, 178; Scheuer, *Osama bin Laden*, 127-128.

[66] Scheuer, *Osama bin Laden*, 116-117.

[67] Al-Bahri and Malbrunot, *Guarding bin Laden*, 217-220; Mashal, "How the Taliban Outlasted a Superpower,"; Scheuer, *Osama bin Laden*, 116-117; Zaeef, *My Life with the Taliban*, 229-231.

[68] Al-Bahri and Malbrunot, *Guarding bin Laden*, 22-23, 163-164, 210-212; Coll, *The Bin Ladens*, 372-373; Worth, "Ex-Jihadist Defies Yemen's Leader."

[69] Khalid al-Hammadi, "Bin Ladin's Former 'Bodyguard' Interviewed on Al-Qa'ida Strategies," *Al-Quds al-Arabi*, 3 August 2004, https://cryptome.org/alqaeda-plans.htm. In this interview with Yemeni journalist Khalid al-Hammadi, Nasser al-Bahri describes al-Qaeda states that, "Some 95 percent of Al-Qa'ida members are Yemenis. The remaining five percent are Yemeni expatriates." Al-Bahri proceeds to state that many of the trainers in al-Qaeda insurgent camps are Yemenis as well as the bulk of the group's field commanders, foot soldiers, and bin Laden's bodyguards, besides the al-Qaeda leader being of Yemeni origin himself.

[70] The fact that bin Laden embraced his Yemeni origins on both sides of his family with his mother Allia Ghanem and her niece, his first wife Najwa, also hailing from a Yemeni immigrant family in Latakia, Syria, despite the discrimination often applied to his fellow Yemenis in societies ruled by *Adnani* Arabs contradicts Flagg Miller's claim that the al-Qaeda chief sought to portray himself as some sort of righteous heir to the throne of Saudi Arabia. Bin Laden does not appear to have made any such claim in any of his public or private statements, and Miller appears to have misinterpreted the words of Nasser al-Bahri in the former bodyguard's memoir pointing to the, "historical legitimacy" of his former boss as compared to his abrasive, Wahhabi-oriented Egyptian colleague al-Zawahiri. Miller errs in assuming that al-Bahri's statement implies that bin Laden tried to portray his family's native Kenda tribe as distant relatives of the al-Saud's or Al Ash Shaykh, the descendants of Abd al-Wahhab, to claim some sort of monarchical legitimacy to the Saudi throne. The Kenda originated in Yemen's Hadramut region and did in fact conquer and dominate the Najd region of central Arabia, the al-Saud's homeland, for a time during the pre-Islamic period before being displaced and driven back into their

ancestral land. As a tribe native to Yemen however, the Kenda are *Qahtanis* and are therefore ethnically distinct from the *Adnani* or "Arabized Arab" al-Sauds and al-Wahhab's family, and neither bin Laden nor his father ever attempted to distort this fact. Bin Laden consistently expressed deep admiration of the early and solid conversion of most Yemenis to Islam and the fiercely tribal and independent nature of rural Yemeni society. Miller follows this assertion by pointing to Ayman al-Zawahiri's pedigree as the descendent of a family of Egyptian religious scholars, inferring that this fact gave bin Laden's second-in-command more legitimacy as a natural leader than the al-Qaeda chief himself. He subsequently contradicts this statement by pointing out correctly that the bin Laden family patriarch, Muhammad, often experienced discrimination in Saudi elite circles, regularly being excluded from public festivals and events while consistently emphasizing the family's Yemeni origins to his sons, as documented in bin Laden's statements and by Steve Coll in his masterpiece *The Bin Ladens: An Arabian Family in the American Century*. Furthermore, al-Bahri consistently conveys a quiet but deep sense of pride in sharing Yemeni origin with the al-Qaeda chief in his memoir, often addressing him affectionately as *khal* or, "uncle" in reference to their shared Yemeni cultural upbringing. Moreover, al-Bahri's statement regarding bin Laden's, "historical legitimacy" refers to the al-Qaeda chief's documented wartime actions, from financing, to construction work, to fighting, in helping the Afghans in their tenacious resistance to the Soviet Army, as the former chief bodyguard reminds his readers. Al-Zawahiri, like the Syrian intellectual Abu Musab al-Suri and the Jordanian takfiri Abu Musab al-Zarqawi, lacked the quiet Saudi's approachability and tended to look down on non-Egyptian Arabs, particularly those from the Arabian Peninsula, and non-Salafi Sunni and Shia Muslims of all races, ethnicities, and nationalities, thereby earning a reputation as a divisive figure rather than a true leader willing and eager to fight alongside the brethren of diverse ethnicities and religious customs on the frontlines. As al-Bahri explains, al-Zawahiri's sole claim to legitimacy stemmed from his association with bin Laden, "a born leader" whose approachability and tolerance of diverse viewpoints prevented the arrogant Egyptian surgeon from losing the limited support that he received from al-Qaeda members. See, al-Bahri and Malbrunot, *Guarding bin Laden*, 74, 138, 212-213, 219; Bin Laden, bin Laden, and Sasson, *Growing Up bin Laden*, 4; Chulov, "My son, Osama,"; Coll, *The Bin Ladens*, 57; Edwards and Stephens, "The house bin Laden built,"; Miller, *The Audacious Ascetic*, 62-63; and Scheuer, *Osama bin Laden*, 21, 26, 195n9.

[71] Al-Bahri and Malbrunot, *Guarding bin Laden*, 163-164. Al-Bahri explains here that he and a small al-Qaeda delegation visited eight tribal leaders during a February 2000 visit to propagandize and enlist the support of Yemeni tribesmen and religious leaders particularly in Sanaa, Aden, and Shabwah province. He also states that while in Yemen the group executed a reconnaissance mission on the Yemeni island of Socotra to spy on alleged U.S. military activity on a strategic Arabian Sea location between the Arabian Peninsula and the Horn of Africa that once reportedly housed a Soviet naval base during the years of Moscow's military presence in South Yemen. See also, Kifner, "SOVIET SAID TO TRY."

[72] Al-Bahri and Malbrunot, *Guarding bin Laden*, 153, 160-161. This marriage to Amal al-Sadah, whose father reportedly received a dowry of $5,000 from bin Laden delivered by Nasser al-Bahri during his February 2000 trip to Yemen, also guaranteed the al-Qaeda leader the protection of her tribe near Taez, a major stronghold of al-Qaeda and Salafism in Yemen, if he ever requested refuge. Bin Laden is said to have fathered at least four

children, two sons and two daughters, with Amal in Pakistan while eluding U.S. and NATO forces in the decade between 9/11 and his death. See, BBC, "Bin Laden 'fathered four children' while on the run," *BBC*, 30 March 2012, https://www.bbc.com/news/world-asia-17560649; SAMAA, "Bin Laden 'fathered four children while on run," *SAMAA*, 30 March 2012, https://www.samaa.tv/news/2012/03/bin-laden-fathered-four-children-while-on-run/.

73 Al-Bahri and Malbrunot, *Guarding bin Laden*, 80; Walker, *Aden Insurgency*, 296-298.

74 Ruthven, "The eleventh of September and the Sudanese mahdiyya," 339-351; Stenersen, *Al-Qaida in Afghanistan*, 162. Stenersen points out that several of these men including Nawaf al-Hazmi, Khaled al-Midhar, Ramsi al-Sheba, and Hani Hanjour had arrived in Afghanistan much earlier, between 1996 and 1997, but began training for their special mission at this time while others involved in the attacks in New York and Washington began basic training in al-Qaeda's camps. Several of these men, mostly Saudis of Yemeni origin native to Saudi Arabia's Asir region, had fought in Afghanistan against the Soviet troops, against the Serbian troops in Bosnia and Kosovo, or alongside the Taleban against Massoud's forces, including Hamza al-Ghamdi, a younger relative of bin Laden's close confidant and fellow Jaji veteran of the same name. Hanjour, another seasoned combat veteran of the anti-Soviet jihad, hijacked and piloted American Airlines Flight 77, crashing the plane into a wing of the Pentagon near Washington, D.C. The group completed their preparations between late 2000 and early 2001 before being dispatched to the United States to execute the 9/11 attacks.

75 Al-Bahri and Malbrunot, *Guarding bin Laden*, 81-82; BBC, "Obituary: Yemen al-Qaeda leader Nasser al-Wuhayshi," BBC, 16 June 2015, https://www.bbc.com/news/world-middle-east-33150212; Campbell, "Yemen,"; Ben Felton, Johanna Kassel, and Richard McGregor, "Bin Laden papers reveal al-Qaeda rifts," *The Financial Times*, 3 May 2012, http://ig-legacy.ft.com/content/1c19c328-952f-11e1-ad38-00144feab49a#axzz6lEYaJsPE.

76 Al-Maqtari, "The evolution of militant Salafism in Taiz,"; Ali Mahmood, "Al Qaeda shows signs of resurgence in Yemen," *MENA*, 9 April 2021, https://www.thenationalnews.com/mena/al-qaeda-shows-signs-of-resurgence-in-yemen-1.1200037; Murad Batal al-Shishani, "Yemen al-Qaeda chief al-Wuhayshi killed in US strike," BBC, 16 June 2015, https://www.bbc.com/news/world-middle-east-33143259; Reuters, "North Korea trying to sell weapons to Houthis, secret UN report reveals," *Arab News*, 4 August 2018, https://www.arabnews.com/node/1350851/world; The Arab Weekly, "Al-Qaeda exploiting security vacuum created by Houthi escalation," *The Arab Weekly*, 18 June 2021, https://thearabweekly.com/al-qaeda-exploiting-security-vacuum-created-houthi-escalation.

77 BBC, "Obituary: Yemen al-Qaeda leader Nasser al-Wuhayshi,"; Al-Maqtari, "The evolution of militant Salafism in Taiz,"; Mark Mazetti and Scott Shane, "For U.S., Killing Terrorists Is a Means to an Elusive End," *The New York Times*, 16 June 2015, https://www.nytimes.com/2015/06/17/world/middleeast/al-qaeda-arabian-peninsula-yemen-nasser-al-wuhayshi-killed.html. Al-Qaeda's steady growth and resilience in Yemen and the Taleban's growing strength in Afghanistan, supported by cadres of al-Qaeda fighters at the local level, appear to contradict the claim by Professor Fawaz Gerges that the group, "was effectively decapitated" following the U.S.- NATO invasion of Afghanistan on 7 October 2001. As Michael Scheuer points out, it seems highly unlikely that bin Laden labored throughout the 1990s to draw U.S. forces into Afghanistan for a protracted war that he and al-Qaeda had long prayed, prepared, and trained for, courtesy

of the Soviet 40th Army, in the hope of replicating the victory over the Soviets via guerrilla warfare if he believed even for a moment that his death or that of the other al-Qaeda top brass amounted to the organization's defeat. Bin Laden also viewed the early 2011 Arab Spring uprisings across much of the Middle East and North Africa as a positive development, moving al-Qaeda closer to its main goals by weakening tyrannical Arab regimes and providing a God-given opportunity to forge connections with local Islamist groups and strengthen their position provided the right amount of patience, careful planning, and avoidance of involvement in counterproductive sectarian strife. Bin Laden advised al-Qaeda fighters and field commanders from Libya, to Syria, to Yemen to follow this path in their efforts to strengthen the local resistance movements against the corrupt Arab rulers in a series of letters that he authored between February and May 2011, including a letter written one week before U.S. troops killed him in Pakistan. See Fawaz A. Gerges, *The Rise and Fall of al-Qaeda* (New York: Oxford University Press, 2014), 108; Johanna Kassel, "Bin Laden supported Arab spring," *The Financial Times*, 3 May 2012, https://www.ft.com/content/a218eb16-9539-11e1-8faf-00144feab49a; and Scheuer, *Osama bin Laden*, 19, 135-136, 235n19.

[78] Al-Bahri and Malbrunot, *Guarding bin Laden*, 81-82, 181-182; Campbell, "Yemen,"; Al-Shishani, "Yemen al-Qaeda chief."

[79] Scheuer, *Osama bin Laden*, 143; Al-Shishani, "Yemen al-Qaeda chief."

[80] Magdy, "Al-Qaida in Yemen claims deadly shooting,"; Reuters Staff, "Bin Laden claims U.S. plane bombing attempt,"; Tucker, "FBI: Shooter at Pensacola Navy Base coordinated with al-Qaida." On 6 December 2019, Saudi naval aviation student Muhammad Said al-Shamrani killed three U.S. sailors and injured eight others in a mass shooting that he conducted at Naval Air Station Pensacola in coordination with AQAP. Given al-Qaeda's continued lethality as indicated by this recent ruthless and successful attack, it appears to be wishful thinking to believe that somehow slowly killing its leaders through courageous but not war-winning hellfire missile drone strikes and Special Forces raids in any way diminishes the insurgent group's operational effectiveness as each leader is consistently replaced by a trained subordinate, often seasoned with Afghan battle experience.

[81] Magdy, "Al-Qaida in Yemen claims deadly shooting,"; Mahmood, "Al Qaeda shows signs of resurgence,"; Al-Maqtari, "The evolution of militant Salafism in Taiz,"; Sean D. Naylor, "U.S. killed a top al-Qaida leader in Yemen, reports say," *Yahoo News*, 31 January 2020, https://news.yahoo.com/us-killed-a-top-al-qaeda-leader-in-yemen-reports-say-21555 5178.html; Sudarsan Raghavan, "As Yemen's war intensifies, an opportunity for al-Qaeda to resurrect its fortunes," *The Washington Post*, 25 February 2020, https://www.washingtonpost.com/world/middle_east/as-yemens-war-intensifies-an-opening-for-al-qaeda-to-resurrect-its-fortunes/2020/02/24/6244bd84-54ef-11ea-80ce-37a8d4266c 09_story.html; Tucker, "FBI: Shooter at Pensacola Navy Base coordinated with al-Qaida." U.S. forces killed al-Raymi on 30 January 2020, but the organization, as is true of any trained insurgency, continues to thrive, threatening U.S. and Western security interests in the region from its solid base in an unconquerable land not unlike Afghanistan. As these newspaper reports and scholarly sources make clear, the ongoing foreign military intervention by the formerly U.S. and UK-backed Saudi-led Arab military coalition and the Houthi rebels' attempts to install a monarchical Shia state, reportedly with Iranian and North Korean support, continue validating bin Laden's lethal legacy and leadership by further alienating Yemen's devout, tribal Sunni majority and driving growing numbers

of young warriors into al-Qaeda's ranks, strengthening the group's effective recruitment mechanism and further entrenching it in the country. Perhaps even more so than the Afghans, the Yemeni people have many internal problems to sort out, but the tribes have consistently succeeded throughout history to defy unpopular central governments and repulse invaders, especially those regarded as apostate rulers or infidel occupiers.

EPILOGUE

[1] Arnett, "Transcript of Osama Bin Ladin interview,"; Miller, "Greetings America. My Name is Osama bin Laden."
[2] Atwan, "My weekend with Osama bin Laden,"; OBL, ARC, 12 September 1994; Miller, "Greetings America. My Name is Osama bin Laden."'
[3] William MacLean, "Loyalty bin Laden inspired leaves lasting risk," *Reuters*, 4 May 2011, https://www.reuters.com/article/us-binladen-loyalties-idUKTRE7436RV20110504.
[4] Jack Moore, "What Is the Taliban's 'Red Unit'? Jihadi Special Forces Are Using Russian, U.S. Tech for Attacks," *Newsweek*, 1 December 2017, https://www.newsweek.com/what-talibans-red-unit-jihadi-special-forces-are-using-russian-us-tech-attacks-711761; Rubin, *Afghanistan*, 246.
[5] Lori Hinnant and Elaine Ganley, "French security forces kill gunmen, end terror rampage," *The Associated Press*, 9 January 2015, https://web.archive.org/web/20150113074036/http://news.yahoo.com/brothers-past-draws-scrutiny-french-manhunt-enters-day-073049780.html.
[6] BBC, "Charlie Hebdo attack: Three days of terror," *BBC*, 14 January 2015, https://www.bbc.com/news/world-europe-30708237.
[7] Those arguing that U.S. and NATO forces should not have been withdrawn from Afghanistan until the Taleban leadership denounced and verifiably expelled al-Qaeda should bear in mind that these two groups are essentially one despite their respectively independent national and ethnic origins. Bin Laden swore an oath of allegiance or *bayat* to Mullah Omar, officially recognizing the Taleban chief as "Commander of the Faithful," in the summer of 1998, essentially fusing al-Qaeda into the Taleban as a multinational guerrilla wing of the same organization, with a growing presence on at least four continents including North America. Despite bin Laden's death, it remains highly unlikely that Mullah Omar's successors can somehow break his pledge to continue sheltering al-Qaeda, as many Islamists regard the oath of allegiance as a very serious religious matter. See al-Bahri and Malbrunot, *Guarding bin Laden*, 134-135, 215-217; Scheuer, *Osama bin Laden*, 123-124. For the deep religious significance of the *bayat* and the title of Commander of the Faithful, see Ibn Khaldun, *The Muqaddimah*, 166-167, 180-183; and Dr. Ali M. as-Sallabi's biography of *Caliph* Omar ibn al-Khattab, a close companion of the Prophet and the first to hold this title, *Umar ibn al-Khattab: His Life & Times*, Vol.1 trans. Nasiruddin al-Khattab (Riyadh: International Islamic Publishing House, 2007), 227-229.
[8] Braithwaite, *Afgantsy*, 333-334, 335; Zaeef, *My Life with the Taliban*, 65.
[9] Galeotti, *Afghanistan*, 4, 6.

AUTHOR'S AFTERWORD TO THE SECOND EDITION

[1] Abd-al-Karim and al-Nur, "Interview with Saudi businessman Usama bin Ladin."

[2] Ibid.; Atwan, "My weekend with Osama bin Laden"; OBL, "Our invitation to Give Advice and Reform," ARC, 12 April 1994; Fisk, "Anti-Soviet Warrior puts his army on the road to peace"; Miller, "Greetings America. My Name is Osama bin Laden"; Nida'ul Islam, "Mujahid Usamah Bin Ladin."

[3] Al-Bahri and Malbrunot, *Guarding bin Laden*, 22-23, 163-164; OBL, "The Banishment of Communism from the Arabian Peninsula," ARC, 11 July 1994; Clark, *Yemen*, 162, 165.

[4] Azzam, "Sheikh Abdullah Azzam said about Usama Bin Ladin," 152-153; Bergen, *Holy War, Inc.*, 18; Nida'ul Islam, "Mujahid Usamah Bin Ladin"; Stenersen, *Al-Qaida in Afghanistan*, 18-19; Tawil, *Brothers in Arms*, 19-20.

[5] Adaki, "Yemeni tribal leader joins AQAP"; Ahmed and Akins, "Making enemies in Yemen"; OBL, "Saudi Arabia supports the communists in Yemen," ARC, 7 June 1994; Boustany, "Civil War in Yemen"; Johnsen, *The Last Refuge*, 42-43.

[6] Peter Bergen, *The Rise and Fall of Osama bin Laden* (New York: Simon & Schuster, 2021), xxvii-xxx, 57-58, 241-243, 244, 245-248; Nelly Lahoud, *The Bin Laden Papers: How the Abbottabad Raid Revealed the Truth about Al-Qaeda, Its Leader and His Family* (New Haven, CT: Yale University Press, 2022), 5-7, 9-12, 282-287. Be that as it may, however, it should also be emphasized here that these two books are, like the authors' other works, splendid texts that are more than worth exploring and are highly recommended to readers. Lahoud's work is particularly excellent and thorough, and on these same pages, she displays admirable courage and wisdom in emphasizing the reasons for which bin Laden remains a threat long after his death as his legacy continues to benefit al-Qaeda and the jihadi group's various global wings throughout the world. Yet notwithstanding their overall splendid works, Lahoud and Bergen also appear to somewhat overemphasize bin Laden's alleged failures as debilitating to the militant Salafist movement that he founded, led, and continues to inspire, particularly as the latter dismisses bin Laden's quite apparent and spectacular successes in Yemen's 1994 Civil War and afterwards as one of the al-Qaeda leader's alleged, "flops." Bergen's assessment here seems somewhat far-fetched, as neither bin Laden nor his anti-Soviet Yemeni guerrilla comrades attempted to install an Islamist regime in their South Arabian homeland once the Riyadh and Pyongyang-backed communists were defeated. Rather, they played the long-term game in the country, wisely focusing on recruitment and guerrilla war training while strengthening al-Qaeda's position and building its solid local support structure among Yemen's tribal majority, a clever tactic that continues benefitting the jihadi group today. It appears, in fact, that bin Laden's experience first in playing a small but, for him and al-Qaeda, key tactical supporting role fighting the Soviets in Afghanistan and second in tactically spearheading the YSP's decisive defeat reflects the impact of his wartime actions and successes on his and al-Qaeda's blueprint for their anti-U.S. strategy in that the Soviet Union's 1991 collapse, an event to which the Afghan insurgents and, to a much lesser extent, their Arab guerrilla allies, had contributed, cost al-Bid's communists their major source of infidel superpower support and helped to ensure their defeat, thereby helping bin Laden to rationally conclude that Islamist fighters armed with enough patience, determination, and practical combat experience could gradually wear down the tyrannical Middle Eastern regimes to which they remained opposed after removing

the ability of superpowers to intervene and bolster the hated regimes' security, a perception that doubtlessly influenced his pragmatic approach to subsequently luring U.S.-U.K. forces into Afghanistan to gradually weaken their governments economically via costly, attritional guerrilla warfare before focusing on the eventual toppling of the al-Sauds and other Arab rulers. For several examples of bin Laden's true motives, tactics, and objectives in Yemen and South Arabia overall, see, OBL, "Saudi Arabia supports the communists in Yemen," ARC, 7 June 1994; OBL, "The Banishment of Communism from the Arabian Peninsula," ARC, 11 July 1994; OBL, *Messages to the World*, 76; MacLeod, "The Paladin of Jihad," 51-52.

[7] Al-Bahri and Malbrunot, *Guarding bin Laden*, 50, 53; Root, "A Sheikh's Life"; Scheuer, *Osama bin Laden*, 73, 82; Worth, "Ex-Jihadist Defies Yemen's Leader."

[8] See Bergen, *Holy War, Inc.*, 176-177.

[9] Bergen, *The Rise and Fall of Osama bin Laden*, 57-58.

[10] Scheuer, *Through Our Enemies' Eyes*, 122.

[11] See Scheuer, *Osama bin Laden*, 80, 97, 221n89.

[12] Johnsen, *The Last Refuge*, 24-25.

[13] Al-Suwaidi et al., *The Yemeni War of 1994*, 62-64, 64-66.

[14] Ginny Hill, *Yemen Endures: Civil War, Saudi Adventurism and the Future of Arabia* (New York: Oxford University Press, 2017), 89-91.

[15] Bergen, *The Rise and Fall of Osama bin Laden*, 57-58; Hill, *Yemen Endures*, 113-115, 117-118, 120; Scheuer, *Osama bin Laden*, 80, 97, 221n89; Al-Suwaidi et al., *The Yemeni War of 1994*, 22, 23-26.

[16] OBL, "The Banishment of Communism from the Arabian Peninsula," ARC, 11 July 1994; Johnsen, *The Last Refuge*, 43-44; Ramani, "North Korea's Balancing Act"; Al-Suwaidi et al., *The Yemeni War of 1994*, 87-88.

[17] Clark, *Yemen*, 232-234; Mackintosh-Smith, *Yemen*, 164-165; The New York Times, "SAUDIS SAY U.A.R. BOMBED VILLAGES"; Van der Bijl, *British Military Operations*, 140; Schmidt, "British in Aden Depart as Egyptians Leave Yemen"; Walker, *Aden Insurgency*, 52, 57, 93, 127.

[18] *Parl. Rec. – House of Commons*, 1st Sess. (1967); Schmidt, "British in Aden Depart as Egyptians Leave Yemen."

[19] *Congressional Record – House of Representatives*, 100th Congress, 2nd Session, pt. (1988), https://babel.hathitrust.org/cgi/pt?id=pst.000014722738&view=1up&seq=1&skin=2021. As discussed in Chapters 2 and 3 of this book, Reagan, Thatcher, and their respective supporters in the U.S. Congress and U.K. Parliament also had to constantly contend, throughout much of the decade, with reluctant lawmakers fearing that the Afghan fighters could not continue resisting the Soviet 40th Army's mechanized, airpower-backed war machine for long, and, while many congressional and parliamentary representatives voted to supply arms and ordnance to the rebels over the course of the decade, Washington's relations with the insurgent factions were further complicated by the demands of some U.S. lawmakers from at least 1987 forward that the Islamist groups within the Afghan resistance, that is, the four major fighting factions, accept a coalition government that included PDPA officials, including President Najibullah himself, and the Afghan royalty that many guerrillas regarded as corrupt, including the deposed King Zahir Shah whose playboy reputation as a womanizing drunkard during his prolonged exile in and frequent visits to Italy rendered him just as unacceptable as the communists in the eyes of many contemporary rural, religious Afghans. The source cited above

includes two congressional debates and hearings before the U.S. House of Representatives Subcommittee on Asian and Pacific Affairs of the Committee on Foreign Affairs during the second session of the 100th U.S. Congress on 17 and 25 February 1988, respectively. Congressman Charlie Wilson of Texas, a staunch congressional supporter of the CIA's efforts to arm the Afghan mujahedin, attended both hearings after having just returned from the embattled Afghan-Pakistani frontier. During the two February 1988 hearings before the House Subcommittee, Chairman Stephen J. Solarz (D-NY) criticized Pakistani President Zia ul-Haq's recent alleged refusal to recognize or sign any agreement with a post-Soviet, "interim government" in Kabul that included members of Najibullah's PDPA regime and the military dictator's ongoing attempts to ensure Islamabad's ability to attain nuclear parity with its hostile Indian, Iranian, and communist neighbors by funding Pakistan's nuclear research program. Congressman Wilson reportedly attended the two hearings, in part, to vote alongside both his fellow Democrat and Republican House colleagues in a successful bipartisan effort to defeat Solarz's proposed amendment to the U.S. aid program through which the New York representative sought to cut U.S. funding to Pakistan, potentially obstructing both Washington, D.C. and Islamabad in the ongoing, joint effort to supply the Afghan resistance just as it appeared, after nearly a decade, that Gorbachev could finally be preparing to publicly commit to a phased withdrawal. As the first debate began, Solarz acknowledged Wilson's presence at the hearing and his tremendous success in working with Director Casey's CIA to supply a considerable amount of material aid to the Afghan warriors, addressing and introducing him as, "an honorary member of the subcommittee, our good friend Field Marshal Wilson. He has just returned from his latest trip to the subcontinent in order to determine how his forces in the field [the Afghan insurgents] are doing and, presumably, to better inform himself on the diplomatic situation which currently exists," before inviting his participation in the debate, to which the Texas representative replied, "I appreciate that, Mr. Chairman." Congressman James "Jim" Leach (R-IA) welcomed Wilson joining in his opposition to the proposed "Solarz amendment," stating, "Let me just say that we [House Republicans] also appreciate Mr. Wilson's participation, particularly because he has chosen to sit on the right side of the aisle," as the representatives attending the debate reportedly burst into good-humored laughter. According to Wilson's biographer George Crile in *Charlie Wilson's War: The Extraordinary Story of How the Wildest Man in Congress and a Rogue CIA Agent Changed the History of Our Times*, Wilson took great pleasure in voting down the Solarz amendment on the House floor to ensure that Operation *Cyclone*, the CIA's covert action aid program to the rebels that relied heavily on channeling arms and ordnance through Pakistan's ISI, could not be obstructed at the last minute as the Soviet Air Force's jet fighter-bombers and attack helicopters reportedly continued mercilessly bombing and seeking to interdict the insurgents' supply caravans, often striking and damaging many Pakistan border villages in the process. As Crile points out, "In the fall of 1982 [nearly three years into the Soviet occupation of Afghanistan], the mujahideen had no congressional champions. In fact, they had no one in any position of power who believed that they had a chance for victory," as many congressional lawmakers and Pakistani officials feared that angering Moscow by providing U.S.-designed arms or a ceaseless flow of support to guerrillas that they viewed as hopelessly doomed could provoke a Soviet invasion of Pakistan or a nuclear escalation with all of its horrific ramifications. This prevailing, fearful assumption that the Afghan fighters decisively disproved through their resilience, perseverance, and tenacity in resisting the

Soviet occupiers even as their homes, mosques, and families were destroyed in the fighting, presented an uphill battle in the U.S. Congress for Reagan, Wilson, Humphrey, and their supporters, and the insistence of some senators and congressman that the Afghan mujahedin parties accept the unacceptable, i.e. an interim government filled with those the guerrillas had long been fighting, only complicated matters further during the Soviet-Afghan War's final years, leading many Afghan commanders, such as bin Laden's friend Yunis Khalis, to utterly resent Washington's perceived, "sell out" and attempt to attach to and impose conditions on further CIA aid to the resistance fighters. Wilson, however, remained determined to prevent such an obstruction of Operation *Cyclone*, and, as stated by Crile, the Texas congressman rhetorically sniped at Solarz in beginning his congressional testimony at the 1988 hearing, stating, "Incidentally, Mr. Chairman, before we start, I would like to congratulate all the friends of India on the acquisition of their peaceful nuclear submarine that has just arrived [from the Soviet Union]," (this set of brackets in the original) in a stinging, sarcastic reference highlighting the Chairman's perceived hypocrisy and counterproductive proposed amendment that undermined Pakistan's already fragile and threatened security even as Moscow continued arming Islamabad's hated enemies in New Delhi. According to Crile, Wilson is said to have described his participation in voting down the Solarz amendment as, "my greatest achievement in Congress," while his considerable success and that of his senatorial ally Gordon Humphrey in rallying many of their respective bipartisan House and Senate colleagues to support the Afghan insurgents had largely resulted from the Texas congressman's key position as a persuasive and influential member of the House of Representatives Defense Appropriations subcommittee, a position that allowed him to begin strengthening the Reagan administration's support for *Cyclone* from 1983 forward as the president's NSDD-75 authorized stronger CIA support for the Afghan fighters. See Crile, *Charlie Wilson's War*, 20, 34-35, 78, 83-84, 111-113, 115, 179, 185, 210, 214, 262, 478; Kamm, "Afghan Rebels Reported Furious"; Ottaway, "Afghan Rebels Assured"; U.S. President, "National Security Decision Directive Number 75."

[20] Clark, *Yemen*, 95-97; Hourani, *A History of the Arab Peoples*, 411, 416-417; Howe, "Southern Yemen blends Marxism"; Hurd and Noakes, "North and South Yemen," 48; *Parl. Rec. – House of Commons*, 1st Sess. (1979); Randal, "Threat to N. Yemen"; Van der Bijl, *British Military Operations*, 206.

[21] Michael H. Armacost, *Reflections on U.S.-Soviet Relations* (Ann Arbor: University of Michigan Library, 1985), 5-7.

[22] Armacost, *Reflections*, 5-7.

[23] Casey, *Scouting the Future*, 116-120.

[24] Ibid., 120-124, 125-129. Italics in the original.

[25] Bergen, *Holy War, Inc.*, 176-177; Coll, *The Bin Ladens*, 373-374; Casey, *Scouting the Future*, 120-124, 125-129; Johnsen, *The Last Refuge*, 8-10; Kifner, "SOVIET SAID TO TRY."

[26] Beckford, "National Archives"; Bowcott, "UK discussed plants to help Mujahideen"; *Parl. Rec. – House of Commons*, 1st Sess. (1980); Thatcher, *The Downing Street Years*, 68; UK Prime Minister, "Afghanistan."

[27] Whitehall History Publishing – Foreign and Commonwealth Office, *Documents on British Policy Overseas Series III, Volume VIII: The Invasion of Afghanistan and UK-Soviet Relations, 1979-1982*, eds. Richard Smith, Patrick Salmon, and Stephen Twigge (London: Routledge, 2012), "No. 17: Record of a meeting between Mrs Thatcher and the Soviet

Ambassador (Mr Lunkov) at No. 10 Downing Street, 3 January 1980, 3 p.m. Confidential (FCO 28/3996, EN 021/1).

[28] Whitehall History Publishing – Foreign and Commonwealth Office, *Documents on British Policy Overseas Series III, Volume VIII*, "No. 41: Minute from Lord Carrington to Mrs Thatcher, 19 January 1980, PM/80/5 Secret (FCO 13/967, PC 295/1)" 92-95n1-5. In his report to Thatcher, after acknowledging that, "They [the Saudis] are playing a leading role, together with Pakistan, in mobilising Moslem opinion against the Soviet action in Afghanistan" Carrington notes here that, "The Saudis are concerned about Soviet influence in both the PDRY [People's Democratic Republic of Yemen/South Yemen] and the YAR [Yemen Arab Republic/North Yemen] and about possible subversion through the many [Yemeni] expatriates in their own country. The Mecca incident was a shock to them," in reference to al-Utaybi's failed November 1979 uprising at Mecca's Grand Mosque. In addition to working closely with the Saudi and Omani royal rulers, the latter of whom, in a rare case for the Arab world, are said to hail from ethnic Yemeni origins native to Yemen's Hadramut region like the bin Ladens, Carrington also advised that Whitehall should seek to obtain U.S. participation in guaranteeing Pakistan's security against a potential Soviet invasion, an alarming possibility from the prevailing contemporary U.S.-U.K. perspective, as the Islamabad leadership remained, "deeply concerned" and continued to, "feel squeezed" over being surrounded on all sides by hostile forces, to which the prime minister, doubtlessly feeling somewhat burdened by the Carter administration's increasingly sour relations with Islamabad over its military regime and nuclear program, firmly objected, stating, "On reflection I am a little unhappy about such a guarantee. It would look as if we were guaranteeing President Zia's regime rather than the territory." The substantive importance here, however, is that the leading U.S.-U.K. officials, like their contemporary Saudi, North Yemeni, and Omani counterparts, regarded Moscow's Afghan incursion and its military presence in South Yemen as a threat, even though it is now known that Brezhnev, Andropov, and Gorbachev had no immediate, aggressive designs on the Arabian Peninsula, at least not at that time. Yet due to the Kremlin's policies such as supporting the hated, dictatorial communist central governments in these devout Muslim countries, bin Laden and his Salafi jihadi comrades in Yemen, Saudi Arabia, and elsewhere, naturally and understandably, shared this logical, defensive perspective at that time, as the al-Qaeda chief later wrote, after emphasizing Moscow's support for Aden's anti-religious Marxist government and Ziad Bari's regime and its public execution of devout Muslim clergymen in nearby Somalia, that, "The Afghans were able to repel the largest invasion of recent times by the forces of disbelief against Islam. We ask Allah to reward them with the best rewards…. Had it not been for the grace of Allah and the people of Afghanistan, the Arabian Gulf states would have fallen into the hands of Communism." See OBL, "Introduction," 80, 81, 82-84; and Scheuer, *Osama bin Laden*, 75, 215n117.

[29] Whitehall History Publishing – Foreign and Commonwealth Office, *Documents on British Policy Overseas Series III, Volume VIII*, "No. 43: Letter from Mrs Thatcher to President Carter, 26 January 1980 Secret (PREM 19/136)," 98-100.

[30] Ibid., "No. 47: Memorandum by East European and Soviet Department on Soviet Foreign Policy after Afghanistan, 31 January 1980 Confidential (FCO 28/3987, EN 020/7)," 106-109.

[31] Ibid., "No. 48: Minute from Mr Mallaby to Mr Ferguson, 1 February 1980 Secret (FCO 49/894, RS 021/7)," 109-110n1-3.

32 Ibid., "No. 55: Partial record of a meeting between Mrs Thatcher and Chancellor Schmidt at 10 Downing Street, 25 February 1980 Secret (FCO 28/4003, EN 021/1)," 123-128, and, for several similar, insightful contemporary views expressed by U.K. officials hoping that President Reagan's landslide presidential election victory on 4 November 1980 signaled an oncoming, welcome shift in Washington, D.C. towards backing the Afghan resistance more effectively, see "No. 78: Minute from Mr Garside (Planning Staff) to Mr Mallaby, 12 November 1980 Secret (FCO 49/893, RS 021/6)," 186-189.

33 Coll, *The Bin Ladens*, 7-8, 10, 11-12; U.S. President, "Ronald Reagan Administration: Statement Welcoming King Fahd of Saudi Arabia (February 11, 1985)," *The White House*, 11 February 1985, *Jewish Virtual Library – A Project of AICE*, https://www.jewishvirtual library.org/president-reagan-statement-welcoming-king-fahd-of-saudi-arabia-february -1985.

34 Jack Reed, "Soviets race to cut rebel supply lines from Pakistan," *UPI*, 1 June 1987, https://www.upi.com/Archives/1987/06/01/Soviets-race-to-cut-rebel-supply-lines-from-Pakistan/1885549518400/; Saira Shah, "SOVIET-AFGHAN CONFLICT. US-supplied missiles boost mujahideen ability," *The Christian Science Monitor*, 18 June 1987, https://www.csmonitor.com/layout/set/amphtml/1987/0618/ojaji.html. Jack Reed's 1 June 1987 newswire story for *UPI* and Saira Shah's 18 June 1987 newspaper report for *The Christian Science Monitor* serve as two highly insightful contemporary sources on the Battle of Jaji and convey to the reader some degree of the fighting's impact on bin Laden's success in acquiring for himself and his Arab guerrilla band key tactical combat experience. Both reports emphasize the Soviet assault as being aimed at the interdiction of the guerrillas' supply caravans entering Afghanistan from Pakistan as Gorbachev's generals persisted in their efforts to sufficiently cripple the resistance to begin the phased withdrawal process while leaving the PDPA in a militarily advantageous position. While Reed's account for *UPI* states, "At least 22 guerrillas have been killed and 80 seriously injured in the attacks, which began last Tuesday [26 May 1987]," these figures likely refer to the overall combined casualties suffered by Sayyaf's Afghan insurgents and bin Laden's Arab fighters at that point in the fighting as bin Laden's guerrilla unit, initially consisting of 120 fighters, appears to have already suffered a loss of 50 men between its two failed raids on the nearby Soviet garrison at Chowni in mid-April and mid-May 1987 respectively, before Afghan Commander Sayyaf, inspired by the Arab holy warriors' tenacity and dogged defiance of the enemy's armored and aerial onslaught, sent 20 fighters to reinforce the Lion's Den and replenish its losses from the day's fighting on the night of 27 May. Reed's report proceeds to quote an anonymous, "Western diplomat" as observing, "320 vehicles, including Soviet T-62 tanks and 152mm self-propelled guns, heading south from the Afghan capital of Kabul toward the Jaji region, where the fighting was reported" as Gorbachev's generals launched the assault, "to cripple rebel supply lines from Pakistan before the snows melt in the towering Hindu Kush mountains" in a three-pronged offensive against the insurgent strongholds. Shah's insightful article emphasizes the participation of Soviet tanks in the assault on Jaji's guerrilla bases, including bin Laden's Lion's Den, while also emphasizing the presence of mujahedin Stinger missiles, weaponry that the Afghans, understandably and naturally, were reportedly unwilling to share with the Arab volunteers at that time, as well as the use of cluster bombing by Soviet planes during the battle, stating, "Commanders deep inside Afghanistan [including bin Laden and his lightly trained Arab guerrillas] have, therefore, missed out on the weapons." Concluding with a brief mention the Soviet Air Force's deployment of cluster

bombs at Jaji, Shah states, "during the Jaji push, the Soviets used 'scatter bombs,' mortar bombs containing hundreds of timed explosive devices" to strike the guerrillas in their mountainside bases and destroy the nearby trees to deny them ambush positions. During his 6 December 1993 interview with British journalist Robert Fisk for the U.K. newspaper *The Independent*, bin Laden recalled that while the heavy Soviet bombing raids caused immense destruction around Jaji, he remained thankful to God that some of the enemy's bombs and shells appear to have been ineffective duds, stating, "I saw a 120mm mortar shell land in front of me, but it did not blow up. Four more bombs were dropped from a Russian plane on our headquarters but they did not explode. We [Islamic guerrillas] beat the Soviet Union. The Russians fled." For bin Laden's recollections to Fisk, see Fisk, "Anti-Soviet warrior puts his army on the road to peace."

35 Bergen, *The Osama bin Laden I Know*, 88-89; Girardet, *Killing the Cranes*, 228-230, 254-255; Simpson, "Simpson on Sunday."

36 Bergen, *The Osama bin Laden I Know*, 26; Bin Laden, bin Laden, and Sasson, *Growing Up bin Laden*, 64, 74-76; OBL, *Messages to the World*, 147; Miller, "Greetings America. My Name is Osama bin Laden"; Scheuer, *Osama bin Laden*, 112-113, 227n32.

37 Al-Bahri and Malbrunot, *Guarding bin Laden*, 74-76; Bin Laden, bin Laden, and Sasson, *Growing Up bin Laden*, 124, 214. Al-Bahri elaborates further on bin Laden's physical health and stamina here, stating that he had seen bin Laden ill only once during his three years as the al-Qaeda leader's chief bodyguard between 1997 and 2000, despite the assertions popularized by Western officials and media outlets. Al-Bahri explains that bin Laden, then in his early 40s, greatly enjoyed hiking and hill-climbing even on, "boiling hot" desert days and often appeared healthier and more physically fit than many younger men, recalling that the almost daily occasions on which bin Laden dressed in his, "long Yemeni turban" signaled the beginning of a long, Spartan trek. Al-Bahri elaborates further, stating that bin Laden ate very little other than dates and an omelet after morning prayers and that on special occasions, such as at al-Qaeda banquets and Islamic festivals, he enjoyed eating and sharing with his guests shoulder of mutton, "like the Prophet," while one of his favorite meals is said to have been Jordanian *Mansaf* that he greatly enjoyed eating together, "with bread made with red wheat." In another possible indication of Ibn Khaldun's influence on bin Laden, al-Bahri also mentions that the al-Qaeda chief firmly believed honey to be God's natural, "remedy for hundreds of illnesses." Complaining about his father's constant desire to go hiking in the arduous White Mountains of eastern Afghanistan, Omar bin Laden, known as one of the al-Qaeda chief's few pro-Western sons that long ago resented and rejected his father's jihadi journey, confirms many of al-Bahri's recollections of Osama's mostly solid physical health, stating that, "There has been much speculation about my father suffering from kidney disorders, including claims that his kidneys were so diseased that is was necessary for him to transport a dialysis machine on the back of a mule. Nothing could be further from the truth," before explaining that while his father, like other members of his extended family, sometimes suffered from extremely painful kidney stones, "his kidneys were strong otherwise." Confirming al-Bahri's comments on Osama suffering from occasional larynx trouble, Omar also recalls, "Although the Russians had deployed chemical gas against my father and his soldiers, the lingering effects were nothing more than occasional bouts of coughing.... He even out-hiked vigorous young men half his age." Crucially, even though Omar broke with his father before 9/11 and al-Bahri is said to have essentially, and indirectly, been fired as Osama sought to placate his Wahhabi-oriented, Egyptian EIJ

lieutenants, such as Ayman al-Zawahiri and Saif al-Adel, that disliked al-Qaeda's Yemeni and Saudi Salafist majority members and thereby prevent a fratricidal, internal conflict from wrecking the jihadi group, neither man shies away from commending Osama on his physical capabilities, Spartan living, approachable and effective management style, and indirect leadership example. In this regard, it is also interesting to note that at the time of writing neither *Guarding bin Laden* nor *Growing Up bin Laden*, despite being two highly insightful primary sources on Osama's life, appear to have yet been translated into Arabic editions, perhaps for the following reason pointed out by Michael Scheuer in his 2011 bin Laden biography, "It will be interesting to see if *Growing Up bin Laden* is published in Arabic, as it would be an engine for winning bin Laden's memory even more love and respect across the Muslim world." For Scheuer's insightful comment, see Scheuer, *Osama bin Laden*, 191-192n42; and for Ibn Khaldun's possible influence on bin Laden's views on the practical uses of honey as a natural remedy and his daily custom of eating only light meals and sharing his food, reportedly a practice of the Prophet's and many of his contemporaries, see Ibn Khaldun, *The Muqaddimah*, 68-69, 387-388.

[38] Al-Bahri and Malbrunot, *Guarding bin Laden*, 22-23; Bin Laden, bin Laden, and Sasson, *Growing Up bin Laden*, 64, 74-76; Scheuer, *Osama bin Laden*, 80.

[39] Abd-al-Karim and al-Nur, "Interview with Saudi businessman Usama bin Ladin"; Bin Laden, bin Laden, and Sasson, *Growing Up bin Laden*, 64, 74-76; OBL, "Open Letter for Sheikh Bin Baz," ARC, 29 December 1994; Scheuer, *Osama bin Laden*, 112-113, 227n32.

[40] Atwan, "My weekend with Osama bin Laden"; Bergen, *The Osama bin Laden I Know*, 59-60; Ibn Khaldun, *The Muqaddimah*, 152-154, 278-279, 351-352; Scheuer, *Osama bin Laden*, 37-38, 51-52, 204n15.

[41] Al-Bahri and Malbrunot, *Guarding bin Laden*, 22-23, 76-77, 105-106, 205, 206-208; al-Batarfi, "Growing up with Osama"; Bin Laden, bin Laden, and Sasson, *Growing Up bin Laden*,10, 266-167.

[42] *Parliamentary Record – House of Commons*, 1st Session (1987), https://hansard.parliament.uk/Commons/1987-12-08/debates/13774fd3-6d24-4327-9774-965bcd6702b3/Afghanistan. In this 8 December 1987 parliamentary debate on the floor of the House of Commons, U.K. MP Lord Alistair Goodlad of Eddisbury expressed his perception that those U.S.-U.K. lawmakers arguing that the Afghan insurgent leaders must agree to an interim government that included the hated PDPA members for the sake of satisfying Moscow and coaxing Gorbachev into publicly committing to a phased withdrawal from the country, essentially threatening to attach unacceptable conditions to further CIA-GID-MI-6 aid to the resistance, were doing little more than parroting the Kremlin's demands that the resistance fighters surrender to the regime against which they had persevered for nearly a decade, a condition that the four major Afghan Islamist insurgent factions could not accept. Pointing out that, "Kabul's reconciliation proposals have not been accepted by any credible Afghan group outside the ruling regime," MP Goodlad proceeded to state emphatically that, "As my noble Friend [Minister of State for Foreign and Commonwealth Affairs] Lord Glenarthur said to the United Nations General Assembly on 10 November, 'it is not reconciliation but capitulation which is on offer,'" before concluding, "I know that yesterday my right hon.[orable] Friend the Prime Minister pressed Mr. Gorbachev for an early withdrawal, and I hope that President Reagan is doing likewise. Soviet withdrawal is essential to a solution to the agony of Afghanistan."

[43] Whitehall History Publishing – Foreign and Commonwealth Office, *Documents on British Policy Overseas Series III, Volume VIII*, "No. 41: Minute from Lord Carrington to Mrs Thatcher, 19 January 1980, PM/80/5 Secret (FCO 13/967, PC 295/1)" 92-95n1-5.
[44] Scheuer, *Osama bin Laden*, 116-117.
[45] Ibid.
[46] Anas and Hussein, *To the Mountains*, 178-179, 180; Bergen, *The Osama bin Laden I Know*, 51-52; Darraz, "Impressions," 95-96, 102-103; Girardet, *Killing the Cranes*, 253-254; Scheuer, *Osama bin Laden*, 61-62; Schultheis, *Hunting bin Laden*, 50-51.
[47] Darraz, "Impressions," 97; Scheuer, *Osama bin Laden*, 63; Tawil, *Brothers in Arms*, 18.
[48] Bergen, *The Osama bin Laden I Know*, 51-52, 53; Scheuer, *Osama bin Laden*, 61-62.
[49] Abd-al-Karim and al-Nur, "Interview with Saudi businessman Usama bin Ladin"; Al-Bahri and Malbrunot, *Guarding bin Laden*, 22-23; OBL, "The Banishment of Communism from the Arabian Peninsula," ARC, 11 July 1994; OBL, ARC, 19 September 1994; Coll, *The Bin Ladens*, 373-374; Scheuer, *Osama bin Laden*, 80.
[50] Bin Laden, bin Laden, and Sasson, *Growing Up bin Laden*, 45; Daily Mail Reporter, "I taught judo to Osama bin Laden"; Loh and Tai, "Osama bin Laden a serious student."
[51] Daily Mail Reporter, "I taught judo to Osama bin Laden"; Darraz, "Impressions," 95-96, 102-103; Loh and Tai, "Osama bin Laden a serious student"; Reed, "Soviets race to cut rebel supply lines"; Shah, "SOVIET-AFGHAN CONFLICT."
[52] Bergen, *The Osama bin Laden I Know*, 51-52; Darraz, "Impressions," 97; Reed, "Soviets race to cut rebel supply lines"; Scheuer, *Osama bin Laden*, 63; Shah, "SOVIET-AFGHAN CONFLICT"; Tawil, *Brothers in Arms*, 18.
[53] Daily Mail Reporter, "I taught judo to Osama bin Laden"; Darraz, "Impressions," 102-103; Loh and Tai, "Osama bin Laden a serious student"; Nida'ul Islam, "Mujahid Usamah Bin Ladin"; Scheuer, *Osama bin Laden*, 61-62.
[54] Al-Bahri and Malbrunot, *Guarding bin Laden*, 22-23; Bergen, *The Osama bin Laden I Know*, 54-55; OBL, "Introduction," 114-115; OBL, "The Banishment of Communism from the Arabian Peninsula," ARC, 11 July 1994; Coll, *The Bin Ladens*, 373-374; Darraz, "Impressions," 109-110; Johnsen, *The Last Refuge*, 24-25; *Parl. Rec. – House of Commons*, 1st Sess. (1987); Reed, "Soviets race to cut rebel supply lines"; Scheuer, *Through Our Enemies Eyes*, 110; Shah, "SOVIET-AFGHAN CONFLICT." During his 8 December 1987 speech on the floor of Britain's House of Commons, MP Goodlad of Eddisbury called his House colleagues' attention to the series of victories that the resistance fighters had won throughout the crucial year as he assessed the demands of Moscow, Kabul, and some U.S.-U.K. lawmakers that the rebels accept an interim government as beyond ridiculous. Goodlad proceeded to argue that, "While these [diplomatic] processes [in Geneva] run their course, contrary to Soviet propaganda, the Soviet and Afghan forces have launched major offensives this year in the Kandahar and Pakhtiar [sic, Paktia] areas. The Kandahar offensive did not secure the city and that in Pakhtiar [sic] was beaten back in a major success for the resistance." Goodlad's insightful House floor observations on the 1987 fighting in Paktia Province, the location of bin Laden's Lion's Den guerrilla base and the Jaji engagements, reveal the importance of the fighting that year in which the zealous Saudi mujahid and his comrades played a key supporting role as they doggedly defied the Soviet juggernaut's merciless assaults and emerged by the battle's end as combat-seasoned guerrilla fighters.
[55] Bergen, *The Rise and Fall of Osama bin Laden*, 57-58; Reuters (Unattributed Report), "Al-Qaeda attack kills 20 Yemeni forces in Abyan, says southern military," *Reuters*, 6

September 2022, https://www.reuters.com/world/middle-east/al-qaeda-attack-kills-20-yemeni-forces-abyan-says-southern-military-2022-09-06/; Jacob Zenn, Brief: Al-Qaeda Affiliates AQIM and AQAP Show Unity with Eid Statement," *The Terrorism Monitor – The Jamestown Foundation*, Vol. 21, Issue 9 (28 April 2023), https://jamestown.org/program/brief-al-qaeda-affiliates-aqim-and-aqap-show-unity-with-eid-statement/.

56 Al-Bahri and Malbrunot, *Guarding bin Laden*, 70; Bergen, *Holy War, Inc.*, 31; Scheuer, *Osama bin Laden*, 69, 166.

57 Bergen, *Holy War, Inc.*, 176-177; Coll, *The Bin Ladens*, 373-374; Johnsen, *The Last Refuge*, 8-10.

58 OBL, "Introduction," 114-115; OBL, "The Banishment of Communism from the Arabian Peninsula," ARC, 11 July 1994; Johnsen, *The Last Refuge*, 24-25.

59 Johnsen, *The Last Refuge*, 25-26, 35-38; Scheuer, *Through Our Enemies' Eyes*, 122.

60 Bergen, *The Rise and Fall of Osama bin Laden*, 56; Scheuer, *Osama bin Laden*, 80.

61 Abd-al-Karim and al-Nur, "Interview with Saudi businessman Usama bin Ladin"; Adaki, "Yemeni tribal leader joins AQAP"; Ahmed and Akins, "Making enemies in Yemen"; Al-Bahri and Malbrunot, *Guarding bin Laden*, 22-23; OBL, "Saudi Arabia supports the communists in Yemen," ARC, 7 June 1994.

62 Al-Bahri and Malbrunot, *Guarding bin Laden*, 22-23; OBL, "Saudi Arabia supports the communists in Yemen," ARC, 7 June 1994; Scheuer, *Osama bin Laden*, 80, 97.

63 OBL, "The Banishment of Communism from the Arabian Peninsula," ARC, 11 July 1994; Root, "A Sheikh's Life"; Scheuer, *Through Our Enemies Eyes*, 122; Worth, "Ex-Jihadist Defies Yemen's Leader."

64 Bergen, *The Osama bin Laden I Know*, 81; Hamid and Farrall, *The Arabs at War in Afghanistan*, 200-202; Scheuer, *Osama bin Laden*, 73-74.

65 Chipman, "Osama bin Laden and Guerrilla War," 163-170; Mitzcavitch, "Al Qaeda and Mao Zedong," 14-18; Zedong, *The Red Book*, 52-53; 64-65.

66 Chipman, "Osama bin Laden and Guerrilla War," 163-170; Mitzcavitch, "Al Qaeda and Mao Zedong," 14-18; Zedong, *The Red Book*, 52-53; 64-65.

67 Coll, *Ghost Wars*, 156-157; MacLeod, "The Paladin of Jihad," 51-52; Miller, "Greetings America. My Name is Osama bin Laden."; Timmerman, "This Man Wants You Dead," 51.

68 *AL-BAB.COM*, "Security incidents in Yemen, 1990-94," https://al-bab.com/security-incidents-yemen-1990-94; Hill, *Yemen Endures*, 113-115; Clark, *Yemen*, 98, 236-241; Al-Suwaidi et al., *The Yemeni War of 1994*, 27-31.

69 *AL-BAB.COM*, "Security incidents in Yemen"; Al-Suwaidi et al., *The Yemeni War of 1994*, 27-31, 37-38.

70 Johnsen, *The Last Refuge*, 21-23, 24-25; Al-Suwaidi et al., *The Yemeni War of 1994*, 37-38.

71 *AL-BAB.COM*, "Security incidents in Yemen"; Johnsen, *The Last Refuge*, 24-25; Al-Suwaidi et al., *The Yemeni War of 1994*, 62-64, 64-66.

72 Al-Suwaidi et al., *The Yemeni War of 1994*, 22, 23-26.

73 *AL-BAB.COM*, "Security incidents in Yemen"; Bergen, *Holy War, Inc.*, 176-177; Scheuer, *Through Our Enemies' Eyes*, 122.

74 *AL-BAB.COM*, "Security incidents in Yemen"; Scheuer, *Osama bin Laden*, 80; Al-Suwaidi et al., *The Yemeni War of 1994*, 22, 23-26.

75 Republic of Yemen – Political Forces Dialogue Committee, "The Document of Pledge and Accord, 1994," *Yemen Times*, 18 January 1994, https://al-bab.com/document-pledge-and-accord-1994.

[76] Republic of Yemen – Political Forces Dialogue Committee, "The Document of Pledge and Accord."
[77] Ibid.
[78] Abd-al-Karim and al-Nur, "Interview with Saudi businessman Usama bin Ladin"; OBL, "Saudi Arabia supports the communists in Yemen," ARC, 7 June 1994; Johnsen, *The Last Refuge*, 35-38; Republic of Yemen – Political Forces Dialogue Committee, "The Document of Pledge and Accord"; Scheuer, *Through Our Enemies Eyes*, 122.
[79] Brian Whitaker, "Fragile union at mercy of outside forces," *The Guardian*, 7 April 1994, https://al-bab.com/articles-section/fragile-union-mercy-outside-forces.
[80] Whitaker, "Fragile union at mercy of outside forces." As Whitaker points out here, al-Bid is also said to have been a descendant of Islam's Prophet, Muhammad, a factor rendering him an ethnic minority ruler as an *Adnani* Arab in *Qahtani*-majority Yemen, in addition to being a member of the ideologically minority Marxists in the overwhelmingly religious, tribal Sunni Muslim country.
[81] See, for example, OBL, "Our invitation to Give Advice and Reform," ARC, 12 April 1994; and Whitaker, "Fragile union at mercy of outside forces." Despite his superb and commendable reporting for *The Guardian* and other newspapers on the Yemeni Civil War of 1994, its origins, and its immediate aftermath, it should be noted here that Whitaker appears to have inadvertently misquoted the Yemenis with whom he spoke on this particular occasion, or, perhaps more likely, somewhat misinterpreted the precise meaning of their words, albeit slightly, as *Mashallah* means "God willed it," referring to a past event, while *Inshallah* means "God willing," referring to the outcome of a potential future event. Regardless, Whitaker is, of course, entirely correct in understanding the basic thrust of the Yemenis' comments, as those with whom he spoke appear to have referred to U.S. President Clinton as having willed the events that had previously transpired to occur due to Washington, D.C. and London's perceived intervention in the South Arabian country's internal affairs, for the sake of stability and the protection of U.S.-U.K. oil interests on the Arabian Peninsula.
[82] *Parliamentary Record – House of Lords*, 1st Session (1994), https://hansard.parliament.uk/Lords/1994-04-18/debates/c02bcf05-df47-4a34-a7ba-cfda2a2b604b/Yemen.
[83] *Parl. Rec. – House of Lords*, 1st Sess. (1994).
[84] Adaki, "Yemeni tribal leader joins AQAP"; Ahmed and Akins, "Making enemies in Yemen"; OBL, "Saudi Arabia supports the communists in Yemen," ARC, 7 June 1994; Boustany, "Civil War in Yemen"; Johnsen, *The Last Refuge*, 42-43.
[85] Ian Black and Brian Whitaker, "Yemen's rival armies turn on each other: failure to unite the two forces lies behind the struggle which is destroying the country from the inside, write Ian Black and Brian Whitaker," *The Guardian*, 6 May 1994, https://al-bab.com/articles-section/yemens-rival-armies-turn-each-other; Hurd and Noakes, "North and South Yemen," 48.
[86] Black and Whitaker, "Yemen's rival armies turn on each other"; Johnsen, *The Last Refuge*, 38-39; Al-Suwaidi et al., *The Yemeni War of 1994*, 83.
[87] Abd-al-Karim and al-Nur, "Interview with Saudi businessman Usama bin Ladin"; Al-Bahri and Malbrunot, *Guarding bin Laden*, 70, 218; Bergen, *Holy War, Inc.*, 31; OBL, "Saudi Arabia supports the communists in Yemen," ARC, 7 June 1994; Scheuer, *Osama bin Laden*, 69, 166.
[88] Abd-al-Karim and al-Nur, "Interview with Saudi businessman Usama bin Ladin"; Black and Whitaker, "Yemen's rival armies turn on each other"; Galeotti, *Afghanistan*, 15;

Johnsen, *The Last Refuge*, 38-39; Malkin, "Reagan and the End of the Cold War"; Al-Suwaidi et al., *The Yemeni War of 1994*, 83; *Wilson Center Digital Archive, Collection 76*, "Excerpt from transcript, CPSU CC Politburo meeting," 20 September 1979.

[89] Abd-al-Karim and al-Nur, "Interview with Saudi businessman Usama bin Ladin"; OBL, "Saudi Arabia supports the communists in Yemen," ARC, 7 June 1994; Howe, "Southern Yemen blends Marxism"; Hurd and Noakes, "North and South Yemen," 48; Ramani, "North Korea's Balancing Act"; Republic of Yemen – Political Forces Dialogue Committee, "The Document of Pledge and Accord"; Scheuer, *Osama bin Laden*, 69, 166; Al-Suwaidi et al., *The Yemeni War of 1994*, 87-88.

[90] Al-Bahri and Malbrunot, *Guarding bin Laden*, 22-23; OBL, "The Banishment of Communism from the Arabian Peninsula," ARC, 11 July 1994; Black and Whitaker, "Yemen's rival armies turn on each other"; Coll, *The Bin Ladens*, 373-374; Johnsen, *The Last Refuge*, 24-25; Scheuer, *Osama bin Laden*, 80.

[91] Black and Whitaker, "Yemen's rival armies turn on each other"; Johnsen, *The Last Refuge*, 35-38, 38-39; Al-Suwaidi et al., *The Yemeni War of 1994*, 87-88.

[92] Black and Whitaker, "Yemen's rival armies turn on each other"; Johnsen, *The Last Refuge*, 38-39.

[93] Nora Boustany, "Foreigners Evacuated From War-Torn Yemen," *The Washington Post*, 8 May 1994, https://www.washingtonpost.com/archive/politics/1994/05/08/foreigners-evacuated-from-war-torn-yemen/894086e5-d65b-406e-a647-eda73b893d70/.

[94] Bergen, *Holy War, Inc.*, 176-177; OBL, "Saudi Arabia supports the communists in Yemen," ARC, 7 June 1994; Johnsen, *The Last Refuge*, 38-39; Scheuer, *Osama bin Laden*, 80, 97.

[95] Boustany, "Foreigners Evacuated." Parentheses in the original.

[96] See, for example, Azzam, "Sheikh Abdullah Azzam said about Usama Bin Ladin," 152-153; Bergen, *The Osama bin Laden I Know*, 51-52, 53, 59-60; OBL, "Introduction," 80, 81, 82-84; Darraz, "Impressions," 95-96, 102-103; Scheuer, *Osama bin Laden*, 75, 215n117; and Al-Qarni, "Bin Laden's Former 'Mufti' Musa Al-Qarni Talks about the Jihad in Afghanistan."

[97] Al-Bahri and Malbrunot, *Guarding bin Laden*, 22-23; OBL, "Saudi Arabia supports the communists in Yemen," ARC, 7 June 1994; OBL, "The Banishment of Communism from the Arabian Peninsula," ARC, 11 July 1994; OBL, "Introduction," 114-115; Bergen, *The Osama bin Laden I Know*, 54-55; Coll, *The Bin Ladens*, 373-374; Darraz, "Impressions," 109-110; Johnsen, *The Last Refuge*, 21-23, 24-25, 35-38, 38-39; Scheuer, *Osama bin Laden*, 80; Al-Suwaidi et al., *The Yemeni War of 1994*, 62-64, 64-66.

[98] Atwan, "My weekend with Osama bin Laden"; Bergen, *Holy War, Inc.*, 176-177; Johnsen, *The Last Refuge*, 35-38, 38-39; Scheuer, *Osama bin Laden*, 80, 216n8-9.

[99] OBL, "Introduction," 114-115; Darraz, "Impressions," 95-96, 102-103, 109-110; Bergen, *The Osama bin Laden I Know*, 51-52, 53, 59-60; Reed, "Soviets race to cut rebel supply lines"; Scheuer, *Osama bin Laden*, 63; Shah, "SOVIET-AFGHAN CONFLICT"; Tawil, *Brothers in Arms*, 18.

[100] Abd-al-Karim and al-Nur, "Interview with Saudi businessman Usama bin Ladin"; Al-Bahri and Malbrunot, *Guarding bin Laden*, 22-23; OBL, "The Banishment of Communism from the Arabian Peninsula," ARC, 11 July 1994; OBL, ARC, 19 September 1994; Coll, *The Bin Ladens*, 373-374; Scheuer, *Osama bin Laden*, 80.

[101] Johnsen, *The Last Refuge*, 35-38; Root, "A Sheikh's Life"; Worth, "Ex-Jihadist Defies Yemen's Leader."

[102] Johnsen, *The Last Refuge*, 35-38, 38-39; Al-Suwaidi et al., *The Yemeni War of 1994*, 62-64, 64-66.
[103] OBL, "Saudi Arabia supports the communists in Yemen," ARC, 7 June 1994; Johnsen, *The Last Refuge*, 35-38, 42-43.
[104] Chris Hedges, "In Yemen's Civil War, South Fights On, Gloomily," *The New York Times*, 16 May 1994, https://www.nytimes.com/1994/05/16/world/in-yemen-s-civil-war-south-fights-on-gloomily.html.
[105] Hedges, "In Yemen's Civil War."
[106] Ibid.
[107] The Russian General Staff, *The Soviet-Afghan War*, 60.
[108] Johnsen, *The Last Refuge*, 35-38, 38-39; Al-Suwaidi et al., *The Yemeni War of 1994*, 62-64, 64-66.
[109] Abd-al-Karim and al-Nur, "Interview with Saudi businessman Usama bin Ladin"; OBL, "Saudi Arabia supports the communists in Yemen," ARC, 7 June 1994; Johnsen, *The Last Refuge*, 35-38; Reuters, "Al Qaeda attack kills 20 Yemeni forces in Abyan"; Zenn, "Brief."
[110] Nora Boustany, "North's Forces Gain Ground in Yemen War," *The Washington Post*, 18 May 1994, https://www.washingtonpost.com/archive/politics/1994/05/18/norths-forces-gain-ground-in-yemeni-war/5bbd6ee5-eec2-4920-abb4-7b204dadab3c/.
[111] Boustany, "North's Forces Gain Ground."
[112] Ibid.
[113] Chris Hedges, "THE WORLD; How Yemen Is Coming Undone," *The New York Times*, 29 May 1994, https://www.nytimes.com/1994/05/29/weekinreview/the-world-how-yemen-is-coming-undone.html.
[114] OBL, "Saudi Arabia supports the communists in Yemen," ARC, 7 June 1994; Hedges, "THE WORLD; Johnsen, *The Last Refuge*, 35-38; Root, "A Sheikh's Life"; Worth, "Ex-Jihadist Defies Yemen's Leader."
[115] Marieke Brandt, *Tribes and Politics in Yemen: A History of the Houthi Conflict* (New York: Oxford University Press, 2017), 7, 11, 15-18; Hedges, "THE WORLD."
[116] Al-Bahri and Malbrunot, *Guarding bin Laden*, 22-23; OBL, "Saudi Arabia supports the communists in Yemen," ARC, 7 June 1994; Boustany, "Civil War in Yemen"; Hedges, "In Yemen's Civil War"; Hurd and Noakes, "North and South Yemen," 48.
[117] *Congressional Record – House of Representatives*, 103rd Congress, 2nd Session (1994), pt.? Government Publishing Office, https://babel.hathitrust.org/cgi/pt?id=pst.000022817129&view=1up&seq=1&skin=2021.
[118] *Cong. Rec. – House of Representatives*, 103rd Cong. 2nd Sess. (1994).
[119] Ibid.
[120] Ibid.
[121] Boustany, "Civil War in Yemen"; *Cong. Rec. – House of Representatives*, 103rd Cong. 2nd Sess. (1994).
[122] OBL, "Saudi Arabia supports the communists in Yemen," ARC, 7 June 1994; OBL, "The Banishment of Communism from the Arabian Peninsula," ARC, 11 July 1994; *Cong. Rec. – House of Representatives*, 103rd Cong. 2nd Sess. (1994); Hurd and Noakes, "North and South Yemen," 48; Ramani, "North Korea's Balancing Act."
[123] Brian Whitaker, "Yemen's north tightens grip," *The Guardian*, 15 June 1994, https://al-bab.com/articles-section/yemens-north-tightens-grip.
[124] Whitaker, "Yemen's north tightens grip." Whitaker's observations here appear to be quite accurate considering Yemen's history and its peoples' record of dogged defiance of

outside invaders, occupiers, and unpopular, foreign-backed central governments. Like the Pashtuns of Afghanistan and Pakistan, South Arabia's indigenous *Qahtanis*, the aboriginal people of all of Yemen, southern Saudi Arabia (about half of the Kingdom's tribal population), and the far western part of Oman, have successfully defied and resisted the repeated attempts of imperial powers to colonize or dominate them since ancient times. Between 26 and 24 BC, Roman forces under Gaius Aelius Gallus invaded the ancient South Arabian Kingdom of Saba, known in the Holy Bible as Sheba, on orders from Caesar Augustus due to the reputation of the region, known to the Romans as *Arabia Felix* meaning "Arabia the Blest" or "Happy Arabia," as hosting abundant, green wooded areas rich in frankincense, myrrh, and cinnamon trees, particularly in bin Laden's ancestral Hadramut Province, the homeland of his father's native Kenda tribe and the location of his family's impoverished home village of al-Rubat Ba'eshn in the valley of Wadi Doan. The ancient Greek geographer Strabo of Amasia, reportedly a close friend and contemporary of Gallus's, discusses in detail the Roman Army's failed incursion in South Arabia in Book 16 of his magisterial *Geography*. Strabo states, "The city of the Sabaeans, Mariaba [Marib], is situated upon a well-wooded mountain; and it has a king who is authority in lawsuits and everything else," and describes the region's cultural caste system that reportedly persists in modern Yemen despite its official abolishment in 1962, stating, "Arabia Felix is split up into five kingdoms [sic, classes], one of which comprises the warriors, who fight for all; another the farmers, who supply food to all the rest; another, those who engage in the mechanical arts; another, the myrrh-bearing country and another the frankincense-bearing country, although the same countries produce cassia, cinnamon, and nard." Nasser al-Bahri's brief, detailed description of Yemen's official class system that continued to unofficially exist well after 1962 bears remarkable resemblance to Strabo's, with the former chief bodyguard for bin Laden providing a detailed description of his family's origins as *qabili* warriors whose tribes had fought for themselves and Yemen's peasants against the British and later resisted the minority rule of both Shia monarchists and descendants of the Prophet, such as the communist al-Bid and his YSP. Strabo states that despite Augustus's high expectations for a quick victory, Gallus's expedition failed due to his army's overextended supply lines and his failure to prepare for a protracted war in the local desert environment that proved more formidable than Rome had expected. The Roman leadership also appears to have underestimated the tenacity and determination of South Arabia's warriors to resist them, as Strabo states that Gallus ordered a retreat to Roman-ruled Egypt after besieging the entrenched local forces at Marib for a week and failing to capture the city. According to the Greek historian Arrian of Nicomedia in his account of Alexander the Great's campaigns, Alexander's armies suffered similar repulses at the hands of the ancient Pashtun tribes as they approached Bactria, the location of the Pashtun dominated parts of modern-day Afghanistan and Pakistan, failing, like other invaders in later history, to impose the central government of their choice on the defiant local tribes. The substantive point here is that powerful rulers, throughout history, have repeated the mistakes of their imperial predecessors in seeking to impose the central governments of their choice on the defiant, tribal peoples of rural Afghanistan and Yemen since pre-Islamic times, and bin Laden's staunch support for the devout Islamic guerrillas in both countries appears to have helped him build a solid personal rapport and strengthen al-Qaeda's local support structure within these fiercely independent warrior societies. Bin Laden, despite being killed in action on 2 May 2011 by U.S. troops in Pakistan, left behind a lethal, anti-Western legacy that crosses official Muslim state borders, and the al-Qaeda chief, therefore, remains a potent threat a dozen years after his death as his example is likely to continue motivating aspiring holy warriors hailing from these countries, as well as their tribal, religious kinsmen in the neighboring rural, ethnic Pashtun and *Qahtani* (South Arabian) parts of Pakistan and Saudi Arabia, respectively, to take up arms against those he deemed the foes of their faith and brethren. See Strabo of Amasia, *Geography: Books 15-16*, trans. Horace Leonard Jones (Cambridge, MA: Harvard University Press, 1930), 237, 309, 347-351, 352-357, 358-362, 364, 365-373; Arrian of Nicomedia, *The Campaigns of Alexander*, trans. Aubrey de Selincourt (New York: Penguin Books, 1971), 237-254; and, for the above biographical information on bin Laden and al-Bahri's familial relations with Yemen's tribes and the country's unofficial caste system, see al-Bahri and Malbrunot, *Guarding bin Laden*, 12-13; and Scheuer, *Osama bin Laden*, 21-22.

[125] OBL, "Saudi Arabia supports the communists in Yemen," ARC, 7 June 1994; Boustany, "Civil War in Yemen"; Hedges, "In Yemen's Civil War"; Hurd and Noakes, "North and South Yemen," 48.
Whitaker, "Yemen's north tightens grip."

[126] Johnsen, *The Last Refuge*, 42-43; Whitaker, "Yemen's north tightens grip."

[127] OBL, "Saudi Arabia supports the communists in Yemen," ARC, 7 June 1994; OBL, "The Banishment of Communism from the Arabian Peninsula," ARC, 11 July 1994; Boustany, "Civil War in Yemen"; Johnsen, *The Last Refuge*, 42-43; Al-Suwaidi et al., *The Yemeni War of 1994*, 87-88.

[128] *Parliamentary Record – House of Commons*, 1st Session (1994), https://hansard.parliament.uk/commons/1994-07-01/debates/6304a043-ba3f-464d-b7e3-dab551dc444d/Yemen.

[129] *Parl. Rec. – House of Commons*, 1st Sess. (1994).

[130] OBL, "The Banishment of Communism from the Arabian Peninsula," ARC, 11 July 1994; Boustany, "Civil War in Yemen"; *Cong. Rec. – House of Representatives*, 103rd Cong. 2nd Sess. (1994); Johnsen, *The Last Refuge*, 43-44; *Parl. Rec. – House of Commons*, 1st Sess. (1994); Ramani, "North Korea's Balancing Act"; Al-Suwaidi et al., *The Yemeni War of 1994*, 87-88.

[131] The Associated Press, "Yemen Claims Victory."

[132] Ibid.

[133] Ibid.

[134] Ibid.

[135] UK Prime Minister, "Mr Major's Press Conference in Naples – 10 July 1994," *John Major Archive*, 10 July 1994, https://johnmajorarchive.org.uk/1994/07/10/mr-majors-press-conference-in-naples-10-july-1994/.

[136] UK Prime Minister, "Mr Major's Press Conference in Naples."

[137] Ibid.

[138] Brian Whitaker, "Yemen reunited by force," *Middle East International*, 22 July 1994, https://al-bab.com/articles-section/yemen-reunited-force.

[139] Al-Suwaidi et al., *The Yemeni War of 1994*, 22, 23-26, 62-64, 64-66; Whitaker, "Yemen reunited by force."

[140] Al-Bahri and Malbrunot, *Guarding bin Laden*, 163-164; Johnsen, *The Last Refuge*, 41.

[141] OBL, "Saudi Arabia supports the communists in Yemen," ARC, 7 June 1994; OBL, "The Banishment of Communism from the Arabian Peninsula," ARC, 11 July 1994; OBL, ARC, 19 September 1994; OBL, "Open Letter for Sheikh Bin Baz," ARC, 29 December 1994; OBL,

Messages to the World, 76; Coll, *The Bin Ladens*, 373-374; *Cong. Rec. – House of Representatives*, 103rd Cong. 2nd Sess. (1994); *Parl. Rec. – House of Commons*, 1st Sess. (1994); Scheuer, *Osama bin Laden*, 80; UK Prime Minister, "Mr Major's Press Conference in Naples."

[142] OBL, "Saudi Arabia supports the communists in Yemen," ARC, 7 June 1994; OBL, "The Banishment of Communism from the Arabian Peninsula," ARC, 11 July 1994; OBL, ARC, 19 September 1994; OBL, "Open Letter for Sheikh Bin Baz," ARC, 29 December 1994; OBL, *Messages to the World*, 76; Coll, *The Bin Ladens*, 373-374; Scheuer, *Osama bin Laden*, 80, 97.

[143] OBL, ARC, 19 September 1994; OBL, "Open Letter for Sheikh Bin Baz," ARC, 29 December 1994; OBL, *Messages to the World*, 76; Coll, *The Bin Ladens*, 373-374; Scheuer, *Osama bin Laden*, 80, 97.

[144] Al-Bahri and Malbrunot, *Guarding bin Laden*, 70, 170-173, 218; OBL, "Saudi Arabia supports the communists in Yemen," ARC, 7 June 1994; OBL, "The Banishment of Communism from the Arabian Peninsula," ARC, 11 July 1994; OBL, ARC, 19 September 1994; OBL, "Open Letter for Sheikh Bin Baz," ARC, 29 December 1994; OBL, *Messages to the World*, 76; OBL, "Jihad Against Jews and Crusaders"; OBL, "Full transcript of bin Ladin's speech"; Lewis, "License to Kill."

[145] OBL, ARC, 19 September 1994; OBL, "Open Letter for Sheikh Bin Baz," ARC, 29 December 1994; OBL, *Messages to the World*, 76-77.

[146] OBL, ARC, 19 September 1994; OBL, "Open Letter for Sheikh Bin Baz," ARC, 29 December 1994; OBL, *Messages to the World*, 76; Coll, *The Bin Ladens*, 373-374; *Cong. Rec. – House of Representatives*, 103rd Cong. 2nd Sess. (1994); *Parl. Rec. – House of Lords*, 1st Sess. (1994); *Parl. Rec. – House of Commons*, 1st Sess. (1994); Scheuer, *Osama bin Laden*, 80; UK Prime Minister, "Mr Major's Press Conference in Naples."

[147] OBL, ARC, 19 September 1994; OBL, "Open Letter for Sheikh Bin Baz," ARC, 29 December 1994; OBL, *Messages to the World*, 76; Black and Whitaker, "Yemen's rival armies turn on each other"; Hurd and Noakes, "North and South Yemen," 48; Johnsen, *The Last Refuge*, 35-38, 38-39; Al-Suwaidi et al., *The Yemeni War of 1994*, 62-64, 64-66.

[148] OBL, ARC, 19 September 1994; OBL, "Open Letter for Sheikh Bin Baz," ARC, 29 December 1994; OBL, *Messages to the World*, 76; Coll, *The Bin Ladens*, 373-374; *Cong. Rec. – House of Representatives*, 103rd Cong. 2nd Sess. (1994); *Parl. Rec. – House of Lords*, 1st Sess. (1994); *Parl. Rec. – House of Commons*, 1st Sess. (1994); Scheuer, *Osama bin Laden*, 80; UK Prime Minister, "Mr Major's Press Conference in Naples."

[149] OBL, "Saudi Arabia supports the communists in Yemen," ARC, 7 June 1994; Boustany, "Civil War in Yemen"; Hedges, "In Yemen's Civil War"; Hurd and Noakes, "North and South Yemen," 48.

[150] Abd-al-Karim and al-Nur, "Interview with Saudi businessman Usama bin Ladin"; OBL, "Saudi Arabia supports the communists in Yemen," ARC, 7 June 1994; Howe, "Southern Yemen blends Marxism"; Hurd and Noakes, "North and South Yemen," 48; Ramani, "North Korea's Balancing Act"; Republic of Yemen – Political Forces Dialogue Committee, "The Document of Pledge and Accord"; Scheuer, *Osama bin Laden*, 69, 166; Al-Suwaidi et al., *The Yemeni War of 1994*, 87-88.

[151] *Cong. Rec. – House of Representatives*, 103rd Cong. 2nd Sess. (1994); Hedges, "In Yemen's Civil War"; *Parl. Rec. – House of Lords*, 1st Sess. (1994); *Parl. Rec. – House of Commons*, 1st Sess. (1994); The Associated Press, "Yemen Claims Victory."; Whitaker, "Yemen's north tightens grip."

[152] Abd-al-Karim and al-Nur, "Interview with Saudi businessman Usama bin Ladin"; Al-Bahri and Malbrunot, *Guarding bin Laden*, 22-23; Azzam, "Join the Caravan," 16-17; Bergen, *The Osama bin Laden I Know*, 51-52; OBL, "Introduction," 77; Darraz, "Impressions," 102; Scheuer, *Osama bin Laden*, 61-62.

[153] OBL, "Saudi Arabia supports the communists in Yemen," ARC, 7 June 1994; Boustany, "Civil War in Yemen"; Hedges, "In Yemen's Civil War"; Hurd and Noakes, "North and South Yemen," 48; Johnsen, *The Last Refuge*, 42-43; Whitaker, "Yemen's north tightens grip."

[154] Bergen, *Holy War, Inc.*, 176-177; Boustany, "Civil War in Yemen"; Hedges, "In Yemen's Civil War"; Hurd and Noakes, "North and South Yemen," 48; Johnsen, *The Last Refuge*, 42-43.

[155] OBL, ARC, 19 September 1994; OBL, "Open Letter for Sheikh Bin Baz," ARC, 29 December 1994; Whitaker, "Yemen reunited by force."

[156] Al-Batarfi, "Growing up with Osama"; Ibn Khaldun, *The Muqaddimah*, 152-154, 351-352; Scheuer, *Osama bin Laden*, 37-38.

[157] Bin Laden, bin Laden, and Sasson, *Growing Up bin Laden*, 19; Ibn Khaldun, *The Muqaddimah*, 278-279; Scheuer, *Osama bin Laden*, 37-38.

[158] Al-Bahri and Malbrunot, *Guarding bin Laden*, 170-173.

[159] Fisk, "10 July 1996: Arab rebel leader warns the British."

[160] Ibid. Bin Laden proceeded to remind Fisk that, "Danger is a part of our life – do you not realise that we [the Afghan and Arab mujahedin collectively] spent 10 years fighting against the Russians and the KGB? ... When we were fighting the Russians here in Afghanistan, 10,000 Saudis came here to fight over a period of 10 years." Although Fisk at the time dismissed bin Laden's reply as being filled with, "contempt," there are several key points that the al-Qaeda chief addressed in his comments that the researcher cannot and should not ignore. Bin Laden, as he had already written in several of his ARC letters and as he did once again in his 1997 and 1998 interviews with Peter Arnett and John Miller respectively, implicitly commended the Soviet Army and KGB on being a formidable opponent whose battlefield ferocity helped teach him and his Arab guerrilla comrades a healthy respect for their vaunted superpower enemies. Moreover, his comment on the 10,000 Saudi guerrilla fighters, many of whom shared his ethnic Yemeni origins and staunch adherence to militant Salafism, seems like a realistic assessment rather than wartime bravado as he recalled in a later interview that, "more than 15,000" Arab fighters had flocked to the guerrilla ranks during the Soviet-Afghan War, nearly all of whom arrived after the 1987 Battle of Jaji, thereby revealing, yet again, his careful, businessman-like calculation that very few Arabs contributed to the holy war effort and ultimate victory over the communists in comparison to their Afghan brethren. Finally, bin Laden's comment to Fisk appears consistent with his other warnings to the U.K. newspaper journalist during the interview in cautioning *The Independent's* readers that the Afghan and non-Afghan Salafi fighters had already persevered against one superpower's merciless, mechanized forces and airpower and that the governments of Britain, France, and the United States should neither, therefore, underestimate nor ridicule the fighting capabilities that the jihadis had acquired over the course of a decade in battle with the Soviet Union's globally feared war machine and intelligence agencies. For bin Laden's consistent comments on these matters in several key letters and other interviews, see Arnett, "Transcript of Osama Bin Ladin interview"; OBL, "Saudi Arabia supports the communists in Yemen," ARC, 7 June 1994; OBL, "The Banishment of Communism from the Arabian Peninsula," ARC, 11 July 1994; OBL, "Open Letter for Sheikh Bin Baz," ARC,

29 December 1994; OBL, *Messages to the World*, 76; MacLeod, "The Paladin of Jihad," 51-52; Miller, "Greetings America. My Name is Osama bin Laden."

[161] Ibid.

[162] Ibid. In this fascinating and insightful newspaper report, Fisk recalls that, "My journey to him [bin Laden] took me across miles of devastated villages and fields in the rocky mountainsides of the country [Afghanistan] where he once fought Soviet invaders, and it culminated in a remote village where dozens of his [Arab] mujahedin, dressed in Afghan clothes, stood guard as he spoke." Fisk reports that bin Laden railed softly but resentfully against the United States, Britain, and Israel, the three main countries on which he subsequently declared war less than a month later and again in 1998, replying to the U.K. journalist's question, "It is not a declaration of war – it's a real description of the situation [from the Salafist perspective]. This doesn't mean declaring war against the west and western people – but against the American regime [and its European allies] which is against every Muslim." After pausing the interview to participate in communal prayer alongside his men, bin Laden returned to elaborate further to Fisk that the Islamist militants, had executed the recent terror attacks on U.S. troops based at the Riyadh and Khobar Towers military housing complexes in Saudi Arabia, "as a result of American behaviour against Muslims," particularly the U.S.-U.K. governments' perceived support for the Israeli leadership's alleged, "massacre of Muslims in Palestine and Lebanon – of Sabra and Shatila and Qana," making no secret of his and al-Qaeda's war motivations to attack the Americans and their Anglo-French allies due to a list of specific governmental policies in the Muslim world, rather than secular, U.S. and Western democratic freedoms, that he and the jihadi group's supporters regarded as unforgiveable Islamophobic assaults. For another example, among the many other sources cited throughout this book, see bin Laden's 1996 interview for the militant Islamist magazine *Nida'ul Islam*, in which the exiled al-Qaeda leader explicitly lists among as his and the international Salafi jihadi movement's grievances, "the recent Qana massacre in Lebanon, and the death of more than six hundred thousands (600,000) Iraqi children because of the shortage of food and medicine which resulted from the boycotts and sanctions against the Muslim Iraqi people, also their [the United States' and UN's] withholding of arms from the Muslims of Bosnian Hercegovina leaving them prey to the Christian Serbians who massacred and raped in a manner not seen in contemporary history…. As for what America accuses us of, of killing the innocent people, they have not been able to offer any evidence, despite the magnitude of their expenditure on their intelligence services. Despite what our history is witnessing in the Afghan phase of the Jihad. This [the anti-Soviet defensive jihad] was also unstained with any blood of innocent [Soviet] people, despite the inhuman Russian campaign against our [Muslim] women, our children, and our brothers in Afghanistan… Similar is our history with respect to our differences with the Saudi regime, all that has been proved is our joy at the killing of the American Soldiers in Riyadh and Khobar, and these are the sentiments of every Muslim." See Nida'ul Islam, "Mujahid Usamah Bin Ladin."

[163] MacLeod, "The Paladin of Jihad," 51-52

[164] Atwan, "My weekend with Osama bin Laden"; Scheuer, *Osama bin Laden*, 80, 216n8-9. Bracket quotes in the original.

[165] See Coll, *The Bin Ladens*, 374; and Scheuer, Osama bin Laden, 80, 216n7.

[166] Worth, "Ex-Jihadist Defies Yemen's Leader."

167 See, for example, Adaki, "Yemeni tribal leader joins AQAP"; Ahmed and Akins, "Making enemies in Yemen"; OBL, "Saudi Arabia supports the communists in Yemen," ARC, 7 June 1994; and Worth, "Ex-Jihadist Defies Yemen's Leader."

168 See, for example, Bergen, *Holy War, Inc.*, 176-177; Coll, *The Bin Ladens*, 373-374; Scheuer, *Osama bin Laden*, ix, 134-135.

169 OBL, "Jihad Against Jews and Crusaders"; OBL, "Full transcript of bin Ladin's speech"; Bergen, *The Osama bin Laden I Know*, 29; Coll, *Ghost Wars*, 156-157; Lewis, "License to Kill"; MacLeod, "The Paladin of Jihad," 51-52; Miller, "Greetings America. My Name is Osama bin Laden"; Scheuer, *Osama bin Laden*, 46, 53-54, 60, 61-62; Timmerman, "This Man Wants You Dead," 52-53.

170 OBL, "Jihad Against Jews and Crusaders"; OBL, "Full transcript of bin Ladin's speech"; MacLeod, "The Paladin of Jihad," 51-52; Miller, "Greetings America. My Name is Osama bin Laden"; Scheuer, *Osama bin Laden*, 46, 53-54, 60, 61-62; Timmerman, "This Man Wants You Dead," 52-53.

171 Atwan, "My weekend with Osama bin Laden"; Al-Bahri and Malbrunot, *Guarding bin Laden*, 22-23; OBL, "Saudi Arabia supports the communists in Yemen," ARC, 7 June 1994; OBL, "The Banishment of Communism from the Arabian Peninsula," ARC, 11 July 1994; OBL, "Introduction," 114-115; Bergen, *The Osama bin Laden I Know*, 54-55; Coll, *The Bin Ladens*, 373-374; Darraz, "Impressions," 109-110; Scheuer, *Osama bin Laden*, 116-117.

172 Rubin, *Afghanistan*, 239-240.

173 David J. Wasserstein, *Black Banners of ISIS: The Roots of the New Caliphate* (New Haven, CT: Yale University Press, 2017), 15-19.

174 Scheuer, *Osama bin Laden*, 134-135, 234n16; Ummat Special Correspondent, "Usama bin Laden Says the Al-Qa'idah Group had Nothing to Do with the 11 September Attacks," *Ummat Karachi*, 28 September 2001, https://scholarship.tricolib.brynmawr.edu/bit stream/handle/10066/4781/OBL20010928.pdf?sequence=3&isAllowed=y.

175 Scheuer, *Osama bin Laden*, ix.

176 See, for example, Adaki, "Yemeni tribal leader joins AQAP"; Ahmed and Akins, "Making enemies in Yemen"; Reuters, "Al Qaeda attack kills 20 Yemeni forces in Abyan"; Staff Writer with AFP, "27 Dead as AQAP Launches Attack"; Zenn, "Brief."

177 OBL, "Jihad Against Jews and Crusaders"; OBL, "Full transcript of bin Ladin's speech"; Ummat Special Correspondent, "Usama bin Laden."

178 RFE/RL, "Interview: Hamid Mir, The Last Man to Interview Osama Bin Laden," *Radio Free Europe/Radio Liberty*, 2 May 2011, https://www.rferl.org/amp/interview_hamid_mir_last_man_to_interview_osama_bin_laden/16800723.html.

179 Stefano Piazza and Luciano Tirinnanzi, "Hamir Mir: When Mullah Omar wanted to send bin Laden to Chechnya," trans. Carol Simonetti, *Panorama*, 21 September 2021, https://www.panorama.it/news/hamid-mir-mullah-omar-bin-laden-chechnya; RFE/RL, "Interview."

180 Fawaz A. Gerges, "The Islamic State Has Become a Resilient Insurgency: The group may no longer have its caliphate, but its far from defeated," *Foreign Policy*, 7 February 2022, https://foreignpolicy.com/2022/02/07/qurayshi-death-leader-islamic-state-current-strength/.

181 Gregory Waters, "ISIS beats back Wagner offensive in central Syria," *Middle East Institute*, 21 April 2023, https://www.mei.edu/publications/isis-beats-back-wagner-offensive-central-syria.

182 Gavin Butler, "ISIS-K Is Waging a New War in Afghanistan – This Time Against China," *Vice News*, 1 March 2023, https://www.vice.com/en/article/dy7aqw/isis-anti-china-war-afghanistan; Ebrahim Noroozi and Dasha Litvinova, "Suicide attack at Russia embassy in Kabul kills 2 diplomats," *AP*, 5 September 2022, https://apnews.com/article/afghanistan-russia-ukraine-explosions-kabul-00bf5815018fb152be8784f6f3af2557.

183 Brian Carter, Kathryn Tyson, Liam Karr, Peter Mills, and Karolina Hird, "Salafi-Jihadi Movement Weekly Update, July 5, 2023," *Critical Threats With ISW*, 5 July 2023, https://www.criticalthreats.org/analysis/salafi-jihadi-movement-weekly-update-july-5-2023.

184 Carter, et al., "Salafi-Jihadi Movement Weekly Update."

185 MEMRI (Unattributed Report), "AQAP Leader Batarfi: Rapprochement Between Saudi Arabia And Iran Indicates Defeat Of Former; Sunnis In Yemen And Saudi Arabia Should Learn From Taliban, Wage Jihad Against 'Agents Of Iran And U.S.'," *MEMRI Jihad & Terrorism Threat Monitor*, 1 May 2023, https://www.memri.org/jttm/aqap-leader-batarfi-rapprochement-between-saudi-arabia-and-iran-indicates-defeat-former-sunnis.

186 MEMRI (Unattributed Report), "Al-Qaeda In The Arabian Peninsula (AQAP) Claims Drone And IED Attacks On High Ranking Yemeni Officer In Shabwah," *MEMRI Cyberterrorism & Jihad Lab*, 31 May 2023, https://www.memri.org/cjlab/al-qaeda-arabian-peninsula-aqap-claims-drone-and-ied-attacks-high-ranking-yemeni-officer; Staff Writer with AFP, "27 Dead as AQAP Launches Attack on Yemen Separatists," *TheDefensePost*, 6 September 2022, https://www.thedefensepost.com/2022/09/06/al-qaeda-attack-yemen-separatists/; The New Arab Staff & Agencies, "Al-Qaeda releases new video of 'seriously ill' UN worker abducted in Yemen," *The New Arab*, 13 June 2023, https://www.newarab.com/news/yemen-al-qaeda-releases-new-video-abducted-un-worker?amp.

187 MEMRI, "Al-Qaeda In The Arabian Peninsula"; Reuters, "Al Qaeda attack kills 20 Yemeni forces in Abyan"; Staff Writer with AFP, "27 Dead as AQAP Launches Attack"; Zenn, "Brief."

188 Bin Laden, bin Laden, and Sasson, *Growing Up bin Laden*, 45; Daily Mail Reporter, "I taught judo to Osama bin Laden"; Loh and Tai, "Osama bin Laden a serious student."

189 Al-Bahri and Malbrunot, *Guarding bin Laden*, 217-220; Mashal, "How the Taliban Outlasted a Superpower"; Moore, "What Is the Taliban's 'Red Unit'?; Rubin, *Afghanistan*, 246; Scheuer, *Osama bin Laden*, 116-117; Zaeef, *My Life with the Taliban*, 229-231.

190 Al-Bahri and Malbrunot, *Guarding bin Laden*, 217-220; Daily Mail Reporter, "I taught judo to Osama bin Laden"; Loh and Tai, "Osama bin Laden a serious student"; Scheuer, *Osama bin Laden*, 116-117.

191 Marx, *The Eighteenth Brumaire*, 15.

192 Scheuer, *Osama bin Laden*, 21-22. As Scheuer and other bin Laden biographers have explained, while bin Laden's mother, Allia, immigrated to the Kingdom from Latakia, Syria to marry his father, Muhammad, her family, like her husband and his family, also hailed from Yemen and had immigrated from the South Arabian nation to Syria at some point before her birth. See also, Bin Laden, bin Laden, and Sasson, *Growing Up bin Laden*, 4, for the brief account of Allia's family's Yemeni origins as recounted by her niece, Osama's first wife, Najwa bin Laden.

193 Arnett, "Transcript of Osama Bin Ladin interview"; Bergen, *The Osama bin Laden I Know*, 29; Coll, *Ghost Wars*, 156-157; MacLeod, "The Paladin of Jihad," 51-52; Miller,

"Greetings America. My Name is Osama bin Laden"; Scheuer, *Osama bin Laden*, 46, 53-54, 60, 61-62; Timmerman, "This Man Wants You Dead," 52-53.

[194] Fisk, "Anti-Soviet Warrior puts his army on the road to peace"; MacLeod, "The Paladin of Jihad," 51-52; Miller, "Greetings America. My Name is Osama bin Laden"; Nida'ul Islam, "Mujahid Usamah Bin Ladin"; Timmerman, "This Man Wants You Dead," 55-57.

[195] Scheuer, *Osama bin Laden*, 116-117.

[196] Marx, *The Eighteenth Brumaire*, 94, 147n43. It should be noted here, as the editors of the 1852 text's 1994 edition explain in note 43 on page 147, that Marx is, himself, paraphrasing the work *Deipnosophistae* or *"Dinner-Table Philosophers"* written by the late second and early third-century Greek scholar Athenaeus of Naucratis, in which the ancient Greek writer describes King Agesilaus of Sparta cautioning Pharoah Tachos of Egypt that while he may seem to the Egyptian ruler as being small in stature, like a mouse, he is, in time, capable of becoming a fierce, formidable lion. On page 94, Marx paraphrases Athanaeus while attributing a similar retort to Napoleon III, stating, "And [France's] parliament, stricken, disintegrated and death-tainted as it was, could not prevail upon itself to see in its duel with the grotesque chief of the Society of December 10 [Louis Bonaparte] anything but a duel with a bedbug. But Bonaparte answered the party of Order as Agesilaus did King Agis [sic, Tachos]: *'I seem to thee an ant, but one day I shall be a lion.'"* Italics in the original. And, as stated in Chapter 2 of this book and the sources cited therein, the name Osama, ironically, means lion.

[197] Darraz, "Impressions," 94; MacLeod, "The Paladin of Jihad," 51-52; Miller, "Greetings America. My Name is Osama bin Laden."; Scheuer, *Osama bin Laden*, 61; Timmerman, "This Man Wants You Dead," 52-53; Weaver, "The real bin Laden."

[198] Bergen, *The Osama bin Laden I Know*, 51-52; OBL, "Introduction," 77; Daily Mail Reporter, "I taught judo to Osama bin Laden"; Darraz, "Impressions," 102; Loh and Tai, "Osama bin Laden a serious student." Scheuer, *Osama bin Laden*, 61-62.

[199] Daily Mail Reporter, "I taught judo to Osama bin Laden"; Darraz, "Impressions," 95-96, 102-103; Loh and Tai, "Osama bin Laden a serious student"; Reed, "Soviets race to cut rebel supply lines"; Shah, "SOVIET-AFGHAN CONFLICT."

[200] Bergen, *The Osama bin Laden I Know*, 53; Darraz, "Impressions," 95-96, 102-103, 109-110; Scheuer, *Osama bin Laden*, 69, 213n95-96.

[201] Bergen, *The Rise and Fall of Osama bin Laden*, 27-28, 34-41, 44-45; Daily Mail Reporter, "I taught judo to Osama bin Laden"; Darraz, "Impressions," 95-96, 102-103; Loh and Tai, "Osama bin Laden a serious student"; Reed, "Soviets race to cut rebel supply lines"; Scheuer, *Osama bin Laden*, 63; Shah, "SOVIET-AFGHAN CONFLICT."

[202] Al-Bahri and Malbrunot, *Guarding bin Laden*, 134-135, 215-217; Scheuer, *Osama bin Laden*, 123-124.

[203] See, for example, OBL, ARC, 11 August 1995; Hamid and Farral, *The Arabs at War in Afghanistan*, 200-202; and Scheuer, *Osama bin Laden*, 73, 97, 221n90.

[204] Cook, "The struggle against terrorism"; Jalali, *A Military History of Afghanistan*, 382-383; Johnson, *Blowback*, 8-11; McGreal, "Fidel Castro claims Osama bin Laden is a US spy"; Moore, "Death, Downtown"; Roy, "The algebra of infinite justice."

[205] Brown, *The Gorbachev Factor*, 221, 235; Gorbachev, *Perestroika*, 162-163; Kaplan, *Soldiers of God*, xx-xxi; National Security Archive, Vol. II, "Episode 20 Soldiers of God"; Yousaf and Adkin, *Afghanistan*, 81-83, 85, 106.

[206] Al-Bahri and Malbrunot, *Guarding bin Laden*, 16-17; Bin Laden, bin Laden, and Sasson, *Growing Up bin Laden*, 74-75, 89; Girardet, *Killing the Cranes*, 255-257; Root, "A

Sheikh's Life"; Simpson, "Simpson on Sunday"; Al-Qarni, "Bin Laden's Former 'Mufti' Musa Al-Qarni Talks about the Jihad in Afghanistan"; Worth, "Ex-Jihadist Defies Yemen's Leader."

[207] *The Bukovsky Archives*, "The Situation in the Democratic Republic," 29 June 1979; *The Bukovsky Archives*, "The situation in Afghanistan and our policy in this respect," 31 October 1979; *Wilson Center Digital Archive, Collection 76*, "Excerpt from transcript, CPSU CC Politburo meeting," 20 September 1979.

[208] Department of the Army, *Soviet Army Operations*, Part II, 3-8, 3-9, 3-10; Galeotti, *Afghanistan*, 18-19; Jalali, *A Military History of Afghanistan*, 395-398; Kalinovsky, *A Long Goodbye*, 38; Kaplan, *Soldiers of God*, 187-188; Nojumi, *The Rise of the Taliban*, 57-59.

[209] *The Bukovsky Archives*, "The Situation in the Democratic Republic," 29 June 1979; *The Bukovsky Archives*, "The situation in Afghanistan and our policy in this respect," 31 October 1979; *Wilson Center Digital Archive, Collection 76*, "Excerpt from transcript, CPSU CC Politburo meeting," 20 September 1979.

[210] Brown, *The Gorbachev Factor*, 221, 235; Gorbachev, *Perestroika*, 162-163; *National Security Archive, Vol. II*, "Episode 20 Soldiers of God."

[211] Amnesty International (Unattributed Report), *Amnesty International Report 1989* (London: Amnesty International Publications, 1989), 9, 159-160, 275, 280-281, 281-282. This same report also discusses the recent atrocities of the North and South Yemeni regimes as both governments reportedly conducted mass arrests of suspected domestic dissidents in the wake of the January 1986 Civil War between the YSP's rival factions and the Moscow-backed faction's subsequent, brutal purge of all alleged internal foes, including those within the Party itself.

[212] Amnesty International, *Amnesty International Report 1989*, 9, 159-160; Kaplan, *Soldiers of God*, 39, 120.

[213] OBL, "Introduction," 78-79, 81; Isby, *War in a Distant Country*, 35-37; Kaplan, *Soldiers of God*, 39, 120.

[214] OBL, "Introduction," 116-117; Miller, "Greetings America. My Name is Osama bin Laden."

[215] OBL, "Introduction," 78-79, 81; Scheuer, *Osama bin Laden*, 104, 224n129.

[216] Abd-al-Karim and al-Nur, "Interview with Saudi businessman Usama bin Ladin"; Alouni, "Transcript of Bin Laden's October interview"; Fisk, "Anti-Soviet Warrior puts his army on the road to peace"; Scheuer, *Osama bin Laden*, 74-75; Yusufzai, "Face to face with Osama."

[217] The Irish Times (Unattributed Report), "Bin Laden will stand his ground, say former comrades: It was 1989, just at the end of the bloody, 10-year-old Soviet occupation of Afghanistan," *The Irish Times*, 29 November 2001, https://www.irishtimes.com/news/bin-laden-will-stand-his-ground-say-former-comrades-1.339617.

[218] The Irish Times, "Bin Laden will stand his ground, say former comrades."

[219] Ibid.

[220] Ibid.

[221] Ibid.

[222] Ibid.

[223] Al-Bahri and Malbrunot, *Guarding bin Laden*, 76, 205, 206-208; Al-Batarfi, "Growing up with Osama"; bin Laden, bin Laden, and Sasson, *Growing Up bin Laden*, 25, 53, 166; Scheuer, *Osama bin Laden*, 64, 73, 68-69, 212-213n91-93.

[224] Scheuer, *Osama bin Laden*, 206-207n33.

225 OBL, "Introduction," 77, 80-81; Bin Laden, bin Laden, and Sasson, *Growing Up bin Laden*, 96-98; Kamm, "Afghan Rebels Reported Furious"; Kaplan, *Soldiers of God*, xx-xxi; Ottaway, "Afghan Rebels Assured"; Scheuer, *Osama bin Laden*, 105-106.

226 See, for example, Hamid Algar, *Wahhabism: A Critical Essay* (Oneonta, NY: Islamic Publications International, 2002), 31-34, 37-40; Delong-Bas, *Wahhabi Islam*, 21, 54-56; Joel Blecher, *Said the Prophet of God: Hadith Commentary Across a Millennium* (Oakland: University of California Press, 2018), 185-188, 194, 243n1, 245n5; Esposito, *The Oxford History of Islam*, 280-281; El Fadl, "Islam and the theology of power," 32; Scheuer, *Osama bin Laden*, 42-43, 174-175.

227 Atwan, *The Secret History of al-Qaeda*, 220; Delong-Bas, *Wahhabi Islam*, 54-56; 93-96; Esposito, *The Oxford History of Islam*, 280-281; El Fadl, "Islam and the theology of power," 32; Wiktorwicz, "Anatomy of the Salafi Movement," 215.

228 Algar, *Wahhabism*, 37-40, 61-65; Atwan, *The Secret History of al-Qaeda*, 220; Blecher, *Said the Prophet of God*, 185-188, 194, 243n1, 245n5; Esposito, *The Oxford History of Islam*, 280-281; El Fadl, "Islam and the theology of power," 32; Scheuer, *Osama bin Laden*, 42-43, 174-175.

229 Atwan, *The Secret History of al-Qaeda*, 220; Rudolph Peters, *Jihad in Classical and Modern Islam: A Reader* (Princeton, NJ: Markus Wiener Publishers, 1996), 7-8, 46; Scheuer, *Osama bin Laden*, 40, 43, 199n62.

230 Al-Bahri and Malbrunot, *Guarding bin Laden*, 76, 205, 206-208; Al-Batarfi, "Growing up with Osama"; OBL, "Introduction," 78-79, 81; El Fadl, "Islam and the theology of power," 32; Peters, *Jihad in Classical and Modern Islam*, 7-8; Scheuer, *Osama bin Laden*, 40, 43, 199n62.

231 Atwan, *The Secret History of al-Qaeda*, 220; Al-Bahri and Malbrunot, *Guarding bin Laden*, 212-214; Bergen, *The Osama bin Laden I Know*, 14; Peters, *Jihad in Classical and Modern Islam*, 46, 116-118; Scheuer, *Osama bin Laden*, 43, 155, 203n112, 241n84-85.

232 Algar, *Wahhabism*, 37-40, 61-65; Blecher, *Said the Prophet of God*, 185-188, 194, 243n1, 245n5; Esposito, *The Oxford History of Islam*, 280-281; El Fadl, "Islam and the theology of power," 32; Peters, *Jihad in Classical and Modern Islam*, 116-118; Scheuer, *Osama bin Laden*, 40, 42-43, 174-175, 199n2; Wiktorwicz, "Anatomy of the Salafi Movement," 215.

233 Al-Bahri and Malbrunot, *Guarding bin Laden*, 76, 205, 206-208; Al-Batarfi, "Growing up with Osama"; OBL, "Introduction," 77, 80-81; Bin Laden, bin Laden, and Sasson, *Growing Up bin Laden*, 103-107.

234 Lenin, *Essential Works*, 116-117, 120, 173-175.

235 Atwan, *The Secret History of al-Qaeda*, 220; OBL, "Introduction," 77, 80-81; Peters, *Jihad in Classical and Modern Islam*, 116-118; Wiktorwicz, "Anatomy of the Salafi Movement," 215.

236 Bin Laden, bin Laden, and Sasson, *Growing Up bin Laden*, 103-107; Lenin, *Essential Works*, 116-117, 120, 173-175; Peters, *Jihad in Classical and Modern Islam*, 47-49, 52, 116-118; Wiktorwicz, "Anatomy of the Salafi Movement," 215.

237 Al-Bahri and Malbrunot, *Guarding bin Laden*, 138-139, 140-143; Gutman, *How We Missed the Story*, 7, 203-204; Peterson, "Osama bin Laden is a 'hero' in Afghanistan"; Scheuer, *Osama bin Laden*, 123-124; Zaeef, *My Life with the Taliban*, 143-144.

238 Weiner, "U.S. Hard Put to Find Proof."

239 U.S. President, "Address to the Nation by the President," *The White House*, Washington, D.C., 20 August 1998, *National Archives and Records Administration*, https://clinton whitehouse6.archives.gov/1998/08/1998-08-20-president-address-to-the-nation.html.

240 OBL, "Jihad Against Jews and Crusaders"; OBL, "Full transcript of bin Ladin's speech"; Lewis, "License to Kill"; U.S. President, "Address to the Nation."
241 Wendy S. Ross, "RICHARDSON: US WORKING TO FREEZE BIN LADIN ASSETS WORLDWIDE (Terrorist leader must not 'rest easy' Richardson says) (510)," *USIS Washington File*, 24 August 1998. As indicated by the title of this contemporary news article, Clinton and Richardson, like later U.S. presidents and U.K. prime ministers and their respective Terrorism Czars, also emphasized the need to cut off al-Qaeda's finances in the misinformed belief that bin Laden could only attract a militant following due to his family's immense wealth rather than the respect that he personally commanded due to his rejection of physical comforts, his adherence to a Spartan lifestyle, and his four-times wounded-in-action guerrilla war record, to no avail as Washington and London's subsequent actions to pressure the Taleban, while persisting in their perceived support for the tyrannical Middle Eastern regimes to which bin Laden remained staunchly opposed, continued to stimulate financing and recruitment, inadvertently boosting al-Qaeda's fortunes and generating more support for the jihadi group on the Arabian Peninsula and elsewhere across the Sunni Muslim world.
242 Kaplan, *Soldiers of God*, 136; Peterson, "Osama bin Laden is a 'hero' in Afghanistan"; Spain, *The Way of the Pathans*, 47-48, 52.
243 Al-Bahri and Malbrunot, *Guarding bin Laden*, 138-139; Gutman, *How We Missed the Story*, 7, 203-204; Peterson, "Osama bin Laden is a 'hero' in Afghanistan"; Scheuer, *Osama bin Laden*, 123-124.
244 Al-Bahri and Malbrunot, *Guarding bin Laden*, 157-159.
245 Ibid, 208-211.
246 Ibid.
247 Ibid.; Bergen, *The Rise and Fall of Osama bin Laden*, 32-33.
248 Azzam, "Join the Caravan," 16-17; Scheuer, *Osama bin Laden*, 4-5, 58-59, 189n5; Tawil, *Brothers in Arms*, 15, 20-24.
249 Gutman, *How We Missed the Story*, 203-204; Scheuer, *Osama bin Laden*, 4-5, 58-59, 189n5; Tawil, *Brothers in Arms*, 15, 20-24; Al-Qarni, "Bin Laden's Former 'Mufti' Musa Al-Qarni Talks about the Jihad in Afghanistan."
250 Al-Bahri and Malbrunot, *Guarding bin Laden*, 138-139; Gutman, *How We Missed the Story*, 7, 203-204; Al-Qarni, "Bin Laden's Former 'Mufti' Musa Al-Qarni Talks about the Jihad in Afghanistan."
251 Anas, *To the Mountains*, 31, 70, 87, 121, 123, 137, 171, 199, 201, 207, 246. As Michael Scheuer and Steve Coll point out, and as mentioned in this book's Preface, Anas's claims seem somewhat inaccurate as the former Algerian jihadi and current political exile in London appears to exude considerable envy at bin Laden's inheriting of Azzam's guerrilla recruitment networks and financial connections after the Palestinian Islamist scholar's 24 November 1989 assassination. His constant Massoud glorification and excessive bin Laden bashing aside, Anas's 2019 memoir *To the Mountains* is, nevertheless, an overall important and somewhat informative source as the former Algerian militant's apparent jealousy does not seem to prevent him from expressing admiration for bin Laden's risking of life and limb alongside his men at their Arab guerrilla base at Jaji in 1987 even as fierce ice storms and snowstorms pounded the mountains incessantly. It is crucial to note here that the researcher should, naturally, always apply a healthy dose of scholarly skepticism in consulting all sources, including Tariq al-Fadhli's February 2010 claim, for example, that he and bin Laden never thought of attacking enemy civilians during the Soviet-

Afghan War, a claim that appears as an obvious attempt at painting both himself and bin Laden as far too angelic and chronically peaceful as the killing of enemy civilians during wartime is, after all, deemed regrettable but acceptable in the Salafist interpretation of Sunni Islamic law to which bin Laden and his senior lieutenants staunchly and consistently adhered from the time of the Soviet-Afghan War forward. See also Coll, *Ghost Wars*, 204; Root, "A Sheikh's Life"; Scheuer, *Osama bin Laden*, 4-5, 58-59, 189n5; and Worth, "Ex-Jihadist Defies Yemen's Leader."

[252] Mark Galeotti, *The Panjshir Valley 1980-86: The Lion Tames the Bear in Afghanistan* (Oxford, UK: Osprey Publishing, 2021), 91-92. Parentheses in the original. To be sure, and in all fairness to an astute, top scholar, Galeotti makes no claim in this book to be a bin Laden biographer and, notwithstanding his incorrect assessment of the al-Qaeda chief as an irrational, chronic Massoud-hater, his 2021 book, like his others on the Soviet-Afghan War, is a commendable and superb text that is highly recommended to readers. As Galeotti correctly points out here, bin Laden succeeded where both the Soviet 40th Army, PDPA, and the Taleban all failed by ordering and directing the assassination of Massoud on 9 September 2001. The timing of bin Laden's success in executing Massoud's assassination two days before the 9/11 terror attacks is considerably impressive considering, as Michael Scheuer points out, that one cannot usually expect things to happen on time in Afghanistan. According to Nasser al-Bahri, whose inside information on this particular occasion reportedly came from fellow Yemeni and Saudi bodyguards of bin Laden with whom he shared a cell during his brief imprisonment in a Yemeni government prison in Sanaa, bin Laden ordered the assassination on 2 September 2001, and, as Scheuer points out, learned about the date that the 9/11 attackers planned to execute their deadly mission three days later, on 5 September. Yet even as he began moving arms, ordnance, and jihadi fighters to advantageous tactical positions from which to execute guerrilla raids and ambushes on the oncoming U.S.-U.K. troops that he prayed could be expected to enter Afghanistan following the attacks in New York City and Washington, D.C., bin Laden managed to execute Massoud's assassination and solidify his position as the Taleban's loyal, protected guest on time before the U.S.-NATO forces began striking Afghanistan. See al-Bahri and Malbrunot, *Guarding bin Laden*, 177-180, 181-182; and Scheuer, *Osama bin Laden*, 126-128, 129-131.

[253] Al-Bahri and Malbrunot, *Guarding bin Laden*, 22-23, 163-164; OBL, "The Banishment of Communism from the Arabian Peninsula," ARC, 11 July 1994.

[254] Al-Bahri and Malbrunot, *Guarding bin Laden*, 76-78.

[255] Chipman, "Osama bin Laden and Guerrilla War," 163-170; Mitzcavitch, "Al Qaeda and Mao Zedong," 14-18; Zedong, *The Red Book*, 52-53; 64-65.

[256] Al-Bahri and Malbrunot, *Guarding bin Laden*, 76-78; Daily Mail Reporter, "I taught judo to Osama bin Laden"; Loh and Tai, "Osama bin Laden a serious student."

[257] Al-Bahri and Malbrunot, *Guarding bin Laden*, 34-37, 76-77, 107-108, 108-110, 110-113; Bergen, *The Osama bin Laden I Know*, 13-15; al-Batarfi, "Growing up with Osama"; Nasiri, *Inside the Jihad*, xi, 206-207, 209-210; Tawil, *Brothers in Arms*, 19.

[258] Al-Bahri and Malbrunot, *Guarding bin Laden*, 34-37, 76-77, 107-108, 108-110, 110-113; Bergen, *The Osama bin Laden I Know*, 13-15; al-Batarfi, "Growing up with Osama"; Nasiri, *Inside the Jihad*, xi, 206-207, 209-210; Tawil, *Brothers in Arms*, 19.

[259] Delong-Bas, *Wahhabi Islam*, 21; Esposito, *The Oxford History of Islam*, 280-281; El Fadl, "Islam and the theology of power," 32; Scheuer, *Osama bin Laden*, 42-43, 174-175; Wiktorwicz, "Anatomy of the Salafi Movement," 215.

[260] Al-Bahri and Malbrunot, *Guarding bin Laden*, 76, 205, 206-208; Al-Batarfi, "Growing up with Osama"; bin Laden, bin Laden, and Sasson, *Growing Up bin Laden*, 25, 53, 166; Scheuer, *Osama bin Laden*, 64, 73, 68-69, 212-213n91-93.

[261] Arnett, "Transcript of Osama Bin Ladin interview"; Bergen, *The Osama bin Laden I Know*, 59; OBL, "Introduction," 116-117; Darraz, "Impressions," 109-110; Gorbachev, *Perestroika*, 162-163; Kaplan, *Soldiers of God*, xx-xxi; Miller, "Greetings America. My Name is Osama bin Laden"; *National Security Archive, Vol. II*, "Episode 20 Soldiers of God"; Scheuer, *Osama bin Laden*, 63-64; Stenersen, *Al-Qaida in Afghanistan*, 18-19; U.S. President, "Address to the Nation"; Yousaf and Adkin, *Afghanistan*, 81-83, 85, 106.

[262] Mashal, "How the Taliban Outlasted a Superpower"; Moore, "What Is the Taliban's 'Red Unit'?; Rubin, *Afghanistan*, 246.

[263] Al-Bahri and Malbrunot, *Guarding bin Laden*, 138-139; Carter, et al., "Salafi-Jihadi Movement Weekly Update"; Gutman, *How We Missed the Story*, 7, 203-204; Peterson, "Osama bin Laden is a 'hero' in Afghanistan"; Ross, "RICHARDSON: US WORKING TO FREEZE BIN LADIN ASSETS WORLDWIDE"; Scheuer, *Osama bin Laden*, 123-124; Wasserstein, *Black Banners of ISIS*, 183-187, 188-189, 205.

[264] Galeotti, *The Panjshir Valley 1980-86*, 91-92; Bill Roggio and Andrew Tobin, "Taliban completes conquest of Afghanistan after seizing Panjshir," *FDD's Long War Journal*, 6 September 2022, https://www.longwarjournal.org/archives/2021/09/taliban-completes-conquest-of-afghanistan-after-seizing-panjshir.php.

[265] Butler, "ISIS-K Is Waging a New War in Afghanistan"; Noroozi and Litvinova, "Suicide attack at Russia embassy in Kabul."

[266] OBL, "Jihad Against Jews and Crusaders"; OBL, "Full transcript of bin Ladin's speech"; Lewis, "License to Kill"; Nida'ul Islam, "Mujahid Usamah Bin Ladin"; Rubin, *Afghanistan*, ix, 239-240, 242, 250-252, 253; Ummat Special Correspondent, "Usama bin Laden'"; Wasserstein, *Black Banners of ISIS*, 183-187, 188-189, 205.

[267] OBL, "Jihad Against Jews and Crusaders"; OBL, "Full transcript of bin Ladin's speech"; Lewis, "License to Kill"; Ummat Special Correspondent, "Usama bin Laden."

[268] Butler, "ISIS-K Is Waging a New War in Afghanistan"; Mashal, "How the Taliban Outlasted a Superpower"; Rubin, *Afghanistan*, 246; Wasserstein, *Black Banners of ISIS*, 183-187, 188-189, 205.

[269] Carter, et al., "Salafi-Jihadi Movement Weekly Update"; Rubin, *Afghanistan*, ix, 239-240, 242, 250-252, 253.

[270] Ross, "RICHARDSON: US WORKING TO FREEZE BIN LADIN ASSETS WORLDWIDE."

[271] Mark Guarino, "Foreign fighters in Ukraine speak out on their willingness to serve: 'I had to go,'" *ABC News*, 6 November 2023, https://abcnews.go.com/International/foreign-fighters-ukraine-speak-willingness-serve/story?id=91671528; Luke Harding, "'It was like in world war one': the foreign volunteers fighting in Ukraine," *The Guardian*, 13 July 2023, https://amp.theguardian.com/world/2023/jul/13/it-was-like-in-world-war-one-the-foreign-volunteers-fighting-in-ukraine.

[272] MacLeod, "The Paladin of Jihad," 51-52; Nida'ul Islam, "Mujahid Usamah Bin Ladin"; Timmerman, "This Man Wants You Dead," 52-53.

[273] Azzam, "Sheikh Abdullah Azzam said about Usama Bin Ladin," 152-153; OBL, "Introduction," 84-85; Darraz, "Impressions," 92-93; Hamid and Farrall, *The Arabs at War in Afghanistan*, 70, 150-151; Scheuer, *Osama bin Laden*, 61-62; Ummat Special Correspondent, "Usama bin Laden."

[274] Guarino, "Foreign fighters in Ukraine"; Harding, "'It was like world war one.'"

275 Gutman, *How We Missed the Story*, 203-204; Scheuer, *Osama bin Laden*, 4-5, 58-59, 63-64, 189n5; Stenersen, *Al-Qaida in Afghanistan*, 18-19; Tawil, *Brothers in Arms*, 15, 20-24; Al-Qarni, "Bin Laden's Former 'Mufti' Musa Al-Qarni Talks about the Jihad in Afghanistan."

276 Galeotti, *The Panjshir Valley 1980-86*, 91-92; Roggio and Tobin, "Taliban completes conquest of Afghanistan."

277 Abd-al-Karim and al-Nur, "Interview with Saudi businessman Usama bin Ladin"; Al-Bahri and Malbrunot, *Guarding bin Laden*, 70, 218; Bergen, *Holy War, Inc.*, 31; OBL, "Saudi Arabia supports the communists in Yemen," ARC, 7 June 1994; OBL, "Introduction," 116-117; Miller, "Greetings America. My Name is Osama bin Laden"; Scheuer, *Osama bin Laden*, 69, 166.

278 Darraz, "Impressions," 109-110; The Irish Times, "Bin Laden will stand his ground, say former comrades."

279 Al-Bahri and Malbrunot, *Guarding bin Laden*, 50, 53; Hamid and Farrall, *The Arabs at War in Afghanistan*, 200-202; Scheuer, *Osama bin Laden*, 73, 97, 221n90.

280 Nir Arielli, *From Byron to bin Laden: A History of Foreign War Volunteers* (Cambridge, MA: Harvard University Press, 2018), 108-114, 114-120.

281 Arielli, *From Byron to bin Laden*, 2, 65, 71, 76, 85-86, 93, 95, 112; Seth Harp and Pedro Brito Da Fonseca, "The Untold Story of Syria's Antifa Platoon: How a ragtag crew of leftist revolutionaries and soldiers of fortune helped defeat ISIS," *Rolling Stone*, 10 July 2018, https://www.rollingstone.com/politics/politics-features/untold-story-syria-antifa-platoon-666159/.

282 Thomas Grove, "Russia Detained Several Senior Military Officers in Wake of Wagner Mutiny," *The Wall Street Journal*, 10 July 2023, https://www.wsj.com/articles/russia-detained-several-senior-military-officers-in-wake-of-wagner-mutiny-35a696e4.

283 Carter, et al., "Salafi-Jihadi Movement Weekly Update"; MEMRI, "Al-Qaeda In The Arabian Peninsula (AQAP) Claims Drone And IED Attacks"; Staff Writer with AFP, "27 Dead as AQAP Launches Attack"; Waters, "ISIS beats back Wagner offensive"; Zenn, "Brief."

284 Al-Bahri and Malbrunot, *Guarding bin Laden*, 74; Bergen, *The Osama bin Laden I Know*, 59; OBL, "Introduction," 116-117; Darraz, "Impressions," 109-110; Miller, "Greetings America. My Name is Osama bin Laden"; Scheuer, *Osama bin Laden*, 63-64; Stenersen, *Al-Qaida in Afghanistan*, 18-19.

285 Brown Pryor, *Reading the Man*, 416-419, 419-421, 421-425.

286 Ibid., 445-447, 447-452, 452-454, 454-456, 456-458, 458-459. Brown Pryor insightfully points out here that Lee's actions, while still exhibiting the accepted white supremacist social norms displayed by many upper class southern American men during the *zeitgeist* of his time, are nevertheless significant in assessing his character as he had even reportedly prayed alongside enslaved men that he inherited from his deceased father-in-law in 1857 before emancipating them and their families, as promised, in 1862 at the height of the American Civil War.

287 Al-Bahri and Malbrunot, *Guarding bin Laden*, 22-23, 76-77, 105-106, 205, 206-208; Al-Batarfi, "Growing up with Osama"; Bin Laden, bin Laden, and Sasson, *Growing Up bin Laden*,10, 266-167; OBL, "Jihad Against Jews and Crusaders"; OBL, "Full transcript of bin Ladin's speech"; Lewis, "License to Kill."

288 Al-Bahri and Malbrunot, *Guarding bin Laden*, 70; Bergen, *The Osama bin Laden I Know*, 51-52; Fisk, "Anti-Soviet Warrior puts his army on the road to peace"; Miller,

"Greetings America. My Name is Osama bin Laden." Nida'ul Islam, "Mujahid Usamah Bin Ladin"; Scheuer, *Osama bin Laden*, 61-62.

[289] Bergen, *The Osama bin Laden I Know*, 51-52, 53; Christopher Hibbert, *Garibaldi: Hero of Italian Unification* (New York: Palgrave MacMillan, 2008), 3, 17-18, 21-22, 220, 291, 324; Scheuer, *Osama bin Laden*, 61-62.

[290] Al-Bahri and Malbrunot, *Guarding bin Laden*, 22-23, 163-164; OBL, "The Banishment of Communism from the Arabian Peninsula," ARC, 11 July 1994; OBL, ARC, 19 September 1994; OBL, "Open Letter for Sheikh Bin Baz," ARC, 29 December 1994; OBL, *Messages to the World*, 76; Coll, *The Bin Ladens*, 373-374; Hibbert, *Garibaldi*, vii-viii, xix, 8, 11, 31, 35, 79.

[291] Hibbert, *Garibaldi*, 9-10, 11, 28-29, 35, 40, 43, 79, 105, 118, 136-139, 143-145, 163, 177, 180, 187-189, 192, 198, 204, 352-353.

[292] Al-Bahri and Malbrunot, *Guarding bin Laden*, 217-220; Mashal, "How the Taliban Outlasted a Superpower"; Scheuer, *Osama bin Laden*, 116-117; Zaeef, *My Life with the Taliban*, 229-231.

[293] Ibn Khaldun, *The Muqaddimah*, 459. Parentheses in the original.

[294] Ibid., 418-420. Parentheses in the original.

[295] Bergen, *Holy War, Inc.*, 226-227; Lahoud, *The Bin Laden Papers*, 5-7, 9-12, 282-287; Scheuer, *Osama bin Laden*, 48-49, 52-54.

[296] Abd-al-Karim and al-Nur, "Interview with Saudi businessman Usama bin Ladin"; Braithwaite, *Afgantsy*, 333-334, 335; Galeotti, *Afghanistan*, 4, 6; MacLeod, "The Paladin of Jihad," 51-52; Nida'ul Islam, "Mujahid Usamah Bin Ladin"; Timmerman, "This Man Wants You Dead," 52-53; Zaeef, *My Life with the Taliban*, 65.

[297] Mashal, "How the Taliban Outlasted a Superpower"; Moore, "What Is the Taliban's 'Red Unit'?; Rubin, *Afghanistan*, ix, 239-240, 242, 250-252, 253.

[298] Arnett, "Transcript of Osama Bin Ladin interview"; Miller, "Greetings America. My Name is Osama bin Laden."

[299] Theodore Roosevelt, "Theodore Roosevelt, 'The Strenuous Life' (10 April 1899)," *Voices of Democracy – The U.S. Oratory Project*, 10 April 1899, https://voicesofdemocracy.umd.edu/roosevelt-strenuous-life-1899-speech-text/.

[300] Ibn Khaldun, *The Muqaddimah*, 152-154, 278-279, 351-352; Scheuer, *Osama bin Laden*, 37-38; Roosevelt, "Theodore Roosevelt 'The Strenuous Life.'"

[301] Ibn Khaldun, *The Muqaddimah*, 152-154, 278-279, 351-352; Scheuer, *Osama bin Laden*, 37-38; Roosevelt, "Theodore Roosevelt 'The Strenuous Life.'"

[302] Abd-al-Karim and al-Nur, "Interview with Saudi businessman Usama bin Ladin"; OBL, "Open Letter for Sheikh Bin Baz," ARC, 29 December 1994; Braithwaite, *Afgantsy*, 333-334, 335; Obama, "Obama's Mideast Speech – Text – The New York Times"; Ross, "RICHARDSON: US WORKING TO FREEZE BIN LADIN ASSETS WORLDWIDE"; *The Bukovsky Archives*, "The situation in Afghanistan," 31 October 1979; U.S. President, "Address to the Nation." To be sure, the CPSU officials' words here refer to the Afghan Islamists resisting their communist puppet regime in Kabul at the end of October 1979. Yet the Politburo's politically-infused comments reflect the beginning of a foolish tendency to ascribe Western or, in the case of the Soviets, perhaps, semi-Western political motives to all Sunni Islamist leaders and groups, including and especially bin Laden and al-Qaeda, a folly-inherent habit that reemerged with President Clinton's August 1998 speech and continued under many U.S. Presidents and their European counterparts at least as late as President Obama's May 2011 speech that he delivered nearly three weeks

after U.S. troops killed bin Laden in Pakistan. Bin Laden, as consistently indicated by many of his written letters and oral statements cited throughout this book, including his March 1994 newspaper interview and December 1994 letter to Saudi Shaykh bin Baz cited here, neither displayed an interest in politics in the Western or Soviet sense of the word nor a liking for politicians, save for men such as the Yemeni Salafists al-Zindani and al-Daylami and their *al-Islah* Party in Yemen. Bin Laden, in short, had little time for political games and seems to have rather rejected such distractions while supporting those whose political parties had little to do with politics in the traditional Western or Eastern definitions of the word but rather sought public office in Yemen and elsewhere solely out of a motivation to gradually promote and implement *Shariah* in their respective Muslim countries, thereby earning bin Laden's comradeship due to his and their genuine, fundamentalist religious convictions rather than political interests that he, and they, appear to have consistently rejected. It is, therefore, a tragic and, perhaps, ultimately self-defeating mistake for Western and Eastern politicians alike, and experts of all stripes, to disregard the genuine and militant religious fervor that served as bin Laden's true motivation for his and al-Qaeda's holy war and the reasons for which he managed to attract and build a following for his guerrilla vanguard in devout, defiant parts of the Sunni Muslim world, such as Yemen, Afghanistan, and the adjacent tribal and rural parts of Pakistan and Saudi Arabia.

BIBLIOGRAPHY

The bulk of the research in this book is drawn from the numerous excellent biographies of bin Laden, the memoirs of his closest associates, many of his own written and oral statements, and several courageous firsthand accounts of the Soviet-Afghan War. Every source that I have cited here has proved indispensable in researching this book, yet several specific works have proved to be especially crucial and informative, and their authors and producers deserve special mention here. In my view, these are the following individuals, in no particular order: Peter L. Bergen, Michael Scheuer, Nasser al-Bahri, Allia Ghanem, Carmen, Najwa, and Omar bin Laden, Dr. Khaled M. al-Batarfi, Tariq al-Fadhli, Steve Coll, Jonathan Randal, Robert D. Kaplan, Shaykh Musa al-Qarni, Debra Denker, Camille Tawil, Abdel Bari Atwan, Rahimullah Yusufzai, John Miller, Robert Fisk, Scott MacLeod, Abdul Salam Zaeef, Edward Girardet, Anne Stenerson, Mohammad Yousaf, Radek Sikorski, Paul Kengor, and Ali Ahmad Jalali. I respectfully disagree with some of the things that they have written, and they may utterly reject what I have written here. Having said that, each of these authors has produced absolutely invaluable work in the biographies, memoirs, interviews, and eyewitness accounts that are cited in this book and these works, having helped to make mine possible, are highly recommended to readers.

Published Primary Sources
of Amasia, Strabo. *Geography: Books 15-16.* Translated by Horace Leonard Jones. Cambridge, MA: Harvard University Press, 1930.
Anas, Abdullah, and Tam Hussein. *To the Mountains: My Life in Jihad, from Algeria to Afghanistan.* London: Hurst & Company, 2019.
Atwan, Abdel Bari. *The Secret History of al-Qaeda.* Berkeley: University of California Press, 2008.
Al-Bahri, Nasser, and Georges Malbrunot. G*uarding bin Laden: My Life in al-Qaeda.* Edited and translated by Susan de Muth. London: Thin Man Press, 2013.
Bergen, Peter L. *The Osama bin Laden I Know: An Oral History of al-Qaeda's Leader.* New York: Free Press, 2006.
Berntsen, Gary, and Ralph Pezzullo. *Jawbreaker: The Attack on bin Laden and al-Qaeda.* New York: Crown Publishers, 2006.
Bin Laden, Carmen. *Inside the Kingdom: My Life in Saudi Arabia.* New York: Grand Central Publishing, 2005.
Bin Laden, Najwa, Omar bin Laden, and Jean Sasson. *Growing Up bin Laden: Osama's Wife and Son Take Us Inside Their Secret World.* London: Oneworld Publications, 2011.

Bin Laden, Osama. *Osama bin Laden: America's Enemy in His Own Words.* Edited and translated by Randall B. Hamud. San Diego: Nadeem Publishing, 2005.

———. *Messages to the World: The Statements of Osama bin Laden.* Edited by Bruce Lawrence. Translated by James Howarth. New York: Verso, 2005.

Borovik, Artyom. *The Hidden War: A Russian Journalist's Account of the Soviet War in Afghanistan.* New York: Grove Press, 2001.

Casey, William J. *Scouting the Future: The Public Speeches of William J. Casey.* Edited and compiled by Herbert E. Meyer. Washington, D.C.: Regnery, 1989.

Department of the Army. *Soviet Army Operations.* Arlington, VA: U.S. Army Intelligence and Threat Analysis Center, 1978.

Gates, Robert M. *From the Shadows: The Ultimate Insider's Story of Five Presidents and How They Won the Cold War.* New York: Simon and Schuster, 1996.

Girardet, Edward. *Killing the Cranes: A Reporter's Journey Through Three Decades of War in Afghanistan.* White River Junction, VT: Chelsea Green Publishing, 2011.

Gorbachev, Mikhail. *Perestroika: New Thinking for Our Country and the World.* New York: Perennial Library, 1988.

———. *Memoirs.* London: Transworld Publishers, 1997.

Hamid, Mustafa, and Leah Farrall. *The Arabs at War in Afghanistan.* London: Hurt & Company, 2015.

Isby, David C. *War in a Distant Country: Afghanistan: Invasion and Resistance.* London: Arms and Armour Press, 1989.

Kaplan, Robert D. *Soldiers of God: With Islamic Warriors in Afghanistan and Pakistan.* New York: Vintage, 2001.

Ibn Khaldun, Abd al-Rahman. *The Muqaddimah – An Introduction to History: The Classic Islamic History of the World.* Edited by N.J. Dawood. Translated by Franz Rosenthal. Princeton: Princeton University Press, 2015.

Al-Kindi, Abu Yusuf. *The Medical Formulary or Aqrabadhin of al-Kindi.* Edited and translated by Martin Levey. Madison: The University of Wisconsin Press, 1966.

Lenin, Vladimir I. *Essential Works of Lenin.* Edited by Henry W. Christman. Mineola, NY: Dover Publications, 1987.

Margolis, Eric S. *War at the Top of the World: The Struggle for Afghanistan, Kashmir, and Tibet.* New York: Routledge, 2002.

Marx, Karl. *The Eighteenth Brumaire of Louis Bonaparte.* New York: International Publishers, 1994.

Al-Muqrin, Abd Al-Aziz. *Al-Qa'ida's Doctrine for Insurgency: Abd Al-Aziz Al-Muqrin's 'A Practical Course for Guerrilla War'.* Translated by Norman Cigar. Dulles, VA: Potomac Books, 2009.

Nasiri, Omar. *Inside the Jihad: My Life with Al Qaeda.* New York: Basic Books, 2008.

Reagan, Ronald. *The Reagan Diaries.* Edited by Douglas Brinkley. New York: Harper Perennial, 2009.

———. *An American Life.* New York: Threshold Editions, 2011.

Sikorski, Radek. *Dust of the Saints: A Journey Through War-Torn Afghanistan*. New York: Paragon House, 1990.

Spain, James W. *The Way of the Pathans*. Karachi: Oxford University Press, 1979.

Thatcher, Margaret. *The Downing Street Years*. New York: HarperCollins, 2012.

The Russian General Staff. *The Soviet-Afghan War: How a Superpower Fought and Lost*. Edited by Lester W. Grau. Translated by Michael A. Gress. Lawrence: The University Press of Kansas, 2002.

Yousaf, Mohammad, and Mark Adkin. *Afghanistan – The Bear Trap: The Defeat of a Superpower*. Barnsley, South Yorkshire: Pen & Sword, 2001.

Zaeef, Abdul Salam. *My Life with the Taliban*. Edited by Alex van Linschoten. Translated by Felix Kuehn. London: Hurst & Company, 2010.

Zedong, Mao. *The Red Book of Guerrilla Warfare*. Edited by Shawn Connors. Translated by Samuel W. Griffith and Foreign Language Press, Peking. El Paso, TX: El Paso Norte Press, 2010.

Digital Primary Sources/Archival Material

Adaki, Oren. "Yemeni tribal leader joins AQAP." *Long War Journal*, 17 June 2014. Accessed 19 May 2020. https://www.longwarjournal.org/archives/2014/06/yemeni_tribal_leader_joins_aqa.php.

Ahmed, Akbar, and Harrison Akins. "Making enemies in Yemen." *Al-Jazeera*, 5 May 2013. Accessed 27 April 2021. https://www.aljazeera.com/opinions/2013/5/5/making-enemies-in-yemen.

AL-BAB.COM. "Security incidents in Yemen, 1990-94." Accessed 12 July 2023. https://al-bab.com/security-incidents-yemen-1990-94.

Alouni, Tayseer. "Transcript of Bin Laden's October interview." *Al-Jazeera*, 5 February 2002. Accessed 29 January 2020. http://edition.cnn.com/2002/WORLD/asiapcf/south/02/05/binladen.transcript/.

Amnesty International (Unattributed Report). *Amnesty International Report 1989*. London: Amnesty International Publications, 1989. Accessed 13 March 2023. https://www.amnesty.org/en/wp-content/uploads/2021/05/POL1000021989ENGLISH.pdf.

Anderson, Jack, and Dale van Atta. "Afghan Rebel Aid Enriches Generals." *The Washington Post*, 8 May 1987. Accessed 17 March 2020. https://www.washingtonpost.com/archive/local/1987/05/08/afghan-rebel-aid-enriches-generals/40243b90-55d4-421b-80b7-929c3e4b1075/.

Armacost, Michael H. *Reflections on U.S.-Soviet Relations*. Ann Arbor: University of Michigan Library, 1985.

Arnett, Peter. "Transcript of Osama Bin Ladin interview by Peter Arnett." *CNN*, March 1997. Accessed 2 December 2019. http://anusha.com/osamaint.htm.

Atwan, Abdel Bari. "My weekend with Osama bin Laden: 'Having borne arms against the Russians in Afghanistan for 10 years, we think our battle with the Americans will be easy by comparison.'" *The Guardian*, 11 November 2001 (1996 interview). Accessed 16 March 2020. https://www.theguardian.com/world/2001/nov/12/afghanistan.terrorism2.

Azzam, Shaykh Abdullah. "Join the Caravan," 15 April 1987. Accessed 27 March 2020. https://ebooks.worldofislam.info/ebooks/Jihad/Join%20the%20Caravan.pdf.

———. "Sheikh Abdullah Azzam said about Usama Bin Laden," in Shaykh Abdullah Azzam, *The Lofty Mountain*, n.d., 151-153. Accessed 19 February 2020. https://ebooks.worldofislam.info/ebooks/Jihad/The%20Lofty%20Mountain.pdf?

Baker, Peter. "Why Did the Soviets Invade Afghanistan? Documents Offer History Lesson for Trump." *The New York Times*, 29 January 2019. Accessed 12 February 2020. https://www.nytimes.com/2019/01/29/us/politics/afghanistan-trump-soviet-union.html.

al-Batarfi, Dr. Khaled M. "Growing up with Osama: 2 youth took different paths." *The Seattle Times*, 6 January 2007. Accessed 24 April 2020. https://www.seattletimes.com/nation-world/growing-up-with-osama-2-youths-took-different-paths/.

BBC. "Bin Laden 'fathered four children' while on the run." *BBC*, 30 March 2012. Accessed 7 August 2020. https://www.bbc.com/news/world-asia-17560649.

———. "Charlie Hebdo attack: Three days of terror." *BBC*, 14 January 2015. Accessed 16 May 2020. https://www.bbc.com/news/world-europe-30708237.

———. "Obituary: Yemen al-Qaeda leader Nasser al-Wuhayshi." *BBC*, 16 June 2015. Accessed March 19, 2020. https://www.bbc.com/news/world-middle-east-33150212.

Beckford, Martin. "National Archives: Britain agreed secret deal to back Mujahideen." *The Telegraph*, 30 December 2010. Accessed 5 December 2019. https://www.telegraph.co.uk/news/worldnews/asia/afghanistan/8215187/National-Archives-Britain-agreed-secret-deal-to-back-Mujahideen.html.

Bin Laden, Osama. "Introduction to 'The battle of the Lion's Den', Afghanistan, 1987," in Shaykh Abdullah Azzam, *The Lofty Mountain*, n.d., 77-92, 113-118. Accessed 28 February 2020. https://ebooks.worldofislam.info/ebooks/Jihad/The%20Lofty%20Mountain.pdf.

———. Advice and Reform Committee Communiques, 1994-1998. *Combating Terrorism Center at West Point*. Accessed 18 May 2020. https://ctc.usma.edu/wp-content/uploads/2013/10/Letter-from-Bin-Laden-Translation.pdf.

———. "Jihad Against Jews and Crusaders: World Islamic Front Statement." 23 February 1998. Accessed 15 February 2020. https://fas.org/irp/world/para/docs/980223-fatwa.htm.

———. "Fight the allies of the devil." *The Guardian*, 12 February 2003. Accessed 8 November 2019. https://www.theguardian.com/world/2003/feb/12/alqaida.terrorism2.

———. "Exposing the New Crusader War – Bin Laden – Statement – February 2003." *Terrorisme.net*, 11 February 2003. Accessed 9 September 2019. https://www.terrorisme.net/pdf/newcrusaderwar.pdf.

———. "Full transcript of bin Ladin's speech." *Al-Jazeera*, 1 November 2004. Accessed 16 October 2019. https://www.aljazeera.com/news/2004/11/1/full-transcript-of-bin-ladins-speech.

———. "Transcript – ABC News." *ABC News*, 6 September 2007. Accessed 16 March 2020. https://abcnews.go.com/images/Politics/transcript2.pdf.

———. "Translation of bin Laden's message." *Al-Jazeera*, 23 October 2007. Accessed 17 August 2021. https://www.aljazeera.com/news/2007/10/23/translation-of-bin-ladens-message.

Black, Ian, and Brian Whitaker. "Yemen's rival armies turn on each other: failure to unite the two forces lies behind the struggle which is destroying the country from the inside, write Ian Black and Brian Whitaker." *The Guardian*, 6 May 1994. Accessed 10 March 2023. https://al-bab.com/articles-section/yemens-rival-armies-turn-each-other.

Boustany, Nora. "Foreigners Evacuated From War-Torn Yemen." *The Washington Post*, 8 May 1994. Accessed 12 July 2023. https://www.washingtonpost.com/archive/politics/1994/05/08/foreigners-evacuated-from-war-torn-yemen/894086e5-d65b-406e-a647-eda73b893d70/.

Boustany, Nora. "Civil War in Yemen Heightens Worries of Wider Instability." *The Washington Post*, 18 June 1994. Accessed 23 June 2021, https://www.washingtonpost.com/archive/politics/1994/06/18/civil-war-in-yemen-heightens-worries-of-wider-instability/94dcbfa8-7655-4659-b8f5-d989c1ee7571/.

———. "Foreigners Evacuated From War-Torn Yemen." *The Washington Post*, 8 May 1994. Accessed 12 July 2023. https://www.washingtonpost.com/archive/politics/1994/05/08/foreigners-evacuated-from-war-torn-yemen/894086e5-d65b-406e-a647-eda73b893d70/.

———. "North's Forces Gain Ground in Yemen War." *The Washington Post*, 18 May 1994. https://www.washingtonpost.com/archive/politics/1994/05/18/norths-forces-gain-ground-in-yemeni-war/5bbd6ee5-eec2-4920-abb4-7b204dadab3c/.

Bowcott, Owen. "UK discussed plans to help mujahideen weeks after Soviet invasion of Afghanistan." *The Guardian*, 29 December 2010. Accessed 17 August 2020. https://www.theguardian.com/uk/2010/dec/30/uk-mujahideen-afghanistan-soviet-invasion.

Brennan, John O. "A New Approach to Safeguarding Americans." *Foreign Policy*, 6 August 2009. Accessed 7 June 2020. https://foreignpolicy.com/2009/08/06/a-new-approach-to-safeguarding-americans/.

Burchill, Julie. "Out of the rubble." *The Guardian*, 20 October 2001. Accessed 19 September 2019. https://www.theguardian.com/world/2001/oct/20/september11.usa1.

Burke, Jason. "Revealed: Secret hideout of world's most feared terrorist." *The Guardian*, 4 July 1999. Accessed 3 February 2020. https://www.theguardian.com/world/1999/jul/04/osamabinladen.alqaida.

Butler, Gavin. "ISIS-K Is Waging a New War in Afghanistan – This Time Against China." *Vice News*, 1 March 2023. Accessed 12 July 2023. https://www.vice.com/en/article/dy7aqw/isis-anti-china-war-afghanistan.

Campbell, Leslie. "Yemen: The Tribal Islamists." *Wilson Center*, 27 August 2015. Accessed 28 May 2021. https://www.wilsoncenter.org/article/yemen-the-tribal-islamists.

Carter, Brian, Kathryn Tyson, Liam Karr, Peter Mills, and Karolina Hird. "Salafi-Jihadi Movement Weekly Update, July 5, 2023." *Critical Threats With ISW*, 5 July 2023. Accessed 12 July 2023. https://www.criticalthreats.org/analysis/salafi-jihadi-movement-weekly-update-july-5-2023.

Chipman, Don D. "Osama bin Laden and Guerrilla War." *Studies in Conflict and Terrorism*, Vol. 26, Issue 3 (2003), 163-170. Accessed 14 July 2020. https://www.tandfonline.com/doi/abs/10.1080/10576100390211400.

Chulov, Martin. "My son, Osama: the al-Qaeda leader's mother speaks for the first time." *The Guardian*, 2 August 2018. Accessed 7 June 2020. https://www.theguardian.com/world/2018/aug/03/osama-bin-laden-mother-speaks-out-family-interview.

Cook, Robin. "The struggle against terrorism cannot be won by military means." *The Guardian*, 8 July 2005. Accessed 30 October 2019. https://www.theguardian.com/uk/2005/jul/08/july7.development.

Daily Mail Reporter. "I taught judo to Osama Bin Laden, claims Taiwanese coach (and here are the pics to prove it)." *Daily Mail*, 7 May 2011. Accessed 6 November 2019. https://www.dailymail.co.uk/news/article-1384682/I-taught-Osama-bin-Laden-judo-claims-Taiwanese-coach.html.

Darraz, Isam, "Impressions of an Arab Journalist in Afghanistan," in Shaykh Abdullah Azzam, *The Lofty Mountain*, n.d., 92-112, 118-128. Accessed 25 February 2020. https://ebooks.worldofislam.info/ebooks/Jihad/The%20Lofty%20Mountain.pdf.

Denker, Debra. "Along Afghanistan's War-Torn Frontier." *National Geographic*, Vol. 167, No. 6, June 1985, 772-797.

Edwards, Haley Sweetland, and Paul Stephens. "The house bin Laden built." *Agence France-Press*, 1 January 2010. Accessed 12 February 2020. https://www.pri.org/stories/2010-01-01/house-bin-laden-built.

El Fadl, Khaled Abou. "Islam and the theology of power." *Middle East Report*, No. 221 (Winter 2001), 32. Accessed 13 January 2020. http://www.mafhoum.com/press2/merip76.htm.

Engel, Pamela. "Osama bin Laden's son wrote this letter to his wife in 2008 outlining his last wishes." *Business Insider*, 20 May 2015. Accessed 16 April 2020. https://www.businessinsider.com/osama-bin-laden-2008-letter-to-his-wife-2015-5.

Felton, Ben, Johanna Kassel, and Richard McGregor. "Bin Laden papers reveal al-Qaeda rifts." *The Financial Times*, 3 May 2012. Accessed 9 August 2020. http://ig-legacy.ft.com/content/1c19c328-952f-11e1-ad38-00144feab49a#axzz6lEYaJsPE.

Fisk, Robert. "Anti-Soviet warrior puts his army on the road to peace: The Saudi businessman who recruited mujahedin now uses them for large-scale building projects in Sudan." *The Independent*, 6 December 1993. Accessed 16 March 2020. https://www.independent.co.uk/news/world/anti-soviet-warrior-puts-his-army-on-the-road-to-peace-the-saudi-businessman-who-recruited-mujahedin-1465715.html.

———. "10 July 1996: Arab rebel leader warns the British: Get out of the Gulf." *The Independent*, 10 July 1996. Accessed 4 June 2020. https://www.independent.co.uk/news/long_reads/robert-fisk-osama-bin-laden-saudi-arabia-afghanistan-war-b1561291.html.

Gerges, Fawaz A. "The Islamic State Has Become a Resilient Insurgency: The group may no longer have its caliphate, but its far from defeated." *Foreign Policy*, 7 February 2022. Accessed 12 July 2023. https://foreignpolicy.com/2022/02/07/qurayshi-death-leader-islamic-state-current-strength/.

Girardet, Edward. "Afghan Rebels Take Hold. KUNAR: A HINT OF THE FUTURE?" *The Christian Science Monitor*, 14 February 1989. Accessed 17

April 2020. https://www.csmonitor.com/1989/0214/okun.html. Accessed 15 May 2020.

Grier, Peter. "Soviets bolster an Arab ally. Military buildup in South Yemen worries US officials." *The Christian Science Monitor*, 11 March 1988. Accessed 4 June 2021. https://www.csmonitor.com/1988/0311/ayem.html.

Grove, Thomas. "Russia Detained Several Senior Military Officers in Wake of Wagner Mutiny." *The Wall Street Journal*, 10 July 2023. Accessed 13 July 2023. https://www.wsj.com/articles/russia-detained-several-senior-military-officers-in-wake-of-wagner-mutiny-35a696e4.

Guarino, Mark. "Foreign fighters in Ukraine speak out on their willingness to serve: 'I had to go.'" *ABC News*, 6 November 2022. Accessed 14 July 2023. https://abcnews.go.com/International/foreign-fighters-ukraine-speak-willingness-serve/story?id=91671528.

al-Hammadi, Khalid. "Bin Ladin's Former 'Bodyguard' Interviewed on Al-Qa'ida Strategies." *Al-Quds al-Arabi*, 3 August 2004. Accessed 18 February 2020. https://cryptome.org/alqaeda-plans.htm.

Hammond, Andrew. "Bin Laden warns U.S. on Israel ties." *Reuters*, 13 September 2009. Accessed 29 April 2020. https://www.reuters.com/article/us-binladen-tape-idUSTRE58D0CX20090914.

Haq, Abdul. "Afghanistan Won't Be a U.S. or Soviet Puppet." *The New York Times*, 9 June 1989. Accessed 17 August 2021. https://www.nytimes.com/1989/06/09/opinion/l-afghanistan-won-t-be-a-us-or-soviet-puppet-628089.html.

Harding, Luke. "'It was like in world war one': the foreign volunteers fighting in Ukraine." *The Guardian*, 13 July 2023. Accessed 14 July 2023. https://amp.theguardian.com/world/2023/jul/13/it-was-like-in-world-war-one-the-foreign-volunteers-fighting-in-ukraine.

Harp, Seth, and Pedro Brito Da Fonseca. "The Untold Story of Syria's Antifa Platoon: How a ragtag crew of leftist revolutionaries and soldiers of fortune helped defeat ISIS." *Rolling Stone*, 10 July 2018. Accessed 13 July 2023. https://www.rollingstone.com/politics/politics-features/untold-story-syria-antifa-platoon-666159/.

Hedges, Chris. "In Yemen's Civil War, South Fights On, Gloomily." *The New York Times*, 16 May 1994. Accessed 14 March 2023. https://www.nytimes.com/1994/05/16/world/in-yemen-s-civil-war-south-fights-on-gloomily.html.

———. "THE WORLD; How Yemen Is Coming Undone." *The New York Times*, 29 May 1994. Accessed 12 July 2023. https://www.nytimes.com/1994/05/29/weekinreview/the-world-how-yemen-is-coming-undone.html.

Hinnant, Lori, and Elaine Ganley. "French security forces kill gunmen, end terror rampage." *The Associated Press*, 9 January 2015. Accessed 12 March 2020. https://web.archive.org/web/20150113074036/http://news.yahoo.com/brothers-past-draws-scrutiny-french-manhunt-enters-day-073049780.html.

Howe, Marvine. "Southern Yemen Blends Marxism With Islam and Arab Nationalism." *The New York Times*, 25 May 1979. Accessed 2 May 2021. https://www.nytimes.com/1979/05/25/archives/southern-yemen-blends-marxism-with-islam-and-arab-nationalism.html.

Hurd, Robert, and Greg Noakes. "North and South Yemen: Lead-up to the Break-up." *Washington Report on Middle East Affairs*, 8 July 1994 (July/August

1994), 48. Accessed 26 May 2021. https://www.wrmea.org/1994-july-august/north-and-south-yemen-lead-up-to-the-break-up.html.

Isby, David C. "Four battles in Afghanistan: Mujahideen destroy myth of Soviet invincibility." *Soldier of Fortune*, April 1988, 32-34. Accessed 5 September 2020. https://archive.org/details/soldieroffortunemagazine/Soldier%20of%20Fortune%20%5B1988%2704%5D/page/n31/mode/2up.

Al-Jazeera (Unattributed Report). "Bin Laden urges end to Gaza closure." *Al-Jazeera*, 19 May 2008. Accessed 12 February 2020. https://www.aljazeera.com/news/2008/5/19/bin-laden-urges-end-to-gaza-closure.

Kamm, Henry. "Afghan Rebels Reported Furious Over Rumors of U.S.-Soviet Deal." *The New York Times*, 24 February 1988. Accessed 24 August 2021. https://www.nytimes.com/1988/02/24/world/afghan-rebels-reported-furious-over-rumors-of-us-soviet-deal.html.

Abd-al-Karim, Ali, and Nur Ahmad al-Nur. "Interview with Saudi businessman Usama bin Ladin." *Al-Quds al-Arabi*, 9 March 1994. Accessed 24 May 2020. https://scholarship.tricolib.brynmawr.edu/bitstream/handle/10066/4733/OBL19940309.pdf.

Kassel, Johanna. "Bin Laden supported Arab spring." *The Financial Times*, 3 May 2012. Accessed 22 February 2020. https://www.ft.com/content/a218eb16-9539-11e1-8faf-00144feab49a.

Kifner, John. "SOVIET SAID TO TRY TO CALM SOUTH YEMEN." *The New York Times*, 17 January 1986. Accessed 24 July 2021. https://www.nytimes.com/1986/01/17/world/soviet-said-to-try-to-calm-south-yemen.html.

Landay, Jonathan. "Bin Laden called for Americans to rise up over climate change." *Reuters*, 1 March 2016 (January 2010 audio recording). Accessed 5 March 2020. https://www.reuters.com/article/us-usa-binladen-climate change-idUSKCN0W35MS.

Lawson, Guy. "Osama's Prodigal Son: The Dark, Twisted Journey of Omar bin Laden." *Rolling Stone*, 20 January 2010. Accessed 19 May 2020. https://www.rollingstone.com/politics/politics-news/osamas-prodigal-son-the-dark-twisted-journey-of-omar-bin-laden-199468/.

Lewis, Bernard. "License to Kill: Usama bin Ladin's Declaration of Jihad." *Foreign Affairs*, 1 November 1998. Accessed 27 August 2019. https://www.foreignaffairs.com/articles/saudi-arabia/1998-11-01/license-kill-usama-bin-ladins-declaration-jihad.

Loh, Nicky, and Ben Tai. "Osama bin Laden a serious student, Taiwan judo coach says." *Reuters*, 7 May 2011. Accessed 4 May 2020. https://in.reuters.com/article/idINIndia-56847220110507.

MacLean, William. "Loyalty bin Laden inspired leaves lasting risk." *Reuters*, 4 May 2011. Accessed 18 September 2020. https://www.reuters.com/article/us-binladen-loyalties-idUKTRE7436RV20110504.

MacLeod, Scott. "The Paladin of Jihad: Fearless and super-rich, Osama bin Laden finances Islamic extremism. A TIME exclusive." *TIME*, Vol. 147, No. 19, 6 May 1996, 51-52. Accessed 19 March 2020. https://time.com/vault/issue/1996-05-06/page/51/.

Magdy, Samy. "Al-Qaida in Yemen claims deadly shooting at Florida's Naval Air Station Pensacola." *Navy Times*, 2 February 2020. Accessed 5 August 2020.

https://www.navytimes.com/news/your-navy/2020/02/02/al-qaida-in-yemen-claims-deadly-shooting-at-floridas-naval-air-station-pensacola/.

Mahmood, Ali. "Al Qaeda shows signs of resurgence in Yemen." *MENA*, 9 April 2021. Accessed 4 June 2021. https://www.thenationalnews.com/mena/al-qaeda-shows-signs-of-resurgence-in-yemen-1.1200037.

Malkin, Lawrence. "Reagan and the End of the Cold War." *The New York Times*, 14 June 2012. Accessed 7 April 2020. https://www.nytimes.com/2012/06/15/opinion/reagan-and-the-end-of-the-cold-war.html.

al-Maqtari, Bushra. "The evolution of militant Salafism in Taiz." *Sana'a Center for Strategic Studies*, 19 September 2017. Accessed 6 November 2020. https://sanaacenter.org/publications/analysis/4843.

Mashal, Mujib. "How the Taliban Outlasted a Superpower: Tenacity and Carnage." *The New York Times*, 26 May 2020. Accessed 15 September 2020. https://www.nytimes.com/2020/05/26/world/asia/taliban-afghanistan-war.html.

Mazetti, Mark, and Scott Shane. "For U.S., Killing Terrorists Is a Means to an Elusive End." *The New York Times*, 16 June 2015. Accessed 17 January 2020. https://www.nytimes.com/2015/06/17/world/middleeast/al-qaeda-arabian-peninsula-yemen-nasser-al-wuhayshi-killed.html.

McDonald, Mark. "New Message Reported From bin Laden." *The New York Times*, 14 September 2009. Accessed 2 June 2020. https://www.nytimes.com/2009/09/15/world/15tape.html.

McGreal, Chris. "Fidel Castro claims Osama bin Laden is a US spy." *The Guardian*, 27 August 2010. Accessed 8 May 2020. https://www.theguardian.com/world/2010/aug/27/fidel-castro-osama-bin-laden-us-spy.

MEMRI (Unattributed Report). "AQAP Leader Batarfi: Rapprochement Between Saudi Arabia And Iran Indicates Defeat Of Former; Sunnis In Yemen And Saudi Arabia Should Learn From Taliban, Wage Jihad Against 'Agents Of Iran And U.S." *MEMRI Jihad & Terrorism Threat Monitor*, 1 May 2023. Accessed 12 July 2023. https://www.memri.org/jttm/aqap-leader-batarfi-rapprochement-between-saudi-arabia-and-iran-indicates-defeat-former-sunnis.

———. "Al-Qaeda In The Arabian Peninsula (AQAP) Claims Drone And IED Attacks On High Ranking Yemeni Officer In Shabwah." *MEMRI Cyber Terrorism & Jihad Lab*, 31 May 2023. Accessed 12 July 2023. https://www.memri.org/cjlab/al-qaeda-arabian-peninsula-aqap-claims-drone-and-ied-attacks-high-ranking-yemeni-officer.

Miller, John. "Greetings America. My Name is Osama bin Laden." *Esquire*, 1 February 1999. Accessed 24 October 2019. http://www.esquire.com/news-politics/a1813/osama-bin-laden-interview/.

Mitzcavitch, Andrew. "Al-Qaeda and Mao Zedong: Analogies of Protracted Warfare." *Counter Terrorist Trends and Analyses*, Vol. 6, No. 4 (May 2014), 14-18. Accessed 19 August 2020. https://www.jstor.org/stable/26351249?seq=1#metadata_info_tab_contents.

Moore, Jack. "What Is the Taliban's 'Red Unit'? Jihadi Special Forces Are Using Russian, U.S. Tech for Attacks." *Newsweek*, 1 December 2017. Accessed 18 September 2020. https://www.newsweek.com/what-talibans-red-unit-jihadi-special-forces-are-using-russian-us-tech-attacks-711761.

Moore, Michael. "Death, downtown." michaelmoore.com, 12 September 2001. Accessed 5 March 2020. https://michaelmoore.com/.

Naylor, Sean D. "U.S. killed a top al-Qaeda leader in Yemen, reports say." *Yahoo News*, 31 January 2020. Accessed 24 April 2020. https://news.yahoo.com/us-killed-a-top-al-qaeda-leader-in-yemen-reports-say-215555178.html?guccounter=1.

Nida'ul Islam (Unattributed Report). "Mujahid Usamah Bin Ladin talks exclusively to Nida'ul Islam about the new powder keg in the Middle East." *Nida'ul Islam* (Call to Islam), Issue 15, 15 January 1997 (1996 interview). Accessed 25 March 2020. https://fas.org/irp/world/para/docs/LADIN.htm.

Noroozai, Ebrahim, and Dasha Litvinova. "Suicide attack at Russia embassy in Kabul kills 2 diplomats." *AP*, 5 September 2022. Accessed 12 July 2023. https://apnews.com/article/afghanistan-russia-ukraine-explosions-kabul-00bf5815018fb152be8784f6f3af2557.

Obama, President Barack. "Obama's Mideast Speech – Text – The New York Times." *The New York Times*, 19 May 2011. Accessed 6 February 2020. https://www.nytimes.com/2011/05/20/world/middleeast/20prexy-text.html.

Ottaway, David B. "Afghan Rebels Assured of More U.S. Support." *The Washington Post*, 13 November 1987. Accessed 21 August 2021. https://www.washingtonpost.com/archive/politics/1987/11/13/afghan-rebels-assured-of-more-us-support/ebdbf011-8283-43f8-aba8-88c5c8b540ca/.

———. "Agreement on Afghanistan Signed in Geneva." *The Washington Post*, 15 April 1988. Accessed 19 July 2020. https://www.washingtonpost.com/archive/politics/1988/04/15/agreement-on-afghanistan-signed-in-geneva/c7288c64-6764-4e73-9bc5-7eeb48f7827d/.

———. "Soviets, Afghan Rebels Pressure U.S. on Arms." *The Washington Post*, 2 October 1988. Accessed 23 June 2020. https://www.washingtonpost.com/archive/politics/1988/10/02/soviets-afghan-rebels-pressure-us-on-arms/1011636c-7396-4a11-ba7a-35259125c258/.

Pear, Robert. "Arming Afghan Guerrillas: A Huge Effort Led by U.S." *The New York Times*, 18 April 1988. Accessed 4 June 2020. https://www.nytimes.com/1988/04/18/world/arming-afghan-guerrillas-a-huge-effort-led-by-us.html.

Peterson, Scott. "Osama bin Laden is a 'hero' in Afghanistan." *The Christian Science Monitor*, 14 December 1999. Accessed 12 April 2020. https://www.csmonitor.com/1999/1214/p7s1.html.

Piazza, Stefano, and Luciano Trinnanzi. "Hamir Mir: When Mullah Omar wanted to send bin Laden to Chechnya." Translated by Carol Simonetti. *Panorama*, 21 September 2021. Accessed 12 July 2023. https://www.panorama.it/news/hamid-mir-mullah-omar-bin-laden-chechnya.

al-Qarni, Musa. "Bin Laden's Former 'Mufti' Musa Al-Qarni Talks about the Jihad in Afghanistan and Says Most Mujahideen in Iraq Are Saudis." *MEMRI TV: Middle East Media Research Institute TV Monitor Project*, 17 March 2006. Accessed 28 September 2019. https://www.memri.org/tv/bin-ladens-former-mufti-musa-al-qarni-talks-about-jihad-afghanistan-and-says-most-mujahideen-iraq/transcript.

Ramani, Samuel. "North Korea's Balancing Act in the Persian Gulf." *HuffPost*, 17 August 2015. Accessed 27 June 2021. https://www.huffpost.com/entry/north-koreas-balancing-ac_b_7995688.

Raghavan, Sudarsan. "As Yemen's war intensifies, an opportunity for al-Qaeda to resurrect its fortunes." *The Washington Post*, 25 February 2020. Accessed 2 November 2020. https://www.washingtonpost.com/world/middle_east/as-yemens-war-intensifies-an-opening-for-al-qaeda-to-resurrect-its-fortunes/2020/02/24/6244bd84-54ef-11ea-80ce-37a8d4266c09_story.html.

Randal, Jonathan C. "Threat to N. Yemen Spurs Saudi Anxiety." *The Washington Post*, 30 March 1979. Accessed 24 July 2021. https://www.washingtonpost.com/archive/politics/1979/03/30/threat-to-n-yemen-spurs-saudi-anxiety/b676aa1b-09e5-48f9-b1a2-3b60cf4c5983/.

Reed, Jack. "Soviets race to cut rebel supply lines from Pakistan." *UPI*, 1 June 1987. Accessed 16 March 2023. https://www.upi.com/Archives/1987/06/01/Soviets-race-to-cut-rebel-supply-lines-from-Pakistan/1885549518400/.

Republic of Yemen – Political Forces Dialogue Committee. "The Document of Pledge and Accord, 1994." *Yemen Times*, 18 January 1994. Accessed 9 March 2023. https://al-bab.com/document-pledge-and-accord-1994.

Reuters (Unattributed Report). "Al Qaeda attack kills 20 Yemeni forces in Abyan, says southern military." *Reuters*, 6 September 2022. Accessed 14 July 2023. https://www.reuters.com/world/middle-east/al-qaeda-attack-kills-20-yemeni-forces-abyan-says-southern-military-2022-09-06/.

Reuters (Unattributed Report). "North Korea trying to sell weapons to Houthis, secret UN report reveals." *Arab News*, 4 August 2018. Accessed 27 June 2021. https://www.arabnews.com/node/1350851/world.

Reuters Staff. "U.S. says Bin Laden son may be dead." *Reuters*, 23 July 2009. Accessed 3 April 2020. https://www.reuters.com/article/us-binbinladen-saad-sb/u-s-says-bin-laden-son-may-be-dead-idUSTRE56M4YK20090723.

———. "Bin Laden claims U.S. plane bombing attempt." *Reuters*, 24 January 2010. Accessed 5 March 2020. https://cn.reuters.com/article/instant-article/idUKTRE60N0L920100124.

RFE/RL. "Interview: Hamir Mir, The Last Man to Interview Osama Bin Laden." *Radio Free Europe/Radio Liberty*, 2 May 2011. Accessed 12 July 2023. https://www.rferl.org/amp/interview_hamid_mir_last_man_to_interview_osama_bin_laden/16800723.html.

Rhee, Joseph, and Rehab el-Buri. "Osama bin Laden Message Surfaces in Wake of 9/11 Anniversary." *ABC News*, 13 September 2009. Accessed 4 June 2020. https://abcnews.go.com/Blotter/osama-bin-laden-message-surfaces-wake-911-anniversary/story?id=8564631.

Roggio, Bill, and Andrew Tobin. "Taliban completes conquest of Afghanistan after seizing Panjshir." FDD's Long War Journal, 6 September 2022. Accessed 14 July 2023. https://www.longwarjournal.org/archives/2021/09/taliban-completes-conquest-of-afghanistan-after-seizing-panjshir.php.

Roosevelt, Theodore. "Theodore Roosevelt, 'The Strenuous Life' (10 April 1899)." *Voices of Democracy – the U.S. Oratory Project*, 10 April 1899. Accessed 17 March 2023. https://voicesofdemocracy.umd.edu/roosevelt-strenuous-life-1899-speech-text/.

Root, Tik. "A Sheikh's Life: What Tariq al-Fadhli's story says about the mixed-up world of Yemeni politics." *The American Prospect*, 30 April 2013. Accessed 2 May 2020. https://prospect.org/world/sheikh-s-life/.

Ross, Wendy S. "RICHARDSON: US WORKING TO FREEZE BIN LADIN ASSESTS WORLDWIDE (Terrorist leader must not 'rest easy' Richardson says) (510)." *USIS Washington File*, 24 August 1998. Accessed 17 March 2023. https://irp.fas.org/news/1998/08/98082403_tpo.html.

Roy, Arundhati. "The algebra of infinite justice." *The Guardian*, 29 September 2001. Accessed 29 January 2020. https://www.theguardian.com/world/2001/sep/29/september11.afghanistan.

Ruthven, Malise. "The eleventh of September and the Sudanese mahdiyya in the context of Ibn Khaldun's theory of Islamic history." *International Affairs*, Vol. 78, Issue 2 (April 2002), 339-351. Accessed 8 June 2020. https://academic.oup.com/ia/article-abstract/78/2/339/2434744?redirectedFrom=fulltext.

SAMAA. "Bin Laden 'fathered four children while on run.'" *SAMAA*, 30 March 2012. Accessed 4 September 2020. https://www.samaa.tv/news/2012/03/bin-laden-fathered-four-children-while-on-run/.

Schmidt, Dana Adams. "British in Aden Depart as Egyptians Leave Yemen; Fighting Begun in 1963 Commandos Depart Accord in Geneva 'Good Fortune' Wished Welcome by U.N. Panel." *The New York Times*, 30 November 1967. Accessed 27 July 2021. https://www.nytimes.com/1967/11/30/archives/british-in-aden-depart-as-egyptians-leave-yemen-fighting-begun-in.html.

Schmitt, Eric. "U.S. Officials Say a Son of bin Laden May be Dead." *The New York Times*, 24 July 2009. Accessed 9 February 2020. https://www.nytimes.com/2009/07/24/world/asia/24pstan.html.

Selbourne, David, and Mary Kenny Deal. "Which side were you on in the last Afghan war?" *The Guardian*, 23 October 2001. Accessed 23 March 2020. https://www.theguardian.com/world/2001/oct/23/afghanistan.terrorism6.

Sennott, Charles M. "Saudi Arabia's Highway 15 Revisited." *GlobalPost*, 6 September 2011. Accessed 22 January 2020. https://www.pri.org/stories/2011-09-06/saudi-arabia-s-highway-15-revisited.

Shah, Saira. "SOVIET-AFGHAN CONFLICT. US-supplied missiles boost mujahideen ability." *The Christian Science Monitor*, 18 June 1987. Accessed 16 March 2023. https://www.csmonitor.com/layout/set/amphtml/1987/0618/ojaji.html.

Shipler, David K. "Reagan Didn't Know of Afghan Deal." *The New York Times*, 11 February 1988. Accessed 9 June 2021. https://www.nytimes.com/1988/02/11/world/reagan-didn-t-know-of-afghan-deal.html.

al-Shishani, Murad Batal. "Yemen al-Qaeda chief al-Wuhayshi killed in US strike." *BBC*, 16 June 2015. Accessed 26 April 2021. https://www.bbc.com/news/world-middle-east-33143259.

Siddique, Haroon. "Bin Laden urges uprising against Musharraf." *The Guardian*, 20 September 2007. Accessed 19 March 2020. https://www.theguardian.com/world/2007/sep/20/alqaida.pakistan.

Simpson, John. "Simpson on Sunday: The day that Osama bin Laden put a price on my head." *The Telegraph*, September 16, 2001. Accessed 31 October 2019. http://www.telegraph.co.uk/news/worldnews/asia/afghanistan/1340688/Simpson-on-Sunday-The-day-that-Osama-bin-Laden-put-a-price-on-my-head.html.

Smith, Martin. "Interview: Dr. Saad al-Fagih." *PBS Frontline Online*, April 1999. Accessed 4 February 2020. https://www.pbs.org/wgbh/pages/frontline/shows/binladen/interviews/al-fagih.html.

Staff Writer with AFP. "27 Dead as AQAP Launches Attack on Yemen Separatists." *TheDefensePost*, 6 September 2022. Accessed 12 July 2023. https://www.thedefensepost.com/2022/09/06/al-qaeda-attack-yemen-separatists/.

Tempest, Rone. "Sen. Humphrey Visits Kabul, Refuses Talks." *Los Angeles Times*, 15 April 1987. Accessed 13 May 2020. https://www.latimes.com/archives/la-xpm-1987-04-15-mn-247-story.html.

The Arab Weekly (Unattributed Report). "Al-Qaeda exploiting security vacuum created by Houthi escalation." *The Arab Weekly*, 18 June 2021. Accessed 28 June 2021. https://thearabweekly.com/al-qaeda-exploiting-security-vacuum-created-houthi-escalation.

The Associated Press. "Yemen Claims Victory in Civil War After Seizing Rebel City." *The New York Times*, 8 July 1994. Accessed 2 May 2021. https://www.nytimes.com/1994/07/08/world/yemen-claims-victory-in-civil-war-after-seizing-rebel-city.html.

The Bukovsky Archives. "Communism on Trial." Accessed 17 August 2021. https://bukovsky-archive.com/2016/07/09/29-june-1979-pb-156ix/.

The Irish Times (Unattributed Report). "Bin Laden will stand his ground, say former comrades. It was 1989, just at the end of the bloody 10-year Soviet occupation of Afghanistan." *The Irish Times*, 29 November 2001. Accessed 17 March 2023. https://www.irishtimes.com/news/bin-laden-will-stand-his-ground-say-former-comrades-1.339617.

The Middle East Forum. "Usama bin Ladin: 'American Soldiers Are Paper Tigers.'" *Middle East Quarterly*, Vol. 5, No. 4 (December 1998), 73-79. Accessed 12 July 2020. https://www.meforum.org/435/usama-bin-ladin-american-soldiers-are-paper-tigers.

The National Security Archive, Volume II. "Episode 20 Soldiers of God: Interview with Frank Anderson – 1997." Accessed 30 October 2019. https://nsarchive2.gwu.edu//coldwar/interviews/episode-20/anderson2.html.

———, Volume II. "Afghanistan: Lessons from the Last War." Accessed 9 October 2019. nsarchive2.gwu.edu/NSAEBB57/us.html.

The New Arab Staff & Agencies. "Al-Qaeda releases new video of 'seriously ill' UN worked abducted in Yemen." *The New Arab*, 13 June 2023. Accessed 12 July 2023. https://www.newarab.com/news/yemen-al-qaeda-releases-new-video-abducted-un-worker?amp.

The New York Times (Unattributed Report). "SAUDIS SAY U.A.R. BOMBED VILLAGES; Break Relations With Cairo in Dispute Over Yemen." *The New York Times*, 7 November 1962. Accessed 27 April 2021. https://www.nytimes.com/1962/11/07/archives/saudis-say-uar-bombed-villages-break-relations-with-cairo-in.html.

———. "Afghans Accept Both Losses and Gains in 'Holy War' Against the Russians." *The New York Times*, 31 October 1985. Accessed 4 June 2021. https://www.nytimes.com/1985/10/31/world/afghans-accept-both-losses-and-gains-in-holy-war-against-the-russians.html.

Timmerman, Kenneth R. "This Man Wants You Dead: Osama bin Laden." *Reader's Digest* (July 1998), 50-57. Accessed 7 March 2020. https://www.rd.com/article/this-man-wants-you-dead-osama-bin-laden/.

Tucker, Eric. "FBI: Shooter at Pensacola Navy base coordinated with al-Qaida." *Military Times*, 18 May 2020. Accessed 19 August 2020. https://www.militarytimes.com/news/your-military/2020/05/18/official-fbi-finds-link-between-pensacola-gunman-al-qaida/.

UK Parliament. *Parliamentary Record – House of Commons. House of Commons Debates*, 27 February 1967. Accessed 9 July 2021. https://www.theyworkforyou.com/debates/?id=1967-02-27a.97.0&s=Aden+1967#g172.3.

———. *Parliamentary Record – House of Commons. House of Commons Debates*, 26 March 1979. Accessed 27 July 2021. https://www.theyworkforyou.com/debates/?id=1979-03-26a.40.1&s=Afghanistan+1980s#g106.1.

———. *Parliamentary Record – House of Commons. House of Commons Debates*, 28 April 1980. Accessed 24 July 2021. https://www.theyworkforyou.com/debates/?id=1980-04-28a.995.0&s=Afghanistan+1980s#g1057.0.

———. *Parliamentary Record – House of Commons. House of Commons Debates*, 18 April 1986. Accessed 28 April 2020. https://www.theyworkforyou.com/debates/?id=1986-06-18a.1082.0&s=Afghanistan+speaker%3A10123#g1129.0.

———. *Parliamentary Record – House of Commons. House of Commons Debates*, 8 December 1987. Accessed 14 March 2023. https://hansard.parliament.uk/Commons/1987-12-08/debates/13774fd3-6d24-4327-9774-965bcd6702b3/Afghanistan.

———. *Parliamentary Record – House of Commons. House of Commons Debates*, 4 March 1988. Accessed 7 June 2021. https://www.theyworkforyou.com/debates/?id=1988-03-04a.1280.0&s=Afghanistan+1980s#g1280.3.

———. *Parliamentary Record – House of Commons. House of Commons Debates*, 1 July 1994. Accessed 16 March 2023. https://hansard.parliament.uk/commons/1994-07-01/debates/6304a043-ba3f-464d-b7e3-dab551dc444d/Yemen.

———. *Parliamentary Record – House of Lords. House of Lords Debates*, 18 April 1994. Accessed 15 March 2023. https://hansard.parliament.uk/Lords/1994-04-18/debates/c02bcf05-df47-4a34-a7ba-cfda2a2b604b/Yemen.

UK Prime Minister. "Afghanistan: FCO letter to No.10 ('Afghanistan: Future Action') [response to Soviet intervention] [declassified 2010]." *Foreign and Commonwealth Office*, London, SW1A 2AH, 28 February 1980. *Margaret Thatcher Foundation*. Accessed 23 July 2020. https://c59574e9047e61130f13-3f71d0fe2b653c4f00f32175760e96e7.ssl.cf1.rackcdn.com/C42D7645C94E4A8A8341AD8E9A688D9F.pdf.

———. "Margaret Thatcher: Interview for ITN (Afghanistan)." *No. 10 Downing Street*, London, 13 December 1985. *Margaret Thatcher Foundation*. Accessed 29 July 2020. https://www.margaretthatcher.org/document/106201.

———. "Mr Major's Press Conference in Naples – 10 July 1994." *John Major Archive*, 10 July 1994. Accessed 16 March 2023. https://johnmajorarchive.org.uk/1994/07/10/mr-majors-press-conference-in-naples-10-july-1994/.

Ummat Special Correspondent. "Usama bin Laden Says the Al-Qa'idah Group had Nothing to Do with the 11 September Attacks." *Ummat Karachi*, 28

BIBLIOGRAPHY
253

September 2001. Accessed 13 July 2023. https://scholarship.tricolib.brynmawr.edu/bitstream/handle/10066/4781/OBL20010928.pdf?sequence=3&isAllowed=y.

U.S. Congress. *Congressional Record – Senate.* 97th Congress, 2nd Session, pt.? 8 March 1982. Government Publishing Office. Accessed 17 March 2020. https://babel.hathitrust.org/cgi/pt?id=mdp.39015011692970&view=1up&seq=1.

———. *Congressional Record – Senate.* 98th Congress, 2nd Session, pt. 98-181, 27 March 1984. Government Publishing Office. Accessed 19 March 2020. https://babel.hathitrust.org/cgi/pt?id=umn.31951d00829084i&view=1up&seq=1.

———. *Congressional Record – House of Representatives.* 100th Congress, 1st Session, pt? 21 May 1987. Government Publishing Office. Accessed 6 April 2020. https://babel.hathitrust.org/cgi/pt?id=pst.000013351069&view=1up&seq=1.

———. *Congressional Record – House of Representatives.* 100th Congress, 2nd Session, pt.? 17 and 25 February 1988. Government Publishing Office. Accessed 13 March 2023. https://babel.hathitrust.org/cgi/pt?id=pst.000014722738&view=1up&seq=1&skin=2021.

———. *Congressional Record – House of Representatives.* 103rd Congress, 2nd Session, pt.? 14 June 1994. Accessed 14 March 2023. https://babel.hathitrust.org/cgi/pt?id=pst.000022817129&view=1up&seq=1&skin=2021.

———. *Congressional Record – Senate.* 100th Congress, 2nd Session, pt. 2, 26 February 1988. Government Publishing Office. Accessed 3 June 2021. https://www.govinfo.gov/content/pkg/GPO-CRECB-1988-pt2/pdf/GPO-CRECB-1988-pt2-8-1.pdf.

———. *Congressional Record – Senate.* 100th Congress, 2nd Session, pt. 100-110, 14 May 1988. Government Publishing Office. Accessed 2 March 2020. https://babel.hathitrust.org/cgi/pt?id=pst.000013390709&view=1up&seq=1.

U.S. President. "Address to the Nation by the President." *The White House*, Washington, D.C., 20 August 1998. *National Archives and Records Administration.* Accessed 17 March 2023. https://clintonwhitehouse6.archives.gov/1998/08/1998-08-20-president-address-to-the-nation.html.

———. "NSDD 75: U.S. Relations with the USSR." *The White House*, Washington, D.C., 17 January 1983. *Ronald Reagan Presidential Library & Museum.* Accessed 14 March 2020. https://www.reaganlibrary.gov/public/archives/reference/scanned-nsdds/nsdd75.pdf.

———. "NSDD 166: U.S. Policy, Programs, and Strategy in Afghanistan." *The White House*, Washington, D.C., 27 March 1985. *Ronald Reagan Presidential Library & Museum.* Accessed 17 April 2020. https://www.reaganlibrary.gov/public/archives/reference/scanned-nsdds/nsdd166.pdf.

———. "NSDD 270: Afghanistan." *The White House*, Washington, D.C., 1 May 1987. *Ronald Reagan Presidential Library & Museum.* Accessed 23 April 2020. https://www.reaganlibrary.gov/public/archives/reference/scanned-nsdds/nsdd270.pdf.

———. "President Reagan Statement Welcoming King Fahd of Saudi Arabia (February 11, 1985)." *The White House*, Washington, D.C., 11 February 1985. *Jewish Virtual Library – A Project of AICE.* Accessed 9 March 2023.

———. "Remarks on Signing the Afghanistan Day Proclamation." *The White House*, Washington, D.C., 20 March 1987. *Ronald Reagan Presidential Library & Museum*. Accessed 23 April 2020. https://www.reaganlibrary.gov/archives/speech/remarks-signing-afghanistan-day-proclamation.

Washington Post Staff. "Afghan Rebel Gains Against Soviets Reported by U.S. Aide." *The Washington Post*, 6 July 1987. Accessed 28 April 2020. https://www.latimes.com/archives/la-xpm-1987-07-06-mn-1274-story.html.

Waters, Gregory. "ISIS beats back Wagner offensive in central Syria." *Middle East Institute*, 21 April 2023. Accessed 13 July 2023. https://www.mei.edu/publications/isis-beats-back-wagner-offensive-central-syria.

Weaver, Mary Anne. "The real bin Laden." *The New Yorker*, 17 January 2000, 32. Accessed 26 February 2020. https://www.newyorker.com/magazine/2000/01/24/the-real-bin-laden.

Weiner, Tim. "U.S. Hard Put to Find Proof Bin Laden Directed Attacks." *The New York Times*, 13 April 1999. Accessed 19 February 2020. https://www.nytimes.com/1999/04/13/world/us-hard-put-to-find-proof-bin-laden-directed-attacks.html.

Whitaker, Brian. "Fragile union at mercy of outside forces." *The Guardian*, 7 April 1994. Accessed 9 March 2023. https://al-bab.com/articles-section/fragile-union-mercy-outside-forces.

———. "Yemen's north tightens grip." *The Guardian*, 15 June 1994. Accessed 14 March 2023. https://al-bab.com/articles-section/yemens-north-tightens-grip.

———. "Yemen reunited by force." *Middle East International*, 22 July 1994. Accessed 15 March 2023.

Whitehall History Publishing – Foreign and Commonwealth Office. *Documents on British Policy Overseas Series III, Volume VIII: The Invasion of Afghanistan and UK-Soviet Relations, 1979-1982*. Edited by Richard Smith, Patrick Salmon, and Stephen Twigge. London: Routledge, 2012.

Wiktorwicz, Quintan. "Anatomy of the Salafi Movement." *Studies on Conflict and Terrorism*, Vol. 29, Issue 3 (August 2006), 207-239. Accessed 11 January 2020. https://www.tandfonline.com/doi/abs/10.1080/10576100500497004?journalCode=uter20.

Wilson Center Digital Archive, Collection 76. "Soviet Invasion of Afghanistan." Accessed 2 October 2019. digitalarchive.wilsoncenter.org/collection/76/soviet-invasion-of-afghanistan.

Worth, Robert F. "Ex-Jihadist Defies Yemen's Leader, and Easy Labels." *The New York Times*, 26 February 2010. Accessed 9 August 2020, https://www.nytimes.com/2010/02/27/world/middleeast/27tareq.html.

Yusufzai, Rahimullah. "Osama bin Laden: Conversation with Terror." *TIME*, 11 January 1999. Accessed 4 March 2020. http://content.time.com/time/magazine/article/0,9171,989958,00.html.

———. "Face to face with Osama." *The Guardian*, 26 September 2001. Accessed 23 June 2020. https://www.theguardian.com/world/2001/sep/26/afghanistan.terrorism3.

———. "Moments that changed the Middle East: The Soviet invasion of Afghanistan." *Arab News*, 19 April 2020. Accessed 28 June 2020. https://www.arabnews.com/node/1661431.

Zenn, Jacob. "Brief: Al-Qaeda Affiliates AQIM and AQAP Show Unity with Eid Statement." *Terrorism Monitor – The Jamestown Foundation*, Vol. 21, Issue 9 (28 April 2023). Accessed 14 July 2023. https://jamestown.org/program/brief-al-qaeda-affiliates-aqim-and-aqap-show-unity-with-eid-statement/.

Secondary Sources

Akram, Agha I. *Khalid bin al-Waleed Sword of Allah: A Biographical Study of One of the Greatest Military Generals in History*. Edited by A. B. al-Mehri. Birmingham, UK: Maktabah Booksellers and Publishers, 2007.

Alexievich, Svetlana. *Boys in Zinc*. Translated by Andrew Bromfield. London: Penguin Modern Classics, 2017.

Algar, Hamid. *Wahhabism: A Critical Essay*. Oneonta, NY: Islamic Publications International, 2002.

Arielli, Nir. *From Byron to bin Laden: A History of Foreign War Volunteers*. Cambridge, MA: Harvard University Press, 2018.

Bergen, Peter L. *Holy War, Inc.: Inside the Secret World of Osama bin Laden*. New York: Simon & Schuster, 2002.

———. *The Rise and Fall of Osama bin Laden*. New York: Simon & Schuster, 2022.

Blecher, Joel. *Said the Prophet of God: Hadith Commentary Across a Millennium*. Oakland: University of California Press, 2018.

Bodansky, Yossef. *Bin Laden: The Man Who Declared War on America*. New York: Prima Publishing, 2001.

Braithwaite, Rodric. *Afgantsy: The Russians in Afghanistan 1979-89*. New York: Oxford University Press, 2013.

Brandt, Marieke. *Tribes and Politics in Yemen: A History of the Houthi Conflict*. New York: Oxford University Press, 2017.

Brown, Archie. *The Gorbachev Factor*. New York: Oxford University Press, 1997.

Brown Pryor, Elizabeth. *Reading the Man: A Portrait of Robert E. Lee Through His Private Letters*. New York: Penguin, 2007.

Clark, Victoria. *Yemen: Dancing on the Heads of Snakes*. New Haven: Yale University Press, 2010.

Cole, Daniel Powell. *Nomads of the Nomads: The Al Murrah Bedouin of the Empty Quarter*. Arlington Heights, IL: AHM Publishing Corporation, 1975.

Coll, Steve. *Ghost Wars: The Secret History of the CIA, Afghanistan, and bin Laden, from the Soviet Invasion to September 10, 2001*. New York: Penguin Books, 2005

———. *The Bin Ladens: An Arabian Family in the American Century*. New York: Penguin Books, 2009.

Crile, George. *Charlie Wilson's War: The Extraordinary Story of how the Wildest Man in Congress and a Rogue CIA Agent Changed the History of Our Times*. New York: Grove Press, 2003.

Delong-Bas, Natana J. *Wahhabi Islam: From Revival and Reform to Global Jihad.* New York: Oxford University Press, 2008.

Esposito, John L. *The Oxford History of Islam.* New York: Oxford University Press, 1999.

Feifer, Gregory. *The Great Gamble: The Soviet War in Afghanistan.* New York: Harper Perennial, 2010.

Gabriel, Richard. *Muhammad: Islam's First Great General.* Norman: University of Oklahoma Press, 2007.

Gaddis, John Lewis. *The Landscape of History: How Historians Map the Past.* New York: Oxford University Press, 2004.

Galeotti, Mark. *Afghanistan: The Soviet Union's Last War.* London: Frank Cass & Co. Ltd., 1995.

———. *The Panjshir Valley 1980-86: The Lion Tames the Bear in Afghanistan.* Oxford, UK: Osprey Publishing, 2021.

Gerges, Fawaz A. *The Rise and Fall of al-Qaeda.* New York: Oxford University Press, 2014.

Gutman, Roy. *How We Missed the Story: Osama bin Laden, the Taliban, and the Hijacking of Afghanistan.* Washington, D.C.: United States Institute of Peace Press, 2013.

Habib, John S. *Ibn Sa'ud's Warriors of Islam: The Ikhwan of Najd and Their Role in the Creation of the Sa'udi Kingdom, 1910-1930.* Riyadh: Mars Publishing House, 1997.

Haqqani, Hussein. *Pakistan: Between Mosque and Military.* Washington, D.C.: Carnegie Endowment for International Peace, 2005.

Hibbert, Christopher. *Garibaldi: Hero of Italian Unification.* New York: Palgrave MacMillan, 2008.

Hill, Ginny. *Yemen Endures: Civil War, Saudi Adventurism and the Future of Arabia.* New York: Oxford University Press, 2017.

Hindley, Geoffrey. *Saladin: Hero of Islam.* Barnsley, South Yorkshire: Pen & Sword, 2015.

Hourani, Albert. *A History of the Arab Peoples.* Cambridge, MA: The Belknap Press of the University of Massachusetts Press, 2002.

Huband, Mark. *Brutal Truths, Fragile Myths: Power Politics and Western Adventurism in the Arab World.* New York: Basic Books, 2004.

Jalali, Ali Ahmad. *A Military History of Afghanistan: From the Great Game to the Global War on Terror.* Lawrence: University Press of Kansas, 2017.

Johnsen, Gregory. *The Last Refuge: Yemen, al-Qaeda, and America's War in Arabia.* New York: W. W. Norton & Company, 2014.

Johnson, Chalmers. *Blowback: The Costs and Consequences of American Empire.* New York: Owl Books, 2001.

Jones, Seth G. *In the Graveyard of Empires: America's War in Afghanistan.* New York: W. W. Norton & Company, 2010.

Kalinovsky, Artemy M. *A Long Goodbye: The Soviet Withdrawal from Afghanistan.* Cambridge, MA: Harvard University Press, 2011.

Kengor, Paul. *The Crusader: Ronald Reagan and the Fall of Communism.* New York: Harper Perennial, 2007.

Lacey, Robert. *Inside the Kingdom: Kings, Clerics, Modernists, Terrorists, and the Struggle for Saudi Arabia.* New York: Penguin Books, 2010.

Lahoud, Nelly. *The Bin Laden Papers: How the Abbottabad Raid Revealed the Truth about Al-Qaeda, Its Leader and His Family.* New Haven, CT: Yale University Press, 2022.

Lings, Martin. *Muhammad: His Life Based on the Earliest Sources.* Rochester, VT: Inner Traditions, 2006.

Mackintosh-Smith, Tim. *Yemen: The Unknown Arabia.* New York: Harry N. Abrams, 2001.

McMichael, Scott R. *Stumbling Bear: Soviet Military Performance in Afghanistan.* London: Brassey's (UK), 1991.

Miller, Flagg. *The Audacious Ascetic: What the bin Laden Tapes Reveal about al-Qa'ida.* London: Hurst & Company, 2015.

of Nicomedia, Arrian. *The Campaigns of Alexander.* Translated by Aubrey de Selincourt. New York: Penguin Books, 1971.

Nojumi, Neamatollah. *The Rise of the Taliban in Afghanistan: Mass Mobilization, Civil War, and the Future of the Region.* London: Palgrave MacMillan, 2002.

Persico, Joseph E. *Casey: The Lives and Secrets of William J. Casey: From the OSS to the CIA.* New York: Penguin Books, 1991.

Peters, Rudolph. *Jihad in Classical and Modern Islam: A Reader.* Princeton, NJ: Markus Wiener Publishers, 1996.

Randal, Jonathan. *Osama: The Making of a Terrorist.* New York: I.B. Tauris, 2012.

Al-Rasheed, Madawi. *A History of Saudi Arabia.* Cambridge: Cambridge University Press, 2002.

Rashid, Ahmed. *Taliban: The Power of Militant Islam in Afghanistan and Beyond.* London: I.B. Tauris, 2010.

Renehan, Jr., Edward J. *The Lion's Pride: Theodore Roosevelt and His Family in Peace and War.* New York: Oxford University Press, 1999.

Reston, Jr., James. *Warriors of God: Richard the Lionheart and Saladin in the Third Crusade.* New York: Anchor Books, 2002.

Rubin, Barnett R. *Afghanistan: What Everyone Needs to Know.* New York: Oxford University Press, 2020.

As-Sallabi, Dr. Ali Muhammad. *Umar ibn al-Khattab: His Life and Times, Vol. 1.* Translated by Nasiruddin al-Khattab. Riyadh: International Islamic Publishing House, 2007.

Scheuer, Michael. *Through Our Enemies Eyes: Osama bin Laden, Radical Islam, and the Future of America.* Washington D.C.: Potomac Books, 2007.

———. *Osama bin Laden.* New York: Oxford University Press, 2012.

Schultheis, Rob. *Hunting bin Laden: How al-Qaeda is Winning the War on Terror.* New York: Skyhorse Publishing, 2008.

Schweitzer, Peter. *Reagan's War: The Epic Story of His Forty-Year Struggle and Final Triumph Over Communism.* New York: Anchor Books, 2003.

Stenersen, Anne. *Al-Qaida in Afghanistan.* Cambridge: Cambridge University Press, 2017.

Al-Suwaidi, Jamal S., Michael Hudson, Paul Dresch, Charles Dunbar, Robert Burrowes, and Mark Katz. *The Yemeni War of 1994: Causes and Consequences.* London: Saqi Books, 1996.

Tawil, Camille. *Brothers in Arms: The Story of Al-Qa'ida and the Arab Jihadists.* London: Saqi Books, 2010.

Trofimov, Yaroslav. *The Siege of Mecca: The 1979 Uprising at Islam's Holiest Shrine.* New York: Anchor Books, 2008.

Urban, Mark. *War in Afghanistan.* London: MacMillan Press, 1988.

Van der Bijl, Nick. *British Military Operations in Aden and Radfan: 100 Years of British Colonial Rule.* Barnsley, South Yorkshire: Pen & Sword, 2014.

Vassiliev, Alexei. *The History of Saudi Arabia.* New York: New York University Press, 2000.

Walker, Jonathan. *Aden Insurgency: The Savage War in Yemen 1962-67.* Barnsley, South Yorkshire: Pen & Sword, 2015.

Wasserstein, David J. *Black Banners of ISIS: The Roots of the New Caliphate.* New Haven, CT: Yale University Press, 2017.

Winder, R. Bayly. *Saudi Arabia in the Nineteenth Century.* New York: St. Martin's Press, 1965.

INDEX

Note: The article "al-" is ignored in alphabetization. For example, "al-Qaeda" appears under the Qs and *"al-Raya"* appears under the Rs, while surnames such as "al-Bahri" and "al-Fadhli" appear under the Bs and Fs, respectively.

Note: Readers will notice that I use the term "Soviet Army" rather than the more popular term "Red Army" throughout this book. This is because the Soviet government changed its army's name from the "Red Army" to the "Soviet Army" in February 1946 and this remained the official title of the Soviet Ground Forces until the Soviet regime's collapse in 1991, although many people worldwide, including Osama bin Laden, frequently used both names, or a combination of them, in reference to the same military force.

Mini-Bio: Focusing his primary research and interests on the life and actions of Osama bin Laden, James Reagan Fancher earned his M.A. in History at the University of Louisiana at Monroe and his Ph.D. at the University of North Texas. His passion is teaching the World History survey course from the sixteenth century to the present. *The Holy Warrior: Osama bin Laden and his Jihadi Journey in the Soviet-Afghan War* is his first book.

A

A Long Goodbye
  The Soviet Withdrawal from Afghanistan (Kalinovsky), 51
A Military History of Afghanistan From the Great Game to the Global War on Terror (Jalali), 40
ABC News, xvii, 170, 173, 186
Abd-al-Nasser, Gamal, 8, 9, 11
Abu Othman hostel, 56
Abyan Governorate, Yemen, 75
al-Adel, Saif, 186
Aden, Yemen, 9, 73, 78, 82, 202, 205

Adnani (branch of Arab peoples), 204, 205
Advice and Reform Committee (ARC), 76
Afgantsy
  The Russians in Afghanistan 1979-89 (Braithwaite), 86
Afghan Air Force, 15
"Afghan Arabs", 13
Afghan Army
  as initial target of Soviet 40th Army, xv, 17
  defections and mutinies in, 27
  desertions and mutinies in, 15

pro-Amin elements initially
    resist Soviets, 18
Soviet advisers embedded with,
    15, 16
trained and equipped by
    Soviets, 17
Afghanistan
    Arab fighters in, 60
    Arab guerrillas in, xvii, xix, 25,
        39, 70, 74
    civil war in, xv, 14, 73, 87
    communist regime in, 42, 74
    factionalism in, 73
    Soviet invasion of, vii, 18, 82
    Soviet occupation of, 19, 28, 43,
        48, 75, 78
    Soviet withdrawal from, 69, 73
    *The Soviet Union's Last War
        (Galeotti)*, 16
    U.S. invasion of, vii
    withdrawal of Soviet troops
        from, 35
*Afghanistan - The Bear Trap
    The Defeat of a Superpower
    (Yousaf)*, 45
"Afghanistan Day", 32, 46
Africa (see also specific countries),
    4
Afridi tribe, 39
Ahmed, Qazi Hussain, 25
AK-47, 43, 72
akh, 5
AKS-74U, 64, 72, 143, 201
Algeria, 201
Amal, 50
Amin, Hafizullah, 17
Amman, Jordan, 7
Anas, Abdullah, x, 25, 68
    as primary source, x, 171
Anderson, Frank, 32, 179
Anderson, Jack, 30
Andropov, Yuri, 14, 15, 16, 17, 29

Angola, 52
apartheid, xii
Armacost, Michael H., 45, 54
Armed Islamic Group (GIA), 201
Armstrong, Sir Robert, 27
asabiyah, 21
al Ash Shaykh, 4, 204
Ashatha, Abu, 201
Asir mountains, 11
Asir Province, Saudi Arabia, 11,
    199, 206
al-Assad family, 186
Atwan, Abdel Bari, 177
Aws (tribe), 74
al-Azman, Muhammad, 62, 63,
    191
Azrow, Afghanistan, 60
Azzam, Abdullah, x, 54, 60, 69
    as primary source, 169, 171

B

Baath Party, 76
badal, 35
Badeeb, Ahmed, 27, 46
al-Bahri, Nasser, xi, 10, 22, 41, 42,
    50, 68, 72, 169, 170, 171, 173,
    177, 186, 198, 201
    as primary source, xi, xvi, 75,
        172, 205
    birth, 10
    contradiction of Omar bin
        Laden's claims, 167
Baluchistan Province, Pakistan, 39
al-Batarfi, Khaled, xi, 11, 22, 159,
    167
    as primary source, xi
Batarfi, Khalid Said, 82
Battle of Jaji, xv, xvi, 60, 61, 64, 65,
    66, 67, 71, 201
Battle of Jalalabad, 70, 71
Battle of Mulayda, 5

Battle of S'bala, 7
Battle of Tora Bora, 82
Beilenson, Anthony, 32
Bennett, Rick, 173
Bergen, Peter, viii, 26, 34, 47, 48, 65, 71, 170, 190
Berntsen, Gary, 197
al-Bid, Ali Salim, 75, 77, 78
Bin Laden
  The Man Who Declared War on America (Bodansky), ix
bin Laden family (see specific individuals), 11, 12, 204
bin Laden, Abdul Rahman, 173, 180
bin Laden, Muhammad bin Awad, 11, 162, 205
bin Laden, Muhammad bin Osama, 168
bin Laden, Najwa, xi, 159
  as primary source, xi, 167
  on Osama's move to Peshawar, 26
bin Laden, Omar, xi, 50
  as primary source, xi, xvi, 167, 173
  on desert hikes with Osama, 41, 195
  on differences between Salafism and Deobandism, 28
  on Osama's alleged relationship with the CIA, 41
  on Osama's move to Peshawar, 26
  On Osama's resentment of the West, 41
bin Laden, Osama, 59, 87, 170
  and Salafi jihadism, 2, 3, 12
  anti-U.S. strategy, xvii, 50
  anti-U.S. strategy of, xvii, 20, 81
  approachability, 170

avoidance of luxuries, 22, 155, 167, 169
birth, xv
bravery, x, 25, 65, 67, 70, 201
command experience, xv, 23, 61, 62, 64, 70
death, viii, xv, xviii, 41, 79, 157, 207
declaration of war, viii, 50, 76, 157, 179
desire for Arab fighters to gain combat experience, xi, 50, 57, 69, 189, 194
emphasis on aiding guerrilla logistics, 24, 62, 70, 72, 168
finances, 49, 55, 75, 177, 184, 205
Gorbachev's temporary escalation as unintended gift for, 51
health, 11, 26, 41, 59, 63, 64, 180
leadership and management skills, xi, xv, xviii, 24, 39, 61, 62, 63, 64, 65, 70, 82, 83, 85, 87
low blood pressure, 63, 64
marriages, 21, 67, 81, 167, 204
napalm inhalation, 64
on Muslim unity and solidarity, 22, 23, 39, 70, 87
on perceived hypocrisy of Saudi regime, 39
on print and digital media as propaganda, 55
on Soviet attempts to sow division in guerrilla ranks, 39
opposition to sectarianism, 4, 50, 158, 168, 186, 207
patience, xvii, 4, 26, 58, 59, 79, 172, 186
persuasiveness, vii, 23, 25, 26, 51, 58, 59, 203

postwar return to Saudi Arabia, 73
practical battle experience, xix, 194
practical battle training, xi, xii, xv, xvii, 20, 23, 35, 63, 67, 68, 71, 76, 82
religious beliefs and piety, 11, 22, 23, 26, 64, 70, 74, 170, 175
resentment of Western governments, 48, 50, 69, 179
return to Afghanistan, 33, 173, 177
rhetorical skills, 166, 193
ruthlessness in warfare, viii, xvii, 3, 158, 186
Salafi jihadism and, 2
Spartan lifestyle, xvi, 21, 22, 155, 167
support for anti-communist Afghan guerrillas, xi, 23, 39, 55, 69, 167
support for anti-communist Yemeni guerrillas, xvii, 73, 75, 76, 77, 78, 83, 167
work ethic, 11, 26, 59, 162
wounded in action, 25, 65, 66, 70
Yemeni tribal connections, xvi, 74
youth, 11, 12
bin Laden, Othman, 56, 189
bin Laden, religious beliefs and piety, 22
bin Laden, Saad
and sale of Osama's remaining properties in Sudan, 177
birth of, 21
death, 180
house arrest in Iran, 180
loyalty to Osama and al-Qaeda, 168, 180
trip to Sudan, 177
Yemeni passport, 177
bin Laden, Salem, 49
bin Laden, Shahira, 169
bin Saud, Abdullah, 5
bin Saud, Muhammad, 3, 4
bin Walid, Khalid, 57
Blowpipe missile, 47, 183
BM-21, 61, 62, 144
Bodansky, Yossef, ix
Boris Ponomarev, 16
Bounoua, Boudejema (Abdullah Anas), x
Braithwaite, Rodric, 44, 86
Brennan, John O., 157
"Brezhnev Doctrine", 18
Brezhnev, Leonid, xi, xv, 14, 16, 17, 43
aid to PDPA regime, 14, 15, 19
expectation to fight Afghan Army not insurgents, 17
reinforcement of 40th Army, 27
Britain, 7, 177
as source of Afghan guerrilla weapons, 30
support for anti-communist Afghan guerrillas, vii, xv, 48
Burchill, Julie, 37
Bush, George W., 185

C

Calcutta, India, 12
Carrington, Lord Peter, 27
Casey, William "Bill", 29, 31, 32, 45, 47, 53
Castro, Fidel, 40, 155, 158
Central Intelligence Agency (CIA), xv, 12, 29, 30, 33, 40, 42, 43, 49, 177
China, 51

as source of Afghan guerrilla weapons, 30
Clinton, Bill, 170, 178
Cohen, Harry, 37
Cold War, 13
Coll, Steve, ix, x, 12, 25, 49, 65, 171, 190, 205
Combating Terrorism Center at West Point, viii
Communist Party of the Soviet Union (CPSU), 16, 17, 60
Congressional Record, viii
Congressional Task Force on Afghanistan, 30
Cook, Robin, 40
Czechoslovakia, 53

D

Darraz, Isam, x
  as primary source, 65, 171
al-Daylami, Abd al-Wahhab, 53, 64, 77, 192
al-Daylami, Hisham bin Abd al-Wahhab, 192
defensive jihad, xii, 7, 15
Denker, Debra, 184
Dhofar Governorate, Oman, 199
Diriyah, Emirate of Diriyah, 5

E

Eastern Province, Saudi Arabia, 191
Egypt
  as source of Afghan guerrilla weapons, 30
Egyptian Islamic Jihad (EIJ), 4, 186, 198
Eid al-Fitr, 64
El Fadl, Khaled Abou, 4
El Salvador, 52

F

al-Fadhli, Tariq, x, 10, 41, 42, 71, 75, 77, 182
  as primary source, xi, xvi, 171
fajr, 64, 175
Federation of South Arabia, 9
FIM-92 "Stinger", 32, 44, 47, 54, 72, 184
First World War (1914-1918), 6
Fisk, Robert, 48, 65
40th Army, 18, 27, 28, 34, 42, 52, 69, 75
France, 177

G

Gaddis, John Lewis, 1
Gailani, Ishaq, 33, 183
Gailani, Ismail, 38
Galeotti, Mark, 16, 17, 44
Gates, Robert, 32, 45
General Intelligence Directorate (GID), 27, 43, 201
Geneva Accords, 36
al-Ghamdi, Hamza (9/11 hijacker), 206
al-Ghamdi, Hamza (al-Qaeda commander), 65, 66, 79, 197
Ghanem, Allia, 204
Ghost Wars
  The Secter History of the CIA, Afghanistan, and bin Laden, from the Soviet Invasion to September 10, 2001 (Coll), ix
Girardet, Edward, 15, 48, 60, 69
Gorbachev, Mikhail, xi, xii, 43, 46, 51
  desire to strengthen PDPA before withdrawing, 34, 35
  desire to withdraw from Afghanistan, 19, 44, 52

temporary escalation of Afghan campaign, 34, 35, 47, 53, 75
Gore, Al, 77
Gorelov, Leonid, 17
Grand Mosque, 11
Grand Mosque siege of 1979, 12, 38, 43
Greater Yemen (see South Arabia), 199
Gromyko, Andrei, 16, 17, 29
Growing Up bin Laden
  Osama's Wife and Son Take Us Inside Their Secret World (Bin Laden, bin Laden, and Sasson), xi
GRU, 16, 39
Guarding bin Laden
  My Life in al-Qaeda (al-Bahri and Malbrunot), xi, 22, 41
Guevara, Ernesto "Che", 158

H

al-Hadhi, Jamal, 10, 64, 75, 76, 77
hadith, 4
Hadramut Region, Yemen, 9, 11, 74, 204
al-Haili, Khidr'haili, 62
halaqat, 26
Hanjour, Hani, 206
Haq, Abdul, 32, 33, 36, 47, 48, 70
Haqqani, Jalaluddin, 44
Harb (tribe), 156
al-Harithi, Abu Ali, 78
Hatem, Mir, 14
al-Hazmi, Nawaf, 206
Hejaz Region, Saudi Arabia, 7, 74
Hekmatyar, Gulbuddin, 14, 32, 33, 34, 35, 64, 70
Herat, Afghanistan, 15
hijra, 5
Hizballah, 50

Holy War, Inc.
  Inside the Secret World of Osama bin Laden (Bergen), viii
Houthi movement, 82, 207
Howe, Sir Geoffrey, 37
Huband, Mark, 177
Humphrey, Gordon J., 30, 32, 33, 45, 46, 53, 177
Hungary, 53
Hunting bin Laden
  How al-Qaeda is Winning the War on Terror (Schultheis), x
Hussein, Saddam, 76, 186
Hyderabad, India, 12

I

Ibn Khaldun, Abd al-Rahman, xvi, 21, 22, 23, 24, 73, 154, 156, 167, 170, 175
Ibn Saud, Abdul Aziz, 5, 6, 7
Ikhwan, 5, 6, 7, 8, 167
IL-76 plane, 70
Imam Yahya of Yemen, 8
imamah, 6
India, 51
  Pakistani tensions with, 47
Inter-Services-Intelligence (ISI), 30, 33, 34, 43, 69
Iraq, 7
Isam Darraz
  as primary source, 192
al-Islah, 75, 77
Islamabad, Pakistan, 30
Islamic Awakening, 8, 12, 76
Israel, 50, 186
  as source of Afghan guerrilla weapons, 30, 198
  similiarities with Pakistan described by Peter Bergen, 47
Italy, 13
Izvestia, 34

J

al-Jadawi, Mohanad, 79
Jaji, Afghanistan, xv, 57, 58, 59, 60
Jalalabad, Afghanistan, xvi, 28, 67, 69, 70
Jalali, Ali Ahmad, 40
Jalil, Mullah, 172
Jamaat-e-Islami, 25
Jandal, Abu (see Nasser al-Bahri), 162
Jawbreaker
　The Attack on bin Laden and al-Qaeda
　　A Personal Account by the CIA's Key Field Commander (Berntsen and Pezzullo), 197
Jazan Province, Saudi Arabia, 8, 199
Jeddah, Saudi Arabia, 10, 22, 23, 56, 76, 167, 169
al-Jihad (magazine), 55, 66
Johnsen, Gregory, 78
Johnson, Chalmers, 40
Jordan, 7

K

Kabul, Afghanistan, 15, 16
Kalinovsky, Artemy, 51
Kandahar Province, Afghanistan, 10, 52
Kandahar, Afghanistan, 22, 24, 29, 31, 34, 35, 38, 68
Kaplan, Robert, 33, 34, 36, 38, 44, 45, 47, 184
Karachi, Pakistan, 30
Karbala, Iraq, 4
Karmal, Babrak, 18, 53
kasat al-ganabel ("grenade spout"), 72

Kaskaz, 34
Katyusha (rocket launcher), 72
Kenda tribe, 204
Kengor, Paul, 54
Kennedy, Edward "Ted", 35, 36
Kenny Deal, Mary, 38
Kenya, 170, 202
KGB, 14, 16, 39
Khalifa, Muhammad Jamal, 59
Khalilzad, Zalmay, 178
Khalis, Muhammad Yunis, 33, 34, 47, 54, 73, 177
Khalq (PDPA faction), 17
Khan, Akhtar Abdul Rahman, 30, 47, 177
Khan, Ismail, 15
Khan, Muhammad Daud, 13
Khan, Nadar, 39
Khartoum, Sudan, 76, 201
Khazraj (tribe), 74
Khomeini, Ruhollah, 2, 33
al-Khulayfi, Muhammad, 76
Killing the Cranes
　A Reporter's Journey Through Three Decades of War in Afghanistan (Girardet), 69
al-Kindi, Abu al-Miqdad (see Khalid Said Batarfi), 82
Kuwait
　support for Yemeni Socialist Party, 78

L

Lahore, Pakistan, 25
Lee Enfield rifle, 18, 43
Lee, Robert E., xvii
Lenin, Vladimir, xviii
Lion's Den (bin Laden's guerrilla base), 58, 59, 61, 62, 64, 194
London, Britain, ix, xviii, 9, 38
Long, Clarence "Doc", 45

M

M-16, 72
madrassa, 3, 10, 82
Madrid, Spain, xviii
Mahmud II (Ottoman Sultan), 4
Makhtab al-Khadamat (MK), 55
Makudor, Redouane, 201
Mandela, Nelson, xii
Margolis, Eric, 173
Marib, Yemen, 75
Marten, Sir Neil, 9
Marx, Karl, xviii, xix
al-Masri, Abu Hafs, 66, 71
Massoud, Ahmed Shah, x, 33, 58, 59, 68, 70, 203, 206
Mazar-e-Sharif, Afghanistan, 28
McCurry, Steve, 69, 71
McMichael, Scott R., 28
Mecca, Saudi Arabia, 5, 7, 11, 12, 13, 26, 43, 198
Medina, Saudi Arabia, 5, 7, 57, 74, 195
melmastia, 79
Mexican-American War (1846-1848), xvii
MI-6, 43, 183
al-Midhar, Khaled, 206
MiG-27, xv, 62, 147, 183
Mil Mi-24 gunship, 18, 24, 25, 31, 34, 52, 61, 62, 63, 69, 183
Miller, Flagg, 204
Miller, John, xvii, 25, 170, 173, 186
Mindanao, 2
Mohammad Yousaf, 40
Moore, Michael, 40
Moscow, Russia, 3, 16, 80
Mozambique, 52
Muhammad (Prophet), 5, 6, 73, 74, 170
Muhammad, Niaz, 14
Muhsin, Ali, 77
mujahid, xi
al-Murrah (tribe), 5
My Life with the Taliban (Zaeef), 29

N

Najd Province, Saudi Arabia, 7, 204
Najibullah, Mohammad, 39, 53, 70
Najran Province, Saudi Arabia, 8, 199
Nangarhar Province, Afghanistan, 52
Narenjack grenade launcher, 72
Nasiri, Omar, 72
National Geographic, 184
National Security Decision Directive Number 75 (NSDD-75), 29
Naval Air Station Pensacola, 207
Nicaragua, 52
9/11 "muscle hijackers", 82
North Atlantic Treaty Organization (NATO), xix, 20, 24, 50, 86
North Korea, 75, 78, 82, 207
NSDD-166, 54
NSDD-270, 54
Nur al-Din, 2

O

Oakley, Phyllis, 178
Oakley, Robert, 178
Obama, Barack, 157, 171, 185
offensive jihad, 2
Omar, Muhammad, Mullah, 22, 172, 178
Operation *17 Ramadan*, 61
Operation *17 Shaban*, 61
Operation *Cyclone*, 30, 31, 40
Operation Storm-333, 18
Osama bin Laden (Scheuer), ix, xvi

Ottoman Empire, 4, 5, 6, 167

P

Pakistan
   fears of Soviet retaliation, 30, 47
   support for anti-communist Afghan guerrillas, vii, xv, 48, 70
Paktia Province, Afghanistan, 52
Panjshir Valley, 68
al-Panshiri, Abu Ubaydah, 66, 71
Parcham (PDPA faction), 18, 53
Paris, France, xviii, 80, 86
Parliamentary Record, viii
Pashtun, 14, 20, 23, 28, 34, 35, 39, 45, 48, 79, 165, 172
Pensacola, Florida, 82
People, 14
People's Democratic Party of Afghanistan (PDPA), 13, 14, 16, 18, 20, 35, 37, 52, 53, 54
   national outreach program of, 33
Percy, Charles "Chuck", 31, 45
Peshawar, Pakistan, 23, 26, 30, 34, 36, 48, 54, 56, 59, 61, 66, 70, 194
Pezzullo, Ralph, 197
PFM-1 "butterfly mine", 31, 52
Poland, 53
Politburo, xii, 13, 15, 16, 17, 19, 29, 164, 186
Ponomarev, Boris, 17
Port Sudan, Sudan, 177
Prentice, Lord Reginald, 8

Q

qabili, 9, 10
Qaddafi, Muammar, 155
Qadir, Abdul, 14
al-Qaeda
   allegations of CIA support for, xiv, xvi, 40, 42, 44
   and practical battle experience, xix, 43, 68, 76, 157, 207
   and practical battle training, xii, xiv, xvii, 19, 20, 35, 43, 50, 51, 53, 64, 65, 67, 71, 72, 81, 82, 83
   as vanguard guerrilla organization, xv, xviii, xix, 12, 43, 72
   established by bin Laden and comrades, xi, xiv, 66, 71
al-Qaeda on the Arabian Peninsula (AQAP), 42, 82, 154, 182, 207
Qahtani (branch of Arab peoples), 13, 58, 74, 162, 199, 205
al-Qarni, Musa, x, 8, 65
   as primary source, xi, xvi, 65, 171
Quetta, Pakistan, 30
Quraish (tribe), 5
Qutb, Said, 3
qutra, 6

R

R-300, 70, 149, 171
Rabbani, Burhanuddin, 26, 33
Randal, Jonathan, 177
al-Rasheed, Madawi, 6
al-Rashidi clan, 5, 6
Rawalpindi, Pakistan, 30
al-Raya (black banner of jihad), 6, 64
al-Raymi, Qasim, 82
"Reagan Doctrine", 32
Reagan, Ronald, xii, 29, 31, 32, 33, 44, 45, 46, 47, 49, 54
Red Star, 34
Renehan, Jr., Edward J., 189
Richardson, Bill, 178

Rippon, Lord Geoffrey, 27
Ritch III, John B., 31
Riyadh, Saudi Arabia, 5, 6, 10, 26, 53
Robert Kaplan, 40
Roosevelt, Theodore "Teddy", 189
Russia (see also Soviet Union), 51
Russian General Staff, 19
Ruthven, Malise, 22
Rwandan Genocide, 78

S

Saadi, Abdullah, 27
Sadaa, Yemen, 75, 188, 200
al-Sadah, Amal, 205
Sadiq, Muhammad, 14
Sahwa (see Islamic Awakening), 8
Saladin, 2
Salafi jihadism, xv, 2, 3, 12, 82
Salafism, 1, 3, 4, 5, 6, 8, 10, 21, 25, 45, 74, 186, 205, 206
Saleh, Ali Abdullah, 53, 74, 75, 77, 78
SAM-7, 72, 183
Sanaa, Yemen, 9, 53, 75, 77, 82, 158, 188, 192, 205
al-Saud royal family (see also specific individuals), 3, 4, 8, 76, 204
al-Saud, Fahd ibn Abd al-Aziz, 11, 39, 53
al-Saud, Faisal ibn Abd al-Aziz, 8, 9, 10, 11, 27
al-Saud, Turki al-Faisal, 27, 46, 73, 162
al-Saud, Turki bin Abdullah, 5
Saudi Air Force, 30
Saudi Arabia
  arrival of U.S. and Western troops in, 51
  fear of communist and national socialist threats, 8, 10
  Salafism at home and abroad, 8
  support for anti-communist Afghan guerrillas, vii, xv, 34, 38, 48, 53
  support for Yemeni Socialist Party, 78, 196
Saudi National Guard, 12
Saudi-Yemeni border war (1934), 8
Sayyaf, Abdul Rasul, 14, 26, 34, 60, 64, 70
Scheuer, Michael, ix, 11, 12, 21, 22, 24, 26, 50, 51, 55, 57, 64, 65, 154, 162, 167, 171, 173, 177, 192, 193, 201, 206
Schultheis, Rob, x, 25, 60
  as primary source, x, 49
Selbourne, David, 37
Senate Congressional Resolution 74, 31
Shabwah Governorate, Yemen, 75, 205
Shah, Zahir, 13
al-Shamrani, Muhammad Said, 207
Shamsi, Nidam al-Deen, 173
Shariah, 23, 74
al-Saud, Khalid ibn Abd al-Aziz, 11
al-Sheba, Ramsi, 206
Shia Muslims, 4, 8, 9, 15, 158, 186, 207
Shultz, George P., 54
Shura, 173, 186
Sikorski, Radek, 184
Simpson, John
  encounter with bin Laden, 49
Sokolov, Sergei, 51
Soldiers of God
  With Islamic Warriors in Afghanistan and Pakistan (Kaplan), 44

Solomon, Gerald, 45
South Africa, xii
South Arabia (region), 13, 78, 82, 199
Soviet Air Force
  air supremacy in Afghanistan, 18
  bombing in Afghanistan, 19, 26, 34, 44, 52, 69, 70
Soviet High Command, 19, 20
Soviet Union
  and goal of stabilizing pro-Soviet Kabul regime, 13, 14
  attempts to sow guerrilla division, 39
  collapse of, xvii
  invasion of Afghanistan, xv
  support for PDPA regime, 70
  withdrawal from Afghanistan, xvii, 35, 36, 69
Spain, 2
Spetsnaz, 28, 34, 52
Stenersen, Anne, 194
Stoessel, Walter J., 31
Storm-333, 19
Su-25, 18, 62, 151, 183
Sudan, 76
sunnah, 4, 74
Sunni Muslims, xii, 1, 2, 3, 4, 9, 10, 39, 201, 207
Supreme Soviet, 16, 29

T

T-55 tank, 72
Taez, Yemen, 81, 82, 188, 205
Taif, Saudi Arabia, 57
Tajik, 33, 79, 201
Tajikistan, 65, 79
takfirism, 76, 159, 186, 196, 198, 201
Taleban

  and bin Laden's return to Afghanistan, 22, 79
  and bin Laden's strategy, 80
  and practical training resisting U.S. invasion, 81, 86
  and resistance to U.S. invasion, 48
  bin Laden's relationship with, 20, 80
  Deobandism and, 28
  origins, 3, 10, 68
Tanzania, 170, 202
Tapsell, Sir Peter, 9
Taraki, Nur Muhammad, 13, 15
Tarnak Farm, 22, 82, 170
Tawil, Camille, 189
Tehran, Iran, 2, 80
Thatcher, Margaret, 27, 35, 47, 183
The Bin Ladens
  An Arabian Family in the American Century (Coll), ix, 65
The Bukovsky Archives, viii
The Eighteenth Brumaire of Louis Bonaparte (Marx), xviii
The Landscape of History
  How Historians Map the Past (Gaddis), 1
The Last Refuge
  Yemen, al-Qaeda, and America's War in Arabia (Johnsen), 78
The Lion's Pride
  Theodore Roosevelt and His Family in Peace and War (Renehan), 189
The Looming Tower
  Al-Qaeda and the Road to 9/11 (Wright), x
The Mail on Sunday, 37
The Muqaddimah - An Introduction to History

The Classic Islamic History of the World (Ibn Khaldun), vii, 21
The National Security Archive, viii
The New York Times, 32, 46, 182
The Osama bin Laden I Know An Oral History of al-Qaeda's Leader (Bergen), ix, 65
The Siege of Mecca The 1979 Uprising at Islam's Holiest Shrine (Trofimov), 199
The Washington Post, 30
The Wilson Center, viii
To the Mountains My Life in Jihad, from Algeria to Afghanistan (Anas), x
Tomsen, Peter, 178
Trofimov, Yaroslav, 199
Trump, Donald, 157
al-Turabi, Hasan, 76, 177
201st Motorized Rifle Division, 27

U

U.S. Air Force, 30
U.S. Army, 201
U.S. Congressional debate
   on CIA aid to Afghan resistance, 31, 35, 46
U.S. Cruise missile, 201
U.S. House of Representatives, 46
U.S. Marines, 202
U.S. Navy SEALs, xv
U.S. Senate, 31, 46
U.S. Senate Committee on Foreign Relations, 31
U.S. State Department, 32, 46, 53
UK House of Commons, 8, 9, 27, 35, 37
UK Parliamentary debate
   on decision to withdraw from Aden, Yemen, 9
   on MI-6 aid to Afghan resistance, 27, 35, 37
   on Soviet military presence in South Yemen, 8
ul-Haq, Muhammad Zia, 44, 47, 177
umra, 26
United States
   as source of Afghan guerrilla weapons, 30
   desire to avenge defeat in Vietnam, 31
   fears of Soviet retaliation, 30
   support for anti-communist Afghan guerrillas, vii, xv, 34, 48, 69
USS *Cole*, 82
Ustinov, Dmitry, 16, 17
al-Utaybi, Juhayman, 12, 43
Uzi, 72, 198

V

van Atta, Dale, 30
Varennikov, Valentin, 52
Vietnam War, 31

W

al-Wadihi, Mukbel, 75, 78
al-Wadihi, Obadah, 10, 64, 75
al-Wahayshi, Nasser, 82
al-Wahhab, Muhammad ibn Abd, 3, 4
Wahhabism, 3
al-Walid, Khalid, 7
Warsaw Pact, 8, 75
Washington, D.C., 33, 45, 54
Waulia, Yemen, 75
Wiktorwicz, Quintan, 4
Wilson, Charles "Charlie", 30, 33, 45, 46, 54, 177

Wilson, Charles "Charlie" Wilson, 32
Wright, Lawrence, x, 25, 159, 171
Wu, Jimmy, 26

Y

Yathrib (see Medina), 5
Yemen
   1986 civil war in, 75
   1993 parliamentary election in, 77
   1994 civil war in, xvii, 77
   al-Qaeda strongholds in, 10, 78
   al-Qaeda training camps in, 75, 76
   civil wars in since 1962, 73
   communist regime in, 8, 42, 43, 51, 71, 73, 74, 75
   Egyptian withdrawal from, 9
   North Yemen Civil War (1962-1970), 8
   reunification of, 75, 78
   Soviet and Warsaw pact troops in, 73, 74
   support for anti-communist Afghan guerrillas, vii, xv, 53, 82
   UK forces in Aden, 9
   UK troop withdrawal from, 9
   UK withdrawal from, 73
Yemeni culture, 11, 82, 205
Yemeni Socialist Party, 75, 77, 78
al-Yemeni, Abu Bashir (see Nasser al-Wahayshi), 82
al-Yemeni, Sorak, 170
Yousaf, Mohammad, 30, 45, 48, 198

Z

Zaeef, Abdul Salam, 29, 68
Zaitsev, Mikhail, 52
al-Zarqawi, Abu Musab, 158, 159, 168, 186
al-Zawahiri, Ayman, 4, 87, 158, 168, 186, 198, 205
Zedong, Mao, 58, 78
al-Zindani, Abd al-Majid, 53, 65, 75, 77

www.ingramcontent.com/pod-product-compliance
Lightning Source LLC
Chambersburg PA
CBHW061435300426
44114CB00014B/1690